NEW YORK
HISTORICAL MANUSCRIPTS:
DUTCH

FIRST PAGE OF WILDWYCK RECORDS

NEW YORK HISTORICAL MANUSCRIPTS: DUTCH

KINGSTON PAPERS

Translated by Dingman Versteeg
(With Revision of Pages 1-171 by Samuel Oppenheim)

Edited by
PETER R. CHRISTOPH
KENNETH SCOTT
And
KENN STRYKER-RODDA

Published under the Direction of
The Holland Society of New York

VOLUME I

Kingston Court Records,
1661-1667

CLEARFIELD

"The Dutch Records of Kingston,"
by Samuel Oppenheim, is excerpted
and reprinted from *Proceedings of the
New York Historical Association*,
Volume XI, 1912.

Reprinted by
Genealogical Publishing Co., Inc.
Baltimore, Maryland
1976

Library of Congress Catalogue Card Number 75-5971

Reprinted for Clearfield Company by
Genealogical Publishing Company
Baltimore, Maryland
1999, 2010

ISBN, Volume I: 978-0-8063-4851-3
Set ISBN: 978-0-8063-0720-6

Made in the United States of America

Publisher's Note

The first 171 pages of this work were revised by Samuel Oppenheim
from translations by Dingman Versteeg and published as "The Dutch
Records of Kingston." The remainder of the work is a continuation of
the records from the point at which Oppenheim's revision terminates.
Indexes to both sections appear at the end of Volume II.

DEDICATED TO
THE HOLLAND SOCIETY
OF NEW YORK

whose prime object is "to collect and preserve information respecting the early history
and settlement of the City and State of New
York by the Dutch and to discover and preserve all still existing documents relating to
their genealogy and history." This purpose,
since 1885, has provided a stimulus for historical research and analysis of the New
Netherland era in America.

TABLE OF CONTENTS

Volume I

Volume II

INTRODUCTION

By PETER R. CHRISTOPH

HISTORY OF THE ESOPUS, 1652-1775

The earliest known sale of land in the region of the Esopus involved a parcel sold by Esopus Indians to Thomas Chambers, a carpenter and farmer residing at that time in Rensselaerswyck. The patent was confirmed on June 5, 1652. That there were settlers in the region soon thereafter is indicated in the minutes of the court of Fort Orange and Beverwyck for June 19, 1653, which record "that some beavers' worth of brandy was sold by Jacob Clomp to the savages at the Esopus, according to the complaint made to (Jan Dircksz van Bremen) by some inhabitants of the Esopus, who declared that they had suffered great annoyance from them in consequence thereof."

Throughout the early history of the settlement the presence of the Indians cast an ominous pall over the whole community. Though they were particularly vulnerable in their scattered houses they were often at fault for the bad relations. Director-General Petrus Stuyvesant recognized the danger to them, and at his urging the settlers signed a bond on May 31, 1658, agreeing to erect a palisaded village and demolish their separate dwellings. Then, on the night of September 20, 1659, a group of settlers and soldiers senselessly shot three Indians, killing one of them. The result was the First Esopus War, which did not end until the signing of a peace treaty on July 15, 1660.

Despite the war and the uneasiness of the ensuing peace, the population of the community continued to grow. By May 2, 1661, the hamlet had been named Wildwyck by Stuyvesant. About May of 1662 a second community was established nearby, called the Nieuw Dorp (New Town), which was settled by former residents of Beverwyck and Wildwyck. Several Huguenots made their homes there.

The fragile peace ended on June 7, 1663, when the Indians burned Nieuw Dorp and attacked Wildwyck. The resulting loss of life, concern for settlers taken hostage, and heavy loss of property had a long-lasting effect upon the community. Troops from New Amsterdam pursued the Indians for many months, eventually rescuing the prisoners. A peace treaty was concluded on May 15, 1664.

Now trouble came to the Esopus from a new source. English forces dispatched by the Duke of York seized New Amsterdam on September 8, and on the 25th Wildwyck was placed under the authority of the Duke. New Netherland and New Amsterdam were renamed New York, and Beverwyck became Albany. The name Wildwyck fell into disuse, the community

xi

generally being referred to as the Town of Esopus. Petrus Stuyvesant retired to the life of a private citizen and the residents of Esopus struggled to adjust to the change in rule.

It was not easy. All the problems of life under an occupation force faced the settlers. They were compelled to board soldiers in their homes and to suffer insults and abuse from the armed troops. Reaction against such treatment culminated in the Esopus Mutiny of February 4, 1667. This armed threat to English rule in the region subsided after a few hours. Governor Richard Nicolls wisely chose to mete out punishment to soldiers as well as civilians, but incidents continued to occur.

On April 6, 1668, Governor Nicolls granted land in a new patent at the Esopus to a number of his soldiers. A village was established there, which under his successor, Francis Lovelace, was named Marbletown on September 17, 1669. On the same day Nieuw Dorp was renamed Hurley, and on September 25 Esopus became Kingston. The official pronouncement was made on April 25, 1670. Thomas Chambers, the original settler in the region, was rewarded by Governor Lovelace by having his house and land enfranchised as the manor of Fox Hall on October 16, 1672.

The war in Europe between England and the Netherlands reached New York when a Dutch force under Anthony Colve recaptured New York City on July 30/August 9, 1673. The Esopus was reduced by the Dutch on August 5/15. Colve became Governor General on September 9/19 and re-established Dutch rule. Among other changes Kingston was renamed Swaenenburgh. However, under the Treaty of Westminster, the colony was returned to English control on October 31/November 10, 1674. Edmond Andros became Governor on that day, and Swaenenburgh became Kingston once again.

The early history of the Esopus, then, could hardly have been more dramatic. Two Indian wars and three changes of allegiance in twenty-three years formed a tumultuous backdrop against which to attempt to develop a stable social and economic community. Certainly these events tended to retard development, discouraging immigration and settlement. The problems were intensified by the existence of four non-integrated ethnic groups: Indians, Dutch, English, and French. Each of these groups sought to preserve its language and customs. The resulting tensions among these groups were not resolved until long after 1675. A realization of this stress is basic to the understanding of the early history of Esopus.

GOVERNMENT IN THE ESOPUS

At first the Esopus fell under the jurisdiction of the court of Fort Orange and Beverwyck. Management of public affairs became the responsibility of the military commander at the garrison after the erection of the palisaded village in 1658. The residents desired a local civil administration, and in response to their request the directors of the Amsterdam Chamber of the Dutch West India Company made the Esopus an independent jurisdiction, appointed Roelof Swartwout as schout, and instructed Director-General Stuyvesant to organize a court. Stuyvesant resisted the order, but after being censured for his recalcitrance, he issued an ordinance on May 16, 1661, establishing the court.

Under the tradition of Roman-Dutch law this inferior court was composed of the schout, representing the sovereign authority, and three (later four) schepens or commissaries, representing the people and selected by the Director-General and Council from a double list presented by the inhabitants. This court was the sole agency of local government and was endowed with both administrative and judicial responsibilities. When it sat as a criminal court the schout presided, bringing the charges and presenting the evidence, while the schepens determined not only guilt or innocence but also the penalty. Execution of the judgment was a duty of the schout, who thus combined the duties of sheriff, chief of police, and public prosecutor. In civil cases the schout sat with the schepens. The court also employed other public officials, including the secretary and court messenger. The secretary was a notary, village clerk, and court recorder, while the messenger's duties included the functions of process server, doorkeeper, and sergeant-at-arms. At first the schout served also as secretary. The separate office of secretary was established on June 14, 1663, the date of Mattheus Capito's appointment.

The arrival of the English did not immediately affect the structure of the court or the village administration. Schout Willem Beeckman and secretary Capito were retained in office. Dutch remained the court language. It was not until 1669 that changes were introduced. On September 9 Governor Lovelace appointed a commission to regulate the government at Esopus, which commission held sessions at Esopus from the 17th to the 29th. It appointed a surveyor-general of highways for Kingston, Hurley, and Marblehead and appointed an officer over the Indians. It ordered the Kingston Court to keep village highways passable, to appoint a person to measure corn and grain for export, to repair the town house, and to keep two men constantly on watch at the redoubt. Christopher Beresford was made chief magistrate over Hurley and Marbletown and instructed to govern by English laws (presumably the Duke's laws), and two overseers were selected for each of the two villages.

Institution of the Duke's laws seems to have been delayed at Kingston until an effort in that direction was made on October 25, 1671. On April 26 the Provincial Council commissioned Thomas Chambers justice of the peace and established a court of sessions for the Esopus consisting of one commissary from each village as well as the justice of the peace. Jurisdiction of the court was limited to suits involving less than £5 and to criminal

xiii

actions, except those punishable by death. Sessions were to be held every half year.

The erection of Fox Hall as a manor on October 16, 1672, introduced new problems. The governor had made Fox Hall "an entire enfranchised Mannor of it selfe," not subject to the town court. Whether this dispensation also included the person of the manor lord remained an open question for some time.

In response to a petition from the residents of Esopus, the Council completed the change to English courts of law on June 12, 1673. However, the reconquest by the Dutch resulted in the suspension of the Duke's laws and the re-establishment of the Dutch form of government at Esopus by an order of August 22/September 1, 1673. The offices established by the order included a schout, secretary, and separate commissaries for Kingston and for Hurley-Marbletown.

With the end of Dutch rule on November 10, 1674, English law was reinstituted. On January 11, 1675, Governor Andros wrote to the inhabitants of Hurley and Marbletown that Thomas Chambers would be justice of the peace and George Hall schout for the three villages together. Uncertainty on the part of the two officeholders as to the delineation between their offices led to misunderstandings and disputes. With the eventual elimination of Dutch offices—the schout itself, for example—these problems were resolved. While that point had not been reached by the end of 1675, the Duke's laws were in force and the court of sessions functioning.

In summary, local administration of the Esopus did not begin until 1661, when the court was created. There were few offices during the period under Roman-Dutch law, but under the Duke's laws numerous offices were created. Demands upon the time of the court commissaries were greatly reduced with the change in legal systems, the frequency of sessions being reduced from every second week to twice yearly.

HISTORY OF THE RECORDS

The original records of the court at Wildwyck begin on page 3 of the first manuscript volume with a copy of the bond of May 31, 1658. Jonathan W. Hasbrouck of Ulster County was of the opinion that the missing pages 1 and 2 contained a copy of the order of Stuyvesant's giving the name Wildwyck to the village, a memorandum of the fact that the court had been established in May 1661 with Roelof Swartwout as schout, and a copy of the order of his appointment by the Amsterdam Chamber of the West India Company. Pages 4 through 10 are blank. Samuel Oppenheim suggests in his introduction to *The Dutch Records of Kingston* that the space had been provided for copies of the commissaries' oaths of office, an "ordinance of the Director General and Council, for the erection of a Court of Justice at Wildwyck," and Roelof Swartwout's commission from the Director-General and Council as schout. The remainder of volume I contains court minutes, first in the handwriting of schout Roelof Swartwout, and thereafter in the hand of secretary Mattheus Capito. Of the records of the court prior to the incorporation of the town of Kingston in 1688, eleven volumes survive, six of court minutes and five of secretary's papers.

The court minutes are a record of the hearings and trials, 1661-1684. The secretary's papers contain copies of legal transactions (contracts, agreements, bonds, wills and powers of attorney) and transfers of real estate for the period 1664-1681. Prior to 1664 no separate secretarial record seems to have been kept, a few deeds and mortgages being entered in the first volume of court minutes. All the existing records were deposited in the Ulster County Clerk's office on December 16, 1686.

These records, along with several others, disappeared from the Ulster County Clerk's office around 1855. The grand jury instituted an investigation and the board of supervisors offered a liberal reward for their return. Around 1880 rumors circulated in Ulster County that the records were on Long Island. The sheriff went to New York with a search warrant, but his well publicized investigation was unsuccessful. Then, one day in June, 1895, an express package containing the long-lost records was delivered at the Ulster County Clerk's office, all carefully packed as though by someone sensible of their value. Investigation revealed only that they had been shipped from Quogue on Long Island by a man unknown to the people at the express company. Wheeler B. Melius in 1905 wrote in his *Index to the Public Records of the County of Albany, State of New York 1630-1894:*

> "A few years ago the compiler of this work became acquainted with a gentleman named Van Alstyne, a resident of Brooklyn, and the descendant of an old Dutch family, of which he was very proud. He was engaged in tracing his family genealogy, and in the course of his researches called at the Albany County Clerk's office, where he met the late Thomas J. Van Alstyne, former Mayor of Albany and ex-Congressman, who at once became interested in the work. In the course of their discussion of family matters, Mr. Van Alstyne, of Brooklyn, alluded to certain Kingston relatives, and incidentally mentioned the disappearance and return of the Kingston records. His language seemed to indicate that he knew something of the matter, and, upon being pressed for an explanation said:
>
>> 'Years ago I, with a few others, became interested in these old Dutch records at Kingston. There was very little interest displayed in their preservation, and, being written more or less illegibly in the old Dutch of that early period, they were as a sealed book to most people. No translation had ever been attempted, officially or otherwise, and as there seemed to be no prospects of a translation,

the records were removed to Brooklyn, where arrangements had been made for a complete translation by an old Dutch scholar. The work was scarcely started when the translator was taken ill and died. Owing to the press of other business, I lost track of the records, but it seems that when the effects of the deceased translator were disposed of, his executors, knowing nothing of the ownership of the records, but being satisfied that they were of a public character, had them packed in a box and removed to the old city hall, where they were left undisturbed for a long time. I was one of the commissioners having in charge the building of the new city hall, and when that edifice was completed and the work of transferring the books and papers was under way, this old box of Kingston records came to light. While the officials, to whom the records were as Greek, were discussing the advisability of consigning the box of 'rubbish' to the junk pile, I happened to come into the room, and at once recognized the records. I had them carefully boxed and shipped to the Ulster County Clerk's office at Kingston. No word was sent with them, because those who had brought them to Brooklyn were unable to complete the work and thought they might be open to censure for removing them from Kingston and then allowing them to lay so long neglected and in danger of destruction. These are the facts of the disappearance and return of the Kingston records, and the mystery is a mystery no longer.' "

The records today remain in the custody of the Ulster County Clerk.

HISTORY OF THE TRANSLATIONS

After the fortuitous return of the records, they were carefully read by Isaac Clearwater, who recognized their importance and believed that they should be translated into English. His son, Judge A. T. Clearwater, presented the matter to the county board of supervisors, suggesting that the county should bear the expense of having a translation made. On December 13, 1895, the supervisors adopted a resolution "that the ancient records of this county, recently returned to the county clerk's office, be translated from the Dutch into English by a competent translator to be selected by the county judge. . . ."

The person selected by Judge Clearwater to translate the records was Dingman Versteeg. Versteeg was a native of the Netherlands (he was born in Zierikzee on January 27, 1867), but had been residing in the United States for several years. He had written a history of the Dutch settlements in Michigan and at Pella, Iowa in 1886, and a pamphlet about the early history of the Bergen (New Jersey) Reformed Church in 1889. In the early 1900s he had become library clerk and official translator for the Holland Society of New York.

Early in 1896 Versteeg began the task of translating the records, com-

,leting the work three years later on January 14, 1899. The translation vas bound in three large folio volumes, as follows:

1. Bond of May 31, 1658 and records of July 12, 1661 - Feb. 16, 1672/73.
2. Records of Feb. 21, 1672/73 - Oct. 23, 1682.
3. Records of Nov. 1, 1682 - Aug. 1, 1684 and various church records, Nov. 13, 1681 - Nov. 28, 1766. Most of the church records concern the poor funds and ordinary administrative expenses of the Reformed Church at Kingston (A. J. F. van Laer thought that Marbletown and New Paltz were also represented). In addition, the church constitution for the Lutheran Church at Loonenburg (now Athens, Greene County) is included, with signatures dated 1736-1746.

After completing this task Versteeg returned to his usual pursuits. He published *The Sea Beggars, Liberators of Holland from the Yoke of Spain* n 1901, a translation of Jonas Michaelius' *Manhattan in 1628* in 1904, nd a journal, *The New Netherland Register*, from 1911 through 1913.)n December 23, 1916, he resigned from his position with the Holland ;ociety. A pamphlet, *New Netherland's Founding*, appeared in 1924. He lied in the Netherlands on November 19, 1947.

Beginning in the mid-nineteenth century, numerous volumes of records elating to New York's colonial history were published. By 1910 transla- ions of Dutch records of New Netherland, New Amsterdam, Schenectady, ;everwyck, and Rensselaerswyck had been prepared by E. B. O'Callaghan, ;erthold Fernow, Jonathan Pearson, and A. J. F. van Laer. The New York Iistorical Association decided that the Kingston records should also be >ublished. After examining Versteeg's translation, the Association decided hat a revision was desirable, and entrusted the task to Samuel Oppenheim.

Oppenheim, who had been born in 1859, was a member of the New 'ork Bar. More importantly, he had long been interested in American iistory and had learned Dutch in order to read the colonial records. He iad published several books and pamphlets, most of which related to udaism in the colonial period. His most important work, *History of the* ews *in New York 1654-1664*, appeared in 1909.

Oppenheim made numerous changes in the translation, primarily in tyle, but occasionally also correcting errors. Unfortunately, the program vas discontinued after he had translated the court minutes only through Vovember 18, 1664. His revision was published in volume XI of the *New* 'ork State Historical Association Proceedings in 1912.

The only portion of the early records of Kingston to have been published, hen, includes less than four full years of the court records, and this >ublication has long been out of print. Photocopies of the Versteeg trans- ation have been available at only a few institutions, and their use has been imited by lack of an index and the occasional difficulty in reading Versteeg's handwriting. The Committee on Publication, therefore, examined the translation in 1974 to determine the feasibility of having it printed.

One problem which Versteeg had discovered is that the original Dutch records appear to be in a state of disorder. On page 37 of Volume II of the translation he wrote:

"It is plain from part of their contents that the pages from which the following translations appear below do not belong where they were put by the party who gathered together what seem to be scattered remnants of other records. It will have been observed, in Vol. I of these translations especially, that there often occurred entries under a certain date which evidently belonged somewhere else in the records, but the pages containing those entries were bound in between other pages, so that, chronologically, many entries are out of place where they occur."

Unfortunately, Versteeg, for whatever reason, did not undertake to reorder the records, a task which would be far simpler for someone working with the originals than for persons restricted to using the translations. To the extent possible, this editor has rearranged those documents which were dated. Because the records after 1675 were too disorganized to permit reorganization by someone working solely from the translation, we have excluded the later material. Fortunately, the records representing the entire period of greatest historical interest could be re-arranged. A major difficulty was posed by the fact that two dating systems were in use in the seventeenth century: the Gregorian year began on January 1 and the Julian on March 25, so that a date such as March 1670 might be either the last month of the Julian calendar or the third month of the Gregorian. Depending upon the calendar, then, this date could refer to either the month before April 1670, or the month before April 1671. The reader should be aware that documents between January 1 and March 25 have sometimes been assigned to a particular year by editorial decision. In undated documents we have followed Versteeg, but the reader should always be ready to seek internal evidence before accepting an implied date.

A second problem concerns errors in translation. These do not appear to be frequent, although Versteeg and Oppenheim were working without the lexicographical tools available to modern translators. Where the context indicates an error the editors have sought the advice and assistance of Charles Gehring, a leading scholar in the area of colonial Dutch linguistics. A list of probable errors is appended at the end of the second volume.

A third problem is posed by Versteeg's tendency to maintain Dutch word order in the translation. While the meaning is seldom obscured, the sentences sometimes read awkwardly. This is unfortunate since in Versteeg's other works in English he exhibited a clear and regular style. In particular, the use of the participle in certain constructions is contrary to good English usage, and in some instances Dr. Scott has changed this to the more natural infinitive. Obvious errors of transcription have been revised without comment.

Despite these problems the Committee recognized several good reasons for publishing these records. First is the importance of the records to historical research. Throughout the colonial period the Esopus was one of the major wheat-growing regions in North America, supplying flour to colonies throughout the Western Hemisphere. These records provide insights into the beginnings of that history. Second, few historians can read 17th-century Dutch, so that the contents of the original records cannot be known to them. Third, the translations are relatively inaccessible. To the best knowledge of the Committee, no copies exist outside New York State. Finally, to encourage research which may eventually lead to a definitive translation, it is necessary to bring the records to public attention.

For these reasons the Committee resolved to publish the records for 1661-1675. Although neither Oppenheim nor Versteeg's work is perfect, it appears to be adequate in expressing the essential meaning. Because Oppenheim's revision eliminated some errors and is preferable in style, it has been included rather than Versteeg's version of the same material. However, most of this publication—the portion commencing at page 172— is the work of Versteeg, in volume representing between 75% and 80%. We hope that the appendices will serve as an acceptable alternative to a full revision, since such revision would delay publication for several years.

THE RESEARCH VALUE OF THE RECORDS

Volume XIII of the *Documents Relating to the Colonial History of the State of New York*, which includes nearly all of the provincial records dealing with Kingston, and which has been a standard source since its publication in 1881, unfortunately contains many errors of translation. Historians should find the related Kingston records a useful check on the earlier publication.

The two publications also present contrasting concerns. Volume XIII represents the viewpoint of Kingston as seen from the level of the colonial executives, while the records in the present publication show the view from the community level. One is concerned with broad policy matters and development in relation to the rest of the colony, while the other shows the life of the ordinary citizen and the development of a sense of community among persons drawn from all over northwest Europe and the middle-Atlantic colonies. The two sources complement each other.

Volume XIII contains over 180 documents which relate to the Esopus in the period 1661-1675, but nearly half of these entries concern a single event, the Second Esopus War of 1663-1664. This imbalance is corrected by the present work, in which the period 1663-1664 forms only a small portion of the total. War is only a small part of any person's life, and we find that in that very period of war the people spent much of their time worrying about more mundane concerns: debts, harvests, personal comfort, and family relationships. One cannot show concern about what the soldiers and Indians are doing off in the woods someplace when his neighbor's hogs are rooting in his cabbage patch. He has to keep a sense of proportion.

We thus see here the events and the times not in their broad historic scope, but on a purely local level and in terms of the humanity of the persons living through them. To the court, the reconquest of 1673 meant only that it changed from court of sessions to schepen court. The record of the first English period brings home to those who have always lived under the United States Constitution the meaning of that amendment forbidding forced quartering of soldiers. We are reminded that we should be eternally grateful for the wisdom of our Founding Fathers in insisting upon that freedom. We are also reminded that the first settlers were not much different from us. They certainly were not saints, and many a proud descendant will be amazed to learn that the noble ancestor was so human as to run up bad debts, argue with his wife, get drunk, punch his neighbor, or neglect his duties. Some today may even have committed these or similar transgressions, and we are chastened to be reminded of the broadest scope of the meaning of humanity. Surely we should not overlook the other, more often remembered side of the coin, that these people were brave to have emigrated and to have remained here in the face of Indian wars, military disturbances, and political upheavals; that they showed a stubborn determination and rough humor in the face of hardship. Albart Heymans Roose does not always behave admirably, but how can we ever forget that moment of grandeur when he faced five armed English soldiers and laid into them with a club like Samson slaying the Philistines.

The settlement at the Esopus was a farming community, unlike the older port village of New Amsterdam or the fur trading center of Beverwyck, and thus offers an interesting contrast to those communities. The chief preoccupation of the residents was with land and crops. The principal symbols of status were those associated with success at farming—large holdings, the number of acres under cultivation, and the ownership of buildings and slaves. The only persons with social status other than well-to-do farmers were the authorities—military officers, the schout and secretary, and elected officials, who were, naturally, prominent farmers of the community. Very quickly the wealthy landowners had gained control of the schepen court. Tjeick Claessen de Wit and his brother-in-law Albert van Steenwyck, Jan Jansen van Oosterhout, Jan Willemsz van Hooghteelingh, and Thomas Chambers all served frequently on the court as schepens.

In such a small community the character of each resident registers sharply. As the reader searches these records many of the personalities come through clearly, and many interesting stories unfold. Captain Thomas Chambers, founder of the community and later Lord of the Manor of Fox Hall, is wealthy, impatient, respected, but not above engaging in a courtroom brawl with the schout. His stepchildren are often mentioned because of the court's role as orphanmaster. We see them grow to adulthood and receive their inheritance, protected over the years for them by guardians who are in turn watched by the court and the stepfather. It is heartening to see these children develop in time into important residents. In contrast, Jan Jansen van Amersfoort is an obstreperous character who is exiled for a year. Although he is guilty of beating his wife, the most shocking crime to the court is his calling his mother-in-law, Chambers' wife, an "old hog." The racy career of Grietje Westerbrook adds spice to the records, but we find that eventually she becomes a settled and accepted resident.

Most interesting is the reaction of the community to the changes of government. A celebration organized by the English soldiers to mark English control of the colony ends in a near riot. Dutch reconquest is accepted (officially, at least) with less enthusiasm than might be expected, and the return of the English accepted noncommitally.

The career of Roelof Swartwout is interesting to follow. Barely past the age of majority (25), he wangled a commission as schout from the West India Company, which set off a dispute between Director-General Stuyvesant and the Company. Eventually Stuyvesant deposed Swartwout, only to have him reappear as a schepen. Swartwout's wife, Eva Bratt, was the widow of Antoni de Hooges, who had been a prominent Rensselaerswyck official. Swartwout was never wealthy, but he did have connections.

There are several possibilities for research in the records. The economic historian will find particularly interesting the fluctuation of prices of grains and other commodities. Agricultural historians will be interested in the tools listed in estate inventories. The medical historian will find useful the catalogue of surgeon Gysbert van Imbroch's library, the inventory of his equipment, and the ideas of the court on the deleterious effects of dead animals in the streets. The social historian will find the reactions of the inhabitants to the Indians and the effects of foreign occupation on the community of importance. The genealogist will find a wealth of material here as well: wills, baptisms, marriages, orphan records, and frequent mention of family relationships in passing. In addition, there are always puzzles to whet the curiosity: who was the "Blue Farmer" and what does the nickname mean?

It is interesting to note the rights accorded to women under Dutch law, which included holding property in their own names and conducting businesses. Even the slaves owned their own personal property and could participate in lawsuits. At the bottom of the social scale were the Indians, whose testimony was considered of questionable value. Unlike the Beverwyck residents, who were dependent upon the Indians for their fortunes and maintained good relations, the people at the Esopus cared little for the aborigines. They engaged in small trade with them, but kept guards posted. The shooting of Indians has already been mentioned.

We can sympathize with those citizens who served on the court, not a professional jurist among them, wrestling with the evidence and their consciences to find truth and justice. We will agree with some decisions and disagree with others, but we must admire the schepens' resolution in ruling on tough questions and applaud their efforts to include other citizens in seeking to re-establish peace between squabbling settlers, often requiring the cooperation of the litigants themselves. It is law by common sense, common law in the best sense. One wonders if we acted in haste in rejecting this portion of Dutch law. Perhaps we should reconsider, in the light of our overworked courts and long delayed trials, the possible value of greater citizen involvement in our court system.

ACKNOWLEDGEMENTS

The goal of the Committee on Publication is to encourage the translation and publication of documents from colonial Netherland America. Following the successful publication in 1974 of four volumes of New Netherland records translated by A. J. F. van Laer in the years 1910-1918, the Committee sought other projects. With the encouragement and assistance of the Holland Society of New York, the State of New York, and the Genealogical Publishing Company three new programs have begun. Mrs. A. C. Hofman-Allema of the Amsterdam, Holland, City Archives is translating colonial deeds and patents. Dr. Charles Gehring is translating and editing records relating to Delaware Valley settlements, while Mrs. Rosemary Conway is transcribing the English records for that region. The present publication is the second Committee project to emerge in print thus far.

Thanks are due to the Holland Society of New York, the State of New York, especially the administration of the New York State Library, the Office of State History, the Cultural Education branch of the State Education Department, the staff of the Manuscripts Division of the State Library and Mr. Kenneth Brock, supervisor of the Local Records unit of the Office of State History, and the Clerk of Ulster County.

The following have assisted in the preparation of the manuscript for publication: Mr. Ralph L. De Groff, Dr. Charles Gehring, William A. Polf, Mrs. Joan Sanger, Dr. Kenneth Scott, Mrs. Dorothy Scutt, Mr. William A. Starna, Dr. Kenn Stryker-Rodda, and Dr. Michael Tepper.

VOLUME I

KINGSTON COURT RECORDS, 1661-1667

THE DUTCH RECORDS OF KINGSTON
BOOK I

[RESOLUTION OF INHABITANTS OF ESOPUS, MAY 31, 1658,
AND
COURT RECORDS OF WILDWYCK, JULY 12, 1661-MAY 6, 1664.]

[Pages 1 and 2 are missing. See Introduction.]

Copy.

Having, through very sad cases and to our general injury, experienced and borne, from time to time, the treacherous and intolerable audacity of the wild and barbarous natives, and realizing the folly of trusting to their promises and our own risk and danger in living separated and far apart from each other among such treacherous and vindictive people,

We, the undersigned inhabitants of the Esopus, in meeting assembled, have, upon the suggestion of the Director General, the Lord Petrus Stuyvesant, and his promise to provide us with a protective guard and, when needed, to assist us with additional troops,

Resolved, that, for the greater security of ourselves, our wives and children, we will, immediately after subscribing to these presents, completely demolish our separate dwellings, and locate at the place designated by the Lord General, and, by our own united efforts, together with the assistance of the Lord Director General, surround the place with palisades of a proper height, in order, with the blessing of the All-Good God, the better to protect ourselves and our property against the hostile assaults of the savages. And, invoking the Divine blessing and help, and using all honorable means, we bind ourselves to enter upon this work at once and to complete it as soon as possible, a fine of one thousand dollars to be paid into the treasury of the community, as a penalty, by any who by word or deed oppose this.

For the greater security whereof we have personally signed
our names hereto, in the presence of the Right Honorable Lord
Director General and Mr. Goovert Loockermans, former Schepen of
the City of Amsterdam in New Netherland.   Done this last of May,
Ao. 1658.

Jacob Jansen Stol, Thomas Chambers, Cornelis Barense
Slecht, the mark (x) of Willem Jansen, made by himself, the mark
(x) of Pieter Dircksen, made by himself, Jan Jansen, Jan Broersen,
his mark (x), made by himself, Dirck Hendricksen Graef, (x) his
mark, made by himself, Jan Lootman.

In presence of the Lord Petrus Stuyvesant and Goovert
Loockermans.

The above copy, made by order of the Commissaries, has been
found, after comparison, to agree with the original.

Attest,

ROELOOF SWARTWOUT, Schout.

[Pages 4 to 10 in original record, blank.   See Introduction as
to probable record intended to be entered here.]

July 12, 1661.

First Ordinary Session, held at Wildtwyck.

Resolved, by the Schepens here present, to hold Court on
Tuesday and thereafter every two weeks, until the further order
of the Director General and Council of New Amsterdam.

On the same day, Sergeant Christiaen Nissen romp informs
the Schout and Schepens here present, that whereas, no grain is to
be had here for the militia, Pieter van Alen, the shoemaker, is
exporting wheat.   Whereupon, deliberation having been had, it is
resolved that the shoemaker shall deliver his remaining grain to
Sergeant Christiaen Nissen romp, who is authorized to pay him on
delivery.

On the same day, the Schout and Schepens appoint one Jacob
Joosten to attend to all kinds of church service and services for the
Court.   He is appointed Court Messenger, provisionally, until the
further order of the Director General, and shall receive for one year
two hundred guilders [one guilder equals forty cents], in zeewant.

Ordinary Session, Tuesday, September 13, 1661.

Present: Evert Pels, Aldert Heymansen, Cornelis Baren Slecht.

The Schout, plaintiff, vs. Coenraedt the soldier, defendant. Default.

Tjirick Classen, plaintiff, vs. Femmetjen. Default .

Hendrick sewant reyger [braider of sewant] plaintiff, vs. Jan Buur. Default.

Mathys Blanchan, plaintiff, vs. Hendrick sewant reyger [braider of sewant].   Default.

Pieter van Alen, plaintiff, vs. Sergeant Christiaen Nissen romp. Default.

Machtelt [Stoffels], plaintiff, vs. Gerrit van Campen. Default.

Femmetjen [Alberts], plaintiff, vs. Gerrit van Campen. Default.

Femmetjen [Alberts] demands payment of twelve guilders, in zeewant.

The Schout, prosecutor and plaintiff, vs. Thomas Chambers, defendant.

The Schout declares that Thomas Chambers drew a knife against his brother-in-law, Jan Janssen, at Cornelis Barentse Slegt's house, which is denied by the defendant. Also that, on the last day of August, Thomas again drew a knife against Jan Janse and wounded him, which also is absolutely denied by the defendant.

Albert, the carpenter, asks for a building lot, which is granted him.

Ordinary Session, held Tuesday, September 28, 1661.

Pieter van Alen, prosecutor and plaintiff, vs. Sergeant Christiaen Nissen romp.

Pieter van Alen complains that the Sergeant beat him in the guard house, and pursued him on the public street. In defense, the Sergeant says that Pieter took brandy into the guard house and sold it there.

Resolved, [rest of page blank].

Catelyn the Walloon, plaintiff, complains of the cowherder, that he does not drive the cows home in time and that he did not drive them home for two days.

In defense, the cowherder says that, as she does not drive her cows to the herd, he cannot take care of them.

Ordered, that Catelyn shall drive her cows to the herd and that the defendant shall then take care of them.

The Schout, plaintiff, declares that Mathys Constapel [the gunner] tapped during the sermon. This the defendant denies, and says it is not true.

Gritedgen [Hillebrants], plaintiff, demands that her master say if he knows aught against her as a reason why he discharged her.

Juriaen Westgaer, the defendant, says that when he was sick she went out every day and returned home late at night, and that he then said to her, "Where you have been during the day, go there also at night."

Tjyrick Classen, plaintiff, vs. Femmetje, defendant. Default. Default.

The Schout plaintiff vs. Poulus Poulssen defendant.

The Schout declares that Poulus drew a knife. This the defendant denies.

The Schout, plaintiff, [blank space in original].

Jan Lammerse asks for a building lot, to be built upon at once.

Ordinary Session, held Tuesday, October 11, Anno 1661.

Present: Cornelis Barense Slecht, Evert Pels, Aldert Heymanse; the Schout, Roeloof Swartwout.

Pieter Jacobsen requests the Schout and Schepens to fix his charges for grinding corn. And whereas the said petitioner leaves it to the decision of the Court, he is allowed to charge for every schepel [about one bushel], eight stivers [one stiver, equals two cents] in zeewant, and as to those who have no zeewant he may deduct a tenth part but no more. This permission is to be for one year, or until the further order of the Director General and Council.

The Lord Schout, plaintiff, vs. Fop Barense. The Schout declares that complaint has been made that Fop Barents created a disturbance in front of the guard house, and there defied the Corporal, knife in hand, the which Corporal Ransou attests and says actually took place. Whereupon, having considered the matter, the Schepens give the officer time until the next Court day to get the Sergeant to testify.

Basje Pieterse, plaintiff, demands payment of Aert Otterspoor of nineteen guilders, in zeewant. Default.

Basjen Pieterse, plaintiff, vs. Fop Barense. Plaintiff demands forty guilders, in zeewant, of Fop Barense who admits owing the same and promises to pay within a month from date, under penalty of execution.

Basje Pieterse, vs. Poulus Poulussen, demands payment of the amount of twenty-three guilders, in zeewant. Default.

Tjirck Classen, plaintiff, demands of Roeloof Swartwout payment of three and a half schepels of wheat, and also of seven schepels of wheat assigned to him by some one else. The Schout is ordered to pay three and a half schepels of seed-corn within eight days, the other seven schepels to be paid within a month.

On this day the Schout submits some written charges against Thomas Chambers, all of which the latter denies.

Ordinary Session, held Tuesday, October 25, [1661].

Present: Evert Pels, the Schout, Cornelis Barense Slecht.

Evert de Waeesman, defendant.

The Commissaries demand a mudde of wheat [about four bushels] and seven guilders, nine stivers, which Evert Pels undertakes to pay, the same to go to the poor.

Evert de Waelsman, plaintiff, demands from William Jansen Stol, as payment for two cows, the amount of two hundred guilders, in corn. William Jansen Stol is ordered to pay within two months.

Evert de Waelsman, plaintiff, demands of Tjirick Clasen payment of wages for nineteen days, and for mowing grass two days. [Defendant] is ordered to pay two schepels of wheat for the mowing of the grass, and two gldrs. in zeewant, per day, for the nineteen days, and to pay the whole amount within six weeks.

Jacob Joosten, plaintiff, vs. Poulus Poulussen. Default.

Jacob Joosten, plaintiff, vs. Aert Jacobsen. Default.

Tjirick Clasen, plaintiff, vs. Pieter Hillebrantsen. Default.

Thomas Chambers requests of the Commissaries further particulars from the Schout of the written charges made against him.

And whereas Thomas requests the same to be in writing, though he has received a copy and he claims that omissions occur therein, the Commissaries have therefore examined said copy, and find the same to be correct and to correspond with the original charges. At the request of the Schout, it is consented that the parties be referred to the Lord Director General and Council of New Amsterdam, or they may await the arrival of the Lord General.

October 26, Anno 1661.

Extraordinary Court Session, called by Thomas Chambers to proceed against the Schout, Roelof Swartwout.

Whereas, Thomas Chambers, by petition, asks the Commissaries, "Why am I, Thomas, not permitted to appear before the Court, notwithstanding the Schout has summoned me?"

The reason why Thomas was summoned is because of the four schepels of wheat which he guaranteed for his servant Poulus Poulussen, and for which he refuses to pay to the Court Messenger sent to him. The Consistory petitioned that the Magistrate should kindly demand the same. The Schout therefore summoned him, Thomas. If his name was not called from the calendar, his default will be opened. Secondly: Whereas, Thomas by a petition has further requested the Commissaries to give reasons why the parties are referred to the Director General and Council, the Commissaries answer that, as Thomas has denied all the charges which the Schout presented against him, and as these concern the Supreme Magistrates, the matter has been referred to the Director General and Council of New Amsterdam.

Thus done, for cause us thereunto moving.

By order of the Commissaries.

Ordinary Session, held Tuesday, November 8, Anno 1661.

Present: The Schout, Evert Pels, Cornelis Barense Slecht. Aldert Heymanse, absent.

The Schout, plaintiff, demands of the Sergeant proof of what he has complained about Fop Barentse. The Sergeant denies this. Fop Barense, the defendant, also declares it to be untrue, and says he was at work.

The Schout, plaintiff, vs. Pieter van Alen, defandant. Default.

The Schout, plaintiff, vs. Tjirick Clasen, defendant. Default.

Matheus Blanchan, plaintiff, vs. Pieter van Alen, defendant. Plaintiff, by virtue of a power of attorney conferred upon him by Fousien Briel, demands payment of Pieter van Alen of the amount of two schepels of wheat. Default.

Jan Aersen, plaintiff, demands of Evert Pels, defendant, payment of the amount of forty gldrs., thirteen stivers. Defendant offers to pay the plaintiff in strung zeewant. The plaintiff, Jan Aersen, is not satisfied with zeewant. He is ordered to show, at the next session of the Court, whether the debt arose in beavers or in zeewant, and, as the defendant does not admit owing in beaver price, Jan Aersen is required to submit a true account.

Gertjen Bouts, plaintiff, demands of Jan Aersen, payment of the quantity of twenty-one schepels of wheat. Jan Aersen admits owing the same and on consent promises to pay one-half within two weeks, and the other half next spring.

Jan Jansen van Eyckelen, plaintiff, demands of Margrita Clabbort payment of the sum of seventy-two guilders.

Margrita, on the other hand, demands payment from Jan Jansen van Eyckelen of rent incurred while living in her house.

The Commissaries having heard the parties, both are referred, under orders from the Schout and Schepens, to two good men to arbitrate the matter as far as possible. For which purpose the Schout and Schepens select Jacob Boerhans and Aldert de Rademaker [the wheelright], who, if a decision should prove too difficult, are permitted to choose a third.

Jan Joosten van Eykelen, plaintiff, demands of Pieter Loockermans the payment of fourteen schepels of wheat and asks to be allowed to attach his money here. Pieter Loockermans says he does not owe him any wheat, and that, besides, he has worked for him two or three days. The Commissaries, having heard the parties, refer them to the judge having jurisdiction.

Jan Janse van Eyckelen, plaintiff, vs. Jan Willemse, defendant. Plaintiff demands of Jan Willemsen payment for the amount of six schepels of wheat. Default.

Basjen [Pieters], plaintiff, vs. Aert Otterspoor. Plaintiff demands of Aert Otterspoor payment of nineteen guilders. Aert Otterspoor admits owing Basjen Pieters nineteen guilders, and assigns to Basjen Pieters [his claim] against Evert Pels who agrees to pay the same.

Basjen Pieters, plaintiff, demands of Poulus Poulussen payment of the amount of twenty-three guilders and assigns one-half of it to the poor or to the church. Third default.

The Schout and Schepens order the defendant to pay within two days, together with the costs accrued under the law relating thereto.

Note. Poulus Poulussen having appeared this day, and having been heard in his defense, denying everything, he saying that he drank there only once, for which the new farmer paid for him, the Commissaries, having heard both parties, order Basjen Pieters to prove the debt, the party found in the wrong to pay the costs.

Femmetjen Alberts, plaintiff, demands of Gerrit van Campen, defendant, payment of the amount of twelve guilders. Second default.

Geertruyt Vosburgh, plaintiff, says that she gave an order to Jan van Breeman for two hundred boards to be delivered here at Wildtwyck. Jan van Breeman, defendant, produces a certificate by two witnesses, that Gysbert van den Bergh would not let the boards go forward until the payment of the money advanced by him thereon.

And as Geertruyt Vosburgh had Jan van Breeman arrested here, and she showed us an extract, dated August 23, whereby the Honorable Commissaries of Fort Orange ordered the defendant either to pay or to deliver the boards at this place, the defendant is ordered to furnish a bond for the remaining one hundred and fifty-two boards, and he offers as surety Juriaen Westgaer. This (x) is the mark of Juriaen Westgaer. And for this reason the parties are referred to the judge having jurisdiction.

Fop Barense, plaintiff, demands of Jan Jansen, defendant, eight schepels of wheat for wages earned by him. Default.

Evert de Wachtsman [the watchman], plaintiff, demands of Juriaen Westgaer, defendant, payment of the amount of forty gldrs. in zeewant.   Defandant admits owing the same and promises to pay within fourteen days.

Gritjen Hillebrants, plaintiff, demands of Juriaen Westgaer payment of her full wages, and says that her master discharged her.   Defendant denies this, and Gritjen is ordered to produce good witnesses at the next session of the Court.

Eymmetjen, defendant, places under attachment the moneys of Jan the weaver, which are in the custody of Cornelis Barense Slecht.

Ymmetjen de Backster [the baker], defendant, places under attachment the moneys of Arent Isacsen, which are in the custody of Cornelis Barense.

First Session, held Wednesday, November 16, Anno 1661.

Present: The Noble Lord General, Petrus Stuyvesant; The Schout, Roelof Swartwout; Commissaries, Evert Pels, Cornelis Barense Slecht, Aldert Heymanse Roosa.

Femmetje Albert, plaintiff, demands twelve guilders of Gerret van Campen, who admits the debt.   The Schout and Schepens order the defendant to pay.

Mathyeu Blanchan, plaintiff, vs. Pieter van Alen, defendant. The third default.

Gritjen Hillebrants, plaintiff, says that her master discharged her, which she offers to prove by two witnesses. They testify that they heard her master say: ''Where you have been during the day, go there also at night.''   Juriaen Westgaer, defendant, says that what the witnesses say is correct.   Both parties having been heard, Juriaen Westgaer is ordered to pay Gritjen Hillebrantsen a quarter year's wages.

Jan Jansen van Eyckelen, plaintiff, demands a receipt and the liquidation of the balance of his account.   He testifies under oath that the debt is just, according to his account.   Arien Symensen, the defendant, is ordered to give plaintiff a receipt and to pay the balance of the debt.

Bart Sybrantse, plaintiff, demands of Lowys Dubo the amount of seven schepels of wheat as payment for the freight of cattle. Lowys Dubo, defendant, says he paid his share.

Whereas, the defendant admits having ordered the cattle of Bart, he is therefore, after deliberation, ordered to pay.

Bart Sybrantsen, plaintiff, demands sixteen guilders in zeewant from Harmen Jansen in payment for passage of himself, wife and children from the Manethans [Manhattan], to the Hesopues [Esopus], also eight guilders paid to Mr. Poulus, besides half a schepel of peas. Harmen Jansen, defendant, admits that he owes the debt, and is ordered to pay, before his departure, twenty-four guilders in zeewant and a half schepel of peas, to Bart Sybrantsen.

Geertruyt Andrissen, plaintiff, demands of Gerrit van Campen payment of two schepels of wheat and eleven guilders in zeewant. Gerrit van Campen, defendant, having been heard in his own defense, is condemned to pay one schepel of wheat and eleven guilders, in zeewant.

Weynant Gerritsen, plaintiff, demands payment of Jan Lammersen, defendant. The first default.

Ordinary Session held Tuesday, November 22, [1661].

Present: The Noble Lord General, Petrus Stuyvesant; Schout Roeloof Swartwout; Commissaries, Evert Pels, Corneiis Barense Slecht, Aldert Heymanse Roosa.

Evert Prys, plaintiff, by a petition, demands the return of the two cows he let to Roeloof Swartwout for one-half of the natural increase, which is testified to by Pieter Jacobsen. Roeloof Swartwout, the defendant, admits having hired the cows, and is permitted to keep said cows untii the expiration of the three years, as contracted for.

Mathyue Blansan, plaintiff, summons Pieter van Alen again, and, by virtue of a power of attorney from Toeryn Briel, demands two schepels of wheat and a sack [zak, or three schepels]. Defendant's third default.

IIe is ordered after the third default to pay to Matheue Blanchan, by virtue of a power of attorney, and the costs of the case.

Wynant Gerritsen, plaintiff, demands thirty guilders in zeewant from Jan Lammersen, defendant, who admits he justly owes the debt. The parties having been heard by the Honorable Court, the defendant is ordered to pay Weynant Gerritsen thirty guilders, the amount claimed, besides the costs accrued herein.

The Schout, plaintiff, demands a fine of Tjirick Clasen because he carted during the harvest. Fined six guilders.

The Schout, plaintiff, demands a fine of Pieter van Alen, because he desecrated the Sabbath by receiving people and selling them brandy during the sermon. The defendant is ordered, on his third default, to pay the legal fine.

Ordinary Session, held at Wildtwyck, December 6, 1661.

Present: The Lord Schout; Evert Pels, Cornelis Barense Slecht, Aldert Heymanse Roosa.

Jonas Ransou, plaintiff, vs. Mathys Roeloofsen, defendant. Plaintiff alleges that defendant murderously attacked him at night, without reason or cause. He accuses him of having been at his wife's bed, and of having overpowered him, so that he would have been murdered if no assistance had come, the which plaintiff says he can prove. Defendant's first default.

Machtelt Stoffels, plaintiff, demands of Altjen Constapel a pettycoat which plaintiff loaned her when she fled from her husband, Mathy Constapel. Defendant's first default.

Christiaen Nissen romp, Sergeant, plaintiff, demands of Magiel Veree eight guilders, heavy money, and also two schepels of loaned wheat. Defendant says he paid the eight guilders of heavy money to My Lord the General. Whereas, Magiel Veere can not prove the payment, therefore the Schout and Commissaries, having heard the parties, order Magiel Feere to pay the aforesaid amount within six weeks.

On the same date, Cornelis Jansen, sawyer, petitions for a lot for a house, which is granted him by the Schout and Schepens, the same to be pointed out to him at the first opportunity.

Ordinary Session, held at Wildtwyck, January 3, Anno, 1662.

Present: The Schout, Roeloof Swartwout, Aldert Heymanse Roosa, Cornelis Barense Slecht.

Tjirick Classen, plaintiff, demands of the Schout, Roeloof Swartwout, the cost of three summonses and also demands, without proof, two schepels of wheat.

Roeloof Swartwout, the defendant, denies owing the two schepels of wheat demanded by the plaintiff. Whereas, Tjirick Clasen cannot prove the debt, his claim is rejected, but the Schout is
ordered to pay for the three summonses.

Tjirick Clasen, plaintiff, demands of Pieter Hillebrantsen,
defendant, eight schepels of wheat. Pieter Hillebrantsen admits
he owes the debt. The Schout and Commissaries, having heard the
parties, order Pieter Hillebrantsen to pay the plaintiff two schepels
every week until the eight schepels are paid.

Huybrecht Bruyn, plaintiff, demands of Tjirick Clasen the
value of six schepels of wheat. The defendant admits he owes the
debt, and promises to pay the same to the Schout within six weeks.

Casper Caspersen, plaintiff, demands of Pieter Jillessen payment of the amount of thirty-two guilders zeewant, as per obligation. The defendant Pieter Jillisse admits he owes the plaintiff.
The Commissaries, having heard the parties, order the defendant
to pay within fourteen days.

Capser Casperse, plaintiff, demands of Jonas Ransou, payment
of the amount of twenty-nine guilders, sixteen stivers, in zeewant,
as per obligation. The defendant admits he owes the debt. The
Schout and Commissaries, having heard the parties, order Jonas
Ransou to pay the amount sued for within eight days.

Mathys Roeloofsen, plaintiff, demands from Albert Gerritsen
payment of the cost of palisades for a lot bought and not built
upon. The defendant answers as follows: The Schout and Commissaries have given me the lot for which I am to pay six schepels
of wheat for expenses incurred for palisades.

Mathys Roelofsen, plaintiff, demands of Aert Aertsen Otterspoor payment of the quantity of ten schepels of wheat, due for
drinks of brandy. The first default.

Huybrecht Bruyn, plaintiff, demands of Barent Gerritsen payment of the value of sixteen schepels of wheat for wages earned
on a lot of work thus undertaken, which Jan Westhoesen is willing
under oath to affirm he heard. The first default.

Albert Gerritsen, plaintiff, demands from Jan Jansen van
Ammerstede payment of the quantity of twenty-seven schepels

of wheat due for wages earned. Defendänt Jän Janse van Amersfoort's [*sic*] first default. Paid.

Jan Jansen van Amersfoort, plaintiff, vs. Willem Haf.   The
first default.

Gerrit van Campen appears and assigns to Jan Barensen
six schepels of wheat which Aldert Heymanse promises to pay.

Matheu Blanchan, plaintiff, demands from Pieter van Alen,
by virtue of an earlier judgement against him, payment of two
schepels of wheat and a sack.   Whereas, Pieter van Alen shows us
a receipt from Toesyn Briel's son-in-law for the debt sued for,
dated November 24, and whereas Matheu Blanchan has pressed the
Schout to issue execution against Pieter van Alen, who has demanded security from Matheu Blanchan, which is conceded as due
to Pieter van Alen, but Matheu Blanchan refuses to give security,
and the parties, at their request, having been heard, Pieter van
Alen is ordered to pay, as aforesaid, provided Matheu Blanchan
gives security on his claim against Pieter van Alen.

January 10, Anno 1662.

Huybrecht Bruyn requests an extraordinary session of the
Court for the purpose of proceeding against Barent Gerretsen, the
party found in the wrong to pay the cost.

Huybrecht Bruyn, plaintiff, demands from Barent Gerritsen,
defendant, payment of the value of sixteen schepels of wheat for
wages earned, for which he had contracted with the defendant.
Barent Garretsen, the defendant, denies owing the value of sixteen
schepels of wheat, but says that he made a contract with Huybrecht
Bruyn for the mason work, for sixteen schepels of oats, of which
he offers to make oath.

Huybrecht Bruyn produces two certificates, one by Jan West-
husen who certifies and declares, at the request of Huybrecht
Bruyn, that Barent Gerretsen contracted for the mason work in
putting up two brandy-stills, and an axle with which to grind, and
a malt kiln, in consideration of sixteen schepels of wheat, or in
oats at the price of wheat, three schepels of oats to be reckoned
equal to one schepel of wheat; and he confirms the same under
oath.

The second certificate, made by Jan Broersen, states that he was present when Huybrecht Bruyn, the mason, demanded sixteen schepels of wheat from Barent Gerritsen, and he confirms the same with his oath.

The plaintiff declares the debt sued for is just, and this he confirms under oath.

The Schout and Commissaries, having considered the matter and having found a great error, thereupon order Barent Gerritsen to pay the demanded quantity of sixteen schepels of wheat, besides the cost of the trial. The defendant is allowed a stay of two weeks.

Ordinary Session, held at Wildtwyck this 17th of January, Anno 1662.

Present: The Schout; Cornelis Barense Slecht, Evert Pels, Aldert Heymanse Roosa.

Jonas Ransou, plaintiff, vs. Evert Prys, defendant. The first default. Paid.

Magiel Feree, plaintiff, vs. Pieter van Alen, defendant. The first default. Paid.

Christiaen Nissen romp, plaintiff, vs. Fop Barense, defendant. The first default.

Barent Gerritsen, plaintiff, vs. Aert Aertsen, defendant. The first default. Paid.

Barent Gerretsen, plaintiff, vs. Hey Olfertsen, defendant. The first default. Paid.

Barent Gerritsen, plaintiff, vs. Jonas Ransou, defendant. The first default. Paid.

Barent Gerretsen, plaintiff, vs. Jacob Jansen, defendant. The first default. Paid.

Jan Jansen, plaintiff, demands from Willem Jansen Hap, defendant, payment of the quantity of thirty schepels of wheat. Against Willem Jansen Stol, defendant. Paid. The first default.

Albert Gerritsen, plaintiff, demands twenty-seven schepels of wheat from Jan Jansen for wages earned. The defendant answers he does not owe any money until he shall have received the money from William Jansen Stol. The plaintiff replies that he will be able to prove that Jan Jansen must pay him.

Mathys Roeloofsen, plaintiff, demands from Dirck Willemse payment of the quantity of ten schepels of wheat, according to account. The defendant admits owing plaintiff ten schepels of wheat, and assigns to him his claim against Tjirick Clasen to receive the value of ten schepels of wheat.

Cornelis Jansen, plaintiff, vs. Pieter van Alen, defendant. The first default.

Jan Dircksen van Breeman, plaintiff, vs. Cornelis Jansen, defendant. The first default.

Jan Dircksen, plaintiff, vs. Jan Lammerse, defendant. The first default.

Hendrick Jochemsen, plaintiff, demands ten and a half schepels of wheat from Jonas Ransou. The first default.

Hendrick Jochemsen attaches the value of six schepels of wheat belonging to Jonas Ransou, in the possession of Dirck Willemsen.

Hendrick Jochemsen, plaintiff, demands payment of Jacob Jansen, defendant. The first default.

Ordinary Session, held Tuesday, January 31, [1662].

Present: The Schout, Roelof Swartwout; Evert Pels, Aldert Heymanse Roosa, Cornelis Barense Slecht.

Albert Gerritsen, plaintiff, demands of Jan Jansen van Amersfoordt, defendant, payment of the quantity of twenty-seven schepels of wheat. Defendant admits he owes no more than sixteen schepels of wheat for work and for making Willem Jansen Stol's harness. He admits still owing eleven schepels of wheat on account of the work of Geertruyt Andrissen, but promises to pay these eleven schepels at the completion of the job. The Schout and Commissaries order the defendant to pay the first half of the sixteen schepels of wheat within two weeks, and the other half one month after date.

Jonas Ransou, plaintiff, demands from Evert Prys payment of the amount of ten schepels of wheat, three half pints, forty-five stivers, on account of brandy delivered to him.

The defendant answers that he owes only for a pint of brandy. The plaintiff says he is ready to prove that the debt sued for is just.

Hey Olfersen, plaintiff, complains that Barent Gerritsen beat and kicked him and trampled upon him, and proves it by four witnesses, viz. Jan Lammersen, Alberent Gerritsen, Gommert Gerritsen, Aert Pietersen Tack.

The defendant, Barent Gerritsen, admits having beaten the plaintiff three times, and says he beat him because plaintiff heaped abuse upon him and said that he, Barent Gerritsen, was a scoundrel. The defendant is granted time until the next session of the Court to prove his assertions.

Jan Jansen van Amersfoort, plaintiff, demands of Willem Jansen Stol, payment of the amount of fifteen schepels of wheat for wages earned. The defendant admits owing plaintiff the amount sued for. The Schout and Commissaries order the defendant to pay the plaintiff the first half within six weeks, and the balance one month after [that] date.

Session, held Tuesday, February 7, 1662.

Present: The Schout, Roelof Swartwout; Cornelis Barense Slecht, Evert Pels, Albert Heymanse Roosa.

Dirck Ariaensen, plaintiff, says he worked for Evert Pels during harvest time, and threshed twenty-seven days. He demands, as daily wages for threshing, two guilders, in zeewant, and, for harvesting, two guilders, ten stivers, in grain, per day. The defendant, Evert Pels, answers he owes the plaintiff no more than one guilder, ten stivers, for threshing, and two guilders, ten stivers for harvesting, both in zeewant.

The Commissaries order the defendant to pay the plaintiff for harvesting, two guilders, ten stivers, in wheat, and, for threshing, one guilder, ten stivers, in zeewant, each per day.

Jan Aersen, plaintiff, demands from Evert Pels payment of the quantity of sixty schepels of oats. The defendant admits owing Jan Aersen the above demanded sixty schepels of oats and promises to pay within fourteen days.

Jan Aersen, plaintiff, demands payment of Roeloof Swartwout. Defendant admits owing the plaintiff and says, if the plaintiff is willing, he will pay him at the opening of navigation.

Hendrick Cornelissen, plaintiff, demands from Albert Gysbertsen payment of the quantity of four and a half schepels of oats for wages earned. The defendant admits owing the amount sued for, and promises to pay within fourteen days, at the option of the plaintiff.

Hendrick Cornelissen, plaintiff, demands a mudde of wheat [about four bushels] or its value from Jan Willemsen for wages earned. The defendant admits owing plaintiff the aforesaid amount, provided plaintiff first completes the work contracted for. The Commissaries order plaintiff first to finish his work and then to demand payment.

Hendrick Corneelissen, plaintiff, demands from Jan Lootman's wife payment of the amount of twelve guilders, in zeewant. The defendant, Jan Lootman, denies the debt, and answers he does not know what his wife has done, but promises the plaintiff eight guilders he owes him. The Commissaries order the defendant to pay plaintiff eight guilders, in zeewant, and the plaintiff to prove the balance of the debt.

Haremen Hendricksen, plaintiff, demands from Pieter Hillebrantsen payment of the amount of eight schepels of wheat, as per obligation assigned to him. The defendant admits owing the quantity demanded. The Commissaries order defendant to pay within three days three and one-half schepels of wheat, and the balance within six weeks.

Storm Albertsen, plaintiff, demands from Baerent Gerritse the quantity of forty schepels of oats in payment for an anker of brandy [about ten gallons]. The defendant, Albert Gerretse, admits owing the amount demanded. The Commissaries sentence defendant to pay plaintiff within one month.

Hey Olfersen, plaintiff, demands of Barent Gerritsen, as per complaint heretofore presented, security for his hurts, physician's fee, and lost time. Barent Gerritsen admits having thrice beaten Hey Olfersen, as heretofore stated, and that he cannot prove anything further. The Commissaries order and refer the parties to two good men within the period of thrice twenty-four hours.

Machiel Feere, plaintiff, demands from Pieter van Alen payment of the amount of two and a half schepels of wheat for wages earned. The defendant, Pieter van Halen, refuses to pay the amount sued for, and says he does not owe it, and has overpaid the plaintiff. The Commissaries having examined the accounts of the parties find that defendant has paid one schepel of wheat too much, on which account the plaintiff is ordered, if he cannot adduce further proof, to pay the defendant one schepel of wheat.

The Schout, as plaintiff, declares that on February 2, Anno 1662, one Jacob Boerhans was found very badly hurt in his own house, and that there were present, Jan van Breemen, Sergeant Christiaen Nissen roemp, Poulus Poulussen, the Norman, of which I demand judicial inquiry.

Christiaen Nissen romp, defendant, says he is not able to say anything about it.

Poulus Thomassen, defendant, says he did not know anything about it until he came in on the morning of the following day, and, seeing what had taken place, went immediately away. He testifies, however, that the Sergeant took a knife from the table, and threatened him, Poulus Tomassen, with the same.

Jan Dircksen van Breeman, defendant, says he was there too, but does not know how Jacob Boerhans happened to get hurt, saying, "I was drunk." He declares that he knew that Sergeant Christiaen Nissen romp and Poulus Tomsen had had trouble, and that Poulus Tomassen had tried to break the Sergeant's sword, and had broken the scabbard to pieces.

Defendant Jan Jansen van Hamersfoort was called upon to testify, but declares that he does not know how Jacob Boerhans happened to get hurt, as he arrived there after it happened.

Christiaen Nissen romp testified: "Poulus Tomassen broke the scabbard of my sword to pieces, and thereupon fell over the bench, and upon me, and thereupon I took a knife from the table and said to him, ' Get off of me.' "

Ordinary Session, held Tuesday this 14th of February, 1662.

Present: The Schout; Evert Pels, Aldert Heymanse Roosa.

Machiel Fere, plaintiff, vs. Pieter van Halen, defendant. The plaintiff demands another two and one half schepels of wheat from Pieter van Halen. Defendant denies owing anything to plaintiff, and even claims a balance in his favor. Whereas, parties have not made up their accounts, the Commissaries refer the parties to two good men, Tomas Chambers and Albert Gerritsen.

Jacob Joosten, plaintiff, demands from Pieter Hillebrantsen payment for the value of four schepels of wheat. Defendant's first default.

Matys Roeloofsen, plaintiff, demands from Jacob Jansen thirty-six schepels of oats. The defendant admits he owes the plaintiff thirty-six schepels of oats. The Commissaries order the defendant to pay within three months.

Mathys Roelofsen, plaintiff, demands from Jacob Barense payment of three schepels of wheat, due for wine delivered to defendant. The defendant admits owing three schepels of wheat, but says he is not able to pay at present, and requests two or three months' time. The Commissaries order the defendant to pay within two months.

Hendrick Janse Looman, plaintiff, demands from Jacob Joosten payment of the value of forty schepels of wheat, due for moneys advanced. The defendant admits he justly owes the plaintiff. The Commissaries order the defendant to pay twenty schepels of wheat within two months, and the balance after that date.

Jacob Joosten, plaintiff, demands from Mathys Roeloofsen, three and a half schepels of wheat for school-money earned by him. The defendant admits owing plaintiff the aforesaid amount and requests four weeks' time, which are allowed him.

As plaintiffs, Aert Aertsen and Pieter Jillessen demand full payment for taking care of the Schout's cows. The Schout answers that they were only to take care of the cows during harvest time, and therefore he refused full payment. The plaintiffs say that as the Schout had the cows brought to his land they were not obliged to receive them again. The Commissaries order the Schout to pay in full.

Albert Gysbertsen, plaintiff, demands from Aert Jacobsen payment of the value of three beavers, wages earned for making a plough. The defendant answers he owes no more than two beavers and a half. The Commissaries find that plaintiff is entitled to his full wages, and thereupon defendant is ordered to satisfy the plaintiff.

Jonas Ransou, plaintiff, vs. Evert Prys, defendant. Default.

Hey Olfertsen, plaintiff, says, Barent Gerritsen has been unwilling to appear before good men to settle his difference with me. The defendant answers that he has not had time. The Commissaries order the defendant to pay to Hey Olfersen, according to the account furnished, eighteen guilders, four stivers, and in addition, for expenses incurred, such as court summons, six gldrs. more, making together twenty-four gldrs., four stivers.

The Commissaries order plaintiff to pay a fine of six gldrs., for the poor.

Mathys Roeloofsen, plaintiff, vs. Barent Gerretsen, defendant.

Plaintiff says he bought of defendant three ankers of distilled waters, one anker [about ten gallons] to be delivered every consecutive week. The defendant answers, and admits he sold plaintiff three ankers of distilled waters and delivered two of them, but says he is not willing to deliver any more until he is first paid. The Commissaries order the defendant to deliver the third anker of wine within a week's time, and further order the plaintiff to pay within a week from date thirteen schepels of wheat and fifty guilders, in zeewant.

Jan Lammersen, plaintiff, demands from Femmetjen Alberts five schepels of wheat, the selling price of a pig.

The defendant, Femmetje Alberts, answers she does not owe more than four schepels of wheat. The plaintiff answers he will be satisfied with four schepels. The Commissaries order defendant to pay one-half within two weeks and the other half two weeks after date.

Jan Barense van Ammeshof, plaintiff, demands from the Schout payment of the value of nineteen schepels of wheat.

Roeloof Swartwout, the defendant, admits the debt and requests time. The Commissaries order defendant to pay within six weeks.

Jacob Joosten, plaintiff, demands from the Schout seven schepels of wheat and one daelder [sixty cents].

The Schout, defendant, admits the debt. The Commissaries order defendant to pay within one month.

Jan Janse Brabander, plaintiff, demands from Aert Jacobsen, defendant, payment of the value of ten schepels of oats. The defendant admits the debt and promises to pay the oats.

Christiaen Nissen romp, plaintiff, demands from Fop Barense, defendant, as payment for a hat, six schepels of wheat and five gldrs., ten st., in zeewant. Defendant admits owing the debt sued for. Plaintiff grants defendant three weeks' time.

The Schout, as plaintiff, again informs the Commissaries that one Jacob Boerhans was very badly wounded in his own house, and requests to be allowed to secure legal evidence concerning the same from the witnesses who were present at the time, viz., Christiaen Nissen romp, Poulus Tomassen, Jan Dircksen van Breeman, and requests that Jan Janse give testimony in regard to the same, as he had come there.

Ordinary Session. held Tuesday, February 28, 1662.

Present: The Schout; Evert Pels, Albert Heymanse Roosa, Cornelis Barense Slecht.

Christiaen Nissen romp, plaintiff, vs. Matys Roeloofsen and Altjen Sybrants, defendants.

Plaintiff demands, as payment for a hat, the value of six schepels of wheat. Defendant admits the debt, but answers he has an account against the plaintiff.

Plaintiff says the account is wrong, and defendant answers that he is able to prove the same.

The Commissaries order the defendant, in accordance with his own request, to prove his account at the next session of the Court.

[No names appear in the following case, but judging from the second entry in the next session it was between Christiaen Nissen romp and Mathys Roeloofsen.]

The plaintiff tells the Court how the defendant, during the night, pushed the drunken savages out of the house, which the defendant admits, saying they rushed, with kettles, in and out of the house.

The plaintiff further says that, because he happened to mention this at the house of Jan Brouwersen, the defendant, and especially his wife, called him, the plaintiff, names, in his own house, on a Sunday before the morning sermon, saying he was a rascal and a thief—"you robber of reputations."

The defendant admits having called plaintiff names, and considers him now just such a person as he was stated to be, and asks if he can prove that I sold brandy to the savages.

On the second count, the Commissaries, upon the plaintiff's demand, order the defendant to prove at the next session of the Court what rascally and thieving acts the plaintiff has committed, under a penalty [to be imposed on] defendant, as an example to others. In addition, the defendant is ordered to prove how the savages obtained the brandy, or he will be punished at the next session of the Court.

Jonas Ransou, plaintiff, demands from Evert Parys, defendant, payment of the amount of ten schepels of wheat and forty-five stivers for sold brandy. Defendant denies the debt. Martin Harmense, a witness, says that Jonas Ransou fetched three cans of brandy for defendant.

Christiaen Nissen romp, a witness, says he heard that Evert Prys promised to pay Jonas Ransou ten schepels of wheat.

The Commissaries order defendant to pay to the plaintiff the amount sued for, within two months, unless the defendant can furnish counter proof.

Evert Parys, plaintiff, vs. Jonas Ransou, defendant. Plaintiff says that Jonas Ransou, in the presence of Poulus Poulussen, Jan Brouwersen and Jan de Brabander, called him a thief and a scoundrel.

The defendant denies having called names, but says that plaintiff did not act right in trying to keep from defendant what belonged to him.

Storm Albertsen, plaintiff, demands from Jonas Ransou, defendant, payment of the amount of ten schepels of oats and two schepels of wheat, as per obligation which ought to have been paid Dec. 10, 1661. The defendant admits the debt. The Commissaries order defendant to pay within two weeks, without further delay, besides the costs.

Aert Pietersen Tack, plaintiff, demands from Aert Jacobsen payment of the amount of eighty-one schepels of oats. Defendant admits the debt but says he is not now able to pay. Requests time.

Commissaries order defendant to pay the plaintiff twenty schepels of oats every two weeks until the debt is paid.

Barent Gerritsen, plaintiff, vs. Matys Roelofsen, defendant. Plaintiff demands from the defendant payment of thirteen schepels of wheat and fifty guilders, in zeewant, for wines delivered to him. Defendant says that, whereas plaintiff did not, in accordance with the judgment, deliver the third anker, he does not now want plaintiff's wines, and requests that the third anker of wine be deducted from the bill. The Commissaries order plaintiff to value the anker of wine at eighty guilders, in zeewant, to be deducted from the bill.

Defendant is ordered to pay plaintiff eight schepels of wheat within two weeks.

Barent Gerritsen, plaintiff, vs. Hey Olfersen, defendant.

Plaintiff presents a petition informing the Commissaries that he gave an order to Hey Olersen, the carpenter, to build a house for him, to be finished without delay, and that he needs it badly. Requests to be allowed to employ another carpenter on it.

The defendant answers that he will have the work done within two weeks, to be ready for occupancy at the pleasure of the plaintiff.

Whereas this matter has already been before the Schout and Schepens, defendant guarantees the completion of the above and, in case of failure, to pay a fine of fifty guilders to the poor, at the pleasure of the Commissaries.

Barent Gerrisen, plaintiff, vs. Jonas Ransou, defendant. Plaintiff demands payment of the value of six schepels of wheat for wine delivered. Defendant demands an account of what has been received for the same. The Commissaries order plaintiff to make out and send in his account.

Dirck Arianese, plaintiff, vs. Evert Pels, defendant. Plaintiff demands payment of twenty-seven guilders, ten stivers, in wheat, and also forty guilders, ten stivers, in zeewant. Defendant answers he paid four schepels of wheat, leaving a balance due of five schepels. The Commissaries order defendant to pay plaintiff two schepels of wheat within eight days, and of the balance, one schepel each week, and to pay the zeewant within three weeks.

Evert Pels. plaintiff, vs. Geertruyt Andrissen, defendant. Plaintiff demands payment of the amount of five hundred guilders, eighteen stivers, to be paid in heavy money.

The defendant answers that he has a counter bill, and also that the accounts do not agree but that there is a considerable difference between them. The parties are allowed by Schout and Commissaries two weeks' time to verify and square their accounts, and are ordered to furnish copies to each other.

Ordinary Session, held Tuesday, March 19, 1662.

Present: The Schout, Roeloof Swartwout; Cornelis Barense Sleght, Evert Pels, Aldert Heymanse Roosa.

Storm Albertsen, plaintiff, vs. Jonas Ransou, defendant. The first default.

Christiaen Nissen romp, plaintiff, vs. Mathys Roeloofsen, defendant. Plaintiff again demands that defendant prove what rascalities and slanders the plaintiff committed.

Defendant requests another two weeks' time to adduce proof. At the request of the defendant, the parties are granted two weeks' time by the Schout and Commissaries.

Geertruyt Andriessen, plaintiff, presents an account against the Schout, and demands fifty lbs. of butter and some beavers, for carting sixteen stack-poles.

The Schout demands a copy of the account with full particulars. The Commissaries allow the parties two weeks' time, and order a copy of the account to be furnished.

Lowys Dubo, plaintiff, vs. Coenraet Jans or Ham and Christiaen Andrissen, defendants.

Plaintiff demands from defendants payment of five schepels of rye, on account of ribbons sold them. Defendants admit the debt. The Commissaries order defendants to pay within three weeks.

Classjen Thunes, plaintiff, demands from Pieter Hillebrantse, defendant, payment of the amount of twenty-two and one half schepels of wheat, due on account of brandy and Spanish wine sold to him. The first default.

I, undersigned, Pieter van Halen, acknowledge owing Pieter van Alen, the amount of one hundred and thirty schepels of good winter wheat, and in default of payment the parties have agreed that Pieter van Halen shall keep at interest the aforesaid one hundred and thirty schepels of wheat for the period of two years, commencing August 1, 1662, and shall pay for the use of said moneys ten schepels of wheat per annum. Pieter van Halen promises to return and repay the aforesaid principal, with the interest thereon, on March 14, 1664. For this purpose, said Pieter van Halen binds and absolutely mortgages his house and lot, situated here, besides all his property, real and personal, present and future, submitting himself to the jurisdiction of all Lords and Courts.

Pieter van Halen.

Ordinary Session, held Tuesday, March 28, 1662.

Present: The Schout, Roeloof Swartwout; Evert Pels, Aldert Heymanse, Cornelis Barense Slecht.

Christiaen Nissen romp, plaintiff, vs. Mathys Roeloofsen, defendant. Default.

The Commissaries allow defendant one more default, for the last time, under penalty of imprisonment.

Cornelis Jansen Houtsager [sawyer], plaintiff, vs. Carsten Carstense. Default.

Cornelis Barense Slecht, plaintiff, vs. Juaraien Westvael. Default.

Cornelis Barense Slecht, plaintiff, demands from Geertruyt Andrisse, defendant, payment of the amount of one hundred and forty-six guilders, ten stivers, heavy money, advanced for building the bridge.

The defendant answers she has a counter bill. The Commissaries order defendant to produce her account at the next session of the Court, and to have it complete.

Ann Bloms, plaintiff, demands from Jan Mertense payment of twenty beavers, according to a delivered obligation, for which defendant's corn, now held by Andries the weaver, has been attached. Defendant answers he knows nothing about the debt, and requests time until his wife arrives here, and lets his grain be held till then.

Philip Hendricksen, plaintiff, demands from Willem Mertense payment of the quantity of two muddes [about four bushels each] of wheat for two thousand bricks delivered by him. Defendant admits having bought the bricks from plaintiff. Whereupon the Schout and Commissaries order defendant to pay plaintiff the two muddes of wheat.

Jeronimus Ebbingh, plaintiff, vs. Cornelis Barense Sleght, defendant. Plaintiff demands from defendant two thousand gldrs., five years' rent for the use of his farm, and now asks to be permitted to enter upon his farm and a restitution of everything, according to lease between both parties. The defendant answers he paid five hundred and fifty-six guilders.

Plaintiff demands a copy of the account, and announces the seizure by the Court Messenger of the threshed and unthreshed grain, the brewing kettle and appurtenances, and the remaining cattle, all of which were in the possession of Cornelis Barense Slecht on March 29.

The Schout and Commissaries, having carefully considered this matter, find a small yield of grain, and therefore resolve that it is unreasonable, as it is not right, in the first year of the lease, to take a farm from the lessee because he is unable, owing to poor crops, to pay the rent which is due, and order defendant to pay the rent of the current year within one week. And as defendant has requested time for the payment of the money due, he promises to pay one thousand guilders within seven months, and engages to pay in addition one-sixth, under penalty of judgment by default.

Jeronimus Ebingh, [the plaintiff], signs appeal papers and requests permission to appeal.

Jeronimus Ebbingh, plaintiff, demands from Willem Mertense payment of the amount of thirty schepels of wheat due in the fall of 1661, on the sale of 150,000 planks. The defendant admits the debt, but answers that he has an account against the Commissaries for the sale of lime. The Commissaries agree to pay Jeronimus Ebbingh thirty schepels of wheat next fall.

Pieter de Reymer, plaintiff, vs. Willem Jansen Stol, defendant. Plaintiff demands payment of the value of eight schepels of wheat, for panes of glass sold and set. Defendant acknowledges the debt and requests time. The Commissaries order him to pay the plaintiff the amount sued for. He promises to pay one-half within three weeks, and the other half in the fall, at plaintiff's option.

Hermen Vedder, plaintiff, demands from Jan Mertense payment of the value of one hundred schepels of oats, and announces the seizure at the house of Andries Barrense of the grain belonging to Jan Mertense. Defendant admits being indebted to Hermen Vedder. The parties decide to come to an agreement.

Barent Pietersen, plaintiff, demands from Barent Gerritsen payment of the amount of ninety-five schepels of wheat, as per obligation payable November 1, 1661. Defendant admits he justly owes the debt, and says he is not able to pay. The Commissaries order defendant to pay the plaintiff the amount sued for.

Barent Pietersen, plaintiff, demands from Willem Mertense payment of the amount of twenty-five schepels of wheat. Defendant admits the debt, and says he has the guarantee of the Commissaries for lime delivered to them. They agree to pay Barent Pietersen twenty-five schepels of wheat next fall for Willem Mertense, if so much is due him.

Elsje Jans, wife of Hendrick Jochemse, had attached the value of six and one-half schepels of wheat in the possession of Aldert Heymanse Roose, belonging to Barent the shoemaker, and now gives notice of the attachment. She also gives notice of another attachment of the value of five schepels of wheat and three and one-half guilders, in zeewant, in the possession of Evert Parys. "The money belongs to Jonas Ransou who owes the above named amount to me." She gives notice of the attachment of the money of Frans Pietersen in the possession of Albert Gysbertse, and "all the money that is coming to him there."

Ordinary Session, held this March 29.

Present: The Schout; Evert Pels, Aldert Heymanse Roose, Cornelis Barense Slecht.

Willem Mertense, plaintiff, vs. Geertryut Andriessen, defendant. Default.

Matheu Blanchan, plaintiff, says he leased to Mathys Roelofsen two oxen for the amount of fifty guilders, for the purpose of carting wood to his house, and that this should have been done last fall. The defendant, Mathys Roeloofsen, says his wife hired the oxen for fifty gldrs., but has not yet carted it all, and therefore refuses to pay. Jan Mertense testifies that the oxen were leased and hired, and that the carting ought to have been finished in the fall at ploughing time, or the oxen returned.

Whereas, Mathue Blanchan says he has another account against her, he is given time until next session of the Court to make out his bill.

Geertruyt Andrissen, plaintiff, vs. Roeloof Swartwout, defendant.

Hey Olfersen, plaintiff, vs. Barent Gerritsen, defendant. Plaintiff says he is building for defendant, and, as the work was given out by contract and there is not sufficient lumber, he is obliged to wait. Defendant says windows and doors are still to be made.

Plaintiff answers that no mention is made in his contract about his making windows and doors. The Commissaries, after calling in carpenters and obtaining their advice, decide that Barent Gerritse shall pay extra for doors and windows.

Jeronimus Ebbing says that, although the grain in possession of Cornelis Barense Slecht has been seized, he will not oppose either its threshing or sowing there, as may be necessary, but asks the Commissaries to supervise the same and to see that the overplus grain be not neglected.

The Commissaries agree to attend to their duty in this matter, according to law.

Ordinary Session, held Tuesday, April 18, 1662.
Present: Roeloof Swartwout, Evert Pels, Aldert Heymanse Roosa, Cornelis Barense Slecht.

Pieter van Halen, plaintiff, demands three and one-half schepels of wheat, in payment for a pair of shoes. Warrenaer Hoorenbeeck, defendant, admits he honestly owes plaintiff the debt. The Commissaries order defendant to pay the amount he is sued for, within a month's time and without further delay.

Volckjen Jans, plaintiff, demands from Jan Aersen the amount of thirty-four schepels of wheat, for one month's board and for zeewant advanced him. Defendant denies owing so much, and demands an itemized account. The Commissaries order the parties to furnish a copy thereof.

Christiaen Nissen romp, plaintiff, demands from Roeloof Swartwout payment of eighteen schepels of wheat. Defendant admits the debt and says he will pay within twenty-four hours with the grain belonging to Storm Albertsen, attached by Christiaen Nissen romp at the Ronduyt [Redoubt].

Christiaen Nissen romp, plaintiff, demands from Juriaen Westgaer payment of the amount of twenty-nine schepels of wheat, according to bill produced in court, due for wages earned.

Defendant admits the debt and promises to pay within two weeks, plaintiff being willing.

Cornelis Barense Slecht, plaintiff, demands from Juriaen Westgaelt payment of the amount of one hundred and fourteen gldrs., heavy money, due for wages earned for brewing.

Defendant Juriaen Westvael admits he honestly owes the debt. The Commissaries condemn defendant to pay within six weeks.

Cornelis Barense Slecht, plaintiff, demands payment from Geertruyt Andrissen of the amount of one hundred and seven gldrs. ten stivers. Defendant admits owing plaintiff the debt. The Commissaries order defendant to pay the amount sued for within six weeks.

Christiaen Nissen romp, plaintiff, demands from Tjirick Classen payment for a cow sold defendant and for wages earned, together amounting to one hundred schepels of oats. Defendant admits the debt, and says he is not able to pay at present as he will be obliged to sow his oats himself. The Commissaries, having heard the parties, order Tjirick Classen to pay plaintiff the amount sued for, and, on default of payment, plaintiff is authorized to seize the cow.

Jan Aersen, plaintiff, demands from Tomas Chambers payment of the amount of one hundred gldrs., heavy money, due for wages earned for smithing.

Defendant admits the debt and requests six months' time. The Commissaries order defendant to pay the amount sued for, within six weeks.

Elsjen Jans, plaintiff, demands from Jonas Ransou five schepels of wheat, and three gldrs., in zeewant. Defendant denies the
debt, and says he does not owe more than one can of brandy, and
one turkey and three musjens [half pints] of brandy. The Commissaries, having heard the parties, order plaintiff to prove the
debt she is suing for and the defendant to pay the debt he has
acknowledged.

Willem Mertense, plaintiff, demands from Geertruyt Andrissen payment of the amount of...... and shows an account. The
defendant and plaintiff decide to agree.

The Schout, as plaintiff, vs. Albert Gysbertse. The first
default.

Volckjen Jans, plaintiff, demands from Juriaen Westvael payment of the amount of fifteen schepels of wheat, according to obligation produced in court. Defendant's first default.

Matthys Roeloofsen, plaintiff, vs. Jacob Barense and Willem
Mertense, defendants. The first default.

Matheu Blanchan, plaintiff, demands for the second time fifty
gldrs., zeewant, for the use of two oxen by Mathys Roelofsen. He
also demands twenty-five gldrs., eleven stivers, zeewant, more, for
milk, butter and brandy supplied to defendant. Default.

Lowys Dubo, plaintiff, vs. Coenraet Ham and Christiaen Andrissen, defendants. Default.

Lowys Dubo, plaintiff, vs. Pieter Hillebrantse, defendant. Default.

Anthony Cruepel, plaintiff, demands from Hendrick Mertense
payment of the amount of twenty-three gldrs., fifteen stivers, in
zeewant, due for wages earned. Defendant admits the debt.

The Schout, Roelof Swartwout, agrees to pay plaintiff for
Hendrick Martense twenty-three gldrs., fifteen stivers, in zeewant,
one-half within two weeks, and the balance one month after that
date.

Anthony Cruepel, plaintiff, vs. Pieter Hillebrantse, defendant.
Default.

The Schout, as plaintiff, vs. Hester Douwens and Hey Olfersen, defendants.

Plaintiff asks Hester Douwens what she has to say against the defendant Hey Olfersen, as she has accused him of theft. She answers: "This is plain enough, because he took out of my house at night some flour and some pieces of meat, as set forth in the summons. I also miss a beaver, an otter, and a half beaver, as well as an anker of small beer, and the person who stole the one I guess must also have taken the other."

Defendant also announces the attachment, at the house of Jan de Brabander, of goods belonging to Hey Olfersen, to serve as security for the stolen goods.

Defendant, Hey Olfersen, admits having taken some meat and flour from Hester Douwens' house at night, because he was hungry. He also says, "As she would not give me food and I was working for her, I tried to procure it, since there was little or no food for sale here."

Whereas, Hey Olfersen requests of the Schout and Commissaries of the Court here, to be allowed to go out on bail, for the purpose of enabling him the better to plead his cause, the Court, therefore, for cause, hereby consents thereto.

For cause, the Commissaries have suspended judgement in the above mentioned case, and also decide to wait until the arrival of the Noble Lord General, so as to enable the parties the better to plead their cause.

Ordinary Session, held Tuesday, May 2, 1662.

Present: The Schout, Roelof Swartwout; Cornelis Barense Slecht, Evert Pels, Aldert Heymanse Roosa.

Anthony Cruepel, plaintiff, demands from Pieter Hillebrantse payment of the amount of two schepels of wheat. Defendant admits owing the plaintiff two schepels of wheat. The Commissaries order defendant to pay plaintiff the amount sued for, within eight days.

Lowys Dubo, plaintiff, demands from Pieter Hillebrantse payment of the amount of two schepels of wheat due for ribbons sold him. Defendant, Pieter Hillebrantsen admits owing the debt to plaintiff. The Commissaries order defendant to pay plaintiff the amount sued for, within two months' time.

Jan Lammersen, plaintiff, demands from Juriaen Westphalen payment of the amount of sixteen scheples of wheat, according to obligation, and procuration received from Volckje Juriaens. Defendant admits the debt, says he is at present unable to pay, requests time, and offers to pay proper interest therefor. ''The principal together with the interest I promise to pay next fall.'' Thus declared, at the pleasure of plaintiff.

Mathys Blahchan, plaintiff, demands from Mathys Roeloofsen payment of fifty gldrs., zeewant, for the use of two oxen, as already mentioned, and as has been proved. Plaintiff in addition demands twenty-five guilders, in zeewant, for goods furnished. Defendant admits the debt of twenty-five gldrs., zeewant, but says he has not had satisfactory use of the oxen, and therefore declines to pay. The Commissaries, after having heard the parties, and the circumstances being known to the Court, order defendant to pay the plaintiff the amount sued for.

Cornelis Jansen van Dost, plaintiff, demands from Aert Jacobsen payment of the amount of sixty-one guilders, zeewant, for wages earned. Defendant admits the debt but says he carted a load of stone for six guilders, zeewant. The Commissaries order defendant to pay plaintiff fifty-five gldrs. zeewant, within fourteen days.

Mathys Roeloofsen, plaintiff, vs. Coeraet Ham, defendant. Default.

In the matter of the elections, the Schout and Commissaries have decided to nominate the following persons to govern us hereafter, subject to the approval of the Very Noble Honorable Lord Director General and the Lord High Councillors: Thomas Chambers, Jan Willemse, Tjirick Classen de Wit, Albert Gysbertsen, Aert Jacobsen.

The Noble Lord Director General and High Councillor Gerret Decker were this day here present. The Lords Director General and Councillor continued Evert Pels and Aldert Heymanse Roose as Commissaries, and from the nominees above mentioned appointed Albert Gysbertsen and Tjirick Classen deWit.

Below stood,

April 27, Ao. 1662, Pieter Stuyvesant.

On May 3, the newly appointed Commissaries took their oaths before the Schout and the old Commissaries, and were installed into office by order of the Noble Lord Director General and the Lord Councillor Gerrit Decker, who were here present.

Ordinary Session, held Tuesday, May 16, 1662.

Present: The Schout, Roelof Swartwout; Evert Pels, Allert Heymanse Roose, Albert Gysbertse.

Jan Broersen, plaintiff, demands from Cornelis Barense the amount of six schepels of wheat and says he sold him hops therefor. Defendant's first default.

Mathys Roeloofsen, plaintiff, demands from Coenract Ham payment of the amount of eighty-six gldrs., fifteen stivers, eight pennies, in zeewant. Second default.

Hey Olfersen, plaintiff, presents a petition in writing, stating that he would have finished his work at Barent Gerritsen's, but that owing to the absence of materials such as boards, lumber and nails, he was unable to do so, and that he also was refused board. He therefore asks full payment for his contracted work, and restitution of expenses and damages suffered in consequence.

Defendant, Barent Gerritsen, answers that there were boards still there for use, and that he did not refuse him board. The Commissaries order plaintiff to prove that his materials had been used up, as stated in his petition presented to the Court.

Ordinary Session, held Tuesday, June 22, 1662.

Present: The Schout; Evert Pels, Albert Heymanse Roose, Albert Gysbertsen, Tjirick Classen de Wit.

Hey Olfersen, plaintiff, vs. Barent Gerritsen, defendant. Plaintiff demands a total of sixty-four gldrs., heavy money, in restitution of expenses and for lost time and board.

Defendant says he is not liable for the expenses, "but if you, Hey Olfersen, had not failed me, I would certainly have paid you the last time."

The Commissaries order the defendant to pay plaintiff sixty-four gldrs., heavy money, for damages sustained. They also order plaintiff and defendant each to pay twenty-five gldrs. for the poor, as both appeared here February 28, and offered fifty gldrs. to the poor if, at the appointed time, Barent Gerritse's house were not finished. This time having expired, it is more Barent Garritsen's than Hey Olfersen's fault, since he, defendant, made the plaintiff do the work over again, so that plaintiff could not complete the work at the appointed time. All of which is known to the majority of the Commissaries and the Schout; they therefore sentence the parties to each pay twenty-five gldrs., for the poor.

Evert Pels does not believe Barent Gerritse should pay for the time during which Hey was detained for his acknowledged theft.

Counter opinion of the Schout and Commissaries: "We deem Barent Gerritsen to be origin and author of all the trouble."

Christiaen Nissen romp, plaintiff, vs. Mathys Roelofsen, defendant. Plaintiff demands of defendant proof of his account, which he himself once before consented to give, and says defendant's book is false.

By order of the Commissaries, Mathys Roelofsen made out another account and found that it tallied with the first one, and at the instance of plaintiff he affirmed it under oath. The Commissaries order plaintiff to pay defendant the amount sued for.

The Schout, plaintiff, vs. Barent Gerritsen, defendant. Plaintiff again demands from defendant a vindication of his honor before the Commissaries' Court, before whom this case comes for the third time, the magistrate having been called names. Defendant, Barent Gerritsen, once more asks for time, and demands an account of expenses from Hey Olfersen.

The Commissaries for the last time grant him time until the next session of the Court, when he is to show what injustice has been done him.

Ordinary Session, held Tuesday, July 4, 1662,

Present: The Schout; Evert Pels, Aldert Heymanse Roose, Albert Gysbertsen.

Mathys Blanchan, plaintiff, demands vindication of his honor. Says that Juriaen told his wife that it was reported that Dirck Adriaensen said to her he had seen Matheu Blanchan beat Juriaen Westvael's pig. Defendant Juriaen Westvael and his wife admit having heard this from Dirck Adriaensen, and state that Pieter Jansen also heard it.

Defendant Dirck Adriaensen denies this, and says he did not say so. The Schout and Commissaries order the parties to preserve the peace, and sentence Dirck Adriaensen to pay a fine of six gldrs., for the poor.

Mathys Roeloofsen, plaintiff, demands from Coenraedt Ham payment of the amount of eighty-six gldrs., fifteen stivers, eight pennies, in zeewant. Defendant admits owing plaintiff the amount sued for. The Schout and Commissaries order defendant to pay within fourteen days thirty gldrs., and the balance one month after date.

Tjirick Classen, plaintiff, vs. Pieter Jillessen, defendant. Default.

Christiaen Nissen romp, plaintiff, demands from Mathys Roeloofsen vindication of his honor, under an earlier complaint mentioned in this register. Whereupon the Commissaries refer both to two good men, and a third, to consider and decide the matter. And in case the good men are unable to mediate between them, the parties are referred to the Lord Director General and Supreme Council at the city of New Amsterdam. Such is the order of the Commissaries, in the absence of the Schout.

Ordinary Session, held Tuesday, October 4, 1662.

Present: The Schout; Evert Pels, Aldert Heymanse Roose, Albert Gysbertsen, Tjirick Classen de Wit.

Grietjen Westercamp, plaintiff, vs. Pieter Jacobsen, defendant. Default.

Classjen Maertens, plaintiff, vs. Pieter Hillebrantsen, defendant. The second default.

The Schout, plaintiff, vs. Barent Gerritsen, defendant. Default.

Barent Gerritsen, plaintiff, vs. Juriaen Westvael, defendant. Default.

Willem Vredenburgh, plaintiff, vs. Jan Jansen van Amersfoort, defendant. Default.

Extraordinary Session, held at Wildtwyck this 10th of October, 1662.

Present: The Schout; Commissaries, Evert Pels, Aldert Heymanse Roose, Albert Gysbertsen, Tjirick Classen de Wit.

Hans Carrelsen van Langesont, plaintiff, vs. Andries Jochemsen, defendant.

Plaintiff says he took defendant in his yacht up the river, and thence above Fort Orange to the Manathans, and then was not able to collect payment; that he again took defendant to Fort Orange, on his promise to pay there, and not being able to get any money there, the defendant signed an obligation for the amount of seventy-seven gldrs., in zeewant, due for passage money and money advanced at Fort Orange.

Defendant admits that he honestly and truly owes plaintiff the above mentioned debt.

Andries Jochemsen assigns to plaintiff his claim against Cornelis Barense Slecht, on which to collect seventy-seven gldrs., if plaintiff will consent thereto. Plaintiff requests the Commissaries to allow him costs as well, as defendant would not pay the principal before suit. The Schout and Schepens having considered the request, defendant is ordered, within twenty-four hours, to pay twenty gldrs. for costs, in addition to the principal of ninety-nine gldrs.

Ordinary Session, held October 17, 1662.

Present: The Schout; Evert Pels, Albert Gysbertsen, Tjirick Classen de Wit.

Barent Gerretsen, plaintiff, vs. Juriaen Westvael, defendant. Plaintiff demands payment of the amount of three hundred and fifteen gldrs., thirteen stivers, as per obligation to, and assignment by, Evert Pels, the same payable at beaver's price.

Defendant admits the obligation and also that he accepted the assignment, but denies owing the whole debt and says he only owes part of it. The Schout and Commissaries order defendant to pay his signed obligation within six weeks.

Grietjen Hendricks Westercamp, plaintiff, vs. Pieter Jacobsen, defendant. Plaintiff demands of defendant why he denies his child. Defendant answers, and says, "I have my doubts about it."

Plaintiff says that defendant ruined her, and asks that he restore her to honor.

Defendant denies that he ruined her, and says "she must prove this to me," and also denies that he promised to marry her.   He asks her when she became pregnant, and when she was delivered.

Plaintiff says that defendant made her pregnant eight days before Christmas, 1661, and that she was delivered eight days before Kermis [the Fair], 1662.   Plaintiff says she conceived at the mill-house of Pieter Jacobsen.   Defendant requests two weeks' time.   The Schout and Commissaries grant the defendant two weeks' time, and order plaintiff to prove at the next session that defendant ruined her.

Maerten Gerretsen, plaintiff, vs. Pieter Hillebrantsen, defendant.   Plaintiff demands from defendant payment of twenty-two schepels of wheat due for debts for liquor.   Defendant admits the debt.   The Schout and Commissaries order defendant to pay within twenty-four hours twenty-five gldrs., in wheat, and to count this from the aforesaid Court day, by virtue of the third default.

Gerrit Herregrins, plaintiff, vs. Roeloof Swartwout, defendant. Plaintiff demands from defendant two schepels of wheat, payment of wages earned by him.   The Commissaries order defendant to pay within twice twenty-four hours two schepels of wheat.   Plaintiff shows a certificate against defendant who requests a declaration. The Commissaries order plaintiff to procure his witnesses at the next session of the Court.

The Schout, plaintiff, vs. Barent Gerrissen, defendant.   Plaintiff asks from the Court a vindication of his honor and reputation, and that the same be maintained, because defendant has abused the Court.

Defendant acknowledges that he has spoken evil, and asks the Commissaries that the matter may be amicably settled between the parties.   The Commissaries resolve and hereby allow the parties to settle their differences amicably.

Ordinary Session, Tuesday, October 31, 1662.

Present: The Schout; Evert Pels, Aldert Heymanse Roose, Albert Gysbertsen, Tjirick Classen de Wit.

Hendrick Cornelissen, plaintiff, vs. Marten Hermensen, defendant. Plaintiff demands from defendant the amount of ten gldrs., ten stivers. The first default.

Barent Sybrantsen van der Hout, plaintiff, vs. Jan Lootman. Plaintiff demands payment of the amount of thirty-six gldrs. zeewant, for freight and board earned by him. The defendant does not deny the debt, and answers that he is willing to pay six schepels of wheat, or thirty-six gldrs., zeewant. The Schout and Commissaries order defendant to pay within ten days.

Jesyntje Verhagen, plaintiff, vs. Jacob Barense, defendant. Default.

Willem Mertense, plaintiff, vs. Hey Olfersen Roseblom, defendant. Plaintiff demands payment for freight from the Manathans to the Hesobes [Esopus], amounting to fourteen gldrs., zeewant. The defendant admits having come here with plaintiff in his vessel. Thereupon the Schout and Commissaries order defendant to satisfy plaintiff.

Sara Pieterse Schepmoes, plaintiff, vs. Huybrecht Bruyn, defendant. Plaintiff demands from defendant payment of the amount of fifty-four gldrs., twelve stivers, and costs, according to judgment and the order given to the Doorkeeper* at the city of New Amsterdam on July 21, 1661. Defendant denies the debt. The Schout and Commissaries order defendant to pay within twenty-four hours, under an earlier sentence of the Burgomasters at the city of New Amsterdam, this at the pleasure of plaintiff. As the defendant denies the debt, he must seek redress before the judge having jurisdiction, at New Amsterdam.

Geertruyt Vosburgh, widow, plaintiff, vs. Marten Harmensen, defendant. Plaintiff demands payment of the amount of fifty-

---

* This word appears here in the Dutch record as *consarsie*, and later as *concergie*, i. e., *concierge*, meaning *doorkeeper*, or the Dutch Court officer, *Deurwaarder*. Though some dictionaries translate *deurwaarder* as a process server, sergeant-at-law, tipstaff, or baliff, in addition to doorkeeper, the revised English translation of Simon van Leeuwen's *Het Rooms-Hollands-regt*, Amsterdam, 1678, by J. G. Kotzé and C. W. Decker, in *Commentaries on Roman-Dutch Law*, London, 1881-1886, renders the word as *Usher* or *Doorkeeper*. The last named form is adopted here and elsewhere in this record as the most appropriate equivalent. The duties of this Court officer, under the Dutch law, differed from those of the Court Messenger or of a Bailiff. The Court Messenger at Wildwyck probably performed the duties of a *deurwaarder*. For some of these duties see *Deurwaarder*, in van Dale's *Groot Woordenboek*.

three gldrs., eight st., due on debt for liquor, as per account produced by her, and which she says has been taken from her husband's book. In addition, there is an account of eighteen gldrs., two st., crossed out in the book. The defendant denies owing her the whole debt, but admits he owes thirty-one gldrs., six st., and says he paid her four beavers on the above itemized bill. The Schout and Commissaries having explained to her, the widow is satisfied with the payment by Marten Harmense of thirty-one gldrs., six st. Accordingly, the defendant is ordered to pay the amount of thirty-one gldrs., six st., and further to prove he paid four beavers.

Tjirick Classen de Wit, plaintiff, vs. Jan Lammersen, defendant. Plaintiff demands payment of the amount of twenty-one gldrs., in zeewant. He admits he received on the account one beaver for twelve gldrs. The defendant admits the debt, but says he worked one day at harvest time, and demands five gldrs. for this. Plaintiff says his other laborers worked for one schepel of buckwheat, and that he pays no more.

The Schout and Commissaries order plaintiff to pay one schepel of buckwheat for one day's work, and defendant to pay plaintiff the balance as demanded.

The Schout, plaintiff, demands a five-fold fine of Jan Barense Amersfort for having, in the presence of two Commissaries, smuggled into this place an anker of wine.

The defendant, Jan Barense Amersfort, denies having smuggled it. He says he will prove that the soldiers at the Ronduyt [Redoubt] permitted him to discharge the wine, and that they said to him, "The Schout and Evert Pels are present."

The Commissaries grant defendant time until the next session of the Court to furnish proof.

Ordinary Session, held Wednesday, November 1, 1662.

Grietjen Hendriks Westercamp, plaintiff, vs. Pieter Jacobse, defendant.

Plaintiff exhibits to the Schout and Commissaries a certificate and deposition by seven women who certify and declare that they were present at the birth of Grietje Westerkamp's child, and that she swore three times that Pieter Jacobse was the father of the child. The plaintiff asks for a vinidiction of her honor.

The defendant says plaintiff did not behave as a decent girl should, and produces a certificate of Juriaen Westvael and his wife who declare that Grietjen Westercamp lay under one blanket with Jan van Breeman, with his daughter between them. Defendant, being interrogated, admits having conversed and lain with plaintiff, but did not promise marriage, and, besides, gave her no money for it, and asks if a woman can be thirteen months and four days in the family way.

The Schout and Commissaries order defendant to bring clearer proof at the Court's next session.

Thomas Chambers, plaintiff, vs. Evert Pels, defendant. Plaintiff demands from defendant payment of the amount of seven hundred guilders, in wheat and in oats, according to bill of sale of a house, barn and lot. The defendant admits the debt, and offers to pay next winter, as his wheat it yet unthreshed.

Plaintiff demands immediate payment.

Defendant answers he is unable to pay at once, and offers to restore plaintiff's property and to pay him a moderate rent for the same, if he is allowed his outlay for repairs.

Plaintiff refuses to take back his property, but says he proposes to recover his money with costs and accrued and accruing damages. The Schout and Commissaries order defendant to pay plaintiff the amount claimed, within the period of . . . . . . etc.

Thomas Chambers, plaintiff, vs. The Schout, defendant. Plaintiff demands payment from defendant of the amount of forty-six schepels of wheat. Defendant admits the debt, and alleges he has a counter claim. The Commissaries order the Schout to liquidate his account with plaintiff and to pay any balance within six weeks.

The Schout, plaintiff, vs. Thomas Chambers, defendant. Plaintiff demands three fines, of six gldrs. each, due from defendant's unwillingness and neglect to cart materials for the parsonage when the Commissaries ordered this to be done.

Defendant admits having thrice neglected to cart materials for the Court, and says he is not disposed to cart materials for the general parsonage, either by order of the Schout or of the Schepens.

Plaintiff demands that the Commissaries impose the fine, and says that, as they promised the fine to the congregation, it ought to have it. Defendant exhibits a certificate in which it is declared that the Schout and some citizens were at the defendants' house, and that the Schout seized some goods there, trying forcibly to take possession of something, and carried it out of the house. For this, defendant now makes a charge of assault against plaintiff, and craves justice. Plaintiff admits he was with others at defendant's house, in order to collect the fine of six guilders for his neglect to cart. He says he received an order and authority from the Commissaries to make no exception as to any offender, this being for the benefit of those who carted.

The Commissaries sentence defendant to pay eighteen gldrs., for thrice neglecting to cart, and empower plaintiff to deduct the amount of the fines from the debt he owes defendant.

Ordinary Session, held on Tuesday, November 14, 1662.

Present: The Schout; Evert Pels, Aldert Heymanse, Albert Gysbertsen. Tjirick Classen. Default.

Isaack d'Foreest, plaintiff, vs. Barent Gerretsen, defendant. Plaintiff demands payment of one hundred and eighty gldrs., zeewant, as per obligation delivered in Court. Defendant admits the debt. The Schout and Commissaries ask plaintiff to accept a mortgage on defendant's house, located in this place, which defendant voluntarilly offers. In case of non payment by April 1, 1663, plaintiff may then take and sell defendant's property until he realizes the amount of the debt of one hundred and eighty gldrs., zeewant, together with costs and interest to the above named date.

Geertruyt Vosburgh, plaintiff, vs. Mathys Roelofsen, defendant. Default.

Hendrick Briesjen, plaintiff, vs. Tjirick Classen, defendant. Default.

Hendrick Bresjes, plaintiff, demands, under power of attorney from Storm Albertse, produced in Court, payment from Barent Gerritsen of the amount of forty schepels of oats, pursuant to judgment of February 7, 1662. The payment not having been made after three warnings, plaintiff asks the court to permit him to proceed with the execution. The Commissaries permit plaintiff so to proceed against defendant, through the Doorkeeper.

Bart Sybrantsen, plaintiff, vs. Hendrick Cornelissen, defendant. Plaintiff demands payment of the amount of three schepels of wheat, due on the sale of some articles. Defendant admits the debt. The Schout and Commissaries order defendant to pay three schepels of wheat within eight days.

Hendrick Briesjes, plaintiff, vs. Jonas Ransou, defendant. Default.

Evert Prys, plaintiff, vs. Albert Gysbertsen, defendant. Plaintiff demands payment of the amount of twenty-five and one-half schepels of wheat, and also twenty-one gldrs., heavy money, for wages earned. Defendant Albert Gysbertsen admits owing the above mentioned debt. The Schout and Commissaries order defendant to pay within six weeks.

Evert Parys, plaintiff, vs. Tjirick Classen de Wit, defendant. Default.

Evert Parys, plaintiff, vs. Aert Pietersen Tack, defendant. Plaintiff demands payment of the amount of eleven and one-half schepels of wheat, for wages earned. Defendant admits the debt, and offers to pay one-half of it within fourteen days, if it so please the plaintiff.

The Schout and Commissaries order defendant to pay the other half within six weeks.

Warrenaer Hoorenbeeck, plaintiff, vs. Jacob Jansen Stoutenburg, defendant. Plaintiff demands two hundred guilders, heavy money, a couple of shirts, a pair of stockings and a pair of shoes, as payment for wages earned. Defendant admits owing plaintiff eighty gldrs., according to the verbal contract between them, and says he paid thirty gldrs. thereof.

Plaintiff admits having received thirty gldrs., and says that as payment has not been made in accordance with the contract, two years having already passed, he requires full payment.

The Schout and Commissaries order defendant to pay plaintiff, as per contract, eighty gldrs., deducting therefrom the amount already paid, unless plaintiff is able to adduce proof of the agreement between them.

Pieter Jillessen, plaintiff, vs. Roeloof Swartwout, defendant. Plaintiff demands payment of the amount of thirteen beavers. Defendant admits the debt. The Commissaries order defendant to pay plaintiff the amount of thirteen beavers within ten days, and that the grain shall be attached until the debt is paid.

Ordinary Session, held Tuesday, November 28, 1662.

Present: The Schout; Evert Pels, Albert Gysbertse, Aldert Heymanse Roose, Tjirick Classen de Wit.

Pieter Couwenoven, plaintiff, vs. Jacob Stoutenburgh, defendant. Plaintiff demands the amount of thirty schepels of oats and four schepels of buckwheat, sold in 1659 for seed-corn, together with the freight charges thereon. Defendant admits having received the corn with Albert Jansen who bought it from the plaintiff.

The Schout and Commissaries order defendant to pay plaintiff the just half of the amount sued for.

Pieter Couwen-oven, plaintiff, vs. Cornelis Barense Slecht, defendant. Plaintiff demands payment of four hundred and thirty-seven gldrs., in corn, for wages earned, as per obligation made out to Albert Jansen. Defendant answers that he paid the obligation, but that it was not cancelled, and requests plaintiff to show his assignment and power of attorney for the same. Cornelis Barense is ordered to furnish written proof.

Symen Jansen, plaintiff, demands payment of twenty-seven gldrs., in zeewant, thirty-one gldrs, ten stivers, in beavers, and thirteen schepels of wheat. Pieter van Halen, the defendant, admits the debt.

The Court orders defendant to pay plaintiff the amount sued for.

Albert Heymanse, plaintiff, demands proof of Pieter van Alen who has accused him of using false weights. Defendant admits [the accusation], and says that he did not receive full weight.

The Court orders defendant under arrest until the accusation shall have been proved.

Symen Jansen Romeyn, plaintiff, vs. Willem Jansen Stol, defendant. Plaintiff demands from defendant payment of the amount of seventy gldrs., Dutch money. The debt was due to his forefather, Claes Hendricksen, deceased, for money borrowed in Holland by Marcus Vogelsaugh on bottomry bond. Defendant offers to pay the principal.

The Court orders defendant to pay plaintiff the principal of the bottomry bond, without interest.

Hendrick Cornelissen, plaintiff, vs. Marten Harmense, defendant. Plaintiff demands of defendant three thousand bricks bought by him but not received. Defendant says he did not deliver any bricks to plaintiff, and admits he owes him eight gldrs., ten stivers.

The Court orders defendant to pay plaintiff the amount of eight gldrs., ten stivers.

Jan Pietersen, plaintiff, demands payment for six schepels, as per assignment by M. [Dr.] Jan. Albert Gysbertsen, defendant, admits the debt.

The Court orders him to pay.

Doctor Jan demands from defendant, Poulus Poulussen, payment of two and one-half schepels of wheat.

Defendant admits having hired Doctor Jan to barber him and give him medical treatment.

The Court orders defendant to pay the amount claimed.

Poulus Martense, plaintiff, demands payment of eighteen schepels of wheat for wages earned. Albert Gysbertsen, defendant, admits the debt.

The Court orders defendant to pay the amount claimed.

Merten Hermensen, plaintiff, demands payment according to judgment which should have been paid within twenty-four [hours]. Defendant, Pieter Hillebrantsen, answers he can make no other payment than what he earns by working for Aert Jacobsen.

Pieter Hillebrantsen, plaintiff, demands from Aert Jacobsen payment of the amount of one hundred and seventy gldrs., in wheat or other grain, for wages earned. Aert Jacobsen, the defendant, admits the debt.

The Court orders defendant to pay the amount claimed.

Barent Gerritsen, plaintiff, vs. Juriaen Westvael, defendant. Plaintiff demands from defendant payment of the amount of three hundred and fifteen gldrs., thirteen stivers, as per an earlier judgment rendered by the Court, here, October 19, 1662.

The Schout and Commissaries order defendant to pay as per former judgment.

Martha Symense, plaintiff, vs. Pieter Jacobsen, defendant. Plaintiff demands from defendant payment of the amount of twenty-eight and one-half gldrs., in heavy money, and seventeen gldrs., in zeewant, besides a shirt, due for wages earned. Defendant admits the debt.

The Court orders defendant to pay plaintiff the amount claimed.

Barent Gerretsen, plaintiff, vs. Albert Gysbertsen, defendant. Plaintiff demands from defendant payment of the amount of ten schepels of oats, nine and one-half schepels of wheat, and forty-six gldrs., zeewant. Defendant admits the debt.

The Schout and Commissaries order defendant to pay.

Gerrit Herregrens, plaintiff, vs. Tjirick Classen de Wit, defendant. Plaintiff demands from defendant payment of two schepels of wheat.

Gerrit Heergrins, plaintiff, vs. Aert Pieterse Tack, defendant. Plaintiff demands from defendant payment of the amount of four schepels of wheat which his son earned while with defednant. Defendant says he hired plaintiff's son for two years, the first year for ten schepels of wheat and a pair of leather breeches, the second year for fifteen schepels of wheat; that plaintiff took his son away from him, and for fear of arrest sent said son to the Mathans [Manhattan]. This having been made known to the Schout and an order of arrest having been asked for, defendant refuses to pay, or wants plaintiff's son to serve out his time; says the mudde of wheat which plaintiff claims for his son is ready. This is affirmed by Poulus Poulussen who is busy winnowing.

The Commissaries, having heard both parties, order plaintiff to send his son back to serve out his time, as he admits he hired him out under a written agreement with defendant, prepared by himself, and according to which defendant is to pay plaintiff a mudde of wheat. For which reason plaintiff is ordered to pay the fine on arrest. He says he himself represents his son.

EVERT PELS,
The mark (x) of ALBERT GYSBERTSEN,
TIERCK CLASZEN DE WITT.

Christiaen Nissen romp, plaintiff, vs. Albert Gysbertsen, defendant.

Plaintiff demands from defendant payment of the amount of twenty schepels of oats, as per assignment, by which defendant engaged to pay for Mathys Roeloofsen the money due for an anker of brandy delivered to the latter.

Defendant admits the debt, requests time or to be allowed to pay at the garrison.

The Court orders defendant to pay within six weeks.

Willem Vredenburgh, plaintiff, vs. Jan Janse van Amersfoort, defendant. Plaintiff demands from defendant payment of nine schepels of wheat. Defendant admits the debt.

The Court orders defendant to pay plaintiff.

Pieter van Halen, plaintiff, vs. Aert Mertense Dorn, defendant. Plaintiff demands payment of twelve schepels of wheat due for shoes made and brandy furnished. Defendant admits he bought the shoes and owes for them, but says he received no more than two cans of brandy.

The Schout and Commissaries order him to pay eight schepels of wheat and the plaintiff to prove the balance of the account or to confirm his book under oath.

[The following entry is in the handwriting of Mattheus Capito, Secretary.]

"This note was neglected to be entered by the ex-Schout and Secretary, Roelof Swartwout, and I have entered the same here at the request of Gysbert van Imbrock. This is a literal copy of the original which reads:

"On the underwritten date, the worthy Aert Pietersen Tack, resident of the village of Wildwyck, appeared before Roelof Swartwout, Schout of Wildwyck, and two Commissaries , and acknowledged and said he appeared before us and admitted and declared that he this day settled and closed his account with Mr. Gysbert van Imbrock, and is truly and justly indebted to him for the sum of five hundred and fifty-eight gldrs., in beavers, with interest on two hundred and sixty four gldrs., as per obligation in favor of Mr. Gysbert, which sum the said Aert Pietersen Tack acknowledges he owes. And, owing to his inability now to pay, he absolutely mortgages his present crop of grain which, by God's grace, is to be harvested in the year 1663, and hereby confers upon him full right, power and authority to do with the same as if personally present, until Mr. Gysbert shall have received his claim out of the same, and in general to properly account for the same. Both appearers hereby admit having made this agreement with each other, and, in pursuance thereof, submitting themselves to the jurisdiction of all courts and judges. The appearer [Tack] shall not be at liberty to alienate, seize or cause to be seized any of the said crops or harvests until Mr. Gysbert van Imbrock shall have been satisfied for what has been above mentioned. In testimony whereof, we have affixed our signatures to these presents at Wildwyck this 21st of December, Anno 1662.

(Signed) This is the mark (x) of Aert Pietersen Tack, This is the mark (x) of Albert Gysbertsen, Tjerck Claesen de Wit.

(Below stood) In my presence. Roelof Swartwout.

After comparison with the original the above has been found to be an exact copy, to which I certify.

MATTHEUS CAPITO, Secretary, October 25, 1664.''

Pieter van Alen, plaintiff, vs. Jonas Ransou, defendant. Default.

The Schout, plaintiff, vs. Jan Barense Amershoff, defendant. Plaintiff demands for the second time one-half an anker of brandy, the fine for smuggling. Defendant answers that he will prove he was at Bestevaer's house, and says that his witnesses are sick.

The Commissaries order defendant to furnish either oral or written proof at the next session of the court.

The Schout, plaintiff, vs. Barent Gerretsen, defendant. Plaintiff demands from defendant a fine of twelve gldrs., because defendant made two exit openings in the fortress or long palisades.

Commissaries order defendant to pay the fine.

EVERT PELS,
TIERCK CLASZEN DE WITT,
The mark (x) of ALBERT GYSBERTSEN.

Willem Jansen Stol, plaintiff, vs. Jan Aersen, defendant. Plaintiff demands payment of the amount of one hundred and fifty gldrs., in beavers, to be paid with wheat at three schepels per beaver, as per obligation therefor shown to the Court. Defendant admits the debt and says he paid twenty beavers on it.

The Court, having heard the parties, orders defendant to pay plaintiff, as per obligation, unless defendant can prove he so paid plaintiff, which shall then be deducted from the amount claimed.

Evert Prys, plaintiff, vs. Hendrick Jochemsen, defendant. Plaintiff demands from defendant the amount of sixty-six gldrs., zeewant. Defendant admits the debt, but shows a bill for sixty gldrs., fourteen stivers, zeewant, which plaintiff accepts in payment.

The Court orders defendant to pay the balance of the account.

Symen Jansen Romeyn asks for an attachment of fifty-four gldrs., Dutch money, in the possession of Jan Aersen Smit, due him from Willem Jansen Stol.

Willem Vredenburgh attaches ...... in the possession of the Noble Lord Director General Pieter Stuyvesant, money due to Evert Parys.

Ordinary Session, held Tuesday, December 12, [1662].

Present: The Schout; Evert Pels, Aldert Heymanse Roose, Albert Gysbertse, Tjirick Classen de Wit.

Barent Hermensen, plaintiff, vs. Albert Gysbertsen, defendant. Plaintiff demands from defendant a receipt for eight schepels of wheat which he says he paid defendant in accordance with a power of attorney and an obligation.

Defendant admits he received the power of attorney, and that he was paid by plaintiff.

The Court orders defendant to return to plaintiff his obligation, together with a receipt.

Barent Gerritsen, plaintiff, vs. Hendrick Cornelissen, defendant. Default.

The Schout, plaintiff, vs. Barent Gerritsen and his wife, defendants. Default.

Plaintiff demands judgment on account of a former complaint, lodged before this Court, that defendants spoke irreverently of the Court in saying that the Commissaries did not give them justice. The Schout having communicated with the Commissaries they know all about the matter.

Whereas, the defendants do not appear before the Court, but have several times poked fun at the Court, the Schout is ordered to put the defendants under arrest until they shall prove they have been unjustly treated by said Court.

EVERT PELS,
ALAERDT HEYMANSZ ROOSE,

This is the mark (x) of ALBERT GYSBERTSEN,

TIERCK CLASZEN DE WITT.

Poulus Poulussen, plaintiff, vs. Aert Pietersen Tack, defendant. Plaintiff demands the amount of thirty schepels of wheat, payment of three months' wages earned.

Defendant answers that plaintiff broke the terms of his contract by leaving him. The Court questions Gommert Gerritsen and Dirck Adriaensen, witnesses who had been summoned, and finds that Poulus Poulussen left Aert Pietersen Tack's service, without the latter's consent.

The Court rejects plaintiff's claim, because he hired himself out for a year and left his place within the stipulated period; and decides that defendant owes plaintiff nothing.

Poulus Poulussen, after the above sentence was read to him, declares that the witnesses testified falsely, and that if he is not paid he will not be receiving justice.

The Commissaries order the Schout to arrest Poulus Poulussen, and to keep him under arrest until he shall prove he has not received justice, and further proved that the witnesses have testified falsely.

EVERT PELS,
ALAERDT HEYMANSZ ROOSE,
ALBERT (x) GYSBERTSEN,
TIERCK CLASZEN DE WITT.

Jan Broersen, plaintiff, vs. Hendrick Martense, defendant. Plaintiff demands payment of six months' house rent, at four gldrs. per month. Defendant answers that plaintiff did not ask any rent, and he therefore refuses to pay.

The Court orders defendant to pay plaintiff twenty-four gldrs.

Hendrick Jochemse, plaintiff, vs. Evert Parys, defendant. Plaintiff demands of defendant five schepels of wheat and three and one-half gldrs., in zeewant, for which plaintiff has attached defendant.

Defendant answers he knows of no attachment and that he has paid. The Court, having heard the parties, orders defendant to pay plaintiff.

Willem Jansen Stol, plaintiff, vs. Evert Prys, defendant. Plaintiff demands payment of five schepels of wheat. Defendant answers he earned this amount from plaintiff for four days' labor. Plaintiff says defendant only worked three days.

The Commissaries order plaintiff to pay defendant three schepels of wheat for labor done, and defendant to satisfy plaintiff for the balance of the account.

The Schout, plaintiff, vs. Jan Barense Amershof, defendant. Plaintiff demands a fine for the half anker of brandy which defendant smuggled, about which Jacob Boerhans, being also questioned by the Court Messenger, says he saw the brandy taken from the wagon. Defendant says he called at the Collector's house and the Collector not being home, the brandy was carried to his house.

The Court, Commissaries, order the brandy to be confiscated and that defendant pay six gldrs. for the poor.

EVERT PELS,
ALAERDT HEYMANSZ ROOSE.

Thomas Chambers, plaintiff, vs. Aert Pietersen Tack, defendant. Plaintiff demands from defendant payment of the amount of two hundred and ninety-four gldrs. beaver's value, as per obligation. Defendant admits the debt.

The Court, having heard the parties, orders defendant to satisfy plaintiff.

Barent Gerritsen, plaintiff, vs. The Schout, defendant. Default.

Hendrick Jochemsen, plaintiff, vs. Willem Vredenburgh, defendant. Default.

Hester Dowens gives notice of an attachment of three schepels of buckwheat in the hands of Jan Jansen, belonging to Merten Hermensen.

Session of January 9, 1663.
Present: The Schout; Evert Pels, Aldert Heymansz Roose, Albert Gysbertse.

Poulus Poulussen, plaintiff, vs. Jannetje Volckertsen, defendant. Default.

Jan Jansen de Brabander, plaintiff, vs. Evert Pels, defendant. Plaintiff demands payment of seventeen and one-half schepels of wheat and also eighteen and one-half lbs. of butter. Defendant answers he has a bill against this, which plaintiff declines to accept.

The Court orders defendant to pay the amount claimed, and, if defendant has any claim against plaintiff, he may go to Court with it.

Jan Broersen, plaintiff, vs. Thomas Chambers, Elsjen Jans, and Pieter Cornelissen, defendants. Default.

Barent Gerretsen, plaintiff, demands payment of ten schepels of wheat, as per obligation payable Ao. 1663. Defendant, Jan Broersen, admits the debt and requests time.

The Court orders defendant to pay plaintiff the amount claimed, as per obligation of Ao. 1663.

Mr. Gysbert van Imbrogh, vs. Matys Roeloofsen, defendant. Plaintiff demands the six new sacks which he found at the house of defendant, who kept them four weeks. Through the Schout, he ordered the defendant to give the sacks back, and upon his return home Mr. Gysbert took the sacks to the Schout for inspection. There is was found that some of them were rotten and decayed, and one was missing, for which he demands payment. Defendant says he knew nothing about the sacks until the Schout sent for them.

Thereupon the Court was informed by Jan Peerssen that he had directed Louwerens the soldier to take the six sacks to Mr. Gysbert van Imbrogh's.

And whereas, both parties refer to Jan Perssen, it is ordered that the witnesses shall be present or testify in writing.

Mathys Roeloofsen, plaintiff, vs. Anthony de Walter, defendant. Default.

Mathys Roeloofsen, plaintiff, vs. Poulus Tomassen, defendant. Plaintiff demands payment of twenty schepels of wheat due for drinks and goods sold defendant. Defendant admits the debt and requests six weeks' time.

The Court orders defendant to pay plaintiff within six weeks.

The Court, Commissaries, order that the attachment laid on the goods in the possession of Roelof Swartwout, for the amount of twenty schepels of wheat, shall remain in force until full payment by Poulus Tomassen.

The Schout, plaintiff, demands from Mathys Roeloofsen a fine of five hundred gldrs., because the savages were admitted to his house at night through the palisades, all of which the Sergeant and his roundsman declare.

The Court allows the Schout fifty gldrs., and the defendant is ordered to pay the same to the Schout.

Tjirick Classen de Wit and Sergeant Christiaen Nissen, under power of attorney from the Lord General Pieter Stuyvesant, plaintiffs, vs. Cornelis Barense Slecht, defendant.

Plaintiffs inform the Court that whereas, in consequence of a late sentence against Cornelis Barsen, they have become sureties for him for the amount of nineteen hundred gldrs., in beavers, and finding that no corn is forthcoming, they ask the Court to authorize them to appoint one or two guards at the expense of defendant, so as to relieve them of their anxiety.

The Court, after considering the petition, directs plaintiffs to take turns each week, and every day to carefully watch the quantity of corn threshed and delivered there, and also to receive and note the same, to store or cause the same to be stored, and, if this do not suffice, they are authorized to appoint two watchers to watch the corn, at the expense of defendant.

Tjirick Classen deWit sues out an attachment upon one hundred and seven gldrs., beaver's value, in the hands of Juriaen Westvael, belonging to Cornelis Barense Slecht.

Pieter Jacobsen, plaintiff, vs. Grietjen Westercamp. Plaintiff, by petition, asks to be released from defendant, so as to be a free man again and earn his living. Defendant requests fourteen days' time.

The Court again allows defendant fourteen days' time, and if she can not bring proof, plaintiff shall receive the judgment of the Court which, upon request, will mete out justice.

Evert Pels, plaintiff, vs. Juriaen Westvael, defendant. Plaintiff demands of defendant what he has to say against his obligation held by plaintiff, as defendant is not willing to pay it.   Defendant demands a bill of particulars.

Plaintiff answers he is not obliged to give one, because, at the signing of the obligation, they settled their accounts in the presence of Thomas Chambers. He therefore demands payment, or proof by defendant that he does not owe it. Defendant answers he is not disposed to bring any other proof before this court.

The Commissaries order plaintiff to show defendant the origin of the indebtedness, and the defendant to send in his account to plaintiff.

Session, held January 13, 1663.

Present: The Schout; Evert Pels, Aldert Heymanse Roose, Albert Gysbertsen, Tjirick Classen deWit.

Aldert Heymanse, plaintiff, vs. Pieter van Alen, defendant. Plaintiff says that by a previous judgment of the Commissaries, rendered at their session of November 28, defendant was ordered to prove to plaintiff that he used false weights. The defendant, after being under arrest for four days in the hands of the Schout, moves him to bring him to Court.

The Court, Commissaries, resolve and decide to give defendant time until the next session of the Court, and in the meantime he may give bail, or else be detained until then.

EVERT PELS,
TIERCK CLASZEN DE WITT.

Ordinary Session, held Tuesday, January 23, 1663.

Present: The Schout; Aldert Heymanse Roose, Albert Gysbertse, Tjirick Classen de Wit.

Thomas Chambers, plaintiff, vs. Evert Pels, defendant. Both default.

Poulus Poulussen, plaintiff, vs. Annejte Aerts, defendant. Plaintiff demands payment of defendant. Default.

Poulus Poulussen, at the request of Emmetje Volckerts, declares and testifies that, after he left Tack's service, Aert Pietersen Tack promised to pay her.

Jan Broersen, plaintiff, demands a declaration of Thomas Chambers, Pieter Cornelissen and Elsjen Jans. Says that the Sergeant called him a thief. Pieter Cornelissen and Elsjen Jans testify and declare that they did not hear it. Thomas Chambers declares he heard he was taxed with having stolen turnips, which plaintiff admits in Court. The Sergeant added: "Fresh pork tastes good with turnips."

Walraven deMont, plaintiff, vs. Huybrecht Bruyn, defendant. Default.

Gommert Poulussen, plaintiff, vs. Roeloof Swartwout, defendant. Plaintiff demands from defendant payment of fifty-three and one half schepels of wheat, due for goods bought from and wages earned by his deceased brother. Defendant admits the debt.

The Court orders defendant to pay plaintiff one-half within one month and the balance within two months.

EVERT PELS,

ALAERDT HEYMANSZ.

Gommert Poulussen, plaintiff, vs. Aert Mertense Dorn, defendant. Plaintiff demands payment of twenty-five and one-half schepels of wheat, for cloth sold; and also twenty-four schepels of wheat, and eleven gldrs., zeewant, the latter due on an obligation to Willem Mertense for whom Gommert Poulussen is attorney, as is known to Tjirick Classen and Albert Gysbertsen.

Defendant Aert Mertense Dorn admits the debt and requests time. The Court orders defendant to pay within six weeks, and the obligation six weeks afterwards.

Gommert Poulussen, plaintiff, vs. Peter Bruynsen, defendant. Plaintiff demands payment of ten schepels of wheat for goods sold. Defendant admits the debt. The Court orders defendant to pay within six weeks.

Gommert Poulussen, plaintiff, vs. Warrenaer Hoorenbeek, defendant. Plaintiff demands payment of seventeen schepels of wheat, and also three schepels of wheat for interest.

Defendant admits the debt. The Court orders defendant to pay within six weeks.

Mathen Blanchan, plaintiff, vs. Mathys Roeloofsen, defendant. Plaintiff demands the expenses he says he incurred for defendant when defendant was under sentence. Defendant answers he offered to pay plaintiff, but his obstinacy caused him to go to Court.

The Court, after hearing both parties, decides that each pay one-half the expense, so that defendant must pay plaintiff ten gldrs., ten stivers.

Pieter Jacobsen, plaintiff, vs. Grietjen Westercamp, defendant. Default.

The Schout, plaintiff, vs. Barent Gerritse, defendant. Default.

Emmetjen Volckertss, plaintiff, vs. Jacob Barense, defendant. Default.

Jacob Joosten, plaintiff, vs. Jacob Barense, defendant. The plaintiff, as attorney for Jan Verbeeck, demands of defendant payment of the amount of fifteen schepels of wheat. Defendant admits the debt, offers to pay eight schepels of wheat within fourteen days.

The Court, Commissaries, order that the attachment levied by Jacob Joosten on Jacob Barense's corn shall remain in force until the final payment.

Hendrick Jochemsen, plaintiff, vs. Annetje Aerts, defendant.. Plaintiff says that defendant taxed him with keeping false accounts and with selling diluted brandy, and he requests a vindication of his honor.

Defendant admits having said to plaintiff that he sent in a false bill, and also says that plaintiff's wife called her a whore. Plaintiff protests and says, "I shall consider you, defendant, to be a whore until you prove to me that I keep false books."

The Court orders defendant to have proof at its next session, and plaintiff to prove his account.

Mr. Gysbert van Imbrogh, plaintiff, vs. Matthys Roeloofsen, defendant.

Plaintiff demands payment for the six ruined sacks which defendant kept four weeks. Defendant once before declared he knew nothing about the sacks, and now shows an attestation by which Jan Persen and Jan Westhoeven declare that his wife took them filled up, from her own mowers at the Ronduyt.

On this, the Court decides and orders the defendant to pay plaintiff for the sacks, and also to pay as a fine one pound Flemish [six guilders, or $2.40] for the church.

Aldert Heymanse Roose, plaintiff, vs. Pieter van hAlen, defendant. Plaintiff, under an earlier judgment of the Commissaries directing defendant's arrest, requests his apprehension outside his own house, until he has proven plaintiff's weights to be false. Defendant, on an examination by the Commissaries, answers that he did not say that plaintiff's weights were false, but that he had not received full weight. At the former session, November 28, 1662,, he roundly declared it be true that he had said so.

The Commissaries, therefore, decide to refer the parties to three good men, Thomas Chambers, Mr. Gysbert van Imbrogh and Sergeant Christiaen Nissen romp, for the purpose of settling, if possible, the difference between them, otherwise to have the defendant arrested at plaintiff's request; the expenses to be paid by the party decided to be in the wrong.

                    EVERT PELS,
                    TIERCK CLASZEN DE WITT,
                    ALBERT GYSBERTSEN, (x) his mark.

The good men selected not having been able to settle the above dispute, the Commissaries are asked to act as arbitrators.   These state that the parties have come to such an understanding that Pieter van Halen declared in their presence that he knew nothing of Albert Heymanse and his wife but what was honorable and virtuous, and promised to pay through the Schout the expenses incurred in the above matter.

                    EVERT PELS,
                    TIERCK CLASZEN DE WITT,
                    (x) [ALBERT GYSBERTSEN.]

Extraordinary Session, held Saturday, January 29, 1663.

Present: The Schout; Evert Pels, Aldert Heymanse Roose, Albert Gysbertsen, Tjirick de Wit.

Hester Douwens, or her attorney in the absence of her husband, plaintiff, vs. Tjirick Classen deWit, defendant.

Plaintiff demands payment of the amount of three hundred and thirty-two gldrs., eighteen stivers, zeewant, for goods and jewelry furnished to defendant. Defendant reviews the account, says he once verbally settled with her, in the presence of herself and husband, and then owed twenty-six schepels of wheat, a schepel

of onions and a half a thousand brick.   But, owing to plaintiff's
pressure, defendant asks for a copy of the account and fourteen
days' time to examine it.

The Court decides that defendant shall furnish a sufficient
counter-bill within fourteen days, unless he can prove, as claimed, that he settled it with plaintiff.   Plaintiff is also ordered to furnish a copy of his account.

Ordinary Secssion, held Tuesday, February 6, 1663.

Present: The Schout; Evert Pels, Aldert Heymanse, sick,
Albert Gysbertse, Tjirick Classen deWit.

Whereas, the Court has decided to find the rent for the Court
room and thus relieve the community, therefore those who shall
appear before it to plead or seek justice, shall each pay thirty-six
stivers, to be advanced by the plaintiff, at the cost of the loser of the
suit, which moneys shall be used to pay the rent of the place where
the ordinary sessions of the Court are held.

EVERT PELS,
TIERCK CLASZEN DE WITT.

Jan Broersen, plaintiff, vs. Thomas Chambers, Pieter Cornelissen, Elsjen Jans, defendants.   Plaintiff again demands an opportunity to testify as to the truth, and for that purpose summoned
Thomas Chambers, Pieter Cornelissen, and Elsjen Jans who do
not refuse to testify to the truth, but ask the Court to first ascertain whether plaintiff's accuser, Christiaen Nissen romp, will affirm what he said to plaintiff, in which case no witnesses will
be necessary.

Regarding this, the Court decides that plaintiff summon the
respondent and have him either deny or affirm the accusation.

Pieter Jacobsen, plaintiff, vs. Grietjen Westercamp, defendant.
Plaintiff asks, by petition, that the Court grant him justice against
defendant.   Defendant answers that plaintiff is the father of her
child.   He denies this, says it is not his child, and offers to affirm
upon oath.   Which he did before the Court, saying, "I am not the
father of the child: So truly help me God Almighty!"

Therefore, the Court decides to allow plaintiff to marry any
other person he pleases, and it has also thought it proper, in view
of several certificates previously shown by both parties to the

Court, that plaintiff shall, for the nonce, pay defendant two hundred gldrs., on a former acknowledgment made by him that he did not compensate her for lying with her, and he is therefore bound to pay her for that service.

Anthony Cruepel, plaintiff, vs. Roeloof Swartwout, defendant. Plaintiff demands payment of the amount of forty schepels of wheat and thirteen schepels of buckwheat. Defendant admits the debt.

The Court, Commissaries, order defendant to pay plaintiff the amount claimed, within six weeks.

EVERT PELS,
TIERCK CLASZEN DE WITT.

Jan Barense Ammershof, plaintiff, vs. Roeloof Swartwout, defendant. Plaintiff demands payment of twelve schepels of wheat. Defendant admits the debt.

The Court orders defendant to pay plaintiff the amount claimed.

EVERT PELS,
TIERCK CLASZEN DE WITT.

The Schout, plaintiff, vs. Barent Gerritsen, defendant. The first default.

Plaintiff demands payment from defendant of the amount due as per agreement on January 9, made in the presence of the Commissaries. Defendant admits the debt and promises to pay the Schout within twenty-four hours.

The Court orders this to be done, and, if defendant does not comply, the Schout is authorized to enforce the claim.

Roeloof Swartwout, plaintiff, vs. Mathys Roeloofsen, defendant. Plaintiff demands from defendant payment of the amount of seven beavers. Defendant admits the debt, but answers that he assigned to plaintiff his claim against Jonas Rantsou, which plaintiff admits, but says the assignment has not been accepted, and, in consequence, he again enters his claim against the principal [the defendant]. The Court orders defendant to pay and satisfy plaintiff.

EVERT PELS,
TIERCK CLASZEN DE WITT.

Jan Jansen Ammersfoort and Cornelis Slecht, plaintiffs, vs. Aert Jacobsen, Jan Willemsen and Hendrick Jansen Looman, defendants.

Plaintiffs demand from defendants payment for what each has bought at public sale: Jan owes three hundred and fifty gldrs.; Aert Jacobsen is to pay three hundred and forty-five gldrs., and Hendrick Jansen Looman two hundred and ten gldrs., all according to bill of sale. The defendants admit the debt.

The Court, having heard the respective parties, orders defendants, each for himself, to pay plaintiffs for the grain bought of the latter, according to the bill of sale, which is past due.

The Schout, plaintiff, vs. Mattheu Blanchan, defendant. Plaintiff says that defendant, an inhabitant of this village, does not confine himself to distilling, but has dared to violate the ordinances established by the Director General and Supreme Council for this place, and still unrepealed, providing that those who desire to tap must observe said ordinances until further order. Concerning which the Schout states that defendant sold a half anker of brandy to his brother-in-law, Lowys Dubo, and [that] when the Court was at defendant's house to gauge, [the defendant,] to account for what had become of his wine, gave as an answer that he had two or three times boiled over into the ashes [i. e., spoiled the product]. And the Court, being informed that on the great piece some mishap has occurred, went thither with the whole Board on horseback to investigate for the general good how much wine there was and in whose possession it was, and found a half anker of distilled water at the house of Lowys Dubo who admitted and declared, in the presence of the Court, that he bought it from his father. And, whereas, the defendant did not declare the wine, the Schout demands his fine.

EVERT PELS,

TIERCK CLASZEN DE WITT.

Jan Albertsen van Steenwyck appeared before the Commissaries, and asked that he be granted a convenient lot below the fort, on the bank of the Kill to the southward of Barent Gerritsen's to be used as a tannery and garden. The same is hereby granted to him provisionally, on condition of not building thereon, either now or hereafter, any dwellings or breweries. The lot is eleven rods

wide and sixteen rods long.   Thus measured in the presence of the
Court.

EVERT PELS,

ALAERDT HEYMANSZ ROOSE,

ALBERT GYSBERTSEN, (x) his mark,

TIERCK CLASZEN DEWITT.

The matter on the other side [of the page] between the Schout
and Matheu Blanchan having been presented to the Commissaries
and having been considered by them and the Court, they find that
the ordinance must be observed, and in order to prevent the evils
which otherwise might result, and for cause it thereunto moving,
the Court condemns the defendant to pay a fine of one hundred and
twenty-five guilders, to be applied as follows: One third to the
poor, one-third to the Bench, and one-third to the Schout.

EVERT PELS,

ALAERDT HEYMANSZ ROOSE,

ALBERT GYSBERTSEN, (x) his mark,

TIERCK CLASZEN DEWITT.

Ordinary Session, Tuesday, February 20, 1663.

Present: The Schout; Evert Pels, Aldert Heymanse Roose,
Albert Gysbertsen, Tjirick Claesen deWit.

Annetjen Aerts, plaintiff, vs. Hendrick Jochemsen, defendant. Plaintiff demands an accounting from defendant. Defendant
submits a bill for fourteen guilders, whereupon plaintiff claims
four hundred bricks more.

The Court, having heard the parties, through witnesses summoned, and information received from Mr. Gysbert van Imbrogh
and from Jan Aersen, the smith, finds an omission in the account
and orders plaintiff to pay defendant four gldrs., ten stivers, the
defendant to supply four hundred bricks to plaintiff and pay the
costs incurred.

Huybrecht Bruyn, plaintiff, vs. Jan Jansen van Ammersfoort,
defendant. Plaintiff demands from defendant the amount of
twelve schepels of wheat, due for wages earned for mason work.
Defendant admits the debt, but says that the mason has still to

plaster the walls. This the mason denies, saying it was not stipulated as part of the work contracted for.

The Court orders defendant to pay the amount claimed, but if he can prove that plaintiff contracted to plaster the walls, the defendant shall then receive satisfaction.

Mr. Gysbert van Imbrogh, plaintiff, vs. Mathys Roeloofsen, defendant. Plaintiff demands from defendant payment of the expenses incurred in consequence of the judgment given in favor of plaintiff on January 13. Defendant answers that plaintiff attached his money before the judgment was rendered.

The Court, having heard the parties, orders defendant to pay plaintiff fourteen gldrs., eight stivers, for costs incurred.

Evert Prys, plaintiff, vs. Hendrick Jansen Looman, defendant.

Mathys Roeloofsen, plaintiff, vs. Huybrecht Bruyn, defendant. Plaintiff demands payment of the amount of thirteen schepels of wheat due on the sale of some goods. Defendant admits the debt. The Court orders defendant to pay.

Barent Gerritsen, plaintiff, vs. Roeloof Swartwout, defendant. Plaintiff, under a power of attorney shown to the Court, demands payment of the amount of fourteen schepels of wheat. Defendant admits the debt, but says he is entitled to a deduction for two sacks.

The Court orders defendant to pay plaintiff within three weeks.

Barent Gerritsen, plaintiff, vs. Tjirick Classen de Wit, defendent. Plaintiff demands, as per adjustment of accounts shown to the Court, the amount of twenty-six schepels of wheat, thirteen gldrs., five st., in zeewant, and five hundred bricks. Defendant admits the debt, and promises to pay within fourteen days, the whole Bench being present.

On February 28, Matheu Blanchan requested permission to appeal, which was granted by the Court.

He offers Christiaen Nissen romp and Lowys Dubo as sureties for the judgment rendered or to be rendered, with the costs thereof.

CHRISTYAN NISZEN,

LOUYS (x) DUBOIS.

Ordinary Session, held Tuesday, March 6, 1663.

Present: The Schout; Evert Pels, Aldert Heymanse Roose, Albert Gysbertsen, Tjirick Classen deWit.

Pieter Vlamingh, plaintiff, vs. Aert Jacobsen, defendant. Plaintiff demands payment of twenty-one schepels of oats for wages earned. Default.

Gommert Poulussen, plaintiff, vs Evert Prys, defendant. Plaintiff demands payment of twenty-one schepels of wheat. Defendant says he does not owe more than nineteen schepels.

The Court, after hearing both parties, orders defendant to pay nineteen schepels of wheat.

Mr. Gysbert van Imbrogh, plaintiff, vs. Altjen Sybrants, defendant. Plaintiff demands, under an earlier complaint made before this Court, vindication of his honor against defendant. He produces a certificate made by three witnesses who declare they heard defendant call plaintiff a Jew and that she also called him a sucker. They also declare that she struck his chest so that he fell backward, and that her husband, Mathys Roeloofsen, threatened plaintiff, saying, "If I had you elsewhere, I would teach you something."

Defendant in default.

Roeloof Hendricksen, plaintiff, vs. Thomas Chambers, defendant. Plaintiff demands payment of the amount of three schepels of wheat. Defendant answers that, to the best of his knowledge. he paid plaintiff or somebody else on his behalf. Plaintiff offers to testify to the truth of the fact that he never received payment and that he did not authorize any one to collect the debt for him.

The Court, having heard both parties, grants, at their request, an adjournment.

Hendrick Jochemsen, plaintiff, vs. Annetjen Aerts, defendant. Plaintiff demands vindication of his honor; says that defendant called his wife a whore, and charged him with keeping false books, and watering his brandy. Defendant denies the accusation, states that she said he showed her a false account, as is entered in the minutes of February 20, 1662, and demands proof of the accusation and vindication of her honor because plaintiff called her a whore.

Plaintiff requests that justice be done him, or otherwise he will be obliged to seek it elsewhere.

An order had been given by the Court to plaintiff, on February 6, that the parties should produce proofs, and as plaintiff has no other witnesses than his own wife, both parties are ordered to keep the peace. In addition, Hendrick Jochemse is ordered to pay a fine of twenty-five gldrs., and Elsjen Jans and Annetjen Aerts are each also ordered to pay a fine of six gldrs., to go to the poor, for having used vile and nasty language before the Court.

Jacob Boerhans, Collector for this village, plaintiff, vs. Hendrick Jochemse, Wallera deMont, Jonas Rantsou, in default, Willem van Vreedenburgh, in default, Hendrick Jansen Looman, Claes Pietersen, in default, defendants.

Plaintiff demands payment of the excise license for the wine or beer which each defendant has taken in and disposed of. The above named defendants admit the claim.

The Court orders defendants, severally, to pay within eight days, in accordance with the Collector's book, under pain of execution.

Mr. Verleet, for Fop Barense, demands payment of the amount due on settlement of accounts, viz.: Fifty-seven and one-half schepels of wheat and one hundred and fifty-four gldrs., eighteen stivers, in zeewant, which amounts are due Fop Baranse for building the parsonage, as per adjustment November 12, 1661.

The Schout, as plaintiff, against Fop Barense, on complaints made by Domine Blom to the Magistrates, demands that the money due Fop Barense be held under attachment until he shall appear here to defend himself.

Whereas, the Schout has a case against Fop Barentse, arising from some threatening or abusive language used towards the minister, Domine Harmanus Blom, and others, the Commissaries, therefore, declare said attachment to be valid, and specially charge the Schout to officially summon Fop Barense to appear before this Court, either in person or by attorney, within six weeks, to answer the complaint now before the magistrates.   Done at Wildtwyck, March 31, 1663.

Hendrick Jochemse informs the Court that he has a piece of farm land situated near the wood opposite the Kill, bounded by a part of the land of Jeronimus Ebbingh whose lessees cause damage to the petitioner through the pasturing of their horses. He requests that the owners of the meadow lands across the Kill, which are private property, be ordered to fence them in, and to pay for the damage done to the farming land.

The Court orders and directs that every one, who has or intends to have and maintain private meadows on or near cultivated farm lands, shall fence such meadow lands, without encroaching upon his neighbor's property.

We, the undersigned, Aldert Heymanse Roose, Commissary and Elder of the village of Wildtwyck, and Albert Gysberse, Commissary and Deacon of said village, make known that before us appeared the worthy Evert Pels, inhabitant of the village of Wildtwyck, who acknowledged that he actually and in good faith borrowed and received from Roeloof Swartwout and Cornelis Barense Slecht, the appointed guardians of the minor children of the late Mathys Jansen, deceased, the amount of one thousand gldrs., in corn, at beaver's value, which he agrees to hold at interest for two consecutive years, and promises to give as interest one hundred and twenty gldrs., in corn, beaver's value, per annum, being twelve gldrs., per cent, commencing February 15, of the current year, 1663 and terminating February 15, 1665, when he will return and reimburse the aforesaid principal and the second year's interest. For which purpose he, the appearer, specially mortgages his lands, situated near the village Wildtwyck, and his house, standing in the aforesaid village, which he says are free and unincumbered; and he further generally pledges his person and goods, real and personal, present and future, nothing excepted, placing and submitting them and himself to and under the jurisdiction of all courts and judges, adding the costs incurred thereby.

In testimony whereof we, the above named, and the appearer, have subscribed and authenticated these presents with our own signatures. Done at the village of Wildtwyck, this February 15, 1663.

EVERT PELS.

To my knowledge, ALAERDT HEYMANSZ ROOSE.

This is the mark (x) of ALBERT GYSBERTSEN, made by himself.

To my knowledge, TIERCK CLASZEN DE WITT.

Ordinary Session, April 3, Anno, 1663.

Present: The Schout; Evert Pels, Albert Gysbertsen, Tjirick Classen deWit. Aldert Heymanse, absent.

Mathys Roeloofsen, plaintiff, vs. Jan Jansen van Ammersfoort, defendant. Plaintiff demands payment of the amount of fifty-eight gldrs., fourteen st., eight pennies, due on a debt for liquor. Defendant admits the debt.

The Court orders defendant to pay plaintiff within six weeks.

Evert Pels, Commissary, as attorney for Jan Dircksen van Breeman, plaintiff, vs. Mathys Roelofsen, defendant. Plaintiff demands payment of the amount of three hundred and eighty-one gldrs., two st., heavy money, and also twelve schepels of wheat, due for wages and goods sold. Defendant answers that he has a counter claim, and that, after balancing accounts, he would owe twelve gldrs., zeewant.

The Court orders the parties to adjust their accounts between themselves and to inform it, at its next session, of the result.

Johanna Ebbingh, plaintiff, vs. Pieter Bruynsen van Booheemen, defendant. Plaintiff demands payment of four beavers, two and one-half of which had been loaned and one and one-half of which were for goods furnished. Defendant admits he received the goods and the beavers, but says he does not owe plaintiff anything, as the latter did not keep her promise to let him learn a trade. Plaintiff answers that about two years ago they mutually agreed regarding the debt specified above.

The Court, after having heard both parties, orders defendant to pay plaintiff, and to give satisfaction for the amount claimed.

Pieter Mathysse, plaintiff, vs. Aert Jacobsen, defendant. Plaintiff demands payment of the amount of twenty-one schepels of oats, due for wages earned. The second default.

Thereupon the Court orders defendant to deposit the twenty-one schepels of oats in Court as provisional security, and to appear before it a third time.

Ordinary Session, Tuesday, April 17, 1663.

Present. The Schout; Evert Pels, Albert Gysbertsen, Tjirick Classen deWit, Aldert Heymanse Roose, in default.

Geertjen Bouts, plaintiff, vs. Aert Mertense Dorn, defendant. Plaintiff demands payment of the amount of thirty schepels of wheat due on an obligation, and says he journeyed many times to this place to obtain payment. Defendant admits the debt, according to obligation.

The Court orders defendant to pay plaintiff.

Roeloof Hendricksen, plaintiff, vs. Thomas Chambers, defendant. Plaintiff demands payment of the amount of three schepels of wheat for wages earned. Defendant in default.

Whereas, plaintiff and defendant were in Court once before, and requested an adjournment, the defendant is therefore ordered to deposit the three schepels of wheat in Court as provisional security.

Cornelis Barense Slecht, plaintiff, vs. Aert Jacobsen, defendant. Plaintiff demands payment of the amount of eight and one-half beavers on which thirty-three schepels of oats have been paid, due for wages earned. Default.

Cornelis Barense Slecht, plaintiff, vs. Jan Willemse, defendant. Plaintiff demands payment of sixty gldrs. heavy money, and twenty-four gldrs., zeewant. Default.

Albert Gerritsen, plaintiff, vs. Annetjen Aerdts, defendant. Default.

Mr. Gysbert van Imbrogh, plaintiff, vs. Altjen Sybrants, defendant. Plaintiff enters a complaint against defendant for assault and for being called a slanderer. Requests vindication of his honor and punishment of defendant, as provided by law.

Defendant presents a certificate of two witensses who offer to testify that Mr. Gysbert van Imbrogh called Altjen Sybrants a heap of dung, and that thereupon Altjen Sybrants called Mr. Gysbert a Jew and a sucker, and threatened one of the witnesses, and said to Mr. Gysbert, "If I had you elsewhere, I would show you what it means to call me a heap of dung." This complaint of Mr. Gysbert van Imbrogh, now made for the third time, and his former appearance, have preforce moved the Court to proceed to punishment, so as to serve as an example to others. The Court allows each of the parties fourteen days' additional time, without extension, to prove their allegations, and then will give judgment.

Christiaen Nissen romp, plaintiff, vs. Aert Mertense Dorn, defendant. Settled.

Aert Mertense, plaintiff, vs. Roeloof Swartwout, defendant. Plaintiff demands payment of the amount of one hundred and two gldrs., as per settlement of accounts shown to the Court. The defendant admits the debt.

The Court orders defendant to pay plaintiff.

EVERT PELS,

TIERCK CLASZEN DE WITT.

Christiaen Nissen romp, plaintiff, vs. Evert Pels, defendant. Plaintiff, demands payment of the amount of ten schepels of wheat due for servant's wages assigned to him. Defendant answers he does not owe more than three schepels of wheat on the old account, and requests a bill for the thirty gldrs. which Christiaen says he owes for brandy, and says, "I would certainly have paid you if you had not summoned me before the Court."

Plaintiff says he settled with defendant, saying, "If I had you outside I would teach you something." He says his claim is just, and offers to swear to it, as he is voluntarily doing by the oath he has taken.

The Court orders plaintiff to furnish a proper account, and defendant to pay the same within one month after its receipt.

On April 20, 1663, Hester Douwens sued for a writ to attach two horses belonging to Jan Dircksen van Breeman, now with Juriaen Westvael.

Ordinary Session, held Tuesday, May 1, 1663.

Present: The Schout; Albert Gysbertsen and Tjirick Classen deWit. Evert Pels in default.

Roeloof Swartwout, plaintiff, vs. Poulus Tomassen, defendant. Plaintiff alleges that defendant hired and bound himself out, together with Jan Muessen, each as principal, to thresh all the corn, and as the defendant voluntarily allowed his comrade to go, and himself now has also run away from the work he contracted to do, plaintiff therefore, after due protest, requests permission to substitute and keep somebody else at the work, at defendant's cost and expense, to do the threshing contracted for. He also requests payment for a small keg of soap and security for its value and costs incurred.

Defendant answers that plaintiff was willing that his mate should depart. Plaintiff admits he was willing, as he relied on his contract which provides that each shall be liable as principal.

The Court orders and directs defendant to bear three parts of the expenses, provided plaintiff shall put somebody else at defendant's work to finish the threshing, plaintiff to bear the fourth part.

Whereas, there is not a full Bench, plaintiff requests a revision or that defendant give security for arrears.

TIERCK CLASZEN DE WITT,
ALBERT GYSBERTSEN, (x) his mark.

Tjirick Classen deWit, plaintiff, vs. Barent Gerritsen, defendant.

The Court resolves not to decide between parties at present, because only the Schout and one Commissary occupy the bench, but the parties must have their papers ready at the next session, when the matter will be taken up.

Claes Louwrence, plaintiff, vs. Walleraven duMont, defendant. Plaintiff asks why defendant attached his money. Defendant answers, because plaintiff hired a man-servant at the Manathans, and on his arrival here he hired him out to another, and thereby made a profit of fifty-two gldrs., in zeewant, and six schepels of wheat. Plaintiff answers that he is entitled to it for his expenses in relation to the servant, and for his trouble.

The Court, having heard the parties, finds that said servant voluntarily hired himself out to Tjerck Classen de Wit, pursuant to a contract made between both, and decrees that, as Tjerck Classen wants to keep the servant, and pays him higher wages than those at which Claes engaged him at the Manathans, Tjerck Classen shall pay Claes Laurence personally the expenses he incurred, or, otherwise, make him a voluntary present, at the option of the last hirer, but Tjerck Classen shall not deduct said money from the servant's wages, and the servant, in accordance with his contract of employment, shall then complete his term.

Ordinary Session, held Tuesday, May 22, 1663.

Present: The Schout; Evert Pels, Albert Gysbertsen, Tirick Classen deWit.

Copy.

The Director General and Council of New Netherland having received and read the nomination made and delivered by the Schout and Commissaries of the village of Wildtwyck, in the Esopus, have selected and confirmed Thomas Chambers and Gysbert van Imburgh at the said place, in place of those retiring.

Done at Fort Amsterdam, in New Netherland, April 5, 1663.

In conformity with the written instructions, the Court requir- ed the newly appointed Commissaries to take the oath, which was administered by the Court, in the usual manner.

Tirick Classen deWit, plaintiff. vs. Barent Gerritsen, defend- ant.   Default.

Barent Gerritsen, plaintiff, vs. Pieter Jacobsen, defendant. De- fault.

Mathys Roelofsen, plaintiff, vs. Christiaen Nissen, defendant. Plaintiff presents a certificate, and states that the Sergeant seized some merchandise belonging to him.   Under examination, he admits he concealed some lead and wool at the Ronduyt, with the permis- sion of the soldiers quartered there.   Hereupon the Sergeant an- swers, "I don't want to have the Ronduyt turned into a home for you sutlers and suckers of this place, and don't intend to give up the goods until the arrival of the Lord General."

The Court, having heard both parties, orders the Sergeant to return plaintiff's merchandise, provided that, if any contraband goods be found thereunder, defendant shall deposit the same with the Court, and further that he shall require his soldiers not to tolerate any sutlers there but to give information of them to the Court which will deal with them as is proper.   Pending the arrival of the Noble Lord General, the contraband goods shall remain in custody.

Hendrick Jochemsen, plaintiff, vs. Geertuyt Andrissen, defend- ant.   Plaintiff demands payment of the amount of — — due on an obligation made by Jacob Jansen Stol, deceased.   Defendant re- quests time to examine her husband's books, for which purpose the

Court allows her fourteen days, and parties are ordered to compare their accounts and inform the Court.

Domine Hermanus Blom requests the Court that care be taken to have the remaining debt on the parsonage paid, and especially that the money for which he has become surety be collected, as he experiences much trouble on its account, adding, "Otherwise we shall put a stop to it." And he especially recommends the Magistrates to take better care than heretofore of his salary.

The Court resolves to summon the retiring Commissaries to appear before it and render an account of receipts and disbursements for the building of the parsonage, for the benefit of those having claims against the same, and to notify each of them, as some bills have already been sent in and presented to the Court. They are ordered to appear on May 25, 1663, at the house of Thomas Chambers.

Ordinary Session, held at Wildtwyck, June 5, 1663.

Present: The Schout; Albert Gysbertsen, Tjrick Classen deWit, Thomas Chambers, Gysbert van Imbrogh.

Tjirick Classen deWit, plaintiff, vs. Barent Gerritsen, defendant. Plaintiff demands, under a power of attorney from Jan Eversen, payment of the amount of seventy-four gldrs., in beavers, and fourteen schepels good winter wheat, and forty-four gldrs., in zeewant. Defendant admits owing the amount claimed, as per obligation, due January 1, 1662.

The Court, having heard the parties, finds, from the obligation, that defendant must pay plaintiff the amount claimed but, as plaintiff still demands payment of one hundred and sixteen gldrs., in beavers, for expenses incurred, the Court, at the request of defendant, refers the matter of the expenses to two impartial people.

The Schout, plaintiff, vs. Jan Jansen van Oosterhout, defendant. Default.

Barent Gerritsen, plaintiff, vs. Pieter Cornelissen, defendant. Plaintiff demands an amount of thirty-five schepels of wheat. Defendant admits owing thirty-four and one-half schepels. The Court orders him to pay.

Gerrit Voken, plaintiff, vs. Cornelis Barense Slecht, defendant. Plaintiff, through a document whereby Volckert Jansen and Jan Tomassen constitute themselves plaintiffs, presents to the Court a petition against Cornelis Barense Slecht, who is summoned by plaintiff before this Court. Plaintiffs demand restitution of a mare, because it was impounded by the defendant. Upon testimony given by Pieter Jacobsen that, to the best of his knowledge, the horse was driven and chased away, and in consequence thereof died, plaintiffs now conclude and demand that defendant shall be ordered to indemnify them for the said mare, and to pay all costs of suit.

In defense, Cornelis Barense Slecht, the defendant, presents a certificate by Adriaen Gerritsen van Vliet and Hermen Hendricksen who attest, at his request, that they saw him about three hours before nightfall drive six horses away from his land, on an easy trot.

The Court, having heard the parties and examined the papers, orders plaintiffs to adduce clearer and fuller proof.

The Schout, plaintiff, vs. Pieter van Halen, defendant. Default.

A majority of the Commissaries resolve that the Court shall not sit again until there are four or five cases. If necessary for the convenience of the residents, it will sit every week. The reason of this is because, in the absence of a Village or City Hall, the rent for the room can not be met.

(x) [ALBERT GYSBERTSEN],
TIERCK CLASZEN DE WITT,
GYSBERT VAN IMBROCH.

[The preceding minutes, except one entry, as noted, are all in the handwriting of Roeloof Swartwout, Schout. The following are in that of Mattheus Capito, Secretary.]

Ordinary Session, held Tuesday, July 24, 1663.
Present: The Noble Lord Johan de Decker; Roelof Swartwout, Schout; Albert Gysbertsen, Tjerck Classen deWit, Thomas Chambers, Gysbert van Imbroch, Commissaries.

Albert Gysbertsen, plaintiff, vs. Aert Martensen Doorn, defendant.

Albert Gysbertsen says that defendant caused plaintiff's pig to be killed, and presents a certificate to this effect. Defendant answers that he does not know whether it was plaintiff's pig, and offers to pay the owner therefor.

The Commissaries, having heard defendant's confession, order him to deposit with the Court the quantity of six schepels of wheat, for the benefit of him who shall be found to be the lawful owner, or otherwise the Court will dispose of it is it may see fit.

Tjerck Classen deWit, plaintiff, vs. Evert Pels, defendant. Default.

The Schout, in place of the Noble Lord Johan de Decker, plaintiff, vs. Tryntje, wife of Cornelissen Barentsen Slecht, defendant. Plaintiff says that defendant called the Noble Lord de Decker a blood sucker.

Defendant does not deny she spoke evilly of the Noble Lord de Decker, but says she spoke while depressed and discouraged because of the many misfortunes that had befallen her through the savages, and adds that she feels sorry for having slandered him.

The Commissaries, having heard the confession and regrets of defendant, prefer mercy to the severeity of justice, and order her to pay a fine of twenty-five gldrs., in zeewant, for the benefit of the church.

Ordinary Session, held Tuesday, September 18, 1663.

Present: Roelof Swartwout, Schout; Tjerck Classen de Wit, Albert Gysbertsen, Thomas Chambers, Gysbert van Imbroch, Commissaries.

Roelof Swartwout, plaintiff, vs. Aert Martensen Dorn, defendant. Default.

Same, vs. Hendrick Cornelissen Slecht, defendant. Default.

Same, vs. Pieter Bruynsen, defendant. Default.

Same, vs. Cornelis Bransten Vos, defendant. Default.

Same, vs. Hendrick Aertsen, defendant. Default.

Same, vs. Jacob Joosten, defendant. The plaintiff demands from defendant the amount of twenty-five gldrs. fine, for the first offense, and fifty gldrs. fine for the second, for violating the ordinance dated August 4, 1663.

Defendant replies by asking whether he is not permitted to support his family.

The Court, having heard the demand of the aforesaid Schout, and the defence of the defendant, orders defendant to settle with the Schout for the fine due, within eight days, or on default then to expect the judgment of this court.

Same, vs. Harmen Hendericks,	defendant.	Default.
Same, vs. Ariaen Huyberts,	do.	do.
Same, vs. Henderick Jochemsen,	do.	do.
Same, vs. Willem Aertsen,	do.	do.
Same, vs. Jan Broersen,	do.	do.
Same, vs. Jacob Barents Cool,	do.	do.
Same vs. Antoni Crupel,	do.	do.
Same, vs. Henderick Hendericksen,	do.	do.
Same, vs. Jan Jansen van Oosterhout,	do.	do.
Same, vs. Jacob Jansen Stoutenborch,	do.	do.
Same, vs. Jacob Janse de lange,	do.	do.
Same, vs. Aert Jacobs,	do.	do.
Same, vs. Gerret Aertsen,	do.	do.
Same, vs. Evert Prys,	do.	do.
Same, vs. Jan Willemsen,	do.	do.
Same, vs. Teunis Jacobsen,	do.	do.
Same, vs. Warnaer Hoorenbeeck,	do.	do.
Same vs. Jan Gerritsen,	do.	do.
Same, vs. Ariaen Gerritsen,	do.	do.
Same, vs. Mattys Roelofsen,	do.	do.

The plaintiff, Roelof Swartwout, Schout, presents to the Court a certificate, dated June 5, 1663, stating that the defendant, Matthys Roelofsen, sold brandy to the savages, according to the testimony of the savages themselves.

The Commissaries order defendant, pursuant to his offer, to reply to the certificate at the next session of the Court.

Hester Douwesen appears before this Court and demands seven schepels of wheat which Hey Olfertsen, deceased, owed her. The Court, having heard her, proposes to administer the property of the deceased here in Wildwyck and then pay her and the other creditors.

This Court resolves, in obedience to a previous request of the Captain Lieutenant and Council of War, to renew and replace the fallen and damaged palisades around the village, next Wednesday, September 26, with the assistance of all the inhabitants of this place, none excepted, under a penalty of twelve gldrs. for non compliance.

The Court further resolves that it will administer the property of persons who were killed during the troubles of June 7 last, leaving no relatives. Their names are: Willem Jansen Scba, servant; Henderick Jansen Looman, brewer's helper; Dirrick Willemsen, inhabitant.

The Court appoints as administrators, Albert Gysbertsen and Tjerck Classen de Wit, both Commissaries, with orders to immediately inventory all the property of said deceased, and to administer the same until further order, or claims by nearest relatives or creditors.

Inventory, September 18, 1663, taken at Wildwyck, at the house of Juriaen Westphael, in the presence of the Schout, Roelof Swartwout, and two Commissaries, Albert Gysbertsen and Tjerck Classen de Wit, of the property left by Hendrick Looman, found to be as follows:

1 gelding,
1 large brewing kettle, — — tuns,
1 sword and belt.
1 trunk without key, wherein was found
1 letter case containing letters, and a note book with memoranda of outstanding debts and accounts,
1 old gray suit,
1 old gray colored pair of breeches,
1 new gray suit,
2 pair of black woolen stockings,
1 new black hat and hat box,
1 bar lead,
4 small pieces of Haarlem cloth,
1 clothes brush,
1 trunk,
2 cravats,
3 handkerchiefs.

1 package containing about a pound of lead,
1 wagon frame, with iron tires.

Ordinary Session, held Tuesday, October 9, 1663.
Present: Roelof Swartwout, Schout; Albert Gysbertsen,
Tjerck Classen de Wit, Gysbert van Imborch.

The Schout, Roelof Swartwout, requests the Court to pronounce judgment against those whom he had summoned to appear,
but who did not come before this Court and were in default.

Roelof Swartwout, Schout, plaintiff, vs. Aert Mertensen Doorn.
Second default.

Same, vs. Jan Hendericksen, defendant. Second default.

Same, vs. Warnaer Hoorenbeeck, defendant. Second default.

Same, vs. Ariaen Gerretsen van Vliet. Second default.

Same, vs. Henderick Cornelissen Slecht. Second default.

Plaintiff demands that there be imposed, in accordance
with the ordinance dated August 4, last, a fine of twenty-five gldrs.,
for the first offense, and fifty gldrs., for the second, for violating
said ordinance that no one should go out to mow. without the
consent of the Captain Lieutenant and a sufficient convoy.

Cornelis Barentsen Slecht, representing his son Hendrick Cornelissen Slecht, answers that he is not obliged to comply therewith,
saying, "Let me appear before the Court having jurisdiction, the
Supreme Council. I have nothing to say till then."

The Commissaries, having heard the reply of Cornelis Barentsen Slecht, order him to pay the above named fine, since he does
not acknowledge the Inferior Court of Justice here as having jurisdiction, and appeals to the Supreme Council.

Cornelis Barentsen Slecht, standing before the Court and being requested to render an account of the estate of William Jansen
Seba, deceased, a demand therefor having been made of him by the
curators and trustees of said estate, September 18, last, answers
that he is not obliged to render an account of this matter to this
Court, he having once delivered an obligation to the aforesaid
William Jansen Seba.

The Schout thereupon asks the Court that Cornelis Barentsen
Slecht be compelled to render to it an account of the above named

estate of William Jansen Seba, deceased, in the interest of the curators appointed for that purpose, because said obligation has not
been and cannot be found by the curators among the effects of the
deceased. The Court, pursuant to the Schout's request, orders and
directs Cornelis Barentse Slecht to render, at its next session, a
statement of the account between him and the said Wiliam Jansen
Seba, deceased, so that debits and credits may be adjusted in the
proper and customary manner.

After the above was read to him, Cornelis Barentsen Slecht
said that he is not inclined henceforth to render an account to this
Court.

The Court, having seen and heard Cornelis Barentsen Slecht's
unreasonableness in opposing the Court of Justice of this place,
orders him to be confined in the house of the Schout, Roelof Swartwout, who, for this purpose, is directed to put him under arrest
and so keep him until he is ready to render said account.

Having been informed by Schout Swartwout, in the presence
of the Court here, that he should repair to the appointed place of
confinement, Cornelis Barentsen Slecht answered that the Schout
would have to fetch him with two officers and that he would not
voluntarily come, and defied him in the matter. For the threat
aforesaid, the Schout requests the Court to be permitted to lock said
Slecht up; whereupon the Court, having heard the request, directs
him to have said Slecht confined in the guard house.

Roelof Swartwout, Schout, plaintiff, vs. Pieter Bruynsen, Henderick Aertsen, Ariaen Roose, Jan Roose, Willem Aertsen, Cornelis
Brantsen Vos, Jacob Joosten, Ariaen Huybertsen, Harmen Hendericksen, defendants.

Plaintiff demands of the above mentioned defendant fines for
violating the ordinance dated August 4, last, that no one should
venture out to mow without consent and a proper convoy, the
fines being,

For Pieter Bruynsen,	25 gldrs.	
" Henderick Aertsen,	75	"
" Ariaen Roose,	25	"
" Jan Rose,	75	"
" Willem Aertsen,	75	"

" Cornelis Brantsen,   75   "
" Jacob Joosten,   75   "
" Harmen Hendericksen,   75   "
" Ariaen Huybertsen,   75   "

Cornelis Barentsen, on behalf of his farm hands above named, answers that they are not guilty and that they are not disposed to pay the fine, but that the matter must be heard and decided by the judge having jurisdiction, and requests copy thereof.

Cornelis Barentsen Slecht's reply having been heard, the Court here decides it has jurisdiction, and orders the above defendants to pay the fines in full to the plaintiff.

Roelof Swartwout, Schout, plaintiff, vs. Henderick Jochemsen, defendant. Second default.

Plaintiff demands judgment. The Court allows defendant a third default.

Roelof Swartwout, Schout, plaintiff, vs. Jan Gerritsen, Antony Crupel, Henderick Hendericksen, Jacob Stoutenborch, defendants. Plaintiff demands from the aforesaid defendants fines due for violation of the ordinance dated August 4, that no one should venture out to mow, without consent and a proper convoy, the fines amounting,

For Jan Gerritsen,   to 75 gldrs.
"   Antoni Crupel,   " 75   "
"   Henderick Hendericksen,   " 75   "
"   Jacob Stoutenborch,   " 25   "

Juriaen Westphael, representing the above named defendants who were in his employ, says he is not disposed to pay any fine herein, as the promises given him were not fulfilled at mowing time. Plaintiff requests judgment herein.

The Commissaries, having heard plaintiff's demand and the answer of defendants' representative, order defendants to pay the full fine to plaintiff, because their representative's day had been extended through rain and other causes, and the next day, when the weather was favorable, no work was done, yet at a time when, under the general agreement of the community, he ought to have assisted other farmers with his people, he had, notwithstanding the ordinance, had his work continued without giving notice to the Council of War and this Court.

The curators or overseers of the estate of the late Henderick Looman request that Jeuriaen Westphael render an account of the property of the said Henderick Looman. He answers he will not render such account.

This Court orders Juriaen Westphael to make a declaration, and extends his time to do so until its next session.

And whereas, defendant offers to make proof that there was no other property of the aforesaid Looman than is shown by the above mentioned inventory, the same will be received by the Court, otherwise the Court stands by the foregoing decision.

Roelof Swartwout, Schout, plaintiff, vs. Jan Broersen, defendant. Second default.

Plaintiff demands a fine of seventy-five gldrs., and requests judgment. The Court allows defendant a third default.

Roelof Swartwout, Schout, plaintiff, vs. Jacob Barentsen Cool, defendant. Second default. Plaintiff demands a fine of twenty-five gldrs. and requests judgment. The Court allows defendant a third default.

Roelof Swartwout, Schout, plaintiff, vs. Jacob Jansen van Oosterhout, defendant. Second default. Plaintiff demands a fine of seventy-five guilders., and requests judgment. The Court allows defendant a third default.

Roelof Swartwout, Schout, plaintiff, vs. Jacob Jansen de lange [the long], defendant. Second default. Plaintiff demands a fine of seventy-five gldrs., and requests judgment. The Court allows defendant a third default.

Lucas Hendricks, plaintiff, vs. Jan Simonsen, defendant. Default.

Roelof Swartwout, Schout, plaintiff, vs. Jan Willemsen and Teunis Jacobsen, defendants. Plaintiff demands from the first named defendant, Jan Willemsen, twenty-five gldrs., and from Teunis Jacobsen, twenty-five gldrs., due for violation of the ordinance dated August 4, last, that no one should venture out to mow without consent and a proper convoy.

Defendants answer that they are not liable for the payment of a fine herein and await a decision and order of the Court hereupon.

The Court orders defendants to pay the full amount of the fine to the plaintiff.

Roelof Swartwout, Schout, plaintiff, vs. Aert Jacobsen and Gerrit Aertsen, his son, Aert Jacobsen's daughter, Aert Jacobsen's servant, Andries, defendants. Plaintiff demands from the aforesaid defendants, for their violation of the ordinance dated August 4, last, that no one should venture out to mow without consent and a proper convoy, a fine,

From Aert Jacobsen,	of 75 gldrs.
" Gerrit Aertsen,	" 75 "
" Aert Jacobsen's daughter,	" 25 "
" Andries, his man,	" 25 "

Defendants answer they are not liable for the payment of the above fines, and request copy of the judgment.

The Court orders defendants to pay plaintiff the full amount of the fines.

Roelof Swartwout, Schout, plaintiff, vs. Aert Jacobsen, defendant. Plaintiff complains to this Court that defendant said that the Lord God would some time avenge himself upon the Lords who are here on the bench.

Defendant does not deny having said so, and the Commissaries Albert Gysbertsen and Gysbert van Imborch also confirm that they heard him say so, once at the house of Schout Roelof Swartout, and once at the bridge.

The Court of this place orders defendant to submit, at its next session, his reasons for saying that revenge should be called down upon it.

Roelof Swartwout, Schout, plaintiff, vs. Aert Jacobsen, defendant. Plaintiff accuses defendant of being a desecrater of the Sabbath, he having on that day taken a load of beer to his house, for which plaintiff seized defendant's wagon and beer, and that, notwithstanding the seizure, the defendant fetched the wagon and beer to his house.

Defendant denies having attempted to take a wagon load of beer home on a Sabbath or Sunday, but offers to prove that the Sabbath had expired.

The Court allows defendant time until the next session of the Court to prove the above.

Roelof Swartwout, Schout, plaintiff, vs. Evert Prys.

Plaintiff demands from defendant a fine of twenty-five gldrs. for violating the ordinance dated August 4, last. Defendant answers that he had the Captain's consent.

The Court orders defendant to submit proof, at the next session, that he had such consent.

Roelof Swartwout, Schout, plaintiff, vs. Jan Tyssen, defendant. Second default.

Roelof Swartwout, Schout, plaintiff, vs. Harmen Hendricksen, defendant. Second default.

Roelof Swartwout, Schout, plaintiff, vs. Magdalena, the wife of Harmen Hendricks. Plaintiff complains that he was hindered in his official duty, while apprehending Aeltje Claes. Defendant denies this, saying she is able to furnish better proof of the matter than has been given; that she only said, "Swartwout, why do you want to put this woman in prison? Why do you want to disgrace her? She is neither a whore nor a thief, and there is a private place here from which she cannot run away."

The Court orders defendant at the next session to submit evidence which will clear her.

Eechtje Ariaens, plaintiff, vs. Christiaen Niessen romp, defendant. Default.

Roelof Swartwout, Schout, plaintiff, vs. Dirrick Hendericksen, defendant. Default.

Copy

Henderick Jochemsen and Juriaen Westphael, appearing this 9th day of October, 1663, at the Court room of the Honorable Court at Wildwyck, request, on behalf of Cornelis Barentsen Slecht, that the said Slecht be permitted to leave the guard house and go to his home in order the better to prepare the account between himself and Willem Jansen Seba, deceased. They offer themselves as sureties for the body of Cornelis Barentsen Slecht, each as principal, that, at the desire of the Honorable Court, he will return at once to his duly provided place of confinement. For which purpose they bind their persons and property, real and personal, present and future, and to give this more force, have personally subscribed hereto. Done at Wildwyck, the day, year and place above.

(Signed)   Henderick Jochemsen. The mark (x) of Juriaen Westphael.

Agrees with the original. To which I certify.

Witness,

MATTHEUS CAPITO, Secretary.

The following ordinances were passed by the Schout and Commissaries at Wildwyck.

CONCERNING BEER EXCISE.

The Honorable Court having seen that licenses for beer have been discontinued during the late troubles, and finding that very little revenue is produced from wine, and as beer as well as wine is sold at retail, and this does not profit the buyer, the Honorable Court advises that from now on no one shall, under the penalty heretofore announced, sell any more beer without having first duly paid the excise to the Collector, Jacob Boerhans.

Done at Wildwyck, this October 9, 1663, at a meeting of Schout and Commissaries.

CONCERNING WOLF CATCHING.

Whereas, great damage in and about the region of Wildwyck is done to pigs, calves, and other cattle, by that destructive animal, the wolf, tending greatly to retard the inhabitants of this place, who would prefer that their pigs and cattle increase; Now, in order to prevent this damage as much as possible, the Honorable Court, here, has resolved and promises to pay twelve guilders, zeewant, to any one shooting, catching or taking, in any manner, a male wolf, and eighteen guilders, in zeewant, for a she wolf. For the purpose of raising this money, the Schout and Commissaries of the village of Wildwyck order every householder engaged in farming to contribute at once, for every wolf caught and brought in, one guilder in zeewant. The wolf catcher must also bring the captured wolf to the Schout's house for inspection.

Thus done at a meeting of Schout and Commissaries, at Wildwyck, this October 9, 1663.

Roelof Swartwout, Schout, plaintiff, vs. Paulus Tomassen, defendant. Plaintiff complains of defendant, that on October 7, being Sunday, a gun was discharged by one Arent Jansen, which was

heard and seen by Captain Lieutenant Cregier who had him tak-
en to jail, and that immediately thereafter another shot was fired,
at the house of Aert Martensen Doorn. The plaintff hearing this,
went to the aforesaid house, saying, "Friends, it looks as if this had
been done to spite us."

Whereupon defendant answered, "I fired off a gun that was
loaded long ago." To which the plaintiff made answer: "Very
well; if you did it I will know how to get satisfaction
from you for it." The defendant to this replied, "See
here, Schout, I'll shoot you some day." Whereupon plaintiff wanted to arrest him. Defendant at first refused to
go along, but upon arriving at plaintiff's house he resisted plaintiff
with acts as well as words, and while following plaintiff to the
guard house kept threatening and hitting him, and after he had
been put in the guard house defendant went so far as to hit plaintiff on the head, so that he stumbled over.

Whereupon the following interrogatories were had:

Interrogatories to Paulus Tommassen, defendant.

Present—the Honorable Court.

Questions:

1. Did the defendant on Sunday, October 7, at the house of
Aert Martensen Doorn, discharge a gun? Answer. Yes.

2. Was defendant drunk or sober at the time? Answer. He
was drunk.

3. Where did he get the wine? Answer. He had the wine
in his little chest.

4. Did he refuse to go to prison? Answer. The Schout
knows all about this.

5. Did he strike the Schout on the street or at the Schout's
house? Answer. No.

6. Did he strike the Schout at the guard house? Answer. He
denies this.

The Schout requests that defendant be again put in prison.
This is granted by the Honorable Court.

Done at Wildwyck, October 9, 1663.

On Saturday, October 6, a meeting was held by the Honorable
Council of War and the Honorable Court at Wildwyck, at which
were present:

Marten Cregier, Captain Lieutenant; Christiaen Niessen, Ensign; Evert Willem Munnick, Peter Ebel, Jan Peersen, Sergeants; Roelof Swartwout, Schout; Albert Gysbertsen, Tjerck Claesen de Wit, Gysbert van Imborch, Commissaries.

Captain Lieutenant Marten Cregier and the Council of War having, on September 26, given Schout Swartwout an order that no strong drink be sold to the militia or to the Indians, as they wished to hold them in readiness for the coming expedition, the Schout went personally to notify the householders at Wildwyck. On arriving at the house of the wife of gunner Mattys Roelofsen to inform her thereof, she told the Schout that he might cleanse his anus (beg your pardon) with the order. On the complaint of the Schout, the Captain Lieutenant expressed to the Council of War and the Commissaries of Wildwyck, here specially assembled, his regret for the act which, if not done to insult the Council of War and those who commissioned it, is still not to be tolerated in decent places.

Whereas, the Schout has met with insult from the gunner's wife above named, on account of this order, he requests that she be punished therefor, in order that so impudent and shameless a person may, in this case, receive what she deserves, and thus be made an example to others.

Aeltje Sybrants, wife of Mattys Roelofsen, was summoned before the Honorable Council of War and Commissaries at Wildwyck and asked by the Captain Lieutenant in reference to the aforesaid complaint, whether she did not say that the Schout might cleanse his anus with the order mentioned, whereupon she answers that she did not say any such words to the Schout, and that he must prove this; that the Schout lied about the matter, and that he treated her in this manner out of spite.

The Schout called in proof Heyltje Jacobs, wife of Jan Broersen, who testifies before the Council of War that she heard that the wife of Mattys the gunner had some words with the Schout, but is not prepared to say truthfully that she also addressed the aforementioned scandalous words to the Schout.

Grietje Jacobs, wife of Willem Jansen, was also called, and testified before the Council of War that she heard there was much wordy war between the Schout and the gunner's wife above named and that among other things she said to the Schout, kiss my anus.

Aeltje Sybrants was again called to the stand and, being informed of the foregoing testimony, did not deny she had had words with the Schout, nor that she may possibly have said to him, kiss my anus.

The Schout, Swartwout, is ordered to submit additional proof in this matter.

Thus done at the session aforesaid, the day and year above stated.

On Wednesday, October 10, 1663, a session was held at Wildwyck by the Honorable Council of War and the Honorable Court of Wildwyck.

Present: Marten Cregier, Captain Lieutenant; Christiaen Niessen, Ensign; Evert Willem Munnick, Jan Peersen, Sergeants; Roelof Swartwout, Schout; Albert Gysbertsen, Tjerck Claesen de Wit, Gysbert van Imbroch, Commissaries.

The Schout, Swartwout, appearing before the Honorable Council of War and the Honorable Court at Wildwyck, submits, in accordance with the foregoing order, proof, in writing, by Willem Jansen Schut, dated October 8, last, confirmed under oath in the presence of two Commissaries, reading thus:

Deponent above named declares that, at the reading of the order given to the Schout by the Captain Lieutenant, and while leaving the house of Jan Broersen, he heard Aeltje Sybrants, wife of Mattys Roelofsen, say, "Tut, tut, it's only a trifle; cleanse your fundament with it." Deponent does not know the meaning of these words.

Aeltje Sybrants, the defendant, called to the stand and being shown by the Schout the deposition, signed as aforesaid, denies the same, and says she did not say the said words to the Schout.

Having seen and heard the obduracy of defendant, Aeltje Sybrants, in denying the truth of the proofs adduced, which are accepted by the Honorable Council of War and the Honorable Court here, and the Schout also being deemed worthy of belief, officially, the Honorable Council of War and the Honorable Court at Wildwyck, therefore, being desirous of preventing all slander and vile language, and of punishing the same as an example to others, hereby sentence and condemn Aeltje Sybrants, the wife of Mattys Roelofsen, for her use of vile and foul language in contemning and vilipending the order given to the Schout, to pay a fine of one hundred Carolus guilders, and the costs, to be applied as usual, and to be paid within the next fourteen days, under penalty of issuance of execution.

Done at Wildwyck the day and year above mentioned. Signed by the Honorable Council of War and the Honorable Court of Wildwyck.

Note.—The Honorable Council of War and the Honorable Court at Wildwyck decree that the Schout, being prosecutor, shall receive two-thirds of the fine to be paid by Aeltje Sybrants, and that one-third shall be for the Church at Wildwyck. Done at Wildwyck, October 10, 1663.

Roelof Swartwout, Schout, plaintiff, vs. Aert Jansen, defendant. Plaintiff lodges a complaint against defendant for having fired a shot on Sunday. Defendant does not deny he fired once. He is therefore sentenced by the Honorable Council of War and the Honorable Court to pay plaintiff a fine of nine gldrs., being three gldrs., as per ordinance, for each shot, and six gldrs., because he did it on Sunday during the sermon.

Given at Wildwyck this October 10, 1663, at the session of the Honorable Council of War and the Honorable Court at Wildwyck.

Willem Jansen Schut called on October 10, 1663, on the Schout. Roelof Swartwout and complained that he, Schut, had been assailed by Aeltje Sybrants, wife of Mattys Roelofsen, who said to him that in his deposition he testified falsely against her. Wherefore, then, for fuller information in the matter, Jan Peersen, Sergeant, and Jacob Boerhans, Clerk, both officers of the Honorable Company, were dispatched with said Willem Jansen, to ascertain if she would confirm these spoken words. Upon their return they reported that she disavowed her spoken words. Notwithstanding this, the appearer aforenamed requests the Honorable Court here that he may have justice done to him.

Thus entered the day and year above mentioned, at Wildwyck, in the presence of the Captain Lieutenant Marten Cregier. To which I certify.   MATTHEUS CAPITO, Secretary.

Extraordinary Session, held Tuesday, October 16, 1663.

Present: Roelof Swartwout, Schout; Albert Gysbertsen, Tjerck Claesen de Wit, Thomas Chambers, Gysbert van Imbroch, Commissaries.

Resolution passed relative to late comers on the Bench.

To prevent any disorder in convening the Inferior Bench at Wildwyck, it is resolved and ordered by the Honorable Court here, that any of those constituting the Bench arriving later than the hour fixed shall be fined twenty stivers, for the benefit of his colleagues. Done at Wildwyck, as above. In my presence. To which I certify.

MATTHEUS CAPITO, Secretary.

There was presented a note signed by the Captain Lieutenant, Marten Cregier, dated October 10, stating that Lieutenant Henderick Jochemsen has suffered and is yet suffering inconveniences from the militia who use his home as a guard house, which makes it burdensome to him. The Captain Lieutenant therefore requests that the aforesaid Henderick Jochemsen be relieved from this burden, and that the Honorable Court cause a guard house to be built for the militia.

Lieutenant Henderick Jochemsen having been summoned to appear in the Council room of the Court in the matter, and having been asked if he would consent to harbor the militiamen four or six weeks longer in his house, as at present no materials can be had for building a guard house, leaves to the discretion of the Honorable Court here the amount of compensation to be paid him during the period.

The Honorable Court, considering that one inhabitant alone should not bear all the burdens, and that he has consented to suffer the inconvenience of having the militia at his house four or six weeks longer, and as the soldiers have been quartered in his house since June 7, and will continue there four or six weeks longer, has therefore allowed him, as compensation, fifty guilders, in zeewant.

Thus done at the session above mentioned.

Reynier Pietersen Schipper, [skipper], presents an account against Henderick Jansen Looman, amounting to four schepels of wheat, and requests payment.

Roelof Swartwout, Schout, plaintiff, vs. Jacob Janse de lange [the long], defendant. Plaintiff requests that defendant testify in the case of the prisoner Paulus Tomassen, and state if he did not hear the prisoner say, ''Schout, I'll shoot you.'' Defendant answers that the said words were spoken by the prisoner Paulus Tomassen at the house of Aert Martensen Doorn.

Roelof Swartwout, Schout, plaintiff, vs. Dirreck Hendericksen, defendant. Second default.

Gerret Willemsen, Corporal in the service of the Honorable Company, called before the Court here, declares that when the Schout placed Paulus Tomassen in custody in the guard house, said Tomassen struck the Schout's head there, so that the Schout fell over the sweat bench. Paulus Tomassen having been accused at the last session of the Court by the Schout, Roelof Swartwout, is once more interrogated:

1. Whether he said to the Schout, at Aert Martensen Doorn's house, ''Schout, I'll shoot you some day.'' Answers, that he was drunk and does not know whether he said this then, but says he said it later.

2. To be brought to jail, he was at the Schout's house. Whether he did not refuse to go with the Schout to jail. Answers, yes, he refused.

3. Whether he did not strike the Schout in the guard house. Answers, he does not know if he struck the Schout in the guard house, but that he heard from others that he had done so.

4. Whether, being put under arrest by the Schout, he beat the latter on the street and hit him with his fists. Answers, he neither beat the Schout nor knocked against him, but that he warded off the beating which the Schout gave him on the street.

The Schout asks whether this confession by the prisoner Paul. us Tomassen is sufficient. If not, he will produce fuller and stronger testimony. The Honorable Court orders the Schout to submit his demand against the prisoner.

The Schout's Demand.

Roelof Swartwout, Schout, prosecutor, against Paulus Tomassen. The plaintiff demands that, though the prisoner ought to be punished criminally by the Honorable Court, yet, as the Honorable Court has no power to inflict such punishment, the prisoner be

sent to the Director General and Council of New Netherland, there
to be duly punished.

DECISION OF THE HONORABLE COURT.

The Honorable Court, having heard the Schout's demand, as
also the witnesses produced and the confession of the prisoner,
Paulus Tomassen, himself, orders the prisoner, Paulus Tomassen,
to settle this matter with the Schout, or to work for one month on
the dam, at his own expense, and to pay all costs that have been
incurred; and, in case he cannot arrive at a settlement with the
Schout, that he shall give bail to the Court against running away,
or shall be chained while working on the dam.

Resolutions concerning the erection of the fortifications
of this village of Wildwyck.

A note from the Captain Lieutenant, dated October 15, was
read to the Honorable Court requesting that the palisades for this
village of Wildwyck be repaired and renewed, so as to serve for defense. After the reading, the Honorable Court decides that there
is an urgent necessity that this village be properly provided with
good and new palisades, and therefore orders and directs every
farmer to properly fence his lot, renewing the old palisades;
and that the rest of the people, inhabitants or burghers, possessing thirty-nine lots in this village, shall,
from the watergate up and along the curtain walls to Aert
Pietersen Tack's lot, properly repair and replace the old with new
palisades of at least two feet in circumference, the thicker the better, and of a height of thirteen feet, according to the extent of the
locality and as the Honorable Court may deem necessary. This
renovation and enclosing shall commence next Monday, October 22.
Wherefore, every inhabitant of this place is notified to appear on
said day at about seven o'clock, at the gate near Hendrick Jochemsen's house, there to be enrolled, for the purpose of commencing
said work, and to remain at it until completed, on pain, for neglect
or unwillingness, of three guilders for the first offense, twice as
much for the second, and increasing so on three guilders.

Thus done, at the session of the Schout and Commissaries of
this village of Wildwyck, this 16th day of October, 1663.

Ordinary Session, held Tuesday, October 23, 1663.

Present: Roelof Swartwout, Schout; Tjerck Classen de Wit, Thomas Chambers, Gysbert van Imborch, Commissaries.

Roelof Swartwout, Schout, plaintiff, vs. Aert Jacobsen, defendant. Defendant is asked by plaintiff what he has to say to the Honorable Court, in view of the record of the previous session of October 9—handing him the papers. Defendant humbly asks forgiveness, saying that, if he said anything which unguardedly escaped his lips, may the Honorable Court pardon him therefor.

Plaintiff demands that defendant be punished for the aforesaid words, either by a money fine of one thousand guilders, or that he be referred in this matter to the Director General and Council of New Netherland.

The Honorable Court, having heard the Schout's demand and also the humble repentance of defendant, besides his confession, sentences defendant, Aert Jacobsen, to pay a fine of twenty-five gldrs., with costs, the fine to be applied as usual.

Plaintiff requests an appeal hereupon, which is granted by the Court.

Roelof Swartwout, Schout, plaintiff, vs. Aert Jacobsen, defendant. Plaintiff appears against the defendant for desecrating the Sabbath, having appeared against him on October 9, and having handed him a copy of the papers. The defendant appearing, says he has nothing to offer, in view of the foregoing papers, to prove that the Sabbath had expired.

The Honorable Court sentences defendant to pay the plaintiff a fine of one pound Flemish [six guilders or $2.40], in this case.

Roelof Swartwout, plaintiff, vs. Roelof Hendericksen, defendant. Plaintiff demands payment of ten schepels of wheat for thirteen days' carpenter work, according to contract. Defendant says he worked eight and one-half days in reduction of the ten schepels of wheat, and remained idle all summer, during which time he was not sought by plaintiff, and later only after he had become bound to some one else.

The Honorable Court, having heard both parties, orders defendant to satisfy plaintiff for the remainder of the thirteen days, being three and one-half days of work.

Roelof Swartwout, Schout, plaintiff, vs. Jan Broersen, defendant. Plaintiff demands a fine of seventy-five gldrs. for violation of
the ordinance of August 4. Defendant says he is not liable for the
payment of a fine to plaintiff, but that his farmer, Juriaen Westphael, in whose employ he was, must pay the fine.

Roelof Swartwout, Schout, plaintiff, vs. Jacob Barents Cool and
Jan Jansen van Oosthout, defendants. Plaintiff demands from
Jacob Barents twenty-five gldrs., and from Jan Jansen van Oosterhout seventy-five gldrs., fine for violating the ordinance of August
4.

Juriaen Westphael, answering for Jan Broersen, Jacob Barents
Cool and Jan Jansen van Oosterhout, allows himself to be recorded
in their place.

Aeltje Claes, appearing before the Honorable Court, requests
that the estate left by Claesje Teunissen, deceased, be administered by the Honorable Court, which request is granted.

Roelof Swartwout, Schout, plaintiff, vs. Ariaen Gerretsen, defendant. Plaintiff demands from defendant a fine of twenty-five
gldrs. for impounding his horses and carting for Tjerck Classen,
a fine of fifty gldrs. for violating the ordinance of August 4, and
twenty-five gldrs. for refusing to cart in the service of the Honorable Company on the strand.

Defendant answers, regarding the seizure of his horses, that he
was not allowed to keep them in the Fort, but that they had to find
their fodder in the field where his children were. The Schout put
down their names. With regard to the fine of fifty gldrs. for
violating the aforesaid ordinance, he refers to Tjerck Claesen deWit
who employed him at the time. With regard to his refusal to cart
on the strand, he answers he was there at the time and carted the
biggest load.

The Honorable Court, having heard defendant's confession,
orders him to settle with plaintiff, because his children were in
the field with the horses, contrary to the ordinance.

Concerning the fine for driving for Tjerck Claesen, the defendant must show that Tjerck Claesen made himself responsible
therefor, which defendant offers to prove.

Concerning his refusal upon the strand, the Honorable Court
acquits defendant, because he afterwards did his duty.

Tjerck Claesen deWit, plaintiff, vs. Evert Pels, defendant. Plaintiff complains that defendant during harvest time caused one of plaintiff's pigs to be shot. Defendant demands proof. The Honorable Court orders plaintiff to adduce proof.

Evert Pels informs the Court that Juriaen Westphael received a letter from Jochem Ketelheem at Fort Orange, and requests a copy thereof, which is allowed him.

Tjerck Claesen deWit and Albert Gysbertsen, curators of the estate left by Hendrick Looman, having summoned Juriaen West- phael before the Honorable Court here, the question was put to him, Juriaen Westphael, whether he knows any more about the estate left by said deceased than is shown by the inventory. Where- upon the aforenamed Juriaen Westphael declares, upon his word as a man, that he knows no more, unless perhaps that, among the ef- fects of Jan Albertsen, there were uppers for two pairs of shoes.

Hilletje Hendericks, having been summoned before the Honor- able Court, declares under oath she does not know of any other property of Willem Jansen Seba than what has been inventoried. She requests immediate payment of the account she has rendered, and in addition three months' stable rent for Willem Jansen Seba's horse, amounting to two and one-quarter schepels of wheat.

Cornelis Barentsen Slecht, having been summoned before the Honorable Court by the curators of the estate of Willem Jansen Seba, is once more called upon to render an account between him- self and Willem Jansen Seba. He requests for this purpose four- teen days' more time, which the Honorable Court allows him.

Elsje Gerrets, plaintiff, vs. Christiaen Niessen romp, defend- ant. Second default. Plaintiff says that defendant has a pillow belonging to her, which he retains. Requests that he fetch said pillow to Court to compare it with another pillow belonging to plaintiff. Defendant is allowed a third default.

Gysbert van Imbroch, plaintiff, vs. Annetje Ariaens, wife of Aert Pietersen Tack, defendant. Plaintiff demands that, pursuant to mortgage, defendant be not permitted to alienate or estrange the gathered grain before he has first been paid. Defendant an- swers that if plaintiff will undertake to pay her debts she will then get out and leave, and adds thereto that the debts contracted by her for food during harvest time must also be paid, otherwise she could not have taken in the crops.

The Honorable Court, having heard both parties, finds that, according to the obligation, defendant must not appropriate or decrease, much less alienate, any of the grain, without the knowledge and consent of the plaintiff.

Jacob Joosten, plaintiff, vs. Annetje Ariaens, defendant. Plaintiff demands from defendant five schepels of wheat, which defendant admit he owes. The Honorable Court orders defendant to pay plaintiff the said amount.

Roelof Swartwout, Schout, plaintiff, vs. Jacob Jansen de lange [the long], defendant. Third default. Plaintiff demands payment of a fine of seventy-five gldrs., legally due after a third default.

The Honorable Court orders defendant, for not appearing before it after a third default, to pay the full fine to plaintiff, and also to pay the costs.

Roelof Swartwout, Schout, plaintiff, vs. Albert Heymans, defendant. Plaintiff enters suit against defendant on a complaint of the Commissaries, Tjerck Claesen, Albert Guysbertsen and Gysbert van Imbroch, that defendant publicly accused them of being deceitful in carrying out their ordinances, and that they did not do justice in accordance therewith.

Defendant says, that the Court did not act in accordance with the wording of the ordinance, and demands a copy of the record herein.

The Honorable Court orders Tjerck Claesen, Albert Gysbertsen and Gysbert van Imbroch, at its next session, to furnish proof of the foregoing complaint, in conformity with their own statement.

Roelof Swartwout, Schout, plaintiff, vs. Albert Heymans, defendant. A complaint is made to the Schout that on August 30, last Albert Heymans, when lawfully called upon by Gysbert van Imbroch, at a meeting held at the Schout's house, to furnish a horse for the expedition against the savages, would not say "yes" or "no" to the Court, but said he would first see what the gentlemen were going to do, and that, when the Commissary again demanded an answer, the defendant called him a little tattle tale. By reason whereof, the said Commissary, *nomine officio,* pursuant to the said complaint, requests the Court to sustain his action.

The foregoing having been read to defendant, he admits having used the aforesaid words, "little tattle tale," towards the Commissary, at the said place, and requests a copy of the record here, and promises to reply at the next session of the Court.

Roelof Swartwout, Schout, plaintiff, vs. Geertruyd Andriesen, defendant. Plaintiff demands from defendant a fine of fifty gldrs. for violating, for the first time, the ordinance enacted August 4, and a fine of two hundred gldrs. for a second violation, in having harvested with four wagons, and a fine also, for a third offense, in having, on October 26, [*sic*] arbitrarily harvested with two wagons, and having a gun in the field. Also a further fine for carrying fodder for her horses on a Sunday, on which occasion the horses were seized, but nevertheless the matter was settled with the Schout for five schepels of wheat, and a can of brandy for the guard.

Defendant answers that she was several times refused a convoy, and therefore she was obliged to gather in her grain herself without a guard, for fear that the rain would spoil it.

The Honorable Court, having heard both parties, orders defendant to pay the full amount of the fines demanded for violating the ordinance, and to pay plaintiff the agreed fine of five schepels of wheat and a can of brandy.

The Schout, Roelof Swartwout, enters a complaint that the Messenger, Jacob Joosten, is of little or no service to him, and requests the Honorable Court to please give orders relative thereto. Whereupon defendant, Jacob Joosten, answers that he has not been able to collect his money, either as Church or Village Messenger, not having, to the best of his knowledge, received as Village Messenger more than one hundred and fourteen gldrs.

The Honorable Court orders and directs the Village Messenger to be more faithful in his duty, and that he be paid as soon as possible for his services as such.

Meeting of the Council of War and Commissaries, held Tuesday, October 30, 1663.

Present: Marten Cregier, Captain Lieutenant; Christiaen Niessen, Ensign; Evert Willem Munnick, Jan Peersen, Sergeants; Roelof Swartwout, Schout; Tjerck Claesen deWit, Gysbert van Imborch, Tomas Chambers, Commissaries.

Roelof Swartwout, Schout, plaintiff, vs. Henderick Cornelissen Slecht, defendant. Plaintiff demands from defendant a fine of seventy-five gldrs., pursuant to the judgment rendered by the Court under date of October 9, for violating the ordinance enacted August 4, in that he worked in the field without permission and a proper convoy.

Defendant admits having worked in the field without permission and convoy, and says that the Schout came without a convoy to the field and fined him for a second offense. He adds that he was fully able to defend himself, and therefore did not need a guard.

Defendant having been given his choice between paying the full fine to the plaintiff pursuant to said judgment, or arranging with him amicably, answers he would rather pay the full fine than settle with the plaintiff.

The Council of War and Commissaries understand that, according to the aforementioned judgment, defendant is liable for the full fine, as he behaves very obstinately in the matter.

The Same, plaintiff, vs. Pieter Bruynsen, defendant. Plaintiff demands from defendant a fine of twenty-five gldrs. for violating the ordinance dated August 4, in that he worked in the field without permission and a proper convoy, for which he was sentenced by the Honorable Court on October 9.

Defendant admits having worked one day in the field without permission and convoy, and the proposition is made to him whether he would prefer to settle with the plaintiff. He answers he is not willing to settle with the plaintiff, nor does he intend to pay one stiver therefor.

The Council of War and Commissaries order defendant to pay the full fine, in accordance with the judgment dated October 9, and, as he shows himself obstinate and unwilling so to do, that he be confined until he shall have paid the full fine.

Roelof Swartwout, Schout, plaintiff, vs. Henderick Aertsen, defendant. Plaintiff demands from defendant a fine of seventy-five gldrs., pursuant to the judgment rendered by the Honorable Court under date of October 9, for violating the ordinance enacted August 4, in that he worked in the field without permission and a proper convoy.

Defendant admits having worked in the field without consent and a proper convoy, and also says that he had sufficient means of defence there.

The proposition having been made to him to settle with plaintiff, he answers he is not willing to settle with him nor does he intend to pay one stiver.

The Council of War and Commissaries condemn defendant to pay the full fine, in accordance with the judgment of the Court on October 9, and, as defendant shows himself obstinate and is unwilling so to do, that he be confined until he shall have paid the full fine.

Roelof Swartwout, Schout, plaintiff, vs. Ariaen Roose and Jan Roose, defendants. Plaintiff demands from defendants a fine of one hundred gldrs., for violating the ordinance dated August 4, in that they worked in the field without permission and a convoy. Defendants admit having worked in the field without permission and a convoy, and also say they had sufficient means of defence there.

The Council of War and Commissaries decide that, as defendants are still young and minors, they shall be excused in this case.

Roelof Swartwout, Schout, plaintiff, vs. Willem Andriese Rees. defendant. Absent. Default.

Roelof Swartwout, Schout, plaintiff, vs. Cornelis Brantsen Vos, defendant. Plaintiff demands from defendant a fine of seventy-five gldrs., pursuant to judgment rendered by the Court on October 9, for violation of the ordinance of August 4, in that he worked in the field without permission and a convoy. Defendant admits having worked in the field without permission and a convoy, and also says that he had sufficient means of defense there.

After a proposition had been made to defendant to settle the fine with plaintiff, he answers he is not willing so to settle nor does he intend to pay anything, but purposes to bring the case before a higher court.

The Council of War and Commissaries condemn defendant to pay the full fine, pursuant to the judgment rendered by the Court and, as defendant shows himself obstinate and unwilling, that he be placed in confinement until he shall have paid the full fine.

Roelof Swartwout, Schout, plaintiff, vs. Jacob Joosten, defendant. Plaintiff demands from defendant a fine of seventy-five gldrs., pursuant to the judgment rendered by the Honorable Court on October 9, for violating the ordinance dated August 4, in that he worked in the field without permission and a proper convoy. Defendant admits his guilt, but says he must earn his living here or elsewhere.

The Council of War and Commissaries decide, for cause, to excuse defendant this time.

Roelof Swartwout, Schout, plaintiff, vs. Ariaen Huybertsen, defendant. Plaintiff demands from defendant a fine of seventy-five gldrs., pursuant to the judgment rendered by the Court on October 9, for violating the ordinance dated August 4, in that he worked in the field without permission and a convoy. Defendant admits having worked in the field without permission and a convoy, and also says that he had sufficient means of defense there. A proposition was made to defendant, to either pay the full fine or to settle with the Schout, but he answers he does not intend to pay the fine herein.

The Council of War and Commissaries condemn defendant to pay the full fine, pursuant to the foregoing judgment rendered by the Court on October 9.

Roelof Swartwout, Schout, plaintiff, vs. Harmen Hendericksen, defendant. Plaintiff demands from defendant a fine of seventy-five gldrs., pursuant to the judgment rendered by the Honorable Court October 9, for violating the ordinance dated August 4, in that he worked in the field without permission and a convoy.

Defendant admits he worked in the field without permission and a convoy, but adds that he had sufficient means of defense there, and requests the Captain Lieutenant to settle this case for him with plaintiff.

Roelof Swartwout, Schout, plaintiff, vs. Jan Gerretsen, defendant. Plaintiff demands from defendant a fine of seventy-five gldrs., pursuant to the judgment rendered by the Honorable Court on October 9, for violating the ordinance dated August 4, in that he worked in the field without permission and a convoy. Defendant admits he worked in the field without permission and a convoy, but says he was working close by the guard house, and does not owe anything but intends to go higher up.

The Council of War and Commissaries order defendant to pay the full fine, pursuant to the judgment rendered by the Court on October 9.

Roelof Swartwout, Schout, plaintiff, vs. Antoni Crupel, defendant. Absent. Default.

Roelof Swartwout, Schout, plaintiff, vs. Hendcrick Henderick-sen, defendant. Plaintiff demands from defendant a fine of seventy-five gldrs., pursuant to the judgment dated October 9, for violating the ordinance enacted August 4, in that he worked in the field without permission and a convoy. Defendant admits he worked without permission in the field, and says that Juriaen Westphael, who also appeared before the Honorable Court on October 9, and was sentenced by it to pay the full fine, made himself responsible for it, and has filed an appeal therein.

Roelof Swartwout, Schout, plaintiff, vs. Jan Willemsen, defendant. Absent. Default.

Roelof Swartwout, Schout, plaintiff, vs. Teunis Jacobsen, defendant. Plaintiff demands from defendant a fine of seventy-five gldrs., pursuant to the judgment rendered by the Honorable Court, on October 9, for violating the ordinance dated August 4, in that he harvested without permission and a convoy. Defendant denies having been notified by plaintiff that he was to be fined, and says he knows nothing about it.

The Council of War and Commissaries order plaintiff to prove his demand.

Roelof Swartwout, Schout, plaintiff, vs. Aert Jacobsen, defendant. Plaintiff demands from defendant a fine of two hundred gldrs., pursuant to the judgment rendered by the Honorable Court on October 9, for a violation of the ordinance dated August 4, by himself, his son, his daughter and his farm hand, in that he harvested without permission and a convoy. The defendant insists upon an appeal.

Roelof Swartwout, Schout, plaintiff, vs. Jacob Jansen de lange, defendant. Plaintiff demands from defendant a fine of seventy-five gldrs., pursuant to the judgment rendered by the Court on October 9, for violating the ordinance dated August 4, in that he harvested without permission and a convoy. Defendant admits that he harvested without permission and a convoy, and says he does not intend to pay for doing so.

The Council of War and Commissaries condemn defendant to pay the above fine to plaintiff, pursuant to the judgment rendered October 9, and, as he shows himself obstinate and unwilling, that he be placed in confinement until he shall have paid the full fine.

Roelof Swartwout, Schout, plaintiff, vs. Aert Otterspoor, defendant. Plaintiff demands from defendant a fine of twenty-five gldrs., pursuant to the judgment rendered by the Honorable Court under date of October 9, for violating the ordinance dated August 4, in that he worked in the field without permission and a convoy. Defendant admits he worked in the field without permission and a convoy and says he is willing to settle with plaintiff.

Roelof Swartwout, Schout, plaintiff, vs. Henderick Jochemsen, defendant. Plaintiff demands from defendant a fine of twenty-five gldrs., for violating the ordinance dated August 4, in that he was in the field near the bridge, without permission and a convoy. Defendant admits he was at the bridge, as a sentry, as he with others present had to repair the bridge, but being unable to work because of a lame hand he therefore stood sentry for the laborers.

Whereas, the repairers of the bridge received permission from the Captain Lieutenant, the Schout's demand is refused.

Roelof Swartwout, Schout, plaintiff, vs. Ariaen Gerritsen, defendant. Absent. Default.

Roelof Swartwout, Schout, plaintiff, vs. Warnaer Hoorenbeeck, defendant. Plaintiff demands from defendant a fine of twenty-five gldrs., for violating the ordinance of August 4, in that he harvested without permission and a convoy. Defendant refers himself to his mistress, because she represented him at the said session of October 23 [sic]. Plaintiff is ordered to summon her in this matter before the Court.

Roelof Swartwout, Schout, plaintiff, vs Geertruyd Andriessen, defendant. Absent. Default.

The Schout, Roelof Swartwout, requests the Honorable Court to allow him execution in the matter of the judgment rendered by the Commissaries and Council of War on June 27, 1663.

The foregoing request of the Schout is granted by the Court here. Done at Wildwyck, this October 30, 1663.

Order to the Schout and Secretary.

Whereas, on October 23, 1663, Aeltje Claes appeared before the Honorable Court here in Wildwyck, and requested that the estate of Claesje Teunissen, deceased, be administered by the Honorable Court, which the Honorable Court agreed to do, it is therefore ordered that the individual, Roelof Swartwout, Schout, together with the Secretary, Mattheus Capito, repair to the house of the deceased Claesje Teunnissen, there to make a proper inventory of the estate left by her, and, having done so, that they exhibit the same to the Honorable Court here.

Given at Wildwyck, this October 30, 1663.

Report on the foregoing.

On this 30th of October, in the afternoon we, Roelof Swartwout, Schout, and Mattheus Capito, Secretary, pursuant to the order of the Honorable Court here, repaired to the house of Aeltje Claes, for the purpose of taking an inventory of the estate left by Claesje Teunissen, deceased, and questioned Aeltje Claes and also the oldest daughter of the deceased, concerning the estate left. They answered us whether we were joking with them and whether we did not know that the Domine had arranged everything relating to this matter, and that if we wanted to know about it we ought to go to the Domine, who would undoubtedly give us information about the matter. Done at Wildwyck, on the above date in the year 1663.

(Signed) Roelof Swartwout, Mattheus Capito.

Whereas, Cornelis Barentsen Slecht has settled with the Schout Swartwout, for and on behalf of his servants, for violating the ordinance passed on August 4, last, by the Council of War and the Honorable Court, and he has made a request of the aforesaid Court that his servants be set at liberty, it is ordered that the same be granted to said Cornelis Barentsen Slecht, and his servants be released from arrest and be permitted to return home. Done at Wildwyck, November 1, 1663.

(Signed) Marten Kregier.

Whereas Mr. Gysbert van Imbroeck has settled with the Schout Swartwout, for the offence committed by Jacob Jansen in violating the ordinance of the Council of War and the Honorable Court made August 4, last, for which said Jacob Jansen has been placed by the Court in confinement, the said Mr. Gysbert van Imborch requests of said Court that the individual, Jacob Jansen, be discharged, to which the Court consents and discharges the said Jacob Jansen from his arrest for the present.

Done at Wildwyck, November 1, 1663.

(Signed) Marten Kregier.

Ordinary Session, held Tuesday, November 6, 1663.

Present: Roelof Swartwout, Schout; Albert Gysbertsen, Tjerck Claesen de Wit, Gysbert van Imborch, Thomas Chambers, Commissaries.

Eechtje Gerrets, plaintiff, vs. Christiaen Nissen romp, defendant. Plaintiff demands that defendant return to her a cushion of which she shows a duplicate to the Court, having taken from the clothes line at defendant's home a pillow case which she says is hers and which she shows to the Honorable Court.

Defendant says that plaintiff took said pillow case from the clothes line at his house, and requests that she return the same to him. Defendant further denies having a pillow and a pillow case belonging to plaintiff, and says that plenty of goods resemble each other without being owned by the same party.

Plaintiff, having been asked whether she would declare under oath that the pillow is in possession of defendant, answers "Yes." Defendant refuses plaintiff's oath, as he does not consent to her taking one, but requests that she prove that he has a pillow and pillow case belonging to her.

The Honorable Court orders plaintiff to prove that defendant has a cushion belonging to her.

Tjerck Claesen de Wit, curator of the estate left by Willem Jansen Seba, plaintiff, vs. Cornelis Barentsen Slecht, defendant.

Plaintiff requests that defendant make an explanation to the Court and render an account, in the matter between him and Willem Jansen Seba, for which he received an extension of fourteen days on October 23, last.

Defendant answers that the Consistory has enjoined him against rendering an account to the Honorable Court here, in the matter of Willem Jansen Seba.

Jacob Joosten, Village Messenger, being summoned before the Honorable Court and being asked whether, under directions from the Consistory, he has enjoined Cornelis Barentsen Slecht from rendering an account to the Honorable Court here, answers "Yes," and says he notified Cornelis Barentsen Slecht, on said directions, not to pay any bills for Willem Jansen Seba, and that, if he should do so, said payment would not be audited.

The Village Messenger having been sent by the Honorable Court to Domine Hermanus Blom and the Consistory to request them to please appear at the session of the Court, the said Domine answered that he could not attend to-day.

The Consistory, Albert Heymans, appeared, and was asked by the Honorable Court whether the Domine and the Consistory forbade Cornelis Barentsen Slecht and Juriaen Westphael to pay anything to any one for Willem Jansen Seba, deceased, and Hendrick Looman. He answered "Yes."

The Honorable Court resolves to refer this record to the Director General and Council of New Netherland.

Tjerck Claesen de Wit, plaintiff, vs. Evert Pels, defendant. Plaintiff requests an extension until the next session of the Court, as he has not yet ready the proofs he is to adduce against defendant.

The Honorable Court orders plaintiff to submit his proofs at its next session, or the Court will decide between the parties on their papers.

Paulus Paulusen, plaintiff, vs. Eva Swartwout, defendant. Plaintiff desires that defendant substantiate her charge that plaintiff stole twelve chickens.

Roelof Swartwout, representing his wife, Eva, the defendant. demands that plaintiff submit proofs.

The Honorable Court orders plaintiff to produce proof at its next session.

Roelof Swartwout, Schout, plaintiff, vs. Allert Heymans Roose, defendant. Plaintiff asks defendant for the documents demanded of him at the last session of the Court. Defendant submits his answer in writing, which literally reads as follows: Anno 1663, October 23. I was standing in the street near the guard house looking at the people going out, and then asked Tjerck Claesen how many horses would go along with the expedition against the savages, to which Tjerck answered, "sixteen;" whereupon I replied, "There are not as many farmers, unless double farms like those of Tomas Aert, Aert Jacobsen and your own furnish two." Whereupon he said, "Well, farmer, you pay rather much attention to me; well, you did not do so much in the expeditions pursuant to the ordinance, for you rather stood on one wagon with two in it, and I alone on one. Ho, farmer, you lie, I have done as much as you." Thereupon, I answered, "Thus you give the lie to your own ordinance. It is not right." For these words, Mr. Gysbert comes and makes complaint.

(Subscribed) Alaerdt Heymansz Roose.

This matter, on the votes of three Commissaries, is, for cause, referred, for decision, to the Director General and Council of New Netherland.

Roelof Swartwout, Schout, plaintiff, vs. Allert Heymans Roose, defendant. Plaintiff alleges that defendant challenged a member of the Court when sitting in the Council of War at the house of Thomas Chambers, July 7, concerning two Wappinger savages, saying, "If there is anyone at this meeting who is a friend of these savages, I dare him to come outside."

Defendant denies this, and requests a copy of the record.

The Honorable Court orders plaintiff, at next session, to prove his charge.

Tjerck Claesen deWit requests the Honorable Court at Wildwyck to allow him to use, as a garden, the place outside of the retracted curtain wall, up to the place of the old removed curtain wall, lying east of petitioner's lot and west of the lot of Aert Otterspoor.

The Honorable Court grants petitioner's request, subject to the approval of the Honorable Director General and Council of New Netherland.

On this November 13, 1663, this note was handed to the minister, Hermanus Blom:

Rev. Mr. Hermanus Blom.

Whereas, Aeltje Sybrants, wife of Mattys Roelofsen, was ordered by the Council of War and the Court of this village, on October 10, last, to pay a fine of one hundred gldrs., and one-third of said amount was set apart for the Church, the one-third part in wheat, being five and one-half schepels of wheat computed at six gldrs. per schepel, due you, is herewith sent to your Reverence.

Done at Wildwyck, this November 13, 1663.

(Signed) Marten Cregier.

(Beneath) By authority of the above named Court.

(Signed) Mattheus Capito, Secretary.

Ordinary Session, held Tuesday, November 20, 1663.

Present: Roelof Swartwout, Schout; Albert Gysbertsen, Thomas Chambers, Gysbert van Imborch, Commissaries.

The Schout, Roelof Swartwout, presents this complaint against Tjerck Claesen de Wit, reading, according to his understanding, as follows:

Whereas, Aeltje Wygerts and Albert Gysbertsen have complained to me that on November 13, Tjerck Claesen, armed with a drawn knife, openly quarreled in his house, acting as if he wished to kill every man, woman and child, I therefore, on this complaint, inform the Court of the matter, and also decide to exclude him for the present from the Bench, until he shall have cleared himself of the charge, and shall have been declared cleared by the Honorable Court. The advice of the Commissaries is requested herein.

The Honorable Court orders that, whereas, Tjerck Claesen de Wit has already amicably settled the above matter with his accuser, Albert Gysbertsen, and they have come to an agreement regarding it, he shall remain away from the Bench until he shall have settled and adjusted this matter with the Schout.

Tjerck Claesen de Wit, plaintiff, vs. Evert Pels, defendant. Plaintiff produces a written certificate against defendant, signed by Harmen Jansen and Aert Teunissen, dated November 19, 1663. Defendant wants the witnesses to appear, and desires them to affirm their deposition under oath. He also offers, if the attestors affirm the aforesaid declaration under oath, to pay for the killed pig, and will also sue for damage caused by the pigs to his corn.

The Honorable Court orders plaintiff to produce the aforenamed attestors in Court, at the next session, to affirm their declaration there under oath.

Tjerck Claesen deWit, plaintiff, vs. Albert Gysbertsen, defendant. Plaintiff demands that defendant, on his default of payment for land sold him, return the land, the time for payment having expired in the month of April, 1663.

Defendant replies that plaintiff has not delivered a deed of the land to him, and that he will pay plaintiff after the deed has been executed to him, as he has made part payment thereon to the plaintiff.

The Honorable Court orders defendant to pay plaintiff the remainder of the money due for the land, plaintiff to deliver to defendant a perfect deed and conveyance of the land.

Paulus Paulussen, plaintiff, vs. Eva Swartwout, defendant. Plaintiff requests that defendant furnish proof, pursuant to his complaint of November 6, and produces as his witnesses, Gerret Fooken and Pieter Cornelissen, who depose that they did not personally hear that plaintiff stole twelve chickens from her, but that they heard that she said, while plaintiff chased a hen out of the barn, "Whoever would do the one would also do the other."

The Honorable Court orders plaintiff to bring better proof, by a written declaration.

Tjerck Claesen deWit files with the Court an inventory of the estate left by his brother-in-law, Jan Albertsen van Steenwyck, made November 14, 1663, and requests that, besides him, a curator of the said estate and a guardian of the minor children be appointed.

The Honorable Court decides that, whereas, Domine Harmanus Blom, and the Consistory, Allert Heymans Roose, have, through the Village Messenger, forbidden the rendering of an account of the aforementioned estate, to the Honorable Court, and whereas this matter has not yet been decided, the petitioner must therefore wait until a decision shall have been rendered by the Supreme Magistrates, when he will then receive aid.

On November 26, 1663, Tjerck Claesen de Wit appeared before the Honorable Court here, and again filed with it the inventory of the estate left by Jan Alberse van Steenwyck, made November 14, last, with the further request that the Honorable Court please appoint, besides him, a curator of the aforenamed estate and a guardian of the minor children, because at the last session (as the Court had declined to have said estate administered by it), the appearer was referred to Domine Blom and the Consistory, Allert Heymans, and though he went to them, they again referred him to the Honorable Court here, saying, after having read the aforesaid inventory, that they did not want to have anything to do with the estate, as there were heirs.

The Honorable Court, by a majority of votes, decides to appoint and hereby appoints, besides the appearer, Evert Pels as curator for the estate left by Jan Albertsen van Steenwyck, and Hendrick Jochemsen as guardian of the minor children, for the purpose of administering the above estate according to law. Thus done at the session of Schout and Commissaries at Wildwyck, the day and year above mentioned.

The Commissary, Thomas Chambers, for reasons of his own, did not vote in the above case.

Ordinary Session, held Tuesday, December 4, 1663.

Present: Roelof Swartwout, Schout; Albert Gysberts, Thomas Chambers, Gysbert van Imborch, Commissaries.

Gysbert van Imborch, plaintiff, vs. Albert Gysbertsen, defendant. Plaintiff produces an account against defendant for the sum of one hundred and ninety-eight gldrs., in zeewant. Defendant admits the debt, and says he is willing to pay, and requests time.

Whereas, plaintiff refuses time for payment, defendant is ordered to satisfy him.

Eechtje Gerrets, plaintiff, vs. Christiaen Niessen romp, defendant. Both absent. Both in default.

Tjerck Claesen de Wit, plaintiff, vs. Jonas Rantsou, defendant. Plaintiff demands from defendant five schepels of wheat. Defendant answers he has an account against the plaintiff.

The Honorable Court orders both parties to produce written accounts at its next session.

Tjerck Claesen de Wit, plaintiff, vs. Cornelis Barentsen Slecht, defendant. Absent. Plaintiff refusing to pay thirty-six stivers towards the amount agreed to be paid for the Court room, none of the parties summoned by him will be admitted within.

Roelof Swartwout, Schout, plaintiff, vs. Tjerck Claesen de Wit, defendant. Plaintiff submits a written complaint against defendant relating to a former complaint before the Honorable Court on November 20, and demands in regard thereto that, as defendant did not settle with the Schout, plaintiff, for the offenses committed by him, he be punished by banishment and confiscation of his estate. Plaintiff also shows a certificate regarding the offenses committed by defendant, signed November 13, 1663 by Lambert Huybertsen and Pieter Hillebrants.

Defendant demands that the certificate be sworn to by the attestants, before the Honorable Court, and further says that Pieter Hillebrants, one of the attestants to said certificate, is his witness and consequently cannot be permitted by the Court to swear to the certificate.

Lambert Huybertsen and Pieter Hillebrants, having been summoned before the Honorable Court to swear to their certificate, are prepared to swear to the same, but their oath is prevented by defendant himself, who is not willing that they should take it before the Honorable Court.

The defendant requests the Court to allow him four days' time to adjust this matter with the plaintiff.

The Honorable Court grants defendant's request.

Roelof Hendricks, plaintiff, vs. Pieter Jacobs, defendant. Plaintiff demands from defendant the amount of forty-five schepels of wheat and seventeen gldrs., in zeewant, and shows defendant's obligation for the same, five schepels of wheat and one schepel of oats having been credited thereon. He demands payment of the balance.

Pieter Cornelissen, representing his partner, Pieter Jacobsen, admits the debt. Defendant is ordered to pay plaintiff the balance of the obligation.

Juriaen Westphael asks to be allowed to appear before the Court and, having entered, requests the Honorable Court to administer the estate of Hendrick Jansen Looman, deceased, as he is stabling a horse which belonged to the aforesaid Looman, and, winter being near at hand, this will cause great expense to the estate of the deceased.

The Honorable Court resolves that, as Domine Blom and the Consistory forbade Juriaen Westphael, the appearer, and other [representatives of] devoluted estates from rendering an account to the Court, as stated to this Honorable Court on November 6, last, by the Consistory Allert Heymans Roose, Domine Hermanus Blom and the Consistory, Allert Heymans, must legally remove the injunction from the estates, and that, after such removal, the appearer will be aided by the Honorable Court.

Tjerck Claesen de Wit, appearing before the Honorable Court, requests that justice be done him in his case against Albert Gysbertsen, and that therefore his appeal from the said judgment rendered November 20, last, be entered.

The Honorable Court resolves, after plaintiff requested permission to appear and had had his opponent, Albert Gysbertsen, summoned to appear before the Court, as shown by the Court Messenger's record, that plaintiff's request be refused, for the reasons heretofore mentioned, in that he is not willing to do the proper thing about the Court room, for which he himself voted, and that he has forbidden several parties summoned by him, to appear with him before the Honorable Court, and also because he himself has neglected the appeal.

Regarding the undated letter brought to the Honorable Court by the Court Messenger, signed by the Rev. Mr. Hermanus Blom, by the authority of the Consistory, containing a request for a copy of a previous letter sent to him and which he had returned to the Honorable Court refusing the request therein contained, the Honable Court deems it therefore unnecessary to return again the copy asked for by his Reverence for the purpose of renewing the request.

Evert Pels, having requested to be admitted, demands of the

Honorable Court, after Tjerck Claesen deWit had summoned him
four times before the Court and did not himself even appear the
fourth time, that costs may be awarded to him by the Honorable
Court, to be paid by Tjerck Claesen deWit, and also further makes
claim for the damage done last summer by Tjerck Claesen deWit's
pigs to the corn on appearer's land.

The Honorable Court decides that the appearer shall, at its
next session, present to it a written demand herein against his
party, Tjerck Claesen deWit.

Arent Teunissen asks the Honorable Court for a lot in the village of Wildwyck, as he intends to take up his abode here.

The Honorable Court will determine upon a vacant spot for
him in the village of Wildwyck.

The Honorable Court agrees to the proposition made by the Ensign, Cristiaen Niessen, dated December 3, 1663, and to the resolution relative thereto passed by the Council of War, concerning the
setting up of new and renewing of the old palisades around the
village of Wildwyck, within three days, and agrees to the same and
will attend to its duty in the matter and notify the inhabitants
thereof through the Village Messenger. If any damage occurs to
any of the inhabitants in the meanwhile because of the erection, or
if, through the Ensign and Council of War, expenses should be
incurred, the Honorable Court will come to their assistance, so as
to reimburse their expenses.

Ordinary Session, held Tuesday, December 18, 1663.

Present: Roelof Swartwout, Schout; Tjerck Claesen deWit,
Thomas Chambers, Gysbert van Imborch, Commissaries.

Mattheus Capito, Secretary, plaintiff, vs. Jacob Joosten, Court
Messenger, defendant. Plaintiff prays the Honorable Court that,
whereas, he has not as yet received from the defendant, the Court
Messenger, one-half of the fees for summonses, as is the custom in
New Netherland, and the defendant has refused and still refuses
the same to him, the Honorable Court be pleased to act in this
particular.

Defendant answers he is not willing to give the Secretary one-
half of the fees for summonses.

The Honorable Court finds in favor of plaintiff, and orders defendant to give up to the Secretary, at each session of the Court, one-half of the fees for summonses.

The foregoing having been read to the defendant, he again answers that he is not willing to pay the Secretary one-half of the fees for summonses.

Jan Broersen, plaintiff, vs. Ariaen Gerretsen, defendant. Plaintiff demands from defendant five and one-half schepels of wheat, due for wages for work done on the barn of the Noble Lord Director General, and says defendant set him to work. Defendant denies he set plaintiff to work.

The Honorable Court orders plaintiff to prove, at its next session, that defendant set him to work.

Albert Gerretsen, plaintiff, vs. Ariaen Gerretsen, defendant. Plaintiff says that defendant set him to work on the barn of the Noble Lord Director General and that he earned at the said work nine schepels of wheat, of which three schepels have been paid. He also demands from defendant a sack which he loaned him to receive grain in.

Defendant denies having set plaintiff to work, but promises to return the sack.

The Honorable Court orders plaintiff to prove, at its next session, that defendant set him to work.

Albert Gerretsen, plaintiff, vs. Annetje Tacks, defendant. Plaintiff demands from defendant, under a contract dated December 16, 1662, payment of the amount of three hundred and thirty-eight guilders, heavy money, payable in grain, according to the contract aforesaid. Defendant admits the debt, and that she has paid on the same the value of eight schepels of wheat and five schepels of peas.

The Honorable Court orders defendant to pay plaintiff, pursuant to her admission and obligation.

Tjerck Claesen deWit, plaintiff, vs. Jonas Ranstou, defendant. Plaintiff demands from defendant payment of the amount of five schepels of wheat. Defendant says he owes plaintiff four and one-half schepels of wheat, and that plaintiff has attached nineteen guilders, in seewan, with Christiaen Andriesen the soldier.

The Honorable Court orders defendant to prove he did not receive the attached nineteen guilders, in seewan, from Christiaen Andriesen.

Henderick Jochemsen, plaintiff, vs. Albert Gysbertsen, defendant. Absent. Default.

Henderick Jochemsen, plaintiff, vs. Aert Martensen Doorn, defendant. Plaintiff demands from defendant the amount of two hundred and ninety-nine guilders, sixteen stivers, as per obligation signed by Jacob Jansen Stol, deceased, upon which forty-six guilders have been paid, leaving a balance of two hundred and fifty-three guilders, sixteen stivers, to be paid in wheat, at three guilders per schepel.

Geertuyd Andriesen, wife of Aert Martensen Doorn, admits the debt, and promises to pay plaintiff in installments, as she is indebted to others besides him.

The Honorable Court orders defendant to pay plaintiff.

Echje Gerrets, plaintiff, vs. Christiaen Niessen romp, defendant. Plaintiff submits proofs against defendant that her pillow is in his hands, the proofs, dated November 20, 1663, being signed by Magdalena Dirricks and Willem van Vredenborg.

Defendant says that the certificate signed by Magdalena Dirricks is false, and wants both certificates confirmed under oath. He further says that his wife's words, uttered while sick and delirious, cannot be received.

The Honorable Court orders plaintiff to produce the attestants in Court, at its next session.

Evert Pels, plaintiff, vs. Juriaen Westphael, defendant. The matters between the parties remaining unsettled, the Honorable Court notifies them that they will receive a special hearing tomorrow, and that their papers will be examined at such place as they may agree upon.

Tomas Chambers, plaintiff, vs. Roelof Swart, Cornelis Barenssen Slecht, and Jan Jansen van Amersfort, guardians of the minor children of Mattys Jansen, deceased, defendants. Plaintiff prays that he may be legally released from the lease of the lands hired by him from the guardians, or defendants, as he cannot utilize them in these troublous times.

Roelof Swartwout and Cornelis Barentsen Slecht request an extract of the application, as Jan Jansen Amersfort, the third guardian, is now absent, and ask time to answ,er.

The Honorable Court allows defendants until its next session to answer the application.

Thomas Chambers, the Commissary, Captain of the Burghery, intends, after Christmas, to organize, muster and officer the Burghery, because some of the petty officers have died, and some have entered the service of the Honorable Company. He requests the determination of the Court thereon.

The Honorable Court grants the aforesaid request of the above named Captain of the Burghery.

Jacob Boerhans, Collector, will please pay to Jacob Joosten, Court Messenger, fifty guilders, in seewan, out of the excise on wines, and credit his account.

Wildwyck, this December 18, 1663.

The Reverend Consistory, in answer to the Court's note of November 4, Sunday, sent to it through Juriaen Westphael, by order of the Honorable Court, replies that it is really astonished that the Honorable Court meets on Sunday, as there are enough other days in the week, and this is the reason why the Magistrates' pew in the Church is vacant Sunday morning and afternoon, and that the Consistory cannot legally release the estates because they came to it ecclesiastically (not that it was seized by the Consistory, as the Honorable Court dares falsely to assert in its note), and consequently it cannot, under the circumstances, release the same. (Below was written) In the name and by the authority of the Reverend Consistory. (Signed) Hermanus Blom. (In the margin) December 18, 1663, at Wildwyck.

Jacob Joosten, Court Messenger, gives notice of appeal in the case between him and the Secretary, Mattheus Capito, decided December 18, last. Dated December 27, 1663.

Extraordinary Session, held Thursday, December 27, 1663.
Present: Marten Cregier, Captain Lieutenant, President: Mattheus Capito, Provisional Schout; Albert Gysberts, Tjerck Claessen de Wit, Thomas Chambers, Gysbert van Imborch, Commissaries.

Marten Cregier, Captain Lieutenant, in the name of the Noble Lord Director General, P. Stuyvesant, plaintiff, vs. Juriaen West-phael, defendant.

Plaintiff demands from defendant the remaining debts due to the Noble Lord Director General Petrus Stuyvesant, amounting to ten hundred and four guilders, as per account, payable in winter grain, beaver's value, upon which there have been delivered one hundred and five schepels of oats, and requests a speedy payment thereof.

Defendant admits the debt, and says he is willing to pay.

The Honorable Court orders him to pay the aforementioned amount to plaintiff.

Tjerck Claesen deWit, plaintiff, vs. Roelof Swartwout, defend-ant. Absent. Default.

Albert Gerritsen, plaintiff, vs. Ariaen Gerretsen, defendant. Plaintiff demands from defendant the amount of six schepels of wheat for work done and earned on the house and barn of the Hon-orable Lord Director General, and produces as witness, pursuant to the order made by the Honorable Court December 18, last, Jan Broersen, who testifies he heard that Ariaen Gerritsen contracted with plaintiff for said work by the day, and that he promised plain-tiff to pay him therefor.

Defendant admits he set him to work, and says he is willing to pay him if the Honorable Lord Director General will approve of it, as the repairs were made on his Honor's house.

The Honorable Court orders defendant to pay plaintiff the demanded six schepels of wheat, and that defendant recover from the lessor because the work was done on his house.

Mattheus Capito, Provisional Schout, vs. Juriaen Westphael, defendant. The Provisional Schout submits his demand in writing. It reads as follows:

Whereas defendant, Juriaen Westphael, on October 9, last, substituted himself for the below mentioned persons, his workmen, who violated the ordinance proclaimed and published on August 4, last, providing that no one, without permission and a proper con-voy, should venture out to mow, cart, or do any other work, and were detected by the former Schout, Roelof Swartwout, my prede-cessor:

Antoni Crupel,	for	twice,		75 fl.
Henderick Hendericksen,	having	twice,		75 fl.
Jan Gerretsen,	violated	twice,	and	75 fl.
Jacob Stoutenborch,	the	once,	having	25 fl.
Jan Broersen,	aforesaid	twice,	been	75 fl.
Jacob Barents Cool,	ordin-	once,	fined	25 fl.
Jan Jansen van Oosterhout,	ance	twice,		75 fl.

Amounting to a total of...................... 425 fl.

say four hundred and twenty-five guilders, which the defendant was condemned to pay, and the defendant, on October 30, last, appeared before the Honorable Court, for the second time, for said persons, and was again ordered to pay the full amount of the fine, whereupon he gave notice of appeal;

The defendant is therefore asked by the Provisional Schout to show the Court forthwith what he has accomplished in his appeal to the High Court at the Manhatans, the appeal not having been received there. The Provisional Schout, plaintiff, concludes that the defendant, Juriaen Westphael, should be ordered to pay the aforesaid demands and fines, with costs, and that execution thereon issue.

Defendant hereupon says he can not answer, as the promises made to him in regard to harvesting his corn were not fulfilled, and says he has done nothing in the appeal.

The Honorable Court orders defendant to pay the above named fines, unless he agrees with the Schout upon a settlement.

Mattheus Capito, Provisional Schout, vs. Aert Jacobsen, defendant. The Provisional Schout submits a written demand which reads as follows:

Whereas, the defendant, Aert Jacobson, appeared on October 9, last, before the Honorable Court, with his son Gerret, his daughter, and his servant, Andries, he having with them violated the ordinance proclaimed and published on August 4, last, providing that no one should venture out to mow, cart, or do any other work, without permission and a proper convoy, and, through the Schout, Roelof Swartwout, my predecesor, fines were imposed on

The defendant,   of 75 fl.

His son Gerret,   " 75 fl.
His daughter,   " 25 fl.
His servant Andries,   " 25 fl.

amounting to a total of 200 fl., say two hundred guilders, which amount defendant was ordered to pay the aforesaid plaintiff, and the defendant having appeared for the second time before the Court on October 30, last, for himself and the aforenamed persons, regarding the aforesaid fines, gave notice of appeal; the defendant is therefore asked by the Provisional Schout, the plaintiff, to show forthwith what he has done in his appeal before the High Court at the Manhatans, the appeal not having been received there. The Provisional Schout, the plaintiff, concludes that the defendant, Aert Jacobson, should be condemned to pay the foregoing demands and fines, with costs, and that execution issue thereon.

Defendant answers that he did not prosecute the appeal.

The Honorable Court orders defendant to pay the above mentioned fines, unless he agrees with the Schout upon a settlement.

Evert Pels, plaintiff vs. Juriaen Westphael, defendant. Plaintiff demands from defendant the sum of three hundred and seventeen guilders, five stivers, and submits in proof several documents, and requests payment thereof with costs. Defendant requests that the documents be examined.

The Honorable Court decides that the papers and documents of both parties shall be examined, in the presence of the Provisional Schout, Mattheus Capito, by two members of the Court, Thomas Chambers and Gysbert van Imborch, who are authorized to make such examination, and, if possible, to settle the matter, and, if they can not do so, to report in writing at the next Court.

Jan Broersen, plaintiff, vs. Ariaen Gerretsen, defendant. Plaintiff demands from defendant five and one-half schepels of wheat, for wages in helping to carry and carrying, and in other work done on the house of the Honorable Director General. Defendant says he paid plaintiff fourteen schepels of oats as wages.

The Honorable Court orders the parties to settle and liquidate their accounts between themselves, and one to pay what may be due the other.

Roelof Swartwout, retiring Schout, requests that, as Juriaen Westphael and Aert Jacobson, pursuant to the judgment rendered

for violating the ordinance of August 4, last, have not paid their
fines, he, Swartwout, the appearer, may be permitted to himself
exact said fines, and, in case no amicable settlement is made thereof, that compulsion may follow.

The Honorable Court decides that whereas, the Provisional
Schout, Mattheus Capito, has summoned the unwilling persons,
Juriaen Westphael and Aert Jacobson, to appear before it regarding said fines, as to which the Court has rendered judgment, the
retiring Schout, Swartwout, and the incoming Provisional Schout,
Capito, may divide said fines between themselves, or so much
thereof as may be received under an amicable adjustment.

Allert Heymans appears before the Honorable Court, and requests that the minister, Hermanus Blom, be paid his salary, because, he says, the Consistory has made default thereon. He also
shows the contract made between the minister and some of his congregation, dated March 4, 1661.

The Honorable Court decides that the contract, dated March 4,
1661, between the minister and some of his congregation, was entered into for the period of a single current year. For the remaining years still to come the congregation shall agree with the
minister about his salary, to be on a reasonable basis, and they
shall meet at the minister's convenience.

Albert Gerritsen shows the Court an extract from the minutes
of December 18, 1663, against Annetje Tack, in reference to a sum
of three hundred and eighteen guilders, heavy money. He has
had three summonses served for the payment of said allowed claim,
and requests that execution may issue for the same.

The Honorable Court orders the Provisional Schout, Mattheus
Capito, to issue such execution.

Extraordinary Session, Saturday, December 29, 1663.

Present: Marten Cregier, Captain Lieutenant, President;
Mattheus Capito, Provisional Schout; Albert Gysbertsen, Thomas
Chambers, Gysbert van Imborch, Commissaries.

Tjerck Claesen de Wit, plaintiff, vs. Roelof Swartwout, defendant. Plaintiff submits to the Honorable Court a petition in
which he requests that defendant restore to him a horse which he

bought from, and for which he paid, defendant who removed it from the stable without plaintiff's knowledge. Plaintiff further submits a receipted account.

Defendant admits he verbally sold a horse to plaintiff, to be delivered and paid for within six weeks, the said horse to be at defendant's risk, and that, after the lapse of six weeks, plaintiff made no payment to defendant. Defendant also demands copy of the account submitted.

The Honorable Court orders plaintiff to furnish defendant with a copy of the account, and at the same time to adjust the same in the presence of the Provisional Schout, Capito, if possible, and, if not, to bring their case before the Honorable Court again at its next session, as usual.

Extraordinary Session, held Monday, December 31, 1663.
Present: Marten Cregier, Captain Lieutenant, President; Mattheus Capito, Provisional Schout; Albert Gysbertsen, Thomas Chambers, Gysbert van Imborch, Commissaries.

Whereas, the account between Tjerck Claesen deWit, plaintiff, and Roelof Swartwout, defendant, has been adjusted by the Honorable Court, which has found that Tjerck Claesen remains indebted to Roelof Swartwout for the purchased horse in twenty-four schepels of wheat, the Honorable Court therefore orders Roelof Swartwout to deliver the purchased horse to Tjerck Claesen deWit within ten days, the receiver to pay the balance of twenty-four schepels of wheat on receipt of the horse, which is to be at Roelof Swartwout's risk until its delivery and the receipt of the wheat, and if Roelof Swartwout can justly claim anything more as due from Tjerck Claesen, he may summon him to appear before the Court. Tjerck Claesen deWit is ordered to pay the costs herein.

Ordinary Session, held Tuesday, January 15, 1664.
Present: Mattheus Capito, Provisional Schout; Albert Gysbertsen, Tjerck Claesen deWit, Thomas Chambers, Gysbert van Imborch, Commissaries.

Henderick Jochemsen, plaintiff, vs. Albert Gysbertsen, defendant. Absent. Default.

Tjerck Claesen deWit, plaintiff, vs. Jonas Rantsou, defendant. Absent. Default.

Mattys Roelofsen, plaintiff. Absent. Default. vs. Aert Martens Doorn, defendant.

Jan Broersen, plaintiff. Absent. Default. vs. Ariaen Gerretsen, defendant.

On January 21, the following note was handed to the minister, Hermanus Blom:

Rev. Mr. Hermanus Blom.

Whereas, on the evening of January 2, last, Paulus Cornelisen, Jacob Jansen, alias long Jacob, Cornelis Brantsen Vos, and Ariaen Huybertsen, came to an agreement with the Provisional Schout to pay, for the violations committed by them, the sum of one hundred and seventy guilders, in seewan, of which eight guilders are for costs, leaving one hundred and sixty-two guilders, one-third whereof is due to the Church, your Reverence will also receive thereby two schepels of wheat, besides seven schepels of wheat of last week, making in all nine schepels of wheat, reckoned at six guilders per schepel, forwarded on account of the Church at Wildwyck, being the legal one-third of one hundred and sixty-two guilders. Done at Wildwyck, this 21st day of January, 1664.

(Signed) Mattheus Capito.

Ordinary Session, Tuesday, January 29, 1664.

Present: Mattheus Capito, Provisional Schout; Albert Gysbert, Tjerck Claesen deWit, Thomas Chambers, Gysbert van Imborch, Commissaries.

Mattheus Capito, Provisional Schout, in the name of Hermanus Blom, minister, plaintiff, vs. Juriaen Westphael, defendant. Plaintiff demands from defendant fl. 64:6:12, heavy money, the balance of the salary of the aforesaid minister, for the past years 1661 and 1662. Defendant admits the debt. The Honorable Court orders defendant to pay the above debt.

The Same, plaintiff, vs. Cornelis Barentsen Slecht, defendant. Plaintiff demands from defendant one hundred and eight guilders, heavy money, the balance of the salary of the aforenamed minister for the years 1661 and 1662. Defendant admits the debt.

The Honorable Court orders defendant to pay the above debt.

The Same, plaintiff, vs. Aeltje Claes, defendant. **Absent. Default.**

The Same, plaintiff, vs. Jan Lootman, defendant. Plaintiff demands from defendant ten guilders, heavy money, the balance of the salary of the aforenamed minister for the year 1662. Defend-ant denies the debt, saying that, as he is in the service of the Company, he is not obliged to contribute to the minister's salary.

The Honorable Court orders defendant to satisfy the afore-said demand, because, though he is in the service of the Honorable Company, he is also domiciled here.

The Same, plaintiff, vs. Mattys Roelofsen, defendant. Plain-tiff demands from defendant ten guilders, heavy money, the bal-ance of the salary of the aforenamed minister for the year 1662, Defendant admits the debt.

The Honorable Court orders defendant to pay the above debt.

The Same, plaintiff, vs. Aert Martensen Doorn, defendant. Plaintiff demands from defendant fl. 17:2:4, the balance of the aforesaid minister's salary for the years 1661 and 1662. Defend-ant admits the debt.

The Honorable Court orders defendant to pay the above debt

The Same, plaintiff, vs. Harmen Hendericks, defendant. Plaintiff demands from defendant fl. 19:6:8, the balance of the aforesaid minister's salary for the years 1661 and 1662. Defend-ant admits the debt.

The Honorable Court orders defendant to pay the above amount.

The Same, plaintiff, vs. Pieter Jacobs, defendant. **Absent Default.**

The Same, plaintiff, vs. Allert Heymans Roose, defendant Plaintiff demands from defendant eleven guilders, heavy money the balance of the aforesaid minister's salary for the year 1662 Defendant admits the debt.

The Honorable Court learns that defendant owns a double lot He must pay for the double lot twenty guilders, being in propor tion to other single lots which must pay ten guilders, towards th minister's salary, and in addition one guilder, for acreage money

The aforementioned balance amounts to twenty-one guilders, which he is ordered to pay, in heavy money.

The Same, plaintiff, vs. Jan Broersen, defendant,. Absent. Default.

The Same, plaintiff, vs. Jacob Barents Cool, defendant. Plaintiff demands from defendant the sum of ten guilders, heavy money, being the balance for the salary of the aforenamed minister for the year 1662. Defendant admits the debt.

The Honorable Court orders defendant to pay the above debt.

The Same, plaintiff, vs. Henderick Martensen, defendant. Plaintiff demands from defendant the sum of ten guilders, heavy money, balance of the aforenamed minister's salary for the year 1662. Defendant denies he is indebted for the minister's salary, and says that he is in the service of the Company, and therefore not obliged to contribute to the minister's salary. He further says that he has nothing to pay with, having been taken captive by the savages.

The Honorable Court orders defendant to pay the aforenamed demand, for, though in the service of the Honorable Company, he nevertheless has a house and lot here.

The Same, plaintiff, vs. Antoni Crupel, defendant. Plaintiff demands from defendant the sum of fl. 12:10, heavy money, being the balance of the minister's salary for the years 1661 and 1662. Defendant admits the debt.

The Honorable Court orders defendant to pay the foregoing debt.

The Same, plaintiff, vs. Jacob Boerhans, defendant. Plaintiff demands from defendant the sum of ten guilders, heavy money, being the balance of the minister's salary for the year 1662. Defendant says that during the troubles here his house was set on fire and he was not able to save anything from the house, and it is therefore impossible for him to pay.

The Court orders defendant to pay the aforesaid demand.

The Same, plaintiff, vs. Jan Jansen van Oosterhout, defendant. Plaintiff demands from defendant ten guilders, heavy money, being the balance of the minister's salary for the year 1661. Defendant admits the debt, and says that Albert Gysbertse undertook to pay the same for him in the year 1661.

The Honorable Court orders defendant to pay the aforesaid demand.

The Same, plaintiff, vs. Henderick Cornelissen lyendraejer [ropemaker], defendant. Plaintiff demands from defendant the sum of twenty-five guilders, heavy money, being balance of the minister's salary for the year 1662. Defendant admits the debt and says that twenty-four guilders, light money, were assigned to Cornelis Barentsen Slecht, and nine guilders, light money, to Albert Gysbertsen, totaling thirty-three guilders, light money.

The Honorable Court orders defendant to pay the aforesaid demand.

Mattheus Capito, Provisional Schout, in the name of the curators of the estate of Jan Albertsen van Steenwyck, plaintiff, vs. Jan Claesen deWit, defendant. Plaintiff demands from defendant, in his absence, for his guardians, the sum of two hundred and one guilders, light money, for goods bought from the estate.

Tjerck Claesen deWit, one of the guardians present, being one of the heirs of the aforesaid estate, offers himself as surety and principal for his brother Jan Claesen deWit, for the above mentioned amount, to secure any balance if his share be not sufficient, adding the guardian, Henderick Jochemse, as surety.

The Honorable Court decides that as Jan Claesen deWit is a co-heir of the estate of Jan Albertsen, the suretyship of his brother Jan [Tjerck] Claesen deWit, and of Henderick Jochemsen, the curators of the estate, be accepted for the said amount.

The Same, plaintiff, vs. Tjerck Claesen deWit, defendant. Plaintiff demands from defendant the sum of eight hundred and fifty-two guilders, eleven stivers, light money, for goods bought from the estate of Jan Albertsen van Steenwyck.

Defendant admits the debt, and says that he is co-heir of the aforesaid estate, and offers to pay if his share should be less; he also offers as sureties for the aforesaid amount the curator Evert Pels, who is present, and the guardian, Henderick Jochemsen.

The Honorable Court decides that, as defendant is co-heir in the aforesaid estate, he shall furnish security for the aforesaid amount.

The Same, plaintiff, vs. Jan Barents Ameshof, defendant. Absent. Default.

The Same, plaintiff, vs. Ariaen Teunissen, defendant. Plaintiff demands from defendant the sum of sixty-four guilders light money, for goods bought from the estate of Jan Albertsen. Defendant admits the debt.

The Honorable Court orders defendant to pay the aforesaid amount.

The Same, plaintiff vs. Ariaen Gerretsen, defendant. Absent. Default.

The Same, plaintiff, vs. Mattys Roelofsen, defendant. Plaintiff demands from defendant the sum of eight guilders, light money, for goods bought from the estate of Jan Albertsen. Defendant admits the debt.

The Honorable Court orders defendant to pay the aforenamed demand.

The Same, plaintiff, vs. Dirrick Hendericks, defendant. Absent. Default.

The Same, plaintiff, vs. Cornelis Barentsen Slecht, defendant. Plaintiff demands from defendant the sum of one hundred and thirty-one guilders, ten stivers, light money, for goods bought from the estate of Jan Albertsen, two hundred and eight guilders, ten stivers, light money, for one-half of the lot purchased from him for and on account of Jeronimus Ebbingh, for which he is surety, together amounting to three hundred and forty guilders, light money. Defendant admits the debt.

The Honorable Court orders defendant to pay the aforesaid demand.

The Same, plaintiff, vs. Jacob Jansen, alias long Jacob, defendant. Absent. Default.

The Same, plaintiff, vs. Lambert Huybertsen, defendant. Plaintiff demands from defendant the sum of forty-three guilders, ten stivers, light money, for goods bought from the estate of Jan Albertsen. Defendant admits the debt, and requests fourteen days' time.

The Honorable Court allows defendant fourteen days' time to pay the aforesaid amount.

Christiaen Niessen, in the name of the Honorable Lord Director General, Petrus Stuyvesant, plaintiff, vs. Juriaen Westphael, defendant. Plaintiff demands from defendant, for the Hon-

orable Director General aforenamed, payment of the sum of ten
hundred and four guilders, heavy money, beaver's value, being an
old balance due for rent and otherwise, and requests that, as he has
attached all his goods, no corn be permitted to leave defendant's
house until he shall have paid the Lord General. Defendant admits the debt, but says he has a counter claim for a portion.

The Honorable Court orders the attachment to continue, and
that defendant shall pay plaintiff, before any other of his creditors.

Christiaen Niessen, in the name of the Honorable Lord Director General, Petrus Stuyvesant, plaintiff, vs. Ariaen Gerretsen, defendant. Absent. Default. Plaintiff says he attached defendant's
property, and gives notice thereof.

The Honorable Court agrees and declares said attachment is
valid.

Hendrick Jochemsen, plaintiff, vs. Albert Gysbertsen, defendant. Plaintiff presents an account against defendant for forty-four guilders, two stivers, in light money, for the wages of, and
expenses incurred by, his son, and for sixty schepels of oats on
account of Frans Pieterse, which he attached March 28, 1662. Defendant admits the debt.

The Honorable Court orders defendant to pay plaintiff the
above amount.

Evert Pels, plaintiff, vs. Aert Martensen Doorn, defendant.
Plaintiff demands from defendant payment of the sum of two hundred and fifty-six guilders, heavy money. Defendant denies the
debt and answers he has a counter claim.

The Honorable Court orders the parties to adjust their accounts, and, if they cannot do so, that each party shall submit his
claim in writing at the next session of the Court.

Mattys Roelofsen, plaintiff, vs. Pieter Hillebrants, defendant.
Absent. Default.

Mattys Roelofsen, plaintiff, vs. Ariaen Gerretsen, defendant.
Absent. Default.

Mattys Roelofsen, plaintiff, vs. Aert Martensen Doorn, defendant. Plaintiff demands from defendant payment of thirty-one
schepels of wheat. Defendant admits the debt, and requests plaintiff to allow him three weeks' time.

The Honorable Court grants defendant the requested time.

Mattys Roelofsen, plaintiff, vs. Rut Albertsen, defendant. Absent. Default.

Tjerck Claesen deWit, plaintiff, vs. Jonas Rantsou, defendant. Plaintiff again demands from defendant five schepels of wheat, as already demanded in this Court on December 18, 1663. Defendant says that plaintiff attached nineteen guilders which were with Christiaen Andriesen, and, as the latter is dead, defendant requires plaintiff to make oath whether he has not received it, and then offers to pay to plaintiff four and one-half schepels of wheat which he admits he owes him.

The Honorable Court orders plaintiff to declare under oath that he did not receive the nineteen guilders from Christiaen Andriesen, nor in any other manner to be out the said nineteen guilders. Defendant is ordered, if the oath is taken, to pay plaintiff four and one-half schepels of wheat. The plaintiff declines to make oath.

Nicolaes Goselingh, plaintiff, vs. Ariaen Gerretsen, defendant. Absent. Default.

Nicolaes Goselingh, plaintiff, vs. Aert Martensen Doorn, defendant. Plaintiff demands from defendant two schepels of wheat. Defendant admits the debt.

The Honorable Court orders defendant to pay plaintiff.

Jan Pietersen Muller presents to the Honorable Court a power of attorney from Wouter Albertsen, residing at Fort Orange, to collect from the estate of Willem Jansen Seba, deceased, a quantity of nine schepels of wheat. He, at the same time, shows the obligation of Willem Jansen Seba, and requests payment out of the sold property of Willem Jansen Seba, deceased.

Ordinary Session, Tuesday, February 12, 1664.

Present: Mattheus Capito, Provisional Schout; Albert Gysbertsen, Thomas Chambers, Gysbert van Imborch, Commissaries.

Mattheus Capito, Provisional Schout, plaintiff, vs. Thomas Chambers, defendant. Plaintiff presents a petition regarding a quarrel with Paulus Cornelissen, which occurred in the house of Mr. Gysbert van Imborch, and states that they came to blows. He asks that defendant be condemned therefor to pay a double fine of one hundred guilders, he being a judge, in whom this is unseemly.

Defendant admits having used his fist once, and leaves the matter to the Honorable Court.

The Honorable Court having seen the Schout's complaint, and that not more than one blow was struck, condemns defendant to pay a fine of twelve guilders, to be duly applied.

Mattheus Capito, Provisional Schout, plaintiff, vs. Paulus Cornelisen, defendant. Plaintiff presents a petition showing that, at the house of Gysbert van Imborch, defendant came to blows over a dispute with Thomas Chambers, and requests that the defendant be condemned therefor to pay a fine of fifty guilders. Defendant says he does not know anything about this.

The Honorable Court orders plaintiff to bring proof at its next session.

Mattheus Capito, Provisional Schout, plaintiff, vs. Mattheu Blanchan, defendant. Plaintiff demands a fine of fifty guilders from defendant because, after the second beating of the drum, he churned some milk on the day of fasting and prayer. Defendant answers that the drum beat only once, and that he had no milk for his calf, and he never in his life did this before.

The Honorable Court, having examined the Schout's complaint and the answer of the defendant, orders defendant to pay six guilders, one-half for the Church.

Mattheus Capito, Provisional Schout, in the name of the minister Hermanus Blom, plaintiff, vs. Aeltje Claesen, defendant.

Plaintiff demands the sum of ten guilders, heavy money, from the defendant, being the balance of the minister's salary for the year 1662. Defendant answers that the building lots should be exempt, she having paid for her land.

The Honorable Court orders defendant to pay the aforesaid demand, because no money was taken from her for her land in the year 1662, but only for the building lots

The Same, plaintiff, vs. Pieter Jacobsen, defendant. Second default.

The Same, plaintiff, vs. Jan Broersen, defendant. Plaintiff demands from defendant the sum of twenty guilders, heavy money, being the balance for the minister's salary for the years 1661 and 1662. Defendant admits the debt, but says that Albert Gysbertsen undertook to pay ten guilders, heavy money, in 1661. He further says he is not able to pay this year.

The Honorable Court orders defendant to pay the aforesaid demand, and that he may commence suit against Albert Gysbertsen on his claim.

Mattheus Capito, Provisional Schout, in the name of the curators of Jan Albertsen van Steenwyck, plaintiff, vs. Ariaen Gerretsen, defendant. Second default.

The Same, plaintiff, vs. Dirrick Hendericksen, defendant. Second default.

The Same, plaintiff, vs. Tomas Hermensen, defendant. Absent. Default.

Walran duMont, plaintiff, vs. Lambert Huybertsen, defendant. Plaintiff demands from defendant sixty guilders, heavy money for one year house rent, and twenty-seven guilders, heavy money, for smithing. Defendant presents a counter claim amounting to one hundred and one guilders, ten stivers, heavy money.

The Honorable Court orders that defendant, having occupied only one-half of the house, shall pay plaintiff forty guilders, heavy money, for one year's house rent, and also the twenty-seven guilders, heavy money, for smithing, making in all sixty-seven guilders, heavy money, and then that plaintiff shall pay defendant thirty-four guilders, ten stivers, heavy money, being the balance of defendant's counter claim.

Evert Pels, plaintiff, vs. Aert Martensen Doorn, defendant. Plaintiff presents his whole account against defendant for the sum of five hundred and forty-one guilders, seventeen stivers. Defendant shows a counter claim still incomplete.

The Honorable Court orders parties to go to good men, namely, Allert Heymans Roose and Cornelis Barentse Slecht, to adjust the accounts on both sides, if possible, and, if not, to again refer to the Court.

Aert Martensen Doorn, plaintiff, vs. Cornelis Barentsen Slecht, defendant. Plaintiff demands from defendant fifty guilders, heavy money, being his share of the salary of the former Reader, Andries Vandersluys, five sieves and five reels and two winnowing baskets, received from his predecessor, Jacob Jansen Stol, deceased. Defendant answers he does not know whether he paid the above debts, as he settled accounts with his predecessor.

The Honorable Court orders parties to settle their accounts.

In regard to the request of the Ensign, Christiaen Niessen, made to the Honorable Court, in reference to paying the woodchoppers, builders and carters of the palisades for filling in the open spaces between the palisades near Cornelis Barentsen Slecht's and the main guard house, the Collector, Jacob Boerhans, is ordered, out of the excise money, to pay to the Ensign aforenamed the sum of forty-one schepels of wheat.

Done at Wildwyck, this February 12, 1664.

Petition or request of the Reverend Consistory to the
Honorable Magistrates of this place.

The Reverend Consistory here, for the sake of their office and for conscience' sake, request, with due submission, of the Honorable Magistrates of this place, that the public, sinful and scandalous Bacchanalian days of Fastenscen*, coming down from the heathens from their idol Bacchus, the God of wine and drunkenness, being also a leaven of popery, inherited from the pagans, which the Apostle, in 1 Cor. 5, admonishes true Christians to expurge, may, while near at hand, be proscribed in this place by your Honors, by proper ordinances, while we admonish against and publicly reprehend those abominations, so that through God's grace and blessing we shall mutually have done our duty, and we may thereby do some good for this place and its inhabitants, their bodies as well as their souls,—the more so as we are passing through such woeful times of God's judgment over us in this place, inflicted because of our sins —and so that we may not, through such scandalous sins of Fastenseen, and sinful doing, continue to irritate the Lord and still further call down his judgments upon us, for we are still under his rod, and his sword of war still threatens us yet more to try the land and its inhabitants. And shall then the inhabitants be gay in their sins, while the land mourns, and we are called on every month to fast, to weep and to mourn? Joel 2. Therefore it is, that the Reverend Consistory desire of the Honorable Court, that our prayer may be heeded and taken to heart, we being foster fathers of God's

---

* Shrove Tuesday or Mardi Gras

Church and congregation, so that thus sin and abomination may the more and more be banished from this newly developing community, to the glorification of God's name and the edification of this community, as well as the happiness and welfare of the place, upon which we must depend. In the meantime we commend you to God's keeping, and may He bless your office and persons.

Below was written, In the name of the Reverend Consistory. (Signed) Hermanus Blom. (In the margin) February 12, 1664, at Wildwyck.

To the petition or request of the Rev. Mr. Hermanus Blom and the Reverend Consistory to the Honorable Court, the following answer was given:

The Honorable Court will be glad to comply with said request, so far as its instructions permit.

The Honorable Court at Wildwyck hereby again admonishes the retiring Commissaries, to please make out their accounts of the village of Wildwyck, within two weeks, as they were also judicially ordered to do on May 22, 1663, the which has been hindered or delayed by the war, so that the Honorable Lord Director General, upon his arrival, may see the state of this place.

The Collector, Jacob Boerhans, is ordered, out of the excise on wine, to pay Aert Martensen Doorn forty-two guilders in seewan, light money, for room rent of the Honorable Court here, and to enter it in the accounts.

Done, this February 12, 1664.

Ordinary Session, Tuesday, February 26, 1664.

Present: Mattheus Capito, Provisional Schout; Albert Gysbertsen, Tjerck Claesen deWit, Tomas Chambers, Gysbert van Imborch, Commissaries.

Tomas Harmense, plaintiff, vs. Albert Gysbertsen, defendant. Plaintiff demands from defendant a quantity of fifty schepels of wheat for assigned debts. Defendant admits the debt but says he is not able just now to pay.

The Honorable Court orders defendant to pay plaintiff's aforesaid demand.

Tomas Harmensen, plaintiff, vs. Aert Martensen Doorn, defendant. Plaintiff demands the sum of thirty-five guilders, in seewan, from defendant, for goods delivered, and for one and one-half days' wages. Geertruyd Andriesen, in the absence of her husband, the defendant, admits the debt.

The Honorable Court, except Thomas Chambers, orders defendant to pay plaintiff's aforesaid demand.

Thomas Harmensen, plaintiff, vs. Henderick Albertsen, defendant. Absent. Default. Plaintiff has attached four schepels of wheat of defendant's, in the hands of Cornelis Barentsen Slecht, and gives notice thereof.

The Honorable Court allows said attachment as valid.

Albert Gysbertsen, plaintiff, vs. Coenrad Ham, defendant. Absent. Default.

Tjerck Claesen deWit, plaintiff, vs. Evert Pels, defendant. Plaintiff demands from defendant two fimmen [or vimmen, plural of vim, the equivalent of a stack of 104 to 108 sheaves] of oats which he loaned defendant last winter. Defendant admits this, but says he has a counter claim against plaintiff.

The Honorable Court orders parties to liquidate their claims, or, otherwise, that defendant shall submit his counter claim to the Court at its next session.

Gysbert van Imborch, plaintiff, vs. Tjerck Claesen deWit, defendant. Plaintiff demands the sum of one hundred and twenty-four guilders, nineteen stivers, in seewan, from defendant, as per account rendered, and also a quantity of eight schepels of wheat, for account of plaintiff's wife, for merchandise delivered. Defendant admits the debt, but also says that, during the war with the savages, he drove the savages from plaintiff's house.

The Honorable Court orders defendant to pay the aforesaid claim of plaintiff.

Gysbert van Imborch, plaintiff, vs. Annetje Tacks, defendant. Plaintiff demands from defendant payment of two hundred and thirty-four guilders, eight stivers, in beavers, as per account rendered, allowed by the Schepens under date of December 21, 1662, among which are included twenty-six guilders, eight stivers, in beavers, for interest on two hundred and sixty-four guilders, in beavers, and requests that the horse called "Blackie" [het Swartje] be sold, at her expense, under execution.

Defendant admits the debt, but says she is not able at present to pay plaintiff, as she already lacks bread, pork, meat, etc., in her household, and, further, that most of her crops were left on the field last harvest because of the war.

The Honorable Court, having requested defendant to furnish security, which she knows not where to obtain, and plaintiff not being willing to give her an extension, orders defendant to pay plaintiff's aforesaid demand.

Christiaen Niessen, substituted for the Honorable Lord Director General, Petrus Stuyvesant, plaintiff, vs. Ariaen Gerretsen, defendant. Plaintiff demands from defendant, according to obligation issued by him, due March next, payment of sixty schepels of wheat, of which thirty-four have been paid, leaving a balance of twenty-six schepels of wheat. Defendant admits the debt, and promises to pay plaintiff at the specified date.

Paulus Cornelisen, plaintiff, vs. Annetje Tacks, defendant. Plaintiff presents an account against defendant, amounting to two hundred and forty-one guilders, ten stivers, in seewan, and eight beavers, for money advanced and provisions sold and furnished to her last harvest. Defendant admits the debt.

The Honorable Court orders defendant to pay plaintiff the aforesaid amount.

Mattheus Capito, Provisional Schout, in the name of the curators of the estate of Jan Albertsen van Steenwyck, plaintiff vs. Tjerck Claesen deWit, defendant. Plaintiff demands from defendant security, as ordered by the Honorable Court, January 29, last, for goods bought from the estate of Jan Albertsen van Steenwyck, deceased, to the amount of eight hundred and fifty-two guilders, eleven stivers, light money, and requests that defendant be compelled to furnish the same.

Evert Pels, the curator, and Henderick Jochemsen, the guardian, also hereby request the Court to be discharged from their curatorship and guardianship, as they cannot agree with defendant who is a joint guardian. They further request, in case they be not discharged, that the Honorable Court please sustain them.

Defendant says he has not been unreasonable about furnishing security, and that last week, he, with the plaintiff and the curator, Evert Pels, called at the house of the guardian, Henderick Jochemsen, and this matter was not then arranged.

The Honorable Court decides that defendant, on his own account as well as of those for whom he became bondsman, shall furnish security for the full amount, satisfactory to the curator, Evert Pels, and the guardian, Henderick Jochemsen, and further orders the curator, Evert Pels, and the guardian, Henderick Jochemsen, to look more closely after the estate of Jan Albertsen van Steenwyck, so that no one shall be deprived of his rights.

The Same, plaintiff, vs. Ariaen Gerretsen, defendant. Plaintiff demands the sum of fifty guilders, light money, from defendant, for goods bought from the estate of Jan Albertsen van Steenwyck, and requests execution on non payment. Defendant admits the debt.

The Honorable Court orders defendant to satisfy plaintiff within twice twenty-four hours, and, in case of default, that execution against his property shall issue.

The Same, plaintiff, in the name of Hermanus Blom, minister, vs. Pieter Jacobsen, defendant. Plaintiff demands the sum of ten guilders, heavy money, from defendant, being the balance of the minister's salary during the year 1662. Defendant admits the debt, and promises to pay this week.

The Same, plaintiff, vs. Paulus Cornelisen, defendant. Plaintiff demands a fine from defendant, pursuant to previous summons. Defendant denies he fought with Thomas Chambers. Plaintiff adduces in evidence the acknowledgement of Thomas Chambers, and demands judgment thereon.

The Honorable Court orders plaintiff to submit proof.

Request of Hermanus Blom, minister.

I, the undersigned, once more and for the last time, request of the Honorable Court here (as I have even several times before this verbally requested at its sessions, yea, even the other day, through my Elder) to know, in writing, whether or not it intends to collect and pay me my salary, earned for religious duties performed by me in this place for the congregaton; if yea, that it is already high time, and if not, that the Honorable Court be pleased to give me an apostile, so that, in due time, I may acquaint the Supreme Magistrates with it, and complain to them that the Honorable Court here does not, as in duty bound, follow the orders, received from the Supreme Magistrates, to collect my earned salary, and that it does not, through its political power, legally attend to and press the matter, and has not done so to date. The Lord Councillors may thereby then see that the fault lies not alone with the congregation, but more so with the Court here. The Lord Councillors will then well be able to judge how it comes that my salary has not been collected and paid to me, much less that it is not legally enforced and insisted upon. To which request, I, the undersigned, shall expect from the Honorable Court a written answer, to use at the proper time before the Lord Councillors. Which complaint to the Supreme Magistrates, the Honorable Court can still prevent. I leave it to the judgment of the Honorable Court here itself whether it is not a sad and grievous thing that a minister of the Word of God is, as here, compelled, with such trouble and pains, to seek for, and request of and through the Court, his long since earned salary, the which has never been seen or heard of anywhere in Christendom.

February 26, 1664, at Wildwyck.

(Signed) Hermanus Blom.

Apostile on the above request: The Honorable Court will do its duty, as far as possible, to compel those reluctant, and those who, following their voluntary promise, are behind in their payment of the salary. Done at Wildwyck, this February 26, 1664.

Pursuant to the foregoing order, the Court Messenger is directed and ordered to remind the inhabitants of this place of the arrearage of the ministers salary, and also to admonish them, under pain of execution, to carry out their promises to pay the minister's salary for the year 1663. Wildwyck, this February 26, 1664.

Extraordinary Session, held Saturday, March 1, 1664.

Present: Mattheus Capito, Provisional Schout; Albert Gysbertsen, Tjerck Claesen deWit, Thomas Chambers, Gysbert van Imborch, Commissaries.

The Honorable Court having seen and read the signed request of the Council of War, dated February 29, last, answers, first, that the severity of the winter season does not permit any digging of the ground to fill in vacant spaces with palisades, though the palisades obtained for this purpose lie here ready, and that the Honorable Court will do its duty by admonishing those on whose side the open spaces will have to be filled in, and also by taking care to have the gates properly closed. To the second request, concerning the issuance of orders to keep the inhabitants under arms, and to furnish a guard for the one post near Henderick Jochemsen's gate, the Honorable Court requests and orders the Captain of the Burghery, Thomas Chambers, to call the citizens to arms, and at the same time to properly man the one post aforesaid, with as little trouble as possible, and as he and his burgher Council of War shall think proper. Thus done in our extraordinary session at Wildwyck, this March 1, 1664.

The mark (x) of Albert Gysbertsen,

Tierck Claszen de Witt,

Gysbert van Imbroch.

Mr. Gysbert van Imborch has caused to be legally attached the wheat of Gerret Fooken, so that it may not be alienated until he shall have been paid, and gives notice of said attachment, this March 1, 1664.

Henderick Jochemsen has caused to be legally attached five schepels of wheat, in the hands of Pieter Cornelissen Molenaer [Miller], belonging to Abraham Stevensen, alias Crawaet, and gives notice of said attachment, this March 1, 1664.

The Honorable Court allows the validity of said attachment, this March 11, 1664.

Ordinary Session, Tuesday, March 11, 1664.

Present: Mattheus Capito, Provisional Schout; Albert Gysbertsen, Tjerck Claesen, Thomas Chambers, Gysbert van Imborch, Commissaries.

Jan Willemsen Hoochteyling, deacon, presented to the Honorable Court here an account showing that of the Church money one hundred and fifty-five guilders, three stivers, seewan, and from the poor money, three hundred and fifty-nine guilders, in seewan, amounting together to five hundred and fourteen guilders, three stivers, seewan, have been expended for building the parsonage here, and thereupon asks where he can obtain payment thereof.

The Honorable Court decides that, as there is no money in the treasury, and the Commissaries have no authority to provide the means, the deacon be requested to give an extension until the arrival of the Honorable Lord Director General, for the purpose of then seeing by what means the above amount may be paid.

Mattheus Capito, Provisional Schout, plaintiff, vs. Evert Pels, defendant. Plaintiff demands the sum of twenty guilders, four stivers, in sewant, due for scriverner's wage from defendant for account of Juriaen Westphael, and says that defendant engaged him.

Defendant says that Juriaen Westphael must pay the expenses.

The Honorable Court orders defendant to pay the aforesaid demand to plaintiff, and that he may bring suit against Juriaen Westphael.

Evert Pels, plaintiff, vs. Juriaen Westphael, defendant. Plaintiff demands from defendant, as per signed obligation dated December 28, 1663, the amount of two hundred and sixty-two guilders, five stivers, heavy money, and also twenty guilders, four stivers, in seewan, for scrivener's wage, and two guilders, eight stivers, in seewan, for the Court Messenger. Defendant says he has nothing to say against the demand.

The Honorable Court orders defendant to pay plaintiff the aforementioned demand, after the attachment in behalf of the Lord Director General by Christiaen Niessen shall have been satisfied, said attachment having taken place on his Honor's own land.

Evert Pels, plaintiff, vs. Aert Martensen Doorn, defendant. Absent. Default.

Tjerck Claesen deWit, plaintiff, vs. Evert Pels, defendant. Plaintiff demands from defendant two fimmen [or vimmen, plural of vim, the equivalent of a stack of 104 to 108 sheaves] of oats which he loaned him last winter. Defendant answers that he ploughed three days for plaintiff, who replies that defendant ploughed two and one-half days for him, and produces Ju-

riaen Westphael who says that defendant on the first day worked
about eight or nine hours in the field, and as to the other two days
he can not say anything. Plaintiff further says that he again
ploughed one and one-half days for defendant, but defendant says
he ploughed one day.

The Honorable Court orders parties to adjust their dispute
before two good men, or, otherwise, to again appear before the
Court with their proofs and accounts.

Andries Pietersen van Leeuven, plaintiff, vs. Cornelis Barentsen Slecht, defendant. Absent. Default.

Andries Pietersen, soldier, plaintiff, vs. Aert Martensen Doorn,
defendant. Absent. Default.

Gysbert van Imborch, plaintiff, vs. Thomas Harmensen, defendant. Plaintiff demands from defendant four schepels of wheat,
and to secure payment has laid an attachment therefor with Aert
Martensen Doorn. Defendant admits owing him as aforesaid, and
asks that the same be deducted from his wages for harvesting, and
also presents divers accounts of eleven schepels of wheat and two
schepels of peas, being wages for harvesting, six schepels of wheat
and five schepels of wheat for guarding the shop of Annetje Tacks,
and two schepels of peas for threshing. He also says that plaintiff, through the Schout, forbade him to thresh, whereupon he
ceased, and thereupon on the following day plaintiff said, "Why
don't you keep on threshing?"; that then he continued threshing
and delivered the grain to plaintiff's loft. Further, that plaintiff
promised him board, with others, in case Annetje Tacks
refused him board. Plaintiff denies he forbade defendant to thresh,
but had him forbidden to furnish grain to any one else than
himself; whereupon the defendant answered that Annetje Tacks
would not board him; thereupon plaintiff said that if she would
not do so, he would.

The Honorable Court, having heard parties, finds, conform-
ably to the judgment for plaintiff rendered October 23, 1663, that
Annetje Tacks should neither use, decrease nor alienate any of the
grain, without the knowledge and consent of plaintiff aforesaid,
and that plaintiff must deliver to defendant six schepels of wheat
for wages earned during harvest, and two schepels of peas for
wages for threshing, and that he may deduct from defendant the

four schepels of wheat, and that defendant may claim the remaining five schepels of wheat from Annetje Tacks.

Gysbert van Imborch, plaintiff, vs. Gerret Fooken, defendant. Plaintiff demands from defendant a quantity of thirty three and one-half schepels of wheat due him from defendant and his partner Jan Gerretsen, in which sum are included six schepels of wheat for shaving and doctor's bill for Jan Gerrets, for a whole year. He also demands from defendant himself two schepels of wheat for doctor's fee during his sickness after said time.

Defendant submits a receipt showing that he paid plaintiff sixteen and one-half schepels of wheat, and further says that he can not pay for his partner who was killed by the savages during the late troubles. He also claims damages from plaintiff for his outlays for wages and board, caused by plaintiff attaching his grain on March 1, so that he could not properly thresh it.

The Court, having heard the respective parties, decides that defendant shall, in accordance with the foregoing demand, pay plaintiff the just half of the goods received, and in addition the two schepels of wheat for doctor's fee for himself during his sickness, and that defendant has no claim against plaintiff for preventing him threshing, as he only attached the grain so that it could not be alienated.

Paulus Cornelisen demands from the Honorable Court the sum of one hundred and eight guilders in seewan, for bricks furnished for the parsonage. The Honorable Court answers that, as the books of the retired Commissaries have not yet been written up, it therefore does not know how much money there is in the treasury.

Paulus Cornelissen requests execution against Annetje Tacks under the judgment entered February 24, 1664, served by the Court Messenger after citation, summons and renewal. The Doorkeeper is directed to proceed with the execution.

The mark (x)of ALBERT GYSBERTSEN,

THOMAS CHAMBERS,

TIERCK CLASZEN DE WITT,

GYSBERT VAN IMBROCH.

Mattheus Capito, Provisional Schout, plaintiff, vs. Paulus Cornelissen, defendant. The Provisional Schout, Mattheus Capito, plaintiff, pursuant to the order of the Court that he submit proof, submits, in addition to the previous admission of Thomas Chambers, a certificate signed by Sergeant Jan Peersen, reciting how the matter occurred and that the defendant came to blows with Thomas Chambers. Defendant answers that he does not know anything about it, and that he was drunk.

The Honorable Court orders defendant to settle with plaintiff, otherwise judgment will be rendered by the Court.

Mattheus Capito, Provisional Schout, again requests of the Honorable Court that, to enable him to be released by the curator Evert Pels and the guardian Henderick Jochemsen with respect to the auction sale, Tjerck Claesen deWit, as ordered February 26, last, be compelled, on his own account as well as for those for whom he became surety and guardian, to give security for the goods purchased and received by him from the estate of Jan Albertsen van Steenwyck.

The curator Evert Pels and the guardian Henderick Jochemsen also request, in addition, that Tjerck Claesen deWit, joint guardian, give security for the entire amount, on his own account as well as for those for whom he has become surety.

The joint guardian, Tjerck Claesen deWit, says that he is ready to give security for the goods received and purchased by him, and that the account presented by him should be accepted in reduction, but that he will not give bond for his brother Jan Claesen and his sister Amarens Claesen, as he is already bound. He adds that he was twice at Henderick Jochemsen's house to give security.

The plaintiff, and the curator, Evert Pels, say that it is true that they were at the aforesaid house with the joint guardian Tjerck Claesen deWit, but that Tjerck Claesen still did not produce any sureties.

The Honorable Court having learned that the curator Evert Pels and the guardian Henderick Jochemsen, without its knowledge, extended to May 1, of the current year, the time of Amarens Claesen to pay for the goods purchased from the aforesaid estate, and that they were also herein contented with the security given by her brother, Tjerck Claesen, who signed as principal bondsman, whereby the Honorable Court has been slighted with regard to its previous judgment rendered February 26, last, it is therefore hereby ordered that Tjerck Claesen deWit, within twice twenty-four hours, give security on his own account for the goods purchased and received by him from the aforesaid estate, to be satisfactory to the curator, Evert Pels, and the guardian, Henderick Jochemsen.

To the account presented by the Rev. Mr. Hermannus Blom, signed by Commissaries Evert Pels, Tjerck Claesen deWit, and Albert Gysbertsen, for moneys expended by his Reverence for materials and wages for the parsonage here, the Honorable Court answers: As there is no money in the treasury, his Reverence is therefore asked to wait until the arrival of the Honorable Lord Director General, for the purpose of then devising with his Honor the means whereby the said account may be paid.

Mr. Gysbert van Imborch requests execution against Annetje Tacks, under the judgment rendered February 26, last, after service by the Court Messenger of citation, summons and renewal.

The Doorkeeper is directed to proceed with the execution.

The mark (x) of ALBERT GYSBERTSEN,

TIERCK CLASZEN DE WITT,

THOMAS CHAMBERS.

Mr. Gysbert van Imborch, Commissary, asks the Court whether Gerret Fooken may dispose of the estate of his deceased partner, Jan Gerretsen, being the crops of the year 1663.

Mr. Gysbert van Imborch gives notice that he will appeal from the judgment rendered against Gerret Fooken March 11. Done at Wildwyck, this March 12, 1664.

Deed by Jan Broersen and Jan Jansen van Oosterhout to
Thomas Chambers.

On March 21, of the year 1663, appeared before me, Mattheus Capito, Secretary of the village of Wildwyck, Jan Broersen and Jan Jansen van Oosterhout, who declare that they have deeded, ceded and conveyed, as they hereby deed, cede and convey, to Thomas Chambers, a parcel of land situate on the Esopus, below the village of Wildwyck, five morgens [about two acres each], two hundred and thirty rods, in extent, bounded on the north by the land of the children of Mattys Jansen, deceased, and on the south by the land of Mattheus Capito; all as given and granted to the aforesaid grantors by letters patent thereof dated April 25, 1663, and signed by the Director General and Council of New Netherland, to which aforesaid parcel of land, the said Jan Broersen and Jan Jansen van Oosterhout have not reserved to themselves any other right of action or claim, but have absolutely renounced and ceded the same for the use of the above named Thomas Chambers, agreeing that the aforesaid parcel of land shall be received by him, and that he may make the same use thereof as of all his other patrimonial possessions, save the Lord's right, in conformity with what is mentioned in the aforesaid letters patent; the aforesaid grantors, Jan Broersen and Jan Jansen van Oosterhout, promising never to revoke this deed and conveyance, nor in any manner, by themselves or anyone else, to do or cause to be done any act in derogation of the same, submitting their persons and estates, real and personal, present and future, nothing excepted, to the jurisdiction of all courts and judges. And these grantors, have personally signed hereunder in the presence of Albert Gysbertsen and Tjerck Claesen deWit, Commissaries of this village, witnesses hereto invited and requested.

Done at Wildwyck the day and year aforesaid.

The mark (x) of JAN BROERSEN, made by himself,
JAN JANSEN,
The mark (x) of ALBERT GYSBERTSEN, made by himself,
TIERCK CLASZEN DEWITT.
In my presence. To which I certify.
MATTHEUS CAPITO, Secretary.

Letter to the Lord Director General and Lord Councillors of New Netherland.

Honorable Very Worthy Sirs:

As it is customary among well regulated governments to change magistrates every year, and the annual change of magistrates of this village occurs in the month of May, the Provisional Schout and the Commissaries of the village of Wildwyck have therefore noted the most honorable, suitable and able persons among the inhabitants of this village, and have made up a nomination, so that your Honorable Worships may select two out of the four mentioned below.

The nominated persons are the following: Jan Willemsen Hoochteylingh, Cornelis Barentsen Slecht, Aert Jacobsen, Henderick Jochemsen.

Concluding herewith, we commend your Very Honorable Worships, with our greetings, to God's protection, and remain

Your Very Honorable Worships'

Humble Servants,

(Signed)   Mattheus Capito, the mark (x) of Albert Gysbertsen, Tjerck Claesen deWit, Thomas Chambers, Gysbert Van Imborch.

Done at Wildwyck, this March 27, 1664.

On March 28 Jan Evertsen gives notice of an attachment by the Court Messenger at Aert Jacobsen's, having attached two brandy kettles belonging to Hester Douwesen, widow of Barent Gerretsen.

On March 29, Jan Pietersen Muller, under power from Wouter Albertsen Backer, at Fort Orange, gives notice of an attachment by the Court Messenger at Aert Jacobsen's, having attached five schepels of wheat of the wheat from the sale of the cows of Evert Prys.

We, the undersigned, Albert Gysbertsen and Gysbert van Imborch, Commissaries of the village of Wildwyck, make known that there appeared before us Pieter Jacobsen van Holsteyn and Pieter Cornelisen, both partners, and inhabitants in the village of Wildwyck. who acknowledge that they really and truly owe to the worthy Nicolaes Meyer, merchant at the Manhatans, the amount of sixty-one schepels of good winter wheat, with four years' interest thereon, being ten per cent. annually, due in the month of November of this current year, on their promise to pay said sixty-one schepels of wheat, with four years' interest, in the month of November next, and to deliver the same to the aforesaid Nicolaes Meyer, at the Manhatans, free of expense and damage, and to have the same measured by the sworn City Measurer.   And to carry out these presents, the appearers obligate themselves, and specially mortgage their mill, situated at Wildwyck, and they also, in general, submit their persons and goods, real and personal, present and future, nothing excepted, to the jurisdiction of all courts and judges.   And the appearers, with us, have personally subscribed these presents.

Done at Wildwyck, this March 31, 1664.
The mark of (x) PIETER JACOBSEN, made by himself,
The mark of (x) PIETER CORNELISSEN, made by himself,
The mark of (x) ALBERT GYSBERTSEN, made by himself,
GYSBERT VAN IMBROCII.
In my presence.   To which I certify.

MATTHEUS CAPITO.

I, Nicolaes d Meyer, acknowledge having received in all, from what is to be received on the foregoing, seventeen schepels of wheat, in part payment of the interest, say seventeen schepels of wheat.

NICOLAES D MEYER, 1664,

20 Nov.

We, the undersigned, Albert Gysbertsen and Tjerck Claesen deWit, Commissaries of the village of Wildwyck, make known that or this date appeared before us the worthy Juriaen Westphael, resident of Wildwyck, who acknowledges and declares that he is really and truly indebted to Mr. Nicolaes de Meyer, burgher and inhabitant of the city of Amsterdam in New Netherland, for the quantity of eighty schepels of good and pure winter wheat, twenty-eight schepels of oats, and six good whole merchantable beavers, together with thirty-three guilders, three stivers, in seewan, due for merchandise and goods delivered, with ten per cent. per annum interest thereon from July 9, 1663, to final payment. And he promises to pay the aforesaid sums in two installments, one-half on October 1, of the current year, and the other half on March 1, of the next year, 1665, with interest thereon, said amounts in grain and otherwise, as above mentioned, to be delivered at the Manhatans, without expense or damage. For the purpose of carrying out these presents, the appearer specially mortgages his land, situated below the village of Wildwyck, between the land of Thomas Chambers, across the Great Kill, and the land of Aert Martensen Doorn and the lot lying in Wildwyck near the lot of Albert Heymans Roose, on the one side, and next to the lot of Tjerck Claesen deWit, on the other side, being the appearer's whole lot, all of which he, the appearer, says is unencumbered and unrestricted, and also in general [he mortgages] his person and estate, real and personal, present and future, nothing excepted, submitting the same to the jurisdiction of all courts and judges. And the appearer, with us, has thereupon personally signed these presents. Done at Wildwyck, this April 1, Anno 1664.

The mark of (x) JURIAEN WESTPHAEL, made by himself,

The mark of (x) ALBERT GYSBERTSEN, made by himself,

TIERCK CLASZEN DEWITT.

In my presence. To which I certify.

MATTHEUS CAPITO, Secretary.

Ordinary Session, Tuesday, April 1, Anno 1664.

Present: Roelof Swartwout, Schout; Albert Gerretsen, Tjerck Claesen deWit, Thomas Chambers, Gysbert van Imborch, Commissaries.

Frederick Philipsen, plaintiff, vs. Wyntje, wife of Allert Heymans, defendant. Plaintiff demands from defendant fifty-nine schepels of wheat, and the expenses therewith, for which an obligation was delivered on May 4, 1662. Defendant admits the debt, but does not know how much it is, and says he has a counter claim for carting goods.

The Honorable Court having heard the parties, and taking into conisderation that defendant's husband is absent, he having gone to the Manhatans, orders the parties to liquidate their accounts between themselves, and that defendant on his admission of indebtedness pay plaintiff the balance of the account.

Jan Pietersen Muller, plaintiff, vs. Evert Pels, defendant. Plaintiff, under power of attorney from Wouter Albertsen, at Fort Orange, demands from defendant five schepels of wheat, he having attached the aforesaid five schepels of wheat in the hands of Aert Jacobsen. Defendant admits the debt.

The Honorable Court declares the attachment valid, and orders defendant to pay plaintiff the aforesaid demand.

Jan Evertsen, plaintiff, vs. Hester Douwesen, defendant. Plaintiff demands from defendant the amount of seventy-five guilders, in beavers, fourteen schepels of good winter wheat, forty-four guilders in sewan, under a previous judgment, dated June 5, 1663, for which he has lawfully caused to be attached two brandy kettles in the hands of Aert Jacobsen. He gives notice of the attachment, and requests execution thereunder. Defendant admits the debt, but requests four months' time.

The Honorable Court declares the attachment valid, and, as plaintiff does not extend her time, the foregoing request of plaintiff is granted.

Johanna de Laet, wife of Jeronimus Ebbingh, plaintiff, vs. Cornelis Barentsen Slecht, defendant. Plaintiff demands from defendant payment of the sum of twelve hundred twenty-one guilders, sixteen stivers, in beavers, due for rent May 1, of the year 1663, and requests payment thereof.

Defendant admits the foregoing demand, and says he paid on account thereof thirty-five schepels of wheat, and the stiver money.

The Honorable Court orders defendant to satisfy plaintiff for the balance of the foregoing demand.

Plaintiff further requests that the estate and possessions of defendant be inventoried, so that she may be paid in full. She also requests that the purchase made yesterday by Frederick Philipsen, of the lot at Wildwyck, be annulled, and that she be preferred with respect thereto, as also with respect to the assignment made by defendant to Frederick Philipsen of about three hundred guilders to be received from the Honorable Company, regarding which she also attached all of defendant's property.

The Honorable Court decides that plaintiff shall be preferred as to defendant's goods which are on plaintiff's own soil and land, and shall also be permitted to have the same inventoried. Regarding the purchase yesterday by Frederick Philipsen from defendant of the lot at Wildwyck, the same is to remain valid, but plaintiff may bring suit against Frederick Philipsen for the purchase money and on the assignment to Frederick Philipsen of about three hundred guilders, due from the Honorable Company. The attachment made by plaintiff of the goods on her own soil is also declared valid by the Honorable Court.

Jacobus Backer, under power of attorney from the Honorable Lord Director General, Petrus Stuyvesant, plaintiff, vs. Juriaen Westphael, defendant. Plaintiff demands from defendant payment of the sum of ten hundred and four guilders, by virtue of a previous judgment, dated December 27, 1663, and says that one hundred and six schepels of winter wheat have been paid on the same. Requests execution for the balance.

The Honorable Court grants plaintiff's said demand for execution.

Hester Douwesen, plaintiff, vs. Cornelis Barentse Slecht, defendant. Plaintiff demands from defendant, on balance of account, twenty-one and one-half schepels of wheat. Defendant admits the debt, but says he paid on the same five schepels of wheat and one guilder in seewan.

The Honorable Court orders defendant to pay plaintiff the balance of said demand.

Hester Douwesen, plaintiff, vs. Pieter Jacobsen, defendant. Plaintiff demands from defendant thirty-four and one-half schepels of wheat, pursuant to a previous judgment and sentence, dated June 5, 1663, and requests payment. Defendant admits the debt, but says he delivered seven schepels of wheat on account.

The Honorable Court orders defendant to pay plaintiff the balance, pursuant to the said judgment.

Hester Douwesen, plaintiff, vs. Evert Pels, defendant. Absent. Default.

Hester Douwesen, plaintiff, vs. Aert Jacobsen, defendant. Plaintiff demands from defendant, as balance of account, seventeen schepels of wheat. Defendant answers, he paid to the cooper, for a tub belonging to both of them, four schepels of wheat as her half share, and also that he delivered to her one-quarter of a keg of beer.

The Honorable Court orders the parties to have their accounts adjusted by impartial men, if possible, or otherwise to again apply to the Court.

Hester Douwesen, plaintiff, vs. Willem van Vredenborch, defendant. Absent. Default.

Nicolaes Meyer, plaintiff, vs. Jan Jansen van Amersfort, defendant. Absent. Default. As the defendant is absent, plaintiff requests that an extraordinary session may be ordered for his benefit against defendant. The Honorable Court grants plaintiff's foregoing request.

Nicolaes Meyer, plaintiff, vs. Harmen Hendericksen, defendant. Plaintiff demands from defendant twenty-seven guilders, ten stivers, in beavers, to be paid in wheat at market value at Wildwyck, and to be delivered at the Manhatans, according to obligation, and also demands fourteen guilders, ten stivers, in seewan, according to the same obligation. Requests payment and expenses thereunder. Defendant admits owing plaintiff the aforesaid amounts.

The Honorable Court orders defendant to pay plaintiff the aforesaid amounts, according to obligation, and to pay the Court expenses here.

Dirrickje Jans, plaintiff, vs. Jan Jansen van Amersfort, defendant. Absent. Default.

Ensign Christiaen Niessen complains to the Honorable Court, that Jacobus Backer purposes to-day to send out one Mattys Roelofsen, without previous notice to the Council of War and Honorable Court here, and that he told him that he had authority from the Honorable Lord Director General to send him to the mountains and therefore forbids the aforenamed Ensign to detain him. Whereupon the Honorable Court forbids Mattys Roelofsen or his people, under penalty of arrest, to travel from this place in a canoe to any savage nation, unless Jacobus Backer can show the Magistrates or Council of War here orders from the Supreme Magistrates.

Jacobus Backer, appearing before the Honorable Court with Mattys Roelofsen, in consequence of the foregoing order against Mattys Roelofsen, whereby he and his are directed not to travel in a canoe to any nation of savages, answers that he has a special order from the Honorable Lord Director General to dispatch said Mattys Roelofsen to the mountains, and that he is not obliged to show said order to the Magistrates or Council of War here, unless they are authorized thereto, as his order must remain secret, and he assumes responsibility for all the consequences.

The Honorable Court, having heard the foregoing statement of Jacobus Backer, permits him to execute the secret order received by him.

Jacob Joosten, Court Messenger, asks the Honorable Court for thirty or forty guilders, in seewan, for his services.

As there is no money in the treasury, the petition is denied for the present.

The Schout, Roelof Swartwout, shows the Court three ordinances which he brought from the Manhatans, one concerning the desecration of the Sabbath, the second concerning lessees and lessors of land, the third concerning the fencing in and impounding of cattle, and requests that the same be published and also that the previous ordinances of August 4, 1663, be renewed and published.

The Commissaries consent that the ordinances taken along by

the Schout be read and posted, also that the ordinance dated August 4, 1663 be renewed and published.

Jan Hendericks van Bael, plaintiff, vs. Hermannus Blom, defendant. Absent. Default.

Albert Gerretsen asks of the Honorable Court that execution may continue against Annetje Tacks, as the barn has been advertised for sale under execution on April 3, next.

The Honorable Court orders the Doorkeeper, after the expiration of the time, to continue the execution, as usual.

Tjerck Claesen deWit, plaintiff, vs. Evert Pels, defendant. Absent. Default.

Henderick Jochemsen states to the Honorable Court that the Burgher Guard meets at his home, which is therefore used as a guard house, in consequence of which he is deprived of his liberty because of the quarrels of the guardsmen, and he is also not able to use his house as he wishes. He asks the Honorable Court to please direct the guard to remove from his house.

The Honorable Court, having heard foregoing request, agrees with the aforesaid Henderick Jochemsen that, as there are no materials for a guard house at hand, and no money at present in the treasury to purchase materials and build a guard house, the Burghery may one month longer use his house for the Burgher Guard, and promises to pay him therefor twenty guilders, in zeewan.

Cornelis Barentse Slecht petitions the Court to be permitted to build on the lot of Aert Jacobsen Otterspoor, beyond the Mill Gate, as his term expires May next, and he must have a dwelling house.

The Honorable Court refers to its previous decision.

Mr. Gysbert van Imborch petitions the Honorable Court that the execution against Annetje Tacks may be continued, as Albert Gerretsen has delayed the execution against his sold horse.

The Honorable Court adheres to its judgment rendered March 11, last.

On this April 3, Jan Evertsen declares he has attached in the hands of Pieter Jacobsen the balance of the money the latter owes Hester Douwesen, so as to obtain thereby full payment from Hester Douwesen, against whom he has been granted execution upon two kettles in the hands of Aert Jacobsen and also on his entire demand of April 1, 1664.

We, the undersigned, Albert Gysbertsen and Tjerck Claesen de Wit, Commissaries of the village of Wildwyck, make known that before us appeared the worthy Jan Jansen van Amersfort, inhabitant of Wildwyck, who acknowledges that he really and truly owes Mr. Nicolaes deMeyer, burgher and inhabitant of the city of Amsterdam in New Netherland, the sum of one hundred and twelve guilders, in beavers, at eight guilders a piece, with ten per cent. per annum interest thereon from March 27, of the year 1662, to final payment, and also the sum of ninety-seven guilders, in seewan, with ten per cent. per annum interest thereon from April 3, of the year 1664, to final payment, which aforesaid two amounts, the aforesaid sum of one hundred and twelve guilders, in beavers, with interest thereon, and the ninety-seven guilders, in seewan, or wheat, the schepel reckoned at six guilders, at the option of the above named Nicolaes de Meyer, the appearer promises to pay to the aforesaid Nicolaes de Meyer in the month of October of the current year, free of expense or damage, at the Manhatans. For the carrying out of these presents, he, the appearer, specially mortgages his house and lot situated in Wildwyck, and his farm land lying below the village of Wildwyck, which he, the appearer, says is unencumbered, and also, in general, his person and other estates, real and personal, present and future, placing the same under the jurisdiction of all courts and judges. And thereupon the appearer, with us, personally signed these presents. Done at Wildwyck this April 3, 1664.

JAN JANSEN,

The mark (x) of ALBERT GYSBERTSEN,

TIERCK CLASZEN DE WITT.

In my presence. To which I certify.

MATTHEUS CAPITO, Secretary.

On November 24, 1666, the foregoing mortgage was satisfied by substitution of Capt. Tomes Chamberssen, and by an accepted obligation binding himself to pay at the earliest shipping opportunity.

NICOLAES D MEYER.

To me known.

MATTHEUS CAPITO, Secretary.

Hester Douwesen requests execution against Pieter Jacobsen, pursuant to judgment rendered April 1, after the Court Messenger served three citations.

The Honorable Court orders the Doorkeeper to proceed with the execution.

The mark (x) of ALBERT GYSBERTSEN,

TIERCK CLASZEN DE WITT,

THOMAS CHAMBERS,

GYSBERT VAN IMBROCH.

Johanna de Laet, wife of Jeronimus Ebbing, has legally placed with Frederick Philipsen an attachment upon the purchase money for a lot bought by him, at Wildwyck, from Cornelis Barentsen Slecht, and gives notice of the aforesaid attachment.

Jacob Burhans, Collector of the Excise, has legally placed with Aert Jacobsen an attachment against Hester Douwesen who has a claim against Aert Jacobsen, and gives notice of the aforesaid attachment.

On April 3, Anna Bloems attached, through the Court Messenger, two brandy kettles in the hands of Aert Jacobsen, belonging to Hester Douwesen, and gave notice this day.

On April 4, Paulus Cornelissen attached, through the Court Messenger, everything that Hester Douwesen might have at Pieter Jacobsen's.

On April 4, while engaged with the Secretary at Cornelis Barentsen Slecht's house, a dispute arose between the Schout, Roelof Swartwout, and the Commissary, Tjerck Claesen de Wit, and, following it, blows were struck. The aforesaid Schout drew his sword against the Commissary, and challenged him to come outside. Wherefore, the Commissary, Gysbert van Imborch, demands, on the Lord's account, a fine from both. There were present, Ensign Christiaen Niessen, Nicolaes de Meyer, and Commissary Thomas Chambers.

We, the undersigned, Albert Gysbertsen and Tjerck Claesen de Wit, Commissaries of the village of Wildwyck, make known that before us appeared the worthy Roelof Swartwout, resident of Wildwyck, who acknowledges that he really and truly owes Mr. Nicolaes de Meyer, burgher and inhabitant of the city of Amsterdam in New Netherland, the amount of thirty-five schepels of winter wheat, due for merchandise and goods received, with ten per cent. interest thereon per annum, from December 3, of the year 1663, to final payment. And he promises to pay said thirty-five schepels of winter wheat to the aforesaid Nicolaes de Meyer at the Manhatans, on October 1, of the year written below, free of expense or damage. And for the carrying out of these presents, he, the appearer, binds and especially mortgages his house and lot, situated at Wildwyck, and his lands lying below the new village, and also, in general, his person and goods, real and personal, present and future, nothing excepted, submitting them to the jurisdiction of all courts and judges. And the appearer, with us, thereupon personally signed these presents, at Wildwyck, this April 4, of the year 1664.

ROELOOF SWARTWOUT,
The mark (x) of ALBERT GYSBERTSEN,
TIERCK CLASZEN DE WITT,
In my presence. To which I certify.
MATTHEUS CAPITO, Secretary.

The foregoing, signed by Roelof Swartwout, annuls all obligations entered into up to this date, from which I discharge him through this, my signature, when the foregoing is paid. Done at Wildwyck, this April 4, 1664.

NICOLAES D MEYER.
To my knowledge. To which I certify.
MATTHEUS CAPITO, Secretary.

Election held March 31, 1664, by a plurality of votes, for the purpose of sending two delegates from the village of Wildwyck to the Manhatans, to a formal Assembly.

Whereas, according to a written invitation of the Director General and Council of New Netherland to the Schout and Commissaries here, dated March 18, last, it was requested that two delegates from our village of Wildwyck be sent to a formal gathering of an Assembly, the Schout and Commissaries have therefore called upon us, the undersigned inhabitants of Wildwyck, to meet together on the day named below, to select two able persons of the community, and to depute them as delegates to the said meeting which is to take place on April 10. We have therefore selected, by a plurality of votes, the worthy persons, Thomas Chambers and Gysbert van Imborch, to whom we hereby give full power and authority to do what may be necessary for the common interest and that of this place, and also to act in any matter as shall seem to them advisable, confirming what they, the delegates may, according to their obligation, have lawfully done for the common welfare. For which purpose we have personally subscribed to these presents, at Wildwyck, this March 31, 1664.

(Signed)   The mark (x) of Albert Gysbertsen, Tjerck Claesen deWitt, Cornelis Barentsen Slecht, Evert Pels, Albert Gysbertsen, the mark (x) of Juriaen Westphael, the mark (x) of Jan Willemse Hoochteylingh, Aert Jacobs, the mark (x) of Ariaen Gerrtesen van Vliet, the mark (AMD) of Aert Martensen Doorn, the mark (x) of Pieter Jacobsen, the mark (x) of Mattys Roelofsen, the mark (x) of Jan Broersen, the mark (x) of Jacob Barents Cool, Henderick Jochemsen.

Accords with the original.   To which I certify.

MATTHEUS CAPITO, Secretary.

On April 11, Emmetje Volckerts, to obtain her dues, legally attached, in the hands of Aert Jacobsen, everything that Evert Prys can claim of Aert Jacobsen, and gives notice of the attachment.

We, the undersigned, Tjerck Claesen deWit, and Gysbert van Imborch, Commissaries of the village of Wildwyck, make known that before us appeared the worthy Albert Gysbertsen, inhabitant of Wildwyck, who acknowledged that on the date below named, he bought and received from the worthy Cornelis Wyncoop two horses for the sum of four hundred guilders in wheat, the schepel to be reckoned at forty-five stivers. Which aforesaid four hundred guilders the appearer receives at ten per cent interest per annum, for four successive years, commencing on the day below written and ending May 1, 1668, and on his promise to pay annually to said Cornelis Wyncoop the interest due, and to return the principal, with annual interest, at the close and expiration of the four years. For the carrying out of these presents, he, the appearer, binds and specially mortgages twenty morgens [about two acres each] of arable land, lying below the village of Wildwyck and between the lands of Aert Jacobsen and Tjerck Claesen deWit, which he, appearer, says is unencumbered and unrestricted; and also, in general, he, the appearer, binds his person and other estate, real and personal, present and future, nothing excepted, submitting the same to the jurisdiction of all courts and judges, and thereupon the appearer with us personally signed these presents. Done at Wildwyck, this May 1, 1664.

This is the mark (x) of Albert Gysbertsen,

Tierck Claszen de Witt,

Gysbert van Imbroch.

On this May 5, 1664, before the honorable Court at Wildwyck, there being then present the Schout, Roelof Swartwout, and the Commissaries, Albert Gysbertsen, Tjerck Claesen deWit, Thomas Chambers and Gysbert van Imborch, appeared the worthy persons, Jan Cornelisen vander Heyde and Paulus Cornelisen, attorneys for Maritje, widow of Jan Barentsen Wemp, and informed the aforesaid Honorable Court of the following Lord's acknowledgement, with the request to enter the same in the minutes.   It reads word for word as follows:

Before me, Cornelis van Ruyven, Secretary in the service of the Honorable Chartered West India Company in New Netherland, appeared the worthy Aert Piertesen Tack who, in the presence of the Honorable Lord Councillors deSille and Johan de Decker, acknowledged that he is really and truly indebted to the worthy Jan Barentsen Poest as follows:

For two horses, in beaver's value......................	fl. 600
Another horse, 106 schepels of wheat, or in beavers......	fl. 318
For a cow	fl. 115
Also in beavers	fl. 200
Total, in beavers or beaver's value	fl. 1233
Also, for sewant received	fl. 300

Which sum of twelve hundred and thirty-three guilders, in beavers, or its value, and three hundred guilders in seewant, the said Aert Pietersen receives and promises to pay to the aforesaid Jan Barentsen or his attorney, within three years, paying each year a just third, with ten per cent. interest thereon from this day. To secure the aforesaid Jan Barentsen Poest in the full payment hereof, he, the appearer, mortgages and binds his farm lying in the Esopus, between Tjerck Claesen's and Jan Willemsen Schoon's, together with the dwelling house, barn and loft, four horses and one cow, and all other appurtenances thereunto belonging, nothing excepted, and also all his estate, real and personal, present and future, submitting the same to the jurisdiction of all judges and courts. In witness whereof, these presents were subscribed by the appearer in the presence of the above mentioned Lord Councillors at Fort Amsterdam in New Netherland, April 1, 1662. (Below stood) To my knowledge, Cornelis van Ruyven.

After comparison, this has been found to agree with the original. To which I certify.

MATTHEUS CAPITO, Secretary.

Ordinary Session, held Tuesday, May 6, 1664.

Present: Roelof Swartwout, Schout; Albert Gysbertsen, Tjerck Claesen deWit, Thomas Chambers, Gysbert van Imborch, Commissaries.

Johanna de Laet, wife of Jeronimus Ebbingh, plaintiff, vs. Cornelis Barentsen Slecht, defendant. Plaintiff states that, as the lease of the defendant has expired, she would like to arrange with him concerning what has been sown on the land, about which they can not agree.

Defendant requests that what shall be now found by impartial men to have been sown may be appraised. The Honorable Court grants defendant's request.

Plaintiff further demands from defendant, in addition to the bills recently presented, eight hundred guilders, according to contract, for rent from the year 1663, just passed.

Defendant presents an account against plaintiff for damage done and sustained during the said period, through the troubles caused by the savages, amounting to the sum of twenty-eight hundred and fifty guilders, and maintains that he is not liable for the payment of the full rent.

Mrs. de Laet, above mentioned, and Cornelis Barentsen Slecht, request the Honorable Court, as arbiters and good men, to give a decision to their mutual satisfaction, in the foregoing matter of the rent for the last year of the lease. Whereupon the aforesaid Honorable Court, as chosen arbiters, have decided, and it is mutual-

ly agreed by the parties, that Cornelis Barentse Slecht shall pay
Mrs. deLaet, as rent for the last year, the sum of five hundred
guilders, in beavers or corn, beaver's value, according to the contract.

Mrs. deLaet shows an extract from the record of the minutes
of the session of the Director General and Councillors in New Netherland, held April 17, 1664, wherein she asked for an attachment
of the moneys due from the Honorable Company to Cornelis Barentsen Slecht, which attachment was declared valid by their Right
Honorable Worships, and thereupon requests that Cornelis Barentsen be directed to give her an assignment [order] on the Company
for the remaining money attached by her, still held by the Company.

To this the defendant, Cornelis Barentsen Slecht, answers, that
he is not able to give an assignment, as he has already made an
assignment to some one else, viz., Frederick Philipsen, of about
three hundred guilders, in sewant, but, if any more should be
debited to him on the books of the Honorable Company, she shall
receive it from the Honorable Company.

Mrs. deLaet further requests that the judgment rendered
April 1, last, against the aforesaid defendant, be enforced by execution.

Defendant answers that the sown grain must first be appraised,
and maintains that until then the execution must be delayed, so as
to determine what he then must pay in satisfaction.

The Honorable Court refers the parties to good men, to be
selected by themselves, as mutually requested, to appraise what
has been sown, and after the appraisal to make up accounts on both
sides. And plaintiff is also authorized to proceed with the execution against defendant for what may then appear to be due for
the rent. Whereto also the Doorkeeper is directed by the Honorable
Court to act accordingly.

The Honorable Court having seen the request of Cornelis Barentsen Slecht to the Director General and Council of New Netherland, dated November 17, 1663, and the letter written concerning
the same by their Right Honorable Worships, the petitioner is,
in consequence thereof, ordered to show that Aert Otterspoor, from
the lot—

[End of Volume I, as extant—page 336.]

Extraordinary Session, Thursday, June 12, 1664.
    Present: Roelof Swartwout, Schout; Albert Gysbertsen,
Thomas Chambers, Gysbert Van Imbroch, Commissaries.
    Whereas on the 10th inst., at the request of the Rev.
Hermannus Blom, preacher at Wildwyck, his Reverence appeared before the hon. local court, where his Reverence
requested to receive an account of his salary for his
ministry at Wildwyck from the hon. court, therefore the
account was handed to him on the above date, and by which
it appears that at the expiration of his three years'
ministry a balance of 387 gldrs. 6 st. 12 pennies (387-6-
12) in beavers, to be paid in wheat, the sch. valued at
50 st. in beavers, was still coming to him. And whereas
his Reverence on said June 10 presented to the hon. court
a bill for the third /this may be the fourth/ year of his
ministry, amounting to 211 sch. of wheat, valued by his
Reverence at two gldrs. in beavers per sch., the hon.
court could not readily accept the same, because the sch.
is here bought and accepted at 50 st. in beavers by the
hon. company itself. On account of which affair his
Reverence uttered words against one of the court, several
times calling him a "snuyver" (one who sniffs),*and further
calling the other associates liars, and while going out
still saying the following words: "You do no less than
to take care that my salary does not come in," and further,
"If you cannot keep me, then let me go, and dismiss me."
But for the purpose of further negotiating with his
Reverence in a friendly spirit, in order to further have
him stay at Wildwyck, the hon. court is obliged to settle
with his Reverence the question concerning his salary, because so large a salary cannot be paid by the congregation, for reasons most of the residents on account of the
troubles with the savages, if not actually ruined, have at
least suffered very great losses. Taking into consideration that, just at present, the farm house /bouwerye, may
also mean building/ cannot be very well constructed by the
congregation. /He is, after the close of the four years _
of his ministry again offered 200 sch. of wheat annually./
The account having been presented to his Reverence, he
would not accept the same, but afterward, for the purpose
of the better examining the same, said account was kept
by him. Thus his Reverence has not been willing to again
come to an understanding with the hon. court in regard to
his salary, not until the four years of his ministry shall
have been closed.

[This page was out of place in the original records]

[Part of] BOOK II

[Court Records, June 24, 1664—November 18, 1664.]

Ordinary Session, Tuesday, June 24, 1664.

Present: Roelof Swartwout, Schout; Thomas Chambers, Gysbert van Imbroch, Jan Willemsen Hoochteylingh, Henderick Jochemsen, Commissaries.

The Schout shows the Honorable Court the note of the Council of War at Wildwyck, dated June 23, 1664, as more at large appears in the original. The Schout also shows to the Honorable Court a note of Captain Lieutenant Marten Cregier, dated June 13, 1664, from which it appears that the Honorable Court has been pleased to delay the farming out of the tapster excise until the further order of the Director General and Council of New Netherland.

Juriaen Westphael, plaintiff, vs. Albert Gysbertsen, defendant. Both absent. Both in default.

Juriaen Westphael, plaintiff, absent, default, vs. Tjerck Claesen deWit, defendant.

Tjerck Claesen deWit, plaintiff, vs. Roelof Swartwout, defendant.

Plaintiff demands sixty guilders, in beavers, from defendant, for pasturing three cows, also a bridle loaned him last year, valued at sixteen guilders in beavers, also a quantity of wood valued at three schepels of wheat and three guilders in seewan. Defendant denies pasturing three cows, but admits that plaintiff pastured two cows for him, and promises to return the bridle and pay the value of the quantity of wood. He admits he owes the three guilders, in seewan.

Plaintiff replies that, as a fine due to defendant, he had to pasture one cow, but was compelled therefor to pasture four cows for him. To this the defendant answers that he has a counter claim.

The Honorable Court orders defendant to submit his counter claim at its next session.

Tjerck Claesen deWit, plaintiff, vs. Cornelis Barentsen Slecht, defendant. Plaintiff requests that defendant, as in duty bound, shall and demands payment therefor, or another canoe instead.

Defendant admits he borrowed the canoe, and that he did not return it; adds that it was taken by Jan Willemsen's man and was used for the benefit of those who had to be on the arable land.

The Honorable Court orders that all of those who have land across the Kill shall indemnify the plaintiff, or else substitute another canoe, otherwise to apply to the Court.

Roelof Swartwout, Schout, plaintiff, vs. Tjerck Claesen de Wit, defendant.

Plaintiff, by a petition to the Honorable Court, requests that he be sustained, he having been scornfully treated by defendant, as appears by the petition, dated May 6, 1664.

Defendant admits he was fined in the field, but says that the Ensign promised a permanent convoy, and when, early one morning, his people went out to look for their horses, the convoy did not follow. The Ensign and the Schout were at that time with the convoy on Thomas Chambers' land to examine the burnt palisades set on fire by a soldier. On their return, the Ensign and the Schout both became intoxicated and then agreed that the Schout should go with the convoy to fine the defendant for ploughing in the field. Defendant denies he called plaintiff names or threatened him.

The Honorable Court orders plaintiff to submit his proofs in writing.

Roelof Swartwout, Schout, plaintiff, vs. Foppe Barents, defendant. Plaintiff demands from defendant fifteen schepels of wheat, according to obligation, dated May 8, 1664. Defendant admits the debt, but says that as soon as he receives his money from Tjerck Claesen he will pay plaintiff.

The Honorable Court orders defendant to pay plaintiff.

Roelof Swartwout, Schout, plaintiff, vs. Albert Gysbertsen, defendant. Plaintiff requests that defendant, as in duty bound, shall testify to the truth before the Honorable Court, with reference to the differences between plaintiff and Tjerck Claesen deWit, regarding the pasturing of plaintiff's cows, concerning which defendant testifies and declares that he knows that Tjerck Claesen deWit promised to pasture two cows for plaintiff, for which plaintiff was not to advance Tjerck Claesen any money.

Albert Gysbertsen requests that he be permitted to dig a saw-pit in front of his lot.

The Honorable Court grants petitioner's request, upon condition that he cover the saw-pit every evening, so that no accident may occur therefrom to man or beast, and that he fill it up before harvest time.

Foppe Barents, plaintiff, vs. Evert Pels, Allert Heymans Roose, absent, and Cornelis Barentsen Slecht, defendants.

Plaintiff demands from defendants the sum of fifteen guilders, eleven stivers, in seewan, being the balance for carpenter work on the parsonage at Wildwyck.

Cornelis Barentsen Slecht, appearing alone, says that judgment may be rendered and recorded against them, as Evert Pels, in Foppe Barents' presence, so verbally instructed him.

The Honorable Court finds that, as the retired Commissaries have never been willing to render an accounting to the newly installed Commissaries, and the new Commissaries know nothing about the receipts and expenditures, the credits or the debits, the newly installed Commissaries are therefore not willing to accept any bills until the retired Commissaries have rendered their accounts.

And for cause, the appearers, Cornelis Barentsen Slecht and Evert Pels, are ordered by the Honorable Court to pay the aforesaid demand of the plaintiff who is a country man and a stranger, and therefore must not be delayed.

Cornelis Barentsen Slecht requests the Honorable Court to please show him, after adjournment, where he may erect his dwelling house.

The Schout requests that, as many complaints have reached him regarding Henderick Jansen Looman's estate, the Honorable Court please order the curators of the said estate to render to it an accounting of the receipts and expenditures.

The Honorable Court orders the curators of the estate of Henderick Jansen Looman and Willem Jansen Seba to render at its next session an accounting of their curatorships.

Jan Cornelisen van der Heyde asks the Honorable Court to permit him to take along with him the horses for account of Aert Pietersen Tack, pursuant to directions from his mother-in-law, Marietje Meynderts.

The Honorable Court decides that petitioner must proceed according to law against the estate of Aert Pietersen Tack.

Paulus Cornelissen requests payment for the goods furnished for the parsonage at Wildwyck, and the freight.

Jacob Joosten, Court Messenger, requests payment for his services, or else to be released from such service.

The Honorable Court orders the petitioner to send in his bill to it.

Extraordinary Session, Thursday, July 10, 1664.

Present: Roelof Swartwout, Schout; Gysbert van Imborch, Jan Willemsen Hoochteylingh, Henderick Jochemsen, Commissaries.

Sweerus Teunissen, successor of Jan Barentsen Wemp, deceased, requests the Honorable Court to permit him to obtain his money from Aert Pietersen Tack who has absented himself from this place, as he is his principal creditor. And he further requests that the real and personal estate of Aert Pietersen Tack be sold under execution to satisfy his mortgage, especially as the risk of the horses, cattle and grain in the field operates to the prejudice of the creditors. Among these horses, also, is a mare, two years old, delivered by his predecessor, Jan Barentsen Wemp, to Aert Pietersen Tack, on the condition, previously stipulated in a contract dated September 7, 1661, that the purchaser should keep said mare, at the seller's risk, for six years and then return it to the seller. Wherefore, he, Sweerus Teunissen, requests possession of the horse and that Aert Pietersen Tack's claim be rated by impartial men. Requests speedy justice with reference to the foregoing, as he is a stranger.

The Honorable Court decides, that, as Aert Pietersen Tack has absented himself, and his wife, not wishing to have anything further to do with the estate, has had an inventory made thereof, he shall be summoned according to law, either by ringing of bell or on holidays. But having learned that the grain in the field, the horses and the cattle are held at great risk to the creditors, the Honorable Court therefore decides to sell these at auction to the highest bidder next Monday, July 14, and to hold the proceeds on deposit as provisional security. The real estate, the Honorable Court decides, shall, after due citation and non appearance of Aert Pietersen Tack, be sold at auction to the highest bidder. Regarding the request for the possession of the mare, the Honorable Court decides that said claim shall be appraised by impartial appraisers, and for that purpose Evert Pels and Aert Jacobsen are chosen to appraise the same as near as possible according to its value; all this being in accordance with the contract relating thereto.

Extraordinary Session, Monday, July 14, 1664.

Present: Willem Beeckman, Schout; Thomas Chambers, Gysbert van Imbroch, Jan Willemsen Hoochteylingh, Henderick Jochemsen, Commissaries.

The Commissioner and Schout, Willem Beeckman, exhibits the commission and instructions given to him by the Honorable Lord Director General and Council of New Netherland.

In clauses seven and eight of these instructions provisions regarding the farming out of the tapster and burgher excise are included, which farming out is postponed to a more propitious time because of the troublous and deplorable condition of the country.

The Honorable Schout suggested that the fortifications be properly completed and repaired, as the savages are again gathering up the river. Also that six or seven of the free men should watch, as the garrison at present is weak. It was resolved to commence work tomorrow.

It was further suggested by Captain Thomas Chambers, that the free men are entirely unprovided with powder and shot, and he therefore requested of Commissioner Beeckman that powder and shot be furnished. This was agreed to, upon condition that, if the Director General and Council require payment therefor, the same shall be made; which was accepted, and that the seven or eight men are to watch.

Swerus Teunissen, appearing, requests that the sale of the grain lying in the field, and the horses and cattle of his debtor, Aert

Pietersen Tack, may proceed, according to the decision of the Court, dated July 10.

Thomas Chambers says he was not present on July 10, and is of opinion that Aert Pietersen Tack must first be condemned according to law, ere his property can be sold under execution.

Mr. Gysbert, Jan Willemsen and Henderick Jochemsen are of the same opinion, but for reasons set forth in the decision of July 10, adhere to their resolution.

The matter having been reviewed, it is decided, for cause, that the sale shall proceed, if reasonable prices are obtainable thereat.

On July 14, the eleven schepels of sown wheat and the additions in the field, together with the horses and cattle, were offered for sale at auction, but were withdrawn by the Honorable Court, as their value could not be reached or realized and this would be very prejudicial to the general creditors. And Swerus Teunissen asks that the horses and cattle be held back until the time appointed for the sale of the farm, the which is consented to.

Ordinary Session, Tuesday, July 22, 1664.

Present: Willem Beeckman, Schout; Thomas Chambers, Gysbert van Imbroch, Jan Willem Hoochteylingh, Henderick Jochemsen, Commissaries.

Juriaen Westphael, plaintiff, vs. Tjerck Claesen deWit, and Albert Gysbertsen, defendants. Plaintiff demands a balance of one hundred and twenty-seven and one-half schepels of wheat from defendants as curators of the estate of Henderick Jansen Looman, appointed by the Honorable Court.

Defendants refer to their account book, exhibited to the Honorable Court, wherefrom it appears that there are more creditors, and the estate apparently will be in debt.

The Honorable Court decides that plaintiff shall receive the whole of his claim relating to the horse, and that for the balance of his account he must share with the other creditors.

Tjerck Claesen deWit, plaintiff, vs. Roelof Swartwout, defendant. Plaintiff still insists upon his former demand of June 24, 1664. Defendant, pursuant to the order of the Honorable Court, exhibits a counter account.

The parties are referred to Evert Pels and Allert Heymans, to bring about, under the supervision of Commissary Henderick Jochemsen, an agreement, if possible, or, otherwise, to report to the Honorable Court.

Roelof Swartwout, plaintiff, vs. Albert Gysbertsen, defendant.

Plaintiff still demands a fine from defendant for violating the ordinance with reference to not going out to plough or work without a convoy.

Defendant says he is ready to prove that he asked Ensign Niessen for a convoy, which the latter promised but did not send.

The case is adjourned to the next session.

FARMING OF THE BURGHER EXCISE.

Terms and conditions upon which the Messieurs Schout and Schepens of the village of Wildwyck, in New Netherland, with the approval of the Right Worshipful Lords, the Director General and Council of New Netherland, intend, according to the laudable custom and order of our Fatherland, to farm out to the highest bidder the burgher excise on wine and beer to be consumed within the jurisdiction of the aforesaid village, by all officers as well as by ordinary burghers, except the Supreme Government and Ministers of the Divine Word.

The one who becomes Farmer of the said excise shall receive from all officers as well as ordinary burghers and inn-keepers, none but those hereinbefore mentioned excepted, as excise for the wines and the beer to be consumed by them:

For an anker of brandy, Spanish wine, distilled waters or others of the same quality, thirty stivers.

For an anker of French wine, Rhine wine, wormwood wine or others of the same quality, fifteen stivers, a hogshead to be reckoned as five ankers.

For a tun of good beer, one guilder.

For a tun of small beer, six stivers.

Larger or smaller casks in proportion.

The impost shall be laid and the excise be paid to the Farmer, between August 17, 1664, and August 10, 1665. No excise shall be received after the date last above mentioned.

The excise shall be paid to the Farmer in good braided sewan, at twelve white or six black beads for one stiver.

The Farmer must promptly every three months pay the lawful quarter of the amount promised for the farming, in good current payment, at twelve white or six black beads for one stiver.

The Farmer must furnish for the promised farming price two sufficient money sureties.

	Tjerck Claesen bids	fl.	50
	Tomas Harmens bids	fl.	75
	Tjerck Claesen bids	fl.	100
	Tomas Harmens bids	fl.	125
	Evert Pels bids	fl.	150
Received fl. 3 seewan	Roelof Swartwout bids	fl.	175
Received fl. 3 seewan	Evert Pels bids	fl.	200
Received fl. 3 seewan	Tomas Harmensen bids	fl.	225
Received fl. 3 seewan	" " bids	fl.	250
Received fl. 6 seewan	Roelof Swartwout bids	fl.	275
Received fl. 6 seewan	Tomas Harmensen bids	fl.	300
Received fl. 6 seewan	" " bids	fl.	325
Received fl. 9 seewan	" " bids	fl.	350

Being put up at [Dutch] auction,* with a limit of three hundred guilders,** (received another nine guilders seewan), Tomas Harmensen becomes the Farmer for the sum of three hundred and fifty-seven guilders, and furnishes as sureties Tjerck Claesen deWit and Walran du Mont, jointly and severally, as principals, all of whom together have subscribed, this August 16, 1664, at Wildwyck.

(Subscribed)   Tomas Harmens, Tjerck Claesen deWit, Walran du Mont.

(Below)

In my presence.

WILLEM BEECKMAN.

On this August 18, Evert Pels and Albert Heymans reported, in regard to the arbitration between Roelef Swartwout and Tjerck Claesen deWit, that there was no prospect of bringing about an agreement between them.

---

*The auctioneer beginning with a high price, and gradually reducing it till he receives a bid.

**As the lowest price.

The Schout and Schepens here give notice and command, that henceforth no inn-keeper or vender of wine and beer shall be allowed to sell until, following the custom in our Fatherland, he shall have obtained from the Honorable Court a license for said business, which every inn-keeper shall renew quarter yearly and for which he shall pay every time for the use of the respective judges one pound Flemish, under penalty of suspension of his business for open and wilful neglect. Done at Wildwyck this August 19, 1664.

The Schout and Schepens further order that those who make a business of brewing and of distilling brandy, shall henceforth no longer tap or sell wine by measure, on pain of confiscation of the broached liquor and fine of fifty guilders for each violation discovered. Done at Wildwyck, August 19, 1664. (Signed) Willem Beeckman.

It was resolved by the Honorable Court at Wildwyck that the burghery and inhabitants shall again keep watch, as, owing to the approach of the English, the militia have been relieved therefrom by the Director General and Council. Done at Wildwyck, this September 1, 1664. (Signed) Willem Beeckman.

Extraordinary Session, Wednesday, September 4, 1664.

Present : Willem Beeckman, Schout : Gysbert van Imbroch, Jan Willemsen Hoochteylingh, Henderick Jochemsen, Commissaries.

On the proposition made by the Honorable Schout what to do in case the English should approach our village of Wildwyck, it is resolved that, at the discharge of a cannon, all the burghery shall repair to the head watch, there to receive further orders, and that in the meantime the Honorable Schout, together with the Honorable Court, shall seek to parley with said English beyond the gates. Meanwhile, the burgher officers are recommended to ascertain what powder and shot there are among the burghery, as we can not tell how the savages will act in these circumstances. Thus done by the Schout and Commissaries at Wildwyck, the day and year above mentioned.

Ordinary Session, Tuesday, October 7, 1664.

Present; Willem Beeckman, Schout; Thomas Chambers, Jan Willemsen Hoochteylingh, Commissaries.

Emmetje Volckerts, plaintiff, vs. Jacob Barentsen Cool, defendant. Plaintiff demands from defendant an amount of thirty-five schepels of wheat, two guilders, ten stivers, in sewan, whereof, according to her account, one schepel of wheat and four guilders, ten stivers, have been paid.

Defendant and his wife deny a portion of the debt, and thereupon submit items of a counter reckoning.

The Honorable Court directs the parties to Roelof Swartwout and Walran du Mont, good men, to bring the parties to an agreement, if possible, and, if not, to report to the Honorable Court.

Walran du Mont, plaintiff, absent, default, vs. Jacob Barentsen Cool, defendant.

Walran du Mont, plaintiff, absent, default, vs. Dirrick Hendericksen, defendant. Absent. Default.

Jan Tyssen, plaintiff, vs. Annetje Ariaens Tack, defendant. Plaintiff demands from defendant, for wages for two and one-half months, seventy guilders, heavy money, and thereupon has attached, at Thomas Chambers', as many schepels of wheat as long Jacob, the defendant's servant, has earned with the aforesaid Thomas Chambers.

Defendant refers the matter to the estate, because the wages earned by the plaintiff were earned under her husband, and she maintains that the wages earned by her servant with Thomas Chambers are due to her.

The Honorable Court decides that, as the wages of defendant's servant, earned with Thomas Chambers, were concealed, the same shall be transferred to the estate, and plaintiff shall stand on a par with the other creditors after the sale of Aert Pietersen Tack's property.

Thomas Harmensen, plaintiff, vs. Sara Gillissen, defendant. Plaintiff demands from defendant the full fine due for smuggling, and also the wine he found with her at her place.

Defendant answers she did not know that there was so much wine in the anker, that there should have been, according to her mother, about twenty cans of wine, and now there have been found about twenty-four cans.

The Honorable Court decides the wine to be a prize, and thereupon, on the Farmer's demand for two hundred guilders, impose upon the defendant a fine of one hundred guilders in sewan, to be duly applied.

Mattheus Capito, plaintiff, vs. Jan Lootman and Michael Verbrugge, defendants.

Plaintiff says that some time ago, at the house of Walran du Mont, he was insulted by the defendants, who said he had caused them loss by overcharging their account with the Company.

Michael Verbrugge answers that in his account there have been deducted by the Honorable Secretary van Ruyven a blanket and two pair of fine stockings, which he should have received from Mattheus Capito in the Esopus, as appears by his books.

Jan Lootman answers that about one hundred guilders were deducted on his account, and that, complaining about this, the Honorable Secretary van Ruyven referred to the books at Esopus or the keeper thereof.

The parties are referred to the bookkeeper of the Honorable Company and to the Honorable Secretary van Ruyven, in order to settle their differences.

Tjerck Claesen deWit, plaintiff, vs. Roelof Swartwout, defendant. Plaintiff sues for the pasturing of three cows, according to the demand of June 29, last.

Defendant admits that plaintiff pastured two cows for him, for which he ought to pay like any one else, and that plaintiff was to pasture two more cows for him, in payment of the fine due from him, under an agreement with him made in the presence of Albert Gysbertsen who, on June 29, last, testified and stated before the Honorable Court, and now confirms under oath, that Tjerck Claesen was to pasture for defendant two cows in payment of the fine due.

The Honorable Court again refers the parties to the decision of Everts Pels and Allert Heymans, good men, to bring the parties to an agreement, if possible, or else to report to the Honorable Court.

Roelof Swartwout, plaintiff, vs. Tjerck Claesen de Wit, defendant. Plaintiff declares he has attached fifteen schepels of wheat of Foppe Barents in the hands of defendant, whereupon defendant told the Village Messenger that he had assigned to his brother-in-law, Jan Tomassen, at Fort Orange, his claim on account of the aforesaid fifteen schepels of wheat of Foppe Barentsen.

Defendant admits that he verbally assigned the above mentioned fifteen schepels of wheat to his brother-in-law, Jan Tomassen.

Roelof Swartwout further says that for this he also lawfully arrested Foppe Barentsen, and that said Foppe Barentsen, after said arrest, went away.

Extraordinary Session, Saturday, October 18, 1664.

Present: Willem Beeckman, Schout; Thomas Chambers, Gysbert van Imbroch, Jan Willemsen Hoochteylingh, Commissaries.

The Honorable Schout asks how the minister's salary is to be paid.

It is resolved that the old and first book of the retired Commissaries be first made up, so as to show the situation to the newly appointed Commissaries. It is further resolved, that, in accordance with the previous order of the Honorable Director General, every resident householder shall, for each year of the past four years, contribute towards the minister's salary one guilder for every morgen, and other inhabitants ten guilders, heavy money, in wheat, for every single lot at Wildwyck, the schepel to be reckoned at fifty stivers, and that the inhabitants shall be commanded herein to make payment within three weeks, on pain of [issuance of] execution.

The Honorable Schout submits:

1. That it is necessary to send some of the Honorable Judges to the Manhatans, to ask of the Governor there a warrant of authority for the continuance of the Court here.

2. Also, that the farming of the beer and wine excise be continued until the village debt, caused by the heavy wars, shall have been paid.

3. Further, that the delegates arrange with the Governor there with reference to the quartering of soldiers at Wildwyck.

4. And further, that the delegates also ask for linen and blankets for the soldiers quartered here, who have made request therefor, as the inhabitants here are unable to provide them therewith, because a great deal has been destroyed by the heavy war.

5. Also, that, pursuant to the articles of peace concluded with them, the savages be not permitted to come or trade on this

side of the Kill near the Redoubt, nor on the lands about the village.

Upon the foregoing propositions, there are chosen from the Magistrates the Honorable Officer, Willem Beeckmen, and Schepen, Jan Willemsen Hoochteylingh, who are herewith commissioned and authorized to promote the said propositions with the Governor at New York, as they are considered necessary for this place.

The Commissary, Gysbert van Imbroch, requests that as, at the late Assembly, he and Thomas Chambers, delegates for the village of Wildwyck, incurred expenses and lost their own time, the money be promptly paid them by the inhabitants, according to contract with the latter, as also their expenses for clerical work at the Manhatans.

The Honorable Court decides that the inhabitants be ordered to pay the foregoing demand and debt, within fourteen days.

Ordinance forbidding trade with the savages on this side of the Kill near the Redoubt.

Whereas, the Honorable Court at Wildwyck has been informed that some of the residents here have attempted to sell to, or buy from, the savages, meats or other merchandise on this side of the Kill near the Redoubt, by which acts the savages have been encouraged to show themselves in and near the village and dwelling houses here, in violation of the wholesome articles of peace, the Honorable Court, therefore, in order to guard against any calamity, hereby prohibits any one here to attempt to trade with the savages on this side of the above named Kill, under a penalty of one hundred guilders for the first offense, double for the second, and arbitrary punishment for the third, one-third of the above stated fine to go to the informer. Thus enacted at a meeting of Schout and Schepens of the village of Wildwyck, this October 18, 1664.

October 20, 1664.

The Magistrates of the village of Wildwyck again announce that all those importing any strong drink into this place shall, before delivering the same to any house, obtain a permit from the Farmer, and then, before being allowed to sell the same at retail, obtain from the Secretary a license and pay therefor six guilders, and to the Farmer the excise. Said license must also be renewed every three months by those who hold them, who shall, each time, pay one pound Flemish therefor.

Ordinary Session, Tuesday, October 21, 1664.

Present: Willem Beeckman, Schout; Thomas Chambers, Gysbert van Imbroch, Jan Willemsen Hoochteylingh, Commissaries.

Henderick Cornelissen, rope maker, plaintiff, vs. Sara Gillissen, defendant.

Plaintiff says that defendant's mother is indebted to him in the sum of forty guilders, in sewan, and six schepels of wheat, under an assignment by Jan Barentsen Ameshof.

Defendant answers that she is not indebted to defendant, and that plaintiff must therefore look to her mother for the aforesaid claim.

The Honorable Court denies plaintiff's claim on the defendant. And if defendant's mother should have any goods or outstanding debts here, plaintiff may then attach said debts and goods, and pursue his claim thereon.

Magdalena Dirricks, plaintiff, vs. Dirrick Storm, defendant. Plaintiff says that defendant has appropriated the effects of the barber, Marten van der Hage, and that plaintiff claims thereof three schepels of wheat as pay for washing, as her husband was referred by the said barber at the Manhatans to these very goods.

Defendant in reply exhibits a letter of attorney from Marten van der Hage regarding the seizure of the chest, and says that he paid said van der Hage, at the Manhatans, about thirty guilders above his claim of the twenty-eight guilders.

Defendant, having been asked whether he is willing to accept the trunk and to pay plaintiff's claim, answers, No, and says that he wishes to speak with plaintiff about it, and thereupon stepped out.

Dirrick Storm, plaintiff, vs. Albert Jansen van Steenwyck, defendant. Plaintiff, under a power of attorney from Roelof Harmensen, demands from defendant payment of three schepels of wheat.

Defendant admits his indebtedness to Roelof Harmensen and adds that Roelof Harmensen also gave a power of attorney to Andries Pietersen, who accepted it.

The Honorable Court decides that defendant pay to plaintiff the aforesaid demand, for the reason that Andries Pietersen did not prosecute his case before the Honorable Court.

Whereas, the old retired Commissaries have several times been admonished to liquidate the village accounts, they are therefore hereby again ordered and directed either to do so, or to have the same done, within eight days, under penalty of fifty guilders.

Whereas, the Honorable Schout and Schepens of the village of Wildwyck feel concerned over the delay in making up the village accounts, and understand that Roelof Swartwout, retired Schout, is negligent in giving up papers, and information relative thereto, said Roelof Swartwout, is therefore ordered immediately to deliver up all such account papers and documents relating to the village of Wildwyck, and, with the old Commissaries, to report to the Secretary, to make up the old accounts of the village.

Jacob Jansen van Etten, farm hand of Aert Pietersen Tack, requests that he also be paid out of the estate of Aert Pietersen Tack, according to account rendered.

Honorable Mr. Beeckman.

Whereas, the Commissaries understand that your Honor has been ordered to send to the Manhatans the powder and shot belonging to the Honorable Company still here, we, the Commissaries, therefore, deeming its necessary to the welfare of the village, request that your Honor be pleased to leave the packages of powder and shot here, until the English Governor at the Manhatans shall have sent us other packages of powder and shot, because, among the congregation or inhabitants here, no powder or shot can be found or procured, so that, in case of unexpected danger from the savages, the inhabitants may be provided therewith. Awaiting your Honor's written and immediate reply.

Done at Wildwyck at a meeting of the Commissaries, this October 27, 1664.

On October 27, Evert Prys lawfully attached [property of] Jonas Rantsou, and hereby gives notice of said attachment.   ,

Under date of November 6, Cornelis Cornelissen Vernoy lawfully attached twenty guilders, in sewan, in the hands of Jan Jansen Oosterhout for Jonas Rantsou, and hereby gives notice thereof.

Extraordinary Session, Friday, November 14, 1664.

The Officer, Willem Beeckman, reported to the Honorable Court what had been accomplished by him and the Commissary,

Jan Willemsen Hoochteylingh, at the Manhatans, with the Governor General, and thereover showed the Court a Warrant given him by the aforesaid Governor. The Honorable Court thereupon resolved to publish said Warrant to the community, which, translated from English into Dutch, reads as follows:—

Regarding the welfare and the tranquility of matters in the Esopus, the following instructions are hereby ordered to be published and observed:

1. That the present officers and Schepens shall on all occasions, as heretofore, be obeyed as authorities, until the contrary appears over my signature.

2. That the minister's arrears be promptly paid, and he shall continue his service as heretofore.

3. That no one shall sell brandy or liquor to the savages, under penalty of five hundred guilders.

4. That the Indians or savages shall be permitted to peacefully enter the Esopus or the village of Wildwyck during the day time, to sell venison and other merchandise, and that no evil or injury be done them, because I have agreed with the Sachems, for themselves as well as for their subjects, that no injury or violence shall be done to the subjects of his Majesty of England.

5. That the soldiers shall be quartered by the Magistrates in the houses of the inhabitants, to whom I shall give good pay, to be fixed by agreement.

6. That the inhabitants and the soldiers shall dwell together in amity and friendship, so that, in occasions or time of need, they may act together as one man.

7. In case any difference should occur between a soldier and an inhabitant, the same shall, after complaint to the officers or Magistrates, be settled and decided by the officers and Magistrates alone.

Given over my signature, October 26, Old Style, 1664, at Fort James, in New York.

(Signed)   RICHARD NICOLA [NICOLLS].

It was also proposed, and thereupon resolved, that, by public notice to the inhabitants here of the mischief and damage that may result from fire, the householders living near the Mill gate shall be forbidden to carry their straw and rubbish, for the purpose of being burnt, close to the village palisades, but shall rather take the same across the Mill dam. Whereupon the following placard was posted:

Whereas, experience teaches us the impropriety of throwing out straw and rubbish and of burning the same close by the palisades, wherefrom great danger from fire may be expected, the Schout and Schepens therefore order that straw and rubbish shall be carted across the Mill dam by those living near the Mill gate, under the penalty heretofore fixed for that purpose. Further, all inhabitants here are directed to clear the streets, within four days, of straw and rubbish, so that, through the carrying of a light or the blowing out of a pipe of tobacco, a conflagration, such as the one at Amersfort on Long Island (God shield us), may not occur. And every one must attend every week to the said clearing and cleaning of the streets of the straw in front of his lot, under penalty of ten guilders' fine. Let every one guard against damage.

Ordinary Session, Tuesday, November 18, 1664.

Present: Willem Beeckman, Schout; Thomas Chambers, Gysbert van Imbroch, Jan Willemsen Hoochteylingh, Henderick Jochemsen, Commissaries.

Gysbert van Imbroch, plaintiff, vs. Ariaen Gerretsen, defendant.

Plaintiff demands from defendant the sum of one hundred and forty-eight guilders, nine stivers, in sewan, according to bill rendered.

Defendant admits the debt, and says he is not able now to pay it.

The Honorable Court orders defendant to pay plaintiff the aforesaid sum.

The Honorable Mr. Petrus Stuyvesant, plaintiff, vs. Juriaen Westphael, defendant.

Plaintiff demands from defendant, pursuant to settlement of August 14, last, fifteen hundred and sixty-five guilders, six stivers, in grain, beaver's value, and requests payment of the amount of eleven hundred and sixty-five guilders, six stivers, now due to the knowledge of the Commissaries, and sufficient security for the remaining four hundred guilders, with the costs thereof.

Defendant being absent, he is represented by his wife, who exhibited the contract of lease, and says that the said contract was not carried out by the lessor.

Plaintiff replies that a waiver of re-examination of the accounts was made, to the knowledge of the Commissaries, on April 26, 1662, and that according to extracts from the minutes, dated December 27, 1663 and April 1, 1664, defendant did not deny the debt.

The Honorable Court, having heard parties, orders defendant to pay plaintiff's above mentioned demand, as he did not deny the debt on December 27, 1663, nor take any exception to the contract, and also because, on April 1, 1664, execution on the claim was granted to plaintiff. Wherefore execution is again allowed to plaintiff for the sum of eleven hundred and sixty-five guilders, six stivers, besides the costs herein.

The Honorable Mr. Petrus Stuyvesant, plaintiff, vs. Ariaen Gerretsen, defendant.

Plaintiff demands from defendant, first, seven hundred and fourteen guilders, in sewan, by virtue of the Commissaries' examination, and, further, two years' rent due, amounting to eight hundred guilders, in grain, beaver's value, according to contract of lease, also butter from three cows for two years, sixteen pounds for each cow each year, also two sows, also one cow slaughtered by defendant, and requests payment or execution, with the costs thereof.

Defendant exhibits against the plaintiff an account charged to the Honorable Company for sixty-four guilders, in beavers, and three hundred and sixty-nine guilders, in sewan, also a claim of two hundred and thirty-four guilders, with still other claims against plaintiff, personally, being, first, that plaintiff did not furnish a suitable house and barn to defendant, and, second, the interest for the damage done to his grain, spoiled by water, and floated away at the time he was impressed at the old fort of the savages; also, third, the interest for the damage done to his corn, destroyed in the fields by pigs, as, because of the strict orders, he could not, without a convoy, properly harvest his crops; and, fourth, that he has been put to loss by sending, under orders, horses instead of oxen, up north.

Plaintiff replying hereto says, that, personally, he is not bound to pay for the Honorable Company, and that defendant personally must look for his claim to the Honorable Company; also that, so far as he personally is concerned, he is not obliged to supply defendant with a barn or loft, as appears by the contract of lease, and that the damage to the corn in the field does not concern him, the lessor, and also that he was not bound, according to contract, to deliver horses to defendant as claimed, also that the claim for carting some wood work for the barn has, to the knowledge of the Schepens, been disposed of by a waiver of re-examination of the account.

He further says he is willing to pay the twenty-four guilders, in sewan, for carting two loads of planks, but that defendant must then pay interest on the arrears.

The Honorable Court decides that defendant must look to the Honorable Company for his claim of sixty-four guilders, in beavers, and three hundred and sixty-nine guilders, in sewan, and also that, as to the further claim of damage in the field, the inconvenience of the barn and the lease of a barn and loft, which are not mentioned in the contract, the lessor is not bound to provide the lessee with a barn and loft. The Honorable Court orders defendant to pay plaintiff's aforesaid demand, with the costs herein, but, in case defendant can prove that the oxen were sent to Fort Orange by order of the lessor, the damage sustained by him on this account shall be made good to him by the lessor, after being taxed by two impartial men.

The Hon. Heer Petrus Stuyvesant, Plaintiff
vs. Tjerck Claesen De Wit, Defendant

Plaintiff demands from defendant an amount of 400 gldrs. in sewan, purchase money for two cows and a calf. Defendant admits the debt, but says having paid on the same 25 sch. of oats, representing 50 gldrs. in sewan, and further gives in a bill for some services rendered upon the order of Capt. Lieut. Marten Cregier or the Ld. Dir. Genl., which bill amounts to 147 gldrs. in heavy money, further 126 gldrs. in sewan. He also requests payment of two years' salary as commissary, amounting to 150 gldrs. annually, the same as is being done at Fort Orange.

The hon. heer plaintiff replies and requests speedy payment, or otherwise that the cattle be returned, and the expenses for the same be paid, and further says that he, personally, is not obliged to pay the bills against the hon. company.

The hon. court decides that defendant shall look to the hon. company for his claim of 147 gldrs. heavy money and 126 gldrs. in sewan, as also for the two years' salary as commissary, and is further ordered to satisfy plaintiff's aforenamed demand as per obligation, and by default of payment to immediately return the cattle, and to pay the expenses.

Tjerck Claesen De Wit requests leave to appeal from the above sentence which is granted him.

The commissary Gysbert Van Imbroch makes a complaint before the hon. court against Tjerck Claesen De Wit, and requests that Tjerck Claesen De Wit shall be obliged to prove that he /plaintiff/ is partial, on which account /de Wit/ made him /Imbroch/ leave the bench.

The Noble Heer Petrus Stuyvesant, Plaintiff
vs. Jan Joosten, Defendant

Plaintiff demands from defendant 60 gldrs. in sewan, passage money for taking him, wife, children and baggage in Dirck Smith's yacht from the Manhatans, and further 127 gldrs. 12 stivers in wheat for merchandise sold defendant, the schepel reckoned at 50 stivers. Further restitution of seed corn, being 37 sch. of oats, 5½ sch. of summer barley, 4 sch. of summer wheat, and for the loss of horses plaintiff refers to the contract. Further butter from two cows for two years, each year 16 pounds for each animal. Defendant admits the debt of 127 gldrs. 12 stivers in wheat, the sch. at 50 stivers. As to the 60 gldrs. in sewan for his passage, says that the secretary Van Ruyven allowed him the passage free of cost. Also admits having received the aforenamed seed corn, and also admits owing one year's butter-rent for two cows.

Both parties having been heard, it is decided that defendant shall pay plaintiff 127 gldrs. 12 st. in wheat at 50 st. per sch. Also 32 pounds of butter, also the

seed corn he borrowed, as per specification mentioned before. And as for the 60 gldrs. in sewan that defendant
shall prove that the secretary Van Ruyven allowed him a
free passage; if not he shall pay plaintiff.

Johanna De Laet, Plaintiff
vs. Evert Pels, Defendant

Plaintiff says that defendant has appropriated her
land, being a little island situated near Wildwyck, and
has ploughed the same, and there besides shows a deed,
dated May 24, 1655, /certifying/ that she bought the same
of the savage Nanecop, signed by him and three Christian
witnesses.

Defendant says that the aforenamed island belongs to
him and produces a certificate stating that he bought the
same from the savage Achquanarawyn, signed by Cornelis
Barentsen Slecht, Tryntje the wife of said Slecht and
Hendrick Cornelissen Slecht, and further offers to procure
a deed from the savage.

The case is adjourned by the hon. court till another
time.

Johanna De Laet requests payment from the judicial
sale of the effects of Cornelis Barentsen Slecht.

The hon. court orders and directs Roelof Swartwout,
the vendue-master of the aforementioned judicial sale,
to satisfy Juffrou De Laet.

Johanna De Laet further shows a copy from the minutes
of March 28, 1662, present: the commissaries Evert Pels,
Allert Heymans Roos, Tjerck Claesen De Wit, and Albert
Gysbertsen, and requests payment of 30 sch. of wheat
which the aforesaid commissaries took it upon themselves
to pay.

The hon. court refers Juffr. De Laet to the aforenamed commissaries.

Nicolaes Meyer, Plaintiff
vs. Jan Jansen Van Amersfoort, Defendant

Plaintiff demands from defendant an amount of 142
gldrs. 8 stvrs. in beavers, being the principal and interest of 112 gldrs. in beavers, as also 103 gldrs. 7
stvrs. principal and interest of 97 gldrs. principal in
sewan, to be paid with the costs, without expense and
risks at the Manhatans as per knowledge of schepenen,
dated April 3, 1664.

Defendant admits the debt, but requests plaintiff to
grant him time till next spring, under promise without
fault or exception, to satisfy said claim with the interest on the same, which shall be on March 1, 1665.

Plaintiff assents to defendants request and says
that defendant, in default of the same, shall pay the
exact expenses of his trip and lost time, besides the
claim which defendant agrees to do.

Nicolaes Meyer shows a judgment against Harmen
Hendericks, and requests execution which is granted him,

and consequently the officer is directed to attend to the execution.

Jan Barentsen Kunst, in his absence his wife
Jacomina Slecht, Plaintiff
vs. Aert Martensen Doorn, in his absence his wife
Geertruyd Andriesen, Defendant

Plaintiff demands from defendant an amount of 147 gldrs. heavy money to be paid in wheat, the schepel at three gldrs., being the balance for wages on a barn, and the building of an old barn and four stacks since the year 1658. Defendant says not having liquidated accounts with plaintiff. The hon. court orders parties to liquidate their accounts and to pay plaintiff the balance.

Pieter Bruynsen, attorney for
Cornelis Brantsen Vos, Plaintiff
vs. Ariaen Gerretsen, Defendant

Plaintiff demands from defendant an amount of 16 sch. of barley and three sch. of buckwheat, the balance of grain loaned him. Defendant admits the debt but says that there are some grains laying ready for Cornelis Brantsen Vos which he should get from defendant's house, but that he has neglected to do so.

The hon. court having seen defendant's note, finds that plaintiff took a usuriously high rate of interest for the loaned, being for seed corn, being 8½ schepel loaned, and that defendant shall pay for the same 20 sch. in five months. And for the purpose of, in the future, preventing similar usurious practices, the hon. court orders defendant not to pay any more to plaintiff than what he has received from him, being a balance of 31 gldrs. 10 stvrs. in sewan, or the value in grain.

Henderick Cornelissen, Plaintiff
vs. Evert Pels, Defendant. Absent. Default.

Mattheus Capito, Plaintiff
vs. Michiel Verbrugge and Jan Lootman (absent), Defendants

Plaintiff requests from defendants vindication of his assailed reputation, he, plaintiff, having been taxed by defendants on Oct. 7, 1664, with having cheated them in the account to the hon. company. Defendant still says that he has been informed by the secretary Van Ruyven at the Manhatans, that defendant should have received a blanket and fine stockings in the Esopus.

The hon. court having examined the books of Commissioner Capito finds that no blanket nor fine stockings are charged against Verbrugge.

In accordance with an order of the hon. court, defendant declares that he acknowledges plaintiff as an honest man, and does not know anything against him.

Thomas Harmensen, Plaintiff
vs. Ariaen Gerretsen, Defendant

Plaintiff demands from defendant payment of 15 sch. of wheat for himself personally, and per assignment by

Aeltje Sybrants 10 sch. of wheat, together 25 sch.
Defendant says having rendered some services to
Aeltje Sybrants, and wants to settle with her concerning
the same; concerning the personal debt to plaintiff of
15 sch. of wheat for wages, defendant admits owing the
same.
The hon. court orders defendant to satisfy plaintiff's personal claim of 15 sch. of wheat.

Thomas Harmensen, Plaintiff
vs. Cornelis Barentsen Slecht, Defendant. Absent. Default.

Thomas Harmensen, Plaintiff
vs. Dirrick Hendericksen, Defendant. Absent. Default.

Thomas Harmensen, Plaintiff
vs. Jacob Jansen Van Etten, Defendant
Plaintiff demands from defendant, as per balance
coming to him, 10 sch. of wheat. Defendant admits the
debt, but answers just now not to have it, neither being
able to procure it on account of being sick with fever,
and requests time. Plaintiff grants defendant time until
Aert Pietersen Tack's estate shall have been settled.

Tomas Harmensen, Plaintiff
vs. Pieter Gellissen, Defendant
Plaintiff demands from defendant payment of 23 gldrs.
in sewan. Defendant admits the debt, and answers never
having refused payment.
The hon. court orders defendant to satisfy plaintiff's aforenamed demand.
Pieter Gillissen requests his pay for taking care
of a cow and a heifer from the estate of Aert Pietersen
Tack.
The hon. court orders that said money shall be paid
and be charged to the aforesaid estate.

Tomas Harmensen, Plaintiff
vs. Allert Heymans, Defendant
Plaintiff demands from defendant payment of three
sch. of wheat. Defendant admits the debt, but says
having a bill against it.
The hon. court orders parties to liquidate their
accounts.

Tjerck Claesen De Wit, Plaintiff
vs. Aeltje Wygerts, Defendant
Plaintiff shows a bill of sale of a horse bought by
her husband, Albert Gysbertsen, during his lifetime from
plaintiff for 200 gldrs. in wheat to be paid at such
times and in such payments to the vendue-master as he
has bought it by Lord's execution on April 7, 1664.
Defendant admits the debt and offers to pay 100 sch.
of oats, provisionally, and the balance from the future
next year's (1665) crop, or else to return the horse, and
is willing to pay plaintiff for the use of said horse.
Plaintiff replies not to be satisfied with aforenamed offer.

The hon. court orders defendant to pay plaintiff as per contract.

Roelof Swartwout, vendue-master at the judicial sale of Cornelis Barentsen Slecht's effects, requests, because some of the buyers are negligent in their payment, that the Schout Willem Beeckman will be pleased to assume said claims for the purpose of proceeding as per law against those who failed to pay, so that Johanna De Laet may be satisfied. The hon. court orders the officer to assume said claims and to proceed.

Roelof Swartwout, vendue-master at the judicial sale of Aert Pietersen Tack's effects, says that at the sale of said effects a horse was sold to Tjerck Claesen De Wit, and requests that said claim may be assumed by the Hon. Schout Beeckman and be judicially proceeded against said Tjerck Claesen De Wit, because he is negligent in paying. The hon. court orders the officer to assume said claim and to proceed.

Gysbert Van Imbroch shows an extract from the minutes dated Feb. 26, 1664, against Tjerck Claesen De Wit, by which Tjerck Claesen De Wit was ordered to satisfy plaintiff, and requests execution of the same. The hon. court orders the officer to proceed with the execution, as per aforenamed request.

Aert Jacobsen requests a lot at Wildwyck for the purpose of building a house, barn, and loft, because he has rented his land to someone else. Refused.

Samuel Olivier, Joris Porter, Eduard Chattelton, appearing before the hon. court, say that on last Thursday, being Nov. 3/13 (they being stationed on the redoubt as a guard), Allert Heymans came with his people for the purpose of taking a canoe from the shore which canoe they had been ordered to watch by the guard which they relieved. Ariaen Huybertsen then came and took hold of the canoe for the purpose of shoving it in the water, whereupon Samuel Olivier came with his gun for the purpose of preventing the same, and threatened to shoot said Ariaen Huybertsen. Ariaen Albertsen, in the meantime, took the small shot out of his gun, and reloaded it with ball, and Allert Heymans also challenged the guard to fight them, man against man, and even raised his axe and threatened the soldier Eduart Chattelton to hit him with the same, and make a complaint about the violence committed against them in their quality of guards at the redoubt by the aforementioned persons. Allert Heymans answers that he arrived on the bank with his people, for the purpose of launching their own canoe, and to use it for hunting, whereupon Samuel Olivier, coming from the redoubt, with his gun cocked, spoke to them. They not being able to understand him, Ariaen Huybertsen, nevertheless, intended to float the canoe, whereupon Samuel pointed the gun at his chest, whereupon he, Ariaen, pushed the gun out of

the way, and took hold of his arm, and, this happening,
Eduard Chattelton approached Ariaen, aforementioned, with
an oar and struck at him, whereupon Joris Porter drew his
sword for the purpose of separating parties.   Thereupon
Allert Heymans called from the wagon, "Keep quiet, I
shall immediately come over to you to get the canoe
afloat."   When he came near the canoe, Eduard Chattelton
also came with his gun, holding the thumb on the trigger
and pointed to him to let the canoe alone.   In the meantime, he /Heymans/ took up the axe from the canoe and
threatened him with the same, whereupon Eduard reversed
his gun and threatened him with the butt end.   In the
meantime Ariaen Allerts, seeing this, also took hold of
his gun and loaded it with ball.   Allert Heymans further
went with the others to the redoubt, and there they were
better informed by each other.   The English, then understanding them a little /and understanding/ that it was
their own canoe, thereupon gave them the oars, and allowed the canoe to follow, and even Eduard Chattelton himself assisted them in getting the canoe afloat.   They also
deny having challenged the English soldiers, and further
deny having taken the small shot out of the gun, but /say/
that they simply loaded it with ball, because it was un-
loaded.

Extraordinary Session, Saturday, November 22, 1664.
     Present: Willem Beeckman, Schout; Thomas Chambers,
Gysbert Van Imbroch, Jan Willemsen, Commissaries.
     On this Nov. 22, the hon. Heer Petrus Stuyvesant
showed to the court two extracts from the minutes dated
Nov. 15 last, the one against Juriaen Westphael, the
other against Ariaen Gerretsen, wherein they were both
sentenced to satisfy plaintiff, and requests execution of
the same.   The hon. court orders the officer to proceed
with the execution, as per the foregoing request.
     "Schout and Commissaries' Knowledge" granted to the
hon. Heer Petrus Stuyvesant by Juriaen Westphael.
     /Copy/ "We undersigned schout and commissaries of
the village of Wildwyck make known and know that before
us appeared Juriaen Westphael, farmer or lessee of a farm
of the Heer Petrus Stuyvesant, who declares to have adjusted and settled with the aforenamed Heer, all claims
and accounts, renouncing, consequently, the collecting of
the same, so that appearer declares to honestly and
actually owe as rent for the years 1663 and 1664 the
amount of one thousand guilders in good merchantable
grain, beavers value of which amount (not including the
'schout and commissaries' knowledge' of the year 1662,
April 27) appearer accepts and promises to pay and render
a just third part before the departure of the said Heer
lessor; a just third part between now and the second half
of February next, to be actually paid to such person or

persons as shall be designated by said Heer lessor, the
last third part besides half of the rent of the next year
1665 in the month of October next, or to give surety for
the same, or by default of such, in case appearer should
be remiss in attending to any of the aforenamed payments,
appearer accepts and promises to voluntarily and without
any legal constraint, renunciate and and give up the lease
of the aforenamed Heer lessor's farm, and all crops to
be raised on the same during next year, for the purpose
of securing and receiving from said crops the rent due,
and also that for the coming year 1665 (provided, that,
after received payment he renders to appearer a satisfactory accounting of the balance, in case there should
be no opportunity for publicly selling to the highest
bidder said crops, either standing on the field or laying
in the barn or loft) without appearer being permitted to
appropriate any of the said crops much less to alienate
them, until the aforesaid Heer lessor shall be fully
satisfied and paid. For the purpose of testifying to
the above we have signed the same besides the appearer,
at Wildwyck in the Esopus Nov. 24, N. S. 1664.

The mark ———< of Juriaen Westphael, thus made
Willem Beeckman
(Signed)   Thomas Chambers
Henderick Jochemsen
·Below stood

N.B. Among the forenamed amount of 1,000 gldrs. are included and liquidated 400 gldrs., being the just half of
800 gldrs. which the appearer, as per foregoing "Schout
and Commissaries' knowledge," owes on account of rent
then due, the loss of horses and other items, so that appearer in regard to this owes no more than 400 gldrs.,
besides the rent, to be paid on conditions and at times
more fully set forth in the aforesaid "Schout and Commissaries' knowledge," dated April 27, 1662.

Dated as above. (Signed) Petrus Stuyvesant.

This, having been recorded upon request, has been
found to be an exact copy of the original to which testifies

(Signed) Mattheus Capito, Secretary.

Ordinary session, Tuesday, November 25, 1664.

Present: Willem Beeckman, Schout; Thomas Chambers,
Gysbert Van Imbroch, Jan Willemsen Hoochteylingh, Henderick
Jochemsen, Commissaries.

Willem Beeckman, Schout, Plaintiff
vs. Tomas Harmensen, farmer /of the excise/, Defendant

Plaintiff demands from defendant the three-monthly
amount due for the farming of the excise on beer and
wines. Defendant admits the debt, and says not to be able
to collect his money from others, in relation to the farm
due, and promises to pay in three or four days. The hon.

court orders defendant to satisfy said demand within two
times 24 hours, under penalty of execution.
    Tomas Harmensen, farmer /of the excise/, Plaintiff
           vs. Gysbert Van Imbroch, Defendant
    Plaintiff says that yesterday he announced to de-
fendant that he would have him fined for smuggling and
that the wine is confiscated. Defendant denies that
plaintiff announced to him that he would have him fined,
and says that for the wine, coming from the river bank,
he obtained a permit from the farmer, and further that
Willem Montagnie has declared an anker of wine, and thereupon requested an innkeeper's license, whereupon the collector's wife answered him that he did not need any further permit, because the wine had been declared. Plaintiff answers that, if yesterday, he did not announce to
defendant that he would have him fined, he does do so now
before the hon. court, and further says that defendant
was not permitted to store wine upon his permit, because
defendant is a retailer of the wine and for that purpose
has also taken out a license. Defendant denies being a
tapster or retailer, and says that his brother-in-law
Willem La Montagnie has said business, and also says that
plaintiff has called him a usurer, taking 24 stivers for
a mutje, and requests that plaintiff shall be punished
for said calumny; which plaintiff does not deny having
said. The hon. court adjourns the case till next session
for the purpose of being better informed about this
business.
         Willem Beeckman, Plaintiff
        vs. Jan Gerretsen, Defendant
    Plaintiff demands, for himself personally, from de-
fendant 43 gldrs. 10 st. in sewan, and further 162 gldrs.
15 st. in sewan or wheat, as per vendue of the effects of
Frederick Claesen upon which have been paid as per bill
produced, 50 gldrs., balance in all amounting to 156
gldrs. 5 st., and requests payment of the same with costs,
because already more than six weeks have passed since said
vendue. Defendant admits the debt, but says that at
present he is not able to pay. The hon. court sentences
defendant to satisfy plaintiff's aforenamed demand with
the costs.
      Henderick Cornelissen, ropemaker, Plaintiff
        vs. Evert Pels, Defendant
    Plaintiff demands from defendant 40 gldrs. in sewan
and requests payment. Defendant says not to intend to
pay plaintiff one stiver unless he shows him a bill. The
hon. court orders plaintiff to give defendant a bill.
    Roelof Swartwout requests that he may receive his
money which Foppe Barents owes him, for which he obtained
judgment on June 24, 1664, and /further requests/ that he
may levy on Foppe Barents for same. The hon. court orders
the officer to proceed with the execution.

Johanna De Laet petitions, whereas her barn is situated outside the palisades, that she may surround the
same with palisades and then be permitted to make an
opening through the nowstanding palisades for a wagon
road to said barn. The hon. court answers that it will
first examine the condition of said place.

Willem Beeckman, Schout, Plaintiff
vs. Allert Heymans, Adriaen Huybertsen and Ariaen Allertsen, Defendants

Plaintiff demands from defendants on account of
violence committed on the bank near the redoubt against
the guard there, being for Allert Heymans and Ariaen
Huybertsen 25 gldrs. each for the poor and for Ariaen Ae-
lertsen 50 gldrs. for the poor, because he loaded his gun
with ball, while they were having a quarrel on account of
the taking away of a canoe, and sustains that defendants
were not permitted to be their own judges in their own
behalf. Defendants, having been informed by reading to
them the complaint made on Nov. 18 last by the English
soldiers, and the answers given thereupon, affirm their
foregoing answer, and thereto add that the difference between them originates in their inability to at first
well understand each other, the one party being English,
the other Dutch. The hon. court, upon the advice of Mr.
Christoffel Beresfort, commander of the local garrison,
decides that defendants are not permitted to be their own
judges, but that they ought to have addressed themselves
to the court, and therefore sentences defendant Allert
Heymans to pay 20 gldrs. to the poor and Ariaen Huybertsen 10 gldrs. in sewan.

The hon. schout makes known that he has received a
letter from the hon. heer Secretary Van Ruyven, ordering
to pay Jacob Joosten from the revenues of the tapster
licenses 100 gldrs. in sewan, which is also shown by an
assignment passed to Tomas Harmensen, farmer, dated Nov.
14, 1664. The hon. court decides whereas the general
and councillors allowed the one-half of the revenue from
said farms to be used in the payment of old village
debts, and thus are preferred debtors, therefore refuse
Jacob Joosten the aforesaid assignment, for as far as
receiving his money during the first half year is concerned.

The hon. schout proposes that the payment of the
preacher's salary shall be continued, and that he shall
be paid the balance due for his services. The hon. court
orders that to each inhabitant shall be sent his bill,
and that they shall promptly pay their debt.

The hon. schout also proposes that the expenses incurred by the delegates in April shall be collected. The
hon. court orders that a bill shall be sent to the house
of each of the inhabitants.

Tjerck Claesen De Wit requests execution of the

judgment dated Nov. 18, 1664, against Aeltje Wygerts. The
hon. court having seen the summons sent to Aeltje Wygerts,
decides that **Tierck Claesen** shall first deliver to Aeltje
Wygerts the deed of the land as per contract of the same
dated Dec. 13, 1663, having been shown to the court by
Roelof Swartwout as attorney of Aeltje Wygerts, aforenamed.

Geertruyd Andriesen reports that whereas recently
she was referred by the court to Domine Blom concerning
the payment of a claim for some land sold to Marten Harpertsen, saying, that the aforenamed domine has said not
to have any effect or property of deceased under him, on
which account she addresses herself to the court for payment or restitution of the land. The hon. court will
enquire into said affair.

Geertruyd Andriesen requests the rent for the room,
amounting to 146 gldrs. in sewan, which is allowed her.

On Nov. 27 Marietje Appels seized at Juriaen Westphael's 40 gldrs. in sewan or the value of the same in
grain, on account of Pieter Gillissen.

Letter to the Governor General:

Noble, Honorable, Valliant and very Discreet Lord,

This serves to inform your honor that upon the arrival of Mr. Beresfort, about 14 days ago, we received
three barrels of meat, but without letter, weight and
price. We further respectfully ask that before the frost*
sets in we may still be sent three or four barrels of
pork, besides the weight and the price, and further a keg
of powder (because we learn that the Esopus savages are
again repairing and fortifying their old fort which has
been demolished by the Dutch) so that in time of need,
against any invasion by the savages, the inhabitants,
here, may be provided with powder. Which we trust, and
remain,

Your honor's obedient servants,
The magistrates at Wildwyck and
the country of the Esopus,
(signed) Willem Beeckman

Given at Wildwyck, this Dec. 1, 1664.

Ordinary Session, Tuesday, Dec. 2, 1664.

Present: Willem Beeckman, Schout; Thomas Chambers,
Gysbert Van Imbroch, Jan Willemsen Hoochteylingh, Henderick Jochemsen, Commissaries.

Tomas Harmenson, Plaintiff, Absent, Default
vs. Cornelis Barentsen Slecht, Defendant, Absent, Default.
Tomas Harmensen, Plaintiff
vs. Dirrick Hendericksen, Defendant

Plaintiff demands from defendant payment of three
sch. of wheat. Defendant admits owing plaintiff only two
sch. of wheat, and says that he gave plaintiff brandy for
the other schepel. The hon. court orders defendant to
pay plaintiff for two sch. of wheat.

Tomas Harmensen, Plaintiff
vs. Aeltje Wygerts, Defendent. Absent. Default.
Tomas Harmensen, farmer /of the excise/, Plaintiff
vs. Gysbert Van Imbroch, Defendant

Plaintiff demands against defendant sentence, as per
previous session. Defendant answers in writing, and says
that he did not smuggle: 1) as per declaration of the
farmer's collectress; 2) as per the written permit; 3)
as per the collector's book, and further says that the
farmer, contrary to burgher right and privilege, did not
hesitate, without the order of the hon. court, to confiscate the wines on Nov. 25; and further says that the
farmer on Nov. 26 again came to defendant's house with a
wagon, and tried, against his will, to remove defendant's
effects out of his house, and thereupon even prohibited
him from doing business, and concludes in his writing
that plaintiff shall be sentenced to restore defendant's
reputation and credit, and also to pay the costs of the
suit. Plaintiff, having again been called inside, answers, after having been questioned, that he knew that
defendant had declared the wine, and then went to defendant's house to receive the money for the declared
wines, and intended to deposit the same with the hon.
court; that defendant at his house denied having declared
wines upon a tapster's license, and requests that defendant may be sentenced to pay the full fine for smuggling,
and that the wine may be confiscated. Defendant says that
plaintiff called at his house and was requested by defendant to gauge the wine, because a half-anker was not
full, and then also requested the farmer to allow a half-
anker for his home-consumption, and that he would pay for
the remaining 11 ankers; which plaintiff admits having
taken place. The schout understands that, as per the
permit shown, and the declaration of the collector's
wife in regard to his declaring six half-"aemen" of
wine, Mr. Van Imbroch owes the full excise, and that the
farmer ought to have awaited the judgment of the court,
because he had brought the affair before the same, and
consequently, in the meantime, illegally tried to promote his own case, and on that account owes reparation,
and the schout demands a fine from him. The Commissary
Thomas Chambers advises that he knows nothing about the
farming-business, and refers himself to the judgment of
others who are better acquainted with the /excise/ farming-business. The Commissary Jan Willemsen Hooghteylingh
advises the same as advised by the Commissary Thomas
Chambers. The Commissary Henderick Jochemsen also assents to the advice of the two aforenamed commissaries,
or that parties shall amicably settle their difference,
exclusive of the officer's demand.

Henderick Cornelissen, Plaintiff
vs. Evert Pelse, Defendant

Plaintiff demands from defendant the same amount as was demanded by him at the previous session, being 40 gldrs. in sewan, with the costs of the same. Defendant shows per account to plaintiff not to owe more than 19 gldrs. 10 st. in sewan. The hon. court orders defendant to pay the amount of 19 glrds. 10 st. in sewan besides the costs, and as soon as plaintiff can prove that he can claim more from defendant, this later demand shall be disposed of.

Henderick Cornelissen, Plaintiff
vs. Ariaen Gerretsen, Defendant. Absent. Default.
Jan Tyssen, Plaintiff, Absent.
vs. Jan Cornelissen, Defendant. Absent.
Mattheus Capito, Plaintiff
vs. Jacob Joosten, Defendant

Plaintiff demands of defendant half of the money for the summons, as per sentence of the court of Dec. 18, 1663. Defendant says he only receives 100 gldrs. in sewan annual salary, and that he well earns it, besides the money for the summonses. The hon. court refers to the earlier sentence on Dec. 18, 1663.

The Secretary Matheus Capito requests some payment for making out the account book of the village of Wild-wyck for the old retired commissaries, and leaves it to the pleasure of the court. The hon. court votes afore-named secretary 48 gldrs. in sewan for making out the aforenamed book of accounts.

The hon. Heer Willem Beeckman, plaintiff, vs. Jan Evertsen requests in regard to the previous sentence on Nov. 25 last that said sentence may be executed. The hon. court orders the officer to proceed with the execution of the aforenamed sentence.

Mr. Gysbert Van Imbroch requests to be informed whether the hon. court intends to allow him to carry on his business of tapster with the wines in dispute, be-cause the farmer on Nov. 26 had forbidden him the same, notwithstanding the collector's wife had told him that he needed no other permit, or that he would twice pay the excise. The schout is of the opinion that petitioner is at liberty to retail said wines, because it appears that the wine was declared, provided he pay the farmer's ex-cise. Commissary Thomas Chambers admits not to know any-thing about the /excise/ farm business. The Commissaries Jan Willemsen Hoochteylingh and Henderick Jochemsen say the same.

Thomas Harmenson, plaintiff, vs. Aert Martensen Doorn, Pieter Gillissen and Ariaen Gerretsen requests con-cerning the previous sentence dated Feb. 26, 1664, against Aert Martensen Doorn, and the sentence dated Nov. 18 last against Pieter Gillissen and Ariaen Gerretsen, that said sentences may be executed. The hon. court orders the of-ficer to proceed with the execution of the aforenamed

184

sentences (or judgments).

The hon. schout reports that it has been found out
that some of the inhabitants have harbored savages in
their houses at night, against which a decree ought to
be issued, according to the orders of the Governor General. It is resolved by the court to publish on this
account decrees that the residents shall not be permitted, without the knowledge of the hon. court, to receive savages in their houses at night, under penalty of
100 gldrs. fine, whenever this shall be found to have
taken place. The resolution reads:

Whereas it has been found that some residents of
Wildwyck have dared to shelter savages at night in this
place which is contrary to the good order and the opinion of the hon. Governor General at New York, therefore
Schout and Scheepenen at Wildwyck, willing to see the
aforesaid well-intentioned order observed, do prohibit
by the present, that none of the residents here shall
attempt or be permitted to harbor during the night any
savage or savages, unless with the knowledge of the local
magistrates, under penalty of 100 gldrs. fine for every
violation. Done etc.

The captain and the lieutenant of the burghers ask
how they will have to behave on their rounds, in case
they should happen, by night, to meet any savage or
savages near the curtains, whether outside or inside;
whether they will be permitted to shoot at them, after
having called out three times, and not receiving an answer from them? The hon. court decides, "Yes," if the
savages after three challenges by the round do not answer
or if they cannot be captured by the round.

The Secretary Mattheus Capito requests that he may
be voted some salary and compensation for the services
rendered by him and yet to be rendered. The hon. court
decides, upon occasion, to allow petitioner some salary.

Geertruyd Andriesen gives in a bill of the rent for
the room of the hon. court at Wildwyck, amounting to 146
gldrs. in sewan and requests payment. The hon. court decides that petitioner shall be paid as soon as the
treasury will permit.

Geertruyd Andriesen requests to be permitted to
again take possession of the land sold to Marten Harpertsen, because she did not receive any other payment for the
same than 3,000 bricks, according to her confession. The
hon. court decides that the land shall be sold, on occasion, by vendue to the highest bidder, and that she
shall have preference for her claim of 100 gldrs. in corn.

Ordinary Session, Tuesday, December 9, 1664.
Present: Willem Beeckman, Schout; Thomas Chambers,

Gysbert Van Imbroch, Jan Willemsen Hoochteylingh, Henderick Jochemsen, Commissaries.

Aeltje Claes, Plaintiff
vs. Albert Gerretsen, Defendant

Plaintiff demands from defendant two sch. of wheat,
for deer meat sold him. Defendant says that her husband
used his loft during the winter, and put grain on the
same, and that he has been paid for this, and further
that during the summer some grain laid on his loft, and
consequently maintains that he ought to receive more
than the meat received by him. The hon. court orders
parties to each select a good man for the purpose of
settling this affair.

Henderick Albertsen, Plaintiff
vs. Allert Heymans, Defendant

Plaintiff says that he contracted with defendant
about threshing his grain, from doing which he has been
prevented. Denied by defendant, having prevented plaintiff from threshing, but defendant says that plaintiff
did not proceed fast enough with it. The hon. court,
having heard parties, orders plaintiff to properly attend
to the threshing, and to continue with the same, so that
defendant may not have cause for complaint.

Henderick Cornelissen, Plaintiff, Absent, Default,
vs. Aert Jacobsen, Defendant, Absent, Default.

Henderick Cornelissen, Plaintiff
vs. Pieter Hillebrants, Defendant. Absent. Default.

Henderick Cornelissen, Plaintiff
vs. Aeltje Wygerts, Defendant. Absent, sick.

Henderick Cornelissen, Plaintiff
vs. Jan Broersen, Defendant

Plaintiff demands from defendant 21 gldrs. in sewan,
being three sch. of wheat for money advanced to Andries
Rees, and three gldrs. which he advanced to himself.* Defendant admits the debt, but answers not to be able, just
at present, to pay. The hon. court sentences defendant
to satisfy plaintiff's before-stated demand.

Antoni Crupel, Plaintiff
vs. Aert Martensen Doorn, Defendant

Plaintiff demands from defendant wages for 18 days
labor, three sch. of oats and ½ sch. of peas whereof
have been paid three sch. of wheat, and demands a daily
wage of three gldrs. Defendant says that he paid somebody
else two gldrs. per day, and is willing to pay plaintiff
the same amount per day. Parties having been heard, the
hon. court decides that defendant shall pay plaintiff for
wages as much as he paid another during that time, and
defendant is sentenced to pay plaintiff the three sch.
of oats and ½ sch. of peas.

Antoni Crupel, Plaintiff
vs. Ariaen Gerretsen, Defendant. Absent. Default.

Antoni Crupel, Plaintiff
vs. Roelof Swartwout, Defendant. Absent. Default.
Antoni Crupel, Plaintiff
vs. Henderick Cornelissen, Defendant
Plaintiff demands from defendant immediate payment
of three sch. of wheat which he took upon himself to pay
for Jan Jansen, carpenter. Defendant denies the debt and
says having paid his share of the swine to plaintiff,
having been assigned by Jan Jansen, carpenter. The hon.
court decides that plaintiff shall have to sue Jan Jansen,
carpenter.

Henderick Cornelissen, Plaintiff
vs. Christoffel Davids, Defendant. Absent. Default.
Evert Prys, Plaintiff
vs. Jan Joosten, Defendant. Absent. Default.
The hon. court, having examined the accounts given
in against Aert Pietersen Tack, finds that these are
preferred: 1) The general expenses of the execution.
2) The village of Wildwyck for the general tax for the
preacher's salary and other items. 3) Jeronimus Ebbingh
for the third or last installment for the land. 4) Gysbert Van Imbroch for "schepen knowledge," dated Dec. 21,
1662. 5) Jan Barentsen Wemp, for "Lord's knowledge,"
dated April 1, 1662, and which has been communicated on
May 5, 1664, to the hon. local court. 6) Evert Prys, on
account of schepen sentence. 7) Albert Gerretsen on account of schepen sentence. 8) Jan Tyssen for wages. 9)
Jacob Jansen Van Etten for wages. 10) Paulus Cornelissen
on account of schepen sentence. The remaining creditors
shall be paid pro rata, being: Cornelis Barentsen
Slecht, Jeronimus Ebbingh, Henderick Cornelissen Slecht,
Jan Aertsen Smith, Gommert Paulussen, Pieter Lookermans,
Andries Harpertsen, Wouter Aertsen, Abraham Staets, Barent Reyndersen.

Aert Otterspoor requests to be permitted to keep the
strawberry patch, situated outside the palisades, opposite the house of Aert Jacobsen, because the same has
been granted him before this by the hon. Lord Dir. Genl.
Peter Stuyvesant, and because Aert Jacobsen is trying to
appropriate the same, petitioner makes a complaint. The
hon. court decides, Whereas said parcel of land has been
granted petitioner for the purpose of cultivating the
same as a garden by the hon. Lord Dir. Genl. Stuyvesant,
and he has already fenced it in and possessed it, therefore he is again permitted to appropriate and cultivate
the same.

The bills of the Rev. Mr. Hermannus Blom amounting
to 46 gldrs. 10 st. in sewan, 76 gldrs. 10 st. heavy
money, 76 gldrs. in beavers and 11 sch. of grain having
been received, as also the extract from the minutes
dated March 11 last, granted to his Rev., the payment
shall be attended to as soon as the excise for the wines

shall have been received.

We, the undersigned Gysbert Van Imbroch and Jan
Willemsen Hoochteylingh, shepenen of the village of Wildwyck, make known and know that there appeared before us
the worthy Aert Martensen Doorn, who declares to have
rented of Mr. Willem La Montagnie a horse named the little black for the period of one current year, commencing
on Dec. 11, 1664, and to terminate on Dec. 11, 1665, for
which horse appearer promises to pay the lessor for the
lease for one current year 16 sch. of wheat, precisely at
the termination of the lease. The appearer shall be o-
bliged to again return the aforesaid horse to the lessor
after expiration of the lease in the same condition as he
has now received the same from him, being hale and sound,
the risk for the said horse to be run by the appearer,
either in regard to death or to loss owing to war or anything else. For which rent or loss of the aforenamed horse
the appearer specially mortgages his dwelling at Wildwyck
which is at present occupied by the Heer Willem Beeckman, and further in general his person and other estate,
personal and real, present and future /submitting the
same/ to the jurisdiction of all judges and courts
renouncing by the present all exceptions or defences
which might be in any way contrary to the present. For
the purpose of legalising the present, the appearer, besides ourselves, has signed the same with our own signatures, at Wildwyck this Dec. 11, 1664.
        The mark A M D of Aert Martensen Doorn
            made by himself
(signed)   Gysbert Van Imbroch
        The mark ✻ of Jan Willemsen Hoochteylingh
    In my presence (signed) Mattheus Capito, Secretary.
I acknowledge by this my signature that I have been
satisfied for the contents of the aforenamed "scheepen
knowledge" of Aert Martensen Doorn, and therefore annul
the aforestanding "scheepen knowledge." Done at Wildwyck, this Nov. 18, 1666.
                (signed) Wilh. d La Montag.
Known to me, to which testifies,
                (signed) Mattheus Capito, Secretary.

Ordinary Session, Tuesday, December 16, 1664.
    Present: Willem Beeckman, Schout; Thomas Chambers,
Gysbert Van Imbroch, Jan Willemsen Hoochteylingh, Henderick Jochemsen, Commissaries.
            Willem Beeckman, Plaintiff
        vs. Henderick Cornelissen, Defendant
    Plaintiff demands from defendant an amount of 58
gldrs. light money for him personally and of 69 gldrs.
9 stvrs. heavy money for the estate of Aert Tack.
    Defendant admits the debt, and says being willing
to pay as soon as possible.

The hon. court orders defendant to satisfy plaintiff's aforestated demand.

Willem Beeckman, Schout, Plaintiff
vs. Walran Du Mont and Ariaen Gerretsen, Defendants.

Plaintiff lodges a complaint against defendant Ariaen Gerretsen, on account of having, on the 13th inst., wounded Walran Du Mont with a knife. Defendant twice stuck said knife into said Walran Du Mont's body, and inflicted three cuts across his hand, and requests that defendant may be arrested because the patient, Du Mont, is in danger of losing his life.

Defendant Walran Du Mont, absent, while defendant Ariaen Gerretsen is also absent, in whose place appeared his wife who produced two certificates about what happened.

The hon. court grants the schout's demands, concerning the arrest of Ariaen Gerretsen, and therebesides orders the schout to more closely investigate this affair.

Willem Beeckman, Plaintiff
vs. Ariaen Gerretsen, Defendant

Plaintiff demands from defendant a balance of 165 gldrs. 3 st. in sewan as per bill sent in. Defendant being absent, he is represented by his wife who admits the debt, and says to be willing to pay.

The hon. court orders defendant to satisfy plaintiff's aforestated demand.

Gysbert Van Imbroch, Plaintiff
vs. Tjerck Claesen De Wit, Defendant

Plaintiff says that, after having waited two years, defendant wants to pay him with "dreps," and shows the origin of the debts, and requests in regard to the same that he may be satisfied in wheat, with the interest to the amount of 124 gldrs. in sewan.

Defendant does not deny the debt, but says not to have anything but "opslach" of wheat.

The hon. court orders defendant to pay plaintiff in such grain as he has received from plaintiff.

Mattheus Capito, Plaintiff
vs. Louwies DuBois, Defendant

Plaintiff says that defendant refuses to contribute to the preacher's salary for the two lots of plaintiff's which he occupies.

Defendant answers, having contracted with plaintiff to use the lots till May 1665 in consideration for fencing them in, chopping the trees and manuring the land.

Plaintiff answers and denies the same, and demands that defendant shall quit the lots, in case he remains unwilling to satisfy plaintiff's demand.

The hon. court orders defendant to prove his assertion at the next session.

Henderick Cornelissen, Plaintiff
vs. Christoffel Davids, Defendant
Plaintiff demands from defendant an amount of 21
gldrs. 15 st. to be paid in Indian corn at 30 st. in
sewan and two bottles of brandy, besides the bottles.
Defendant admits the debt, and answers that he has
paid something on the same to Jan Van Bremen, and maintains that he paid Jan Van Bremen and plaintiff more than
the debt amounts to.
The hon. court orders defendant to produce his
counter claims, and that parties then shall settle with
each other.

Evert Prys, Plaintiff
vs. Jan Joosten, Defendant
Plaintiff says that he hired himself out to defendant at 40 gldrs. heavy money for one month, before the
time of the war against the savages, and also demands for
five days spent in looking for lost horses as much as he
earned with him in one month.
Defendant says that plaintiff worked two and one-
half weeks for him, and that his time was cut short
through the war against the savages. He also therefore
paid him as per account 30 gldrs. in heavy money. Concerning the horses, he says having issued a general information to those who might have found the horses, and
having promised a silver ducaton for their return. Also
says not having specially employed plaintiff to look for
the horses.
The hon. court decides whereas plaintiff in his bill
demands pay for making a shirt, and the other shirt was
being made, and then taken by the savages, therefore defendant shall pay plaintiff six gldrs. heavy money.

Antoni Crupel, Plaintiff
vs. Jan Jansen Van Amersfoort, Defendant
Plaintiff demands from defendant three sch. of wheat
for mowing grass.
The defendant admits the debt, but says that he assigned plaintiff six sch. of wheat on Henderick Cornelissen, where upon he has received three sch. of him.
The hon. court orders defendant to satisfy plaintiff's
aforestated demand.

Jan Jansen Van Amersfoort, Plaintiff
vs. Henderick Cornelissen, Defendant
They are trying to settle the case.

Antoni Crupel, Plaintiff
vs. Roelof Swartwout, Defendant. Absent. Default.

Antoni Crupel, Plaintiff
vs. Juriaen Westphael, Defendant. Absent. Default.

Antoni Crupel, Plaintiff
vs. Ariaen Gerretsen, Defendant
Plaintiff demands from defendant two sch. of wheat,
and two sch. of barley for wages during the harvest.

Defendant being absent, he is represented by his wife who says not to owe any more than 18 gldrs. in sewan.

Parties having been heard, the hon. court orders plaintiff to prove that he contracted for more than three gldrs. per day for threshing, and defendant is, in anticipation, ordered to pay plaintiff 18 gldrs. as per defendant's own acknowledgment.

Allert Heymans requests that Tjerck Claesen, Albert Gysbertsen and Aert Jacobsen may be ordered to have their farms fenced in, for the purpose of preventing damage owing to the trespassing of pigs and cattle, on account of which petitioner has, heretofore, sustained much damage.

The hon. court refers to the decree issued in this regard on /left open/.

Allert Heymans complains about the village /tax/ bill, sent to him on account of his lot, saying that it was granted him as a single lot, and on the village bill he finds that the same has been charged against him as a double lot, and requests the decision of the court concerning the same.

The hon. court decides whereas his lot has been found to be larger than two common lots, that petitioner is obliged to contribute to the preacher's salary, and to the other expenses as much as other lots having the same dimensions as his.

Jan Joosten and Jan Willemsen Hoochteylingh show their village bills which were sent to them, having found that they have been debited for the preacher's salary for the whole year 1664, as also the expenses for the diet. And whereas they two did not take hold of Jeronimus Ebbingh's farm until May last, they maintain that they owe nothing for previous times. On this account petitioners request the hon. court's moderation and decision.

The hon. court decides that petitioners are not obliged to contribute for the previous eight months from September 1663 till May 1664 to the preacher's salary, but that their predecessor Cornelis Barentsen Slecht shall pay the same, because he still had the lease of Jeronimus Ebbingh's land. The remaining four months shall be paid by petitioners. Also that they, petitioners, shall be obliged to contribute to the expenses to the diet of the delegates, because the delegates were considering at the diet future and not past affairs.

The schout proposes that orders may be issued to close the small village-gates at night.

The hon. court orders that written decrees concerning this shall be published and that the violator shall be fined three gldrs. for the officer, whenever it shall be found that the small gates are not closed at night. Hereupon the underwritten decree was issued:

"Whereas Schout and Schepenen at Wildwyck perceive

the negligence of the inhabitants here in not closing the
little gates at night and unusual hours; notwithstanding
before this decrees concerning the same have been issued
by Schout and Schepenen, therefore Schout and Schepenen
for the purpose of preventing danger and peril want to
have obeyed the aforeissued orders, conceived for the
well-being of this place, and therefore once more order
all those having small gates in the palisades or curtains
of this place to properly close said little gates by
night and unusual hours either with a lock or with a pin,
upon penalty in case of violation of three gldrs. for the
officer, whenever it shall be found that said little gates
had been left open at night or unusual hours. Let everybody look out for himself. Thus given at the session of
Schout and Schepenen at Wildwyck, this December 16, 1664."

 We, the undersigned, Gysbert Van Imbroch and Jan Willemsen Hoochteylingh, Scheepenen of the village of Wildwyck, make known and know that there appeared before us
the worthy Aeltje Wygerts, widow of Albert Gysbertsen,
deceased, who declares that her husband Albert Gysbertsen, deceased, bought during his lifetime from the estate
of Aert Pietersen Tack, a heifer for the amount of 100
gldrs. heavy money, for which amount of 100 gldrs. heavy
money the appearer has been referred to and promises to
pay to Swerus Teunissen, inhabitant of the colony of
Rensselaerswyck, in good merchantable winter wheat with
the interest of the same, being ten percent during the
time of one current year, commencing Nov. 18, 1664, and
ending on Nov. 18, 1665, the schepel at three gldrs.
For which amount of 100 gldrs. with the current interest
of the same, she, appearer, specially mortgages for the
purpose of precisely, at the above stipulated period,
paying Swerus Teunissen aforementioned, the crop of all
the corn which, by God's blessing, shall, in the coming
year 1665, be brought in from her land, and further in
general her person and further goods, personal and real
estate, present and future, none excepted, submitting the
same to the jurisdiction of all courts and judges. And
hereby renounces all exceptions and pretexts which might
in any way be contrary to the present. For the purpose
of legalizing the present, she, appearer, has besides
ourselves, signed the present with her own hand.
 Given at Wildwyck this December 18, 1664.
                           Aeltien Wychersen
             (signed)   Gysbert Van Imbroch
                           Jan Willemsen Hoochteylingh

Decree against shooting on New Year:
 "Whereas experience has demonstrated that on account of the shooting on New Year's many disasters have
occurred, for which reason, prior to this, similar shoot-

192

ing on New Year has been rigidly prohibted by decrees,
therefore Schout and Scheepenen of this village of Wildwyck once more wanting to see said issued decrees obeyed,
because they were made with the intention of preventing
fire or any other accident through said shooting, once
more prohibit one and all, that anybody shall undertake
to shoot the New Year, under penalty of /a fine/ of three
gldrs. for every shot by him who shall be found to have
fired the same. Thus given at the session of Schout and
Schepenen at Wildwyck, this December 30, 1664.

Ordinary Session, Tuesday, January 6, 1665.
    Present: Willem Beeckman, Schout; Thomas Chambers,
Gysbert Van Imbroch, Jan Willemsen Hoochteylingh, Henderick Jochemsen, Commissaries.
            Walran Du Mont, Plaintiff
         vs. Ariaen Gerretsen, Defendant
    Plaintiff makes a complaint against defendant on ac-
count of a crime committed against him, because defendant
wounded him with a knife in his body on Dec. 13, 1664, and
requests that defendant may be punished for this and pay
for pain and lost time 100 daelders besides 12 schs. of
wheat for physician's fees. Ariaen Gerretsen, defendant,
brings in certificates against plaintiff. Plaintiff replies, saying that said certificates are false and shows
two certificates signed by Jan Jansen Van Amersfoort and
Antoni Crupel and requests that defendant's attestors
judicially confirm their attestation under oath. Also
requests that the hon. court be pleased to take a declaration from Mattheus Blanchan and his wife, near whose house
the aforesaid crime has been committed. Which /declaration/
is as follows:
    Mattheu Blanchan, having been questioned before the
hon. court about what he has seen, after Walran Du Mont
had been fighting with Aert Gerretsen in his house, answers that he thereupon ordered Walran Du Mont to leave
his house, whereupon he went outside, and that Ariaen
Gerretsen followed him right away. After they left, his
wife was going to close the door, and he, Blanchan, has
seen that it appeared to him that Ariaen Gerretsen had
something in his left hand, and they then both saw that
Walran Du Mont fell down on the street near the oven, he
Ariaen Gerretsen being behind the aforesaid Walran, and
then declares that neither one saw anymore.
    Mattheu Blanchan's testimony having been heard, the
hon. court decides that the declarations of the attestors
of both parties shall be examined in the presence of the
Heer Officer and two commissaries from the bench, being
Thomas Chambers and Jan Willemsen Hoochteylingh.
            Juriaen Westphael, Plaintiff
       vs. Tjerck Claesen De Wit, Curator of the
           estate of Henderick Looman, Defendant

Plaintiff requests that defendant (being the curator of the estate of Henderick Jansen Looman) may be made to render an accounting, because plaintiff still has some claims against said estate. Defendant renders his accounting of said estate to the court, and requests to be relieved from said estate.

The hon. court decides, whereas there are some debtors to said estate living at Fort Orange, that they shall be written to.

Evert Pels, Plaintiff
vs. Dirrick Hendericksen, Defendant

Plaintiff being the attorney for the widow of Michiel Jansen, demands from defendant 48 gldrs. 9 st. in wheat, at three gldrs. per sch. Defendant denies the debt, and says that he assigned under his own signature his account with the hon. company to Michiel Jansen while he was alive for the purpose of settling his debt, and that he did not owe Michiel Jansen anything but sewan. Also says that after the assignment on the hon. company he lived two years at the Manhatans, also that he called several times at the house of Michiel Jansen, that he ate and drank with him, and that he has never been talked to about it by Michiel Jansen. Also, in case he should again be handed his account and assignment of the same, that he will himself go to the company for his money.

The hon. court decides and orders that plaintiff shall return to defendant his bill and assignment, and that defendant shall then be obliged to pay plaintiff the debt.

Jan Jansen Van Amersfoort, Plaintiff
vs. Aeriaen Gerretsen, Defendant

Plaintiff says that he is to receive three sch. of wheat of Henderick Cornelissen which defendant has attached. Defendant shows his bill. Plaintiff still owes him a balance of 14 gldrs, and 13 gldrs. 16 st. for expenses, on account of which he had attached aforementioned three sch. of wheat; and also requests that the hon. court be pleased to secure him against lost time.

The hon. court decides whereas plaintiff cites the wife of Willem Jansen Stol who declares to know that plaintiff ordered her husband during his life time to pay defendant three sch. of wheat, wherewith defendant was satisfied at the time, because her husband made shingles and did cooper's work for him on which account he still owes her money, therefore the hon. court orders that said assignment shall be valid, and defendant is refused the expense for the attachment of the three sch. of wheat, and further orders parties to mutually settle and square their accounts.

Gerret Fooken, Plaintiff
vs. Jan Willemsen Hoochteylingh, Defendant

Plaintiff says that during the war against the

savages, in the year 1663 the soldiers took some goods out of his burnt house in the new village, and sold them to defendant, and requests those goods to be returned to him.

Defendant admits having bought some goods from the soldiers in the year 1663, for nine sch. of wheat, and says that, after he had bought the aforenamed goods, plaintiff called upon him and asked him if he had bought any goods from the soldiers, whereupon defendant answered him, "Yes," and then showed him the whole lot and said, "If it was his he would gladly and willingly return it, for what he had promised to pay for the same, or that he would go to the soldiers for the purpose of making an arrangement with them."

Plaintiff replies and says that, at the time, he called at defendant's house for the purpose of enquiring about said goods.

The hon. court decides that plaintiff at the time ought to have spoken about the goods to the sellers and demanded his rights from them, because they were present at the time and knew about it, and defendant Jan Willemsen at the time, and even now yet, offered to return his goods to him, provided plaintiff be willing to return him his advanced nine sch. of wheat. On this account plaintiff's demand against defendant is denied.

Willem Beeckman, Schout, Plaintiff
vs. Foppe Barents, Defendant

Plaintiff says that last Saturday during the evening, a soldier Ridsert Keesschie complained to him that Foppe Barents has bothered him and called him names in his quarters. He first said not to care a snap for all the English, and that the English soldiers had come hither for the purpose of plaguing the farmers, and to rob the country, and he further said, "When spring comes, we shall kill all of you," and while passing through the house, he snapped his nails against his teeth, saying to care as much for the English and for their King.

Defendant denies the foregoing.

The hon. court orders the officer to enquire more closely into this business and to gain information concerning the same.

Annetje Ariaens requests to be relieved from the debts of hers, because the effects she has possessed with her absconded husband have been sold by execution in behalf of the creditors.

The hon. court decides to have no authority for the same, but petitioner will have to address the higher authority to which she is referred.

The hon. schout proposes whereas up to now no or little payment has been made to the preacher for his past services, that the hon. court be pleased to take measures for the payment of the same.

The commissary Gysbert Van Imbroch also complains about the expenses incurred for the last diet of the year 1664 to the Manhatans, and requests the hon. court to take measures for paying said incurred expenses.

The hon. court decides to sell on Friday next to the highest bidder the empty lot of Pieter Van Hael, for the payment of the village debts.

Also to let the house of Gerret Bancken, for the purpose of paying the village debts.

Gysbert Van Imbroch requests execution of the judgment pronounced on Nov. 15, 1664, against Ariaen Gerretsen. The hon. court orders the officer to proceed with the execution.

Further information taken in regard to the affair between Walran Du Mont and Ariaen Gerretsen. And were examined the attestors in behalf of Ariaen Gerretsen, in the presence of Willem Beeckman, Schout, Thomas Chambers and Jan Willemsen Hoochteylingh, Commissaries.

Joris Hael and Eduard Wittiger judicially verified and affirmed under oath their attestation given on Dec. 15, 1664, at the request of Ariaen Gerretsen.

Jacob Burhams, Evert Pels and Jan Jansen Van Amersfoort judicially verified and affirmed under oath their attestation in behalf of Ariaen Gerretsen on Dec. 15, 1664.

Ordinary Session, Tuesday, January 20, 1665.
Present, Willem Beeckman, Schout; Thomas Chambers, Gysbert Van Imbroch, Jan Willemsen Hoochteylingh, Henderick Jochemsen, Commissaries.
Willem Beeckman, Plaintiff
vs. Tjerck Claesen De Wit, Defendant. Absent. Default.
Gysbert Van Imbroch, Plaintiff
vs. Tjerck Claesen De Wit, Defendant. Absent. Default.
Jacob Joosten, Plaintiff
vs. Roelof Swartwout, Defendant
Plaintiff demands from defendant the money coming to him from the sale of the grain of the children of Mattys Jansen, deceased; also the "stiver money" on account of the judicial sale at Cornelis Barentsen Slecht's; also the "stiver money" for the horse sold at the judicial sale at Aert Pietersen Tack's, and, requests to receive an oortje from the stiver. Also demands two sch. of wheat for school money.

Defendant says that plaintiff's demand has no foundation as far as the "stiver money" is concerned, but does not refuse him his daily wage. Defendant also requests whereas in his quality of schout, before this, he also held the office of secretary, that he may receive from plaintiff one-half of the money for the summons till the end of his first year in office, according to the customs of this country.

The hon. court decides that plaintiff shall receive

from defendant in regard to the sales /vendues/ three
gldrs; and in regard to the judicial sales /execution/ six
gldrs. for daily wage. Plaintiff is also ordered to pay
defendant one-half of the money for the summons, in accordance with defendant's request, and /further orders/
parties to settle with each other concerning the same.

Gysbert Van Imbroch, Plaintiff
vs. Annetje Mattysen, Defendant

Plaintiff demands from defendant (in whose place appear the guardians Roelof Swartwout and Cornelis Barentsen
Slecht) the physician's fee, being five beavers. Defendant's guardians answer to have been informed that plaintiff has settled concerning the same with Jan Peersen who
has hurt defendant.

Plaintiff answers and denies having settled, but says
that he had a talk with Jan Peersen, at the time the patient was going to the Manhatans, about having earned five
beavers with her, and if it should cost five more beavers
/said Peersen/ would not object to paying the same if the
patient only should not keep a stiff leg, whereupon
plaintiff, Mr. Gysbert Van Imbroch, answered Jan Peersen,
"If any surgeon at the Manhatans says that the patient has
not been well cured, or that her case should not have been
well treated, he does not want anything for it."

The hon. court decides that plaintiff shall settle
with defendant or her guardians concerning the surgeon's
fee, in consideration of the fact that defendant has been
fully cured at the Manhattans.

Pieter Gillissen, Plaintiff
vs. Ariaen Gerretsen, Defendant

Plaintiff demands from defendant six sch. of wheat
for tending the cattle. Defendant answers having only
yesterday offered plaintiff one-half, which plaintiff was
unwilling to accept. The hon. court orders defendant to
satisfy plaintiff's aforenamed demand.

Tomas Harmensen, Plaintiff
vs. Albert Gerretsen, Defendant. Absent. Default.
and Jan Jacobs Burhans, Defendant

Plaintiff demands from defendant, Jan Jacobs Burhans,
the just share of his excise. Defendant says, having declared to the farmer or plaintiff the excise of half a keg
of good beer, which had been taken into the guardhouse, he
further told him to deduct the excise from the four gldrs.
he owed defendant.

The hon. court orders defendant to pay the plaintiff
the excise for the half keg of good beer and denies plaintiff's further claim because defendant declared the same
to him, and also because he could deduct it from defendant's claimed money.

Tomas Harmensen, Plaintiff
vs. Evert Pels, Defendant

Plaintiff says that defendant summoned him at the last

session of the court, for which he claims his lost time,
saying that he has fooled him. Defendant says that he
wanted plaintiff to appear at the last session to have
plaintiff affirm under oath, why he is not obliged to pay
to Jonas Rantsou 36 gldrs. in sewan, for which reason defendant still claims from plaintiff aforenamed 36 gldrs.
in sewan, unless plaintiff would declare not to owe said
amount to Jonas Rantsou.

The hon. court orders defendant, Evert Pels, to
prove that plaintiff, Thomas Harmensen, has promised to
pay Jonas Rantsou 36 gldrs. in sewan.

Willem Beeckman, Schout, Plaintiff
vs. Walran Du Mont, Defendant

Plaintiff says that defendant refused to pay /his
share of_/ the preacher's salary, amounting, as per account, to 25 gldrs. in beavers. Defendant answers that
the hon. court, last year, gave him permission to cry out
that those having claims against his predecessor Jan
Aertsen should notify him, and consequently asserts, because it is so long ago, that he is not obliged to pay his
predecessor's village debts.

The hon. court orders defendant to pay, with the
other inhabitants, such moneys, as are shown by the bill,
from the village book, and /which bill was_/ sent to his
house, under penalty of execution.

Willem Beeckman, Schout, Plaintiff
vs. Mattheu Blanchan, Defendant

Plaintiff says that defendant has refused to pay /his
contribution to_/ the preacher's salary, being as per bill
20 gldrs. in beavers. Defendant replies that the preacher
does not hold consistory as is done in other congrega-
tions, and further says that the domine has not dealt
justly with him, for which reason he will not contribute
toward the preacher's salary, unless the domine gives him
satisfaction in the case between him and Allert Heymans.

The hon. court orders defendant to pay, like the
other inhabitants, such moneys as are shown by the bill
sent to his house, taken from the village book, under
penalty of execution, and that defendant shall once more
address himself to the consistory, and in case he cannot
get satisfaction there, will be at liberty to apply to
the court.

Henderick Cornelissen, Plaintiff
vs. Evert Pels, Defendant. Absent. Default.
Willem Beeckman, Plaintiff
vs. Henderick Cornelissen Slecht, Defendant

Plaintiff demands from defendant 16 1/3 sch. of
wheat for merchandize sold to him for wheat, for himself,
personally, and still 54 gldrs. 12 st. heavy money from
the effects of Aert Pietersen Tack. Defendant admits the
above debts, and says having some counter claims against
the 54 gldrs. 12 st. from the effects of Tack. In re-

gard to the personal debt, he says that he not really
owes wheat, but maintains that he is at liberty to pay in
other grain.

The hon. court orders defendant to pay plaintiff for
his personal claims one-half in wheat and the balance in
other grain. Concerning the 54 gldrs. 12 st. in heavy
money defendant is ordered to pay the same to plaintiff in
said money.

Walran Du Mont, Plaintiff

vs. Ariaen Gerretsen, Defendant

Plaintiff demands as per foregoing suit on Jan. 6,
1665, from defendant the expenses for surgeon's fee and
pain. Defendant says not to be obliged to pay for surgeon's fee and pain.

The hon. court decides whereas plaintiff Walran Du
Mont has been causa movens, and has twice beaten defendant at the house of Mattheu Blanchan, as per sworn certificate, and also has, with a long stick, driven defendant near the guard house into a corner of the palisades,
and has also taken hold of his hair, and would not release him until Eduard Wittiger threatened to strike
plaintiff with his sword, whereupon he let go and later
on he, plaintiff, assaulted and struck defendant at the
well with a piece of chopped wood, and threw him to the
ground, according to a sworn statement of Eduard Wittiger
and Joris Hael, both soldiers in the Service of the Royal
Majesty of England, whereby it further appeared that defendant was hurt by plaintiff about the head, therefore
plaintiff is refused his demand, and it is decided that
plaintiff as well as defendant shall each bear his own
damage, pain and expenses for surgeon.

Cornelis Pietersen Hoogeboom requests that he may be
granted a lot opposite the mill dam for a brick yard.
The hon. court grants petitioner's request /and decides/
to grant him /a lot/ of about ½ morgen in extent.

Tjerck Claesen De Wit, having on this day been judicially summoned by the court messenger to appear before
the court for the purpose of hearing his testimony in regard to the calling of names between an English soldier
quartered at his house, and Foppe Barentsen, has at the
first summons said to the court messenger that he had no
time because his help was in the woods, at the second
time when the court messenger had again been sent to his
house, to summon him to appear or that the court would
fetch him, he answered that he could not come, "but if
the court will fetch me, it knows where I live," whereupon
the court sent the officer for him, but did not find him
at home.

The hon. court decides whereas Tjerck Claesen, on
account of the aforementioned case, has been summoned before the hon. court, and he obstinately refuses to appear,
and has thereby shown contempt of court, therefore he is

sentenced to pay 50 gldrs. fine, to be applied where it is proper.

The petition of the guardians of the minor children of Mattys Jansen, deceased, having been received, in which it is requested that the money for the preacher's salary amounting to 80 gldrs. and the expenses for the delegates to the diet, amounting to 15 gldrs. in grain, heavy money, may not be levied from them, but from the lessee Thomas Chambers, in the same way and manner as before this has been done in regard to other lessees, and is still done, is replied to:

Whereas it has not been specially stipulated in the lease whether the lessee or the lessor should bear and pay the past village charges for the lands, therefore the hon. court decides that the lessor and the lessee shall each bear and pay one-half of the past village expenses of the lands, but that the lessee shall be responsible for the payment of the full amount of the past village debts, provided the lessee is at liberty to charge one-half of said amount to the lessor.

The hon. Schout Willem Beeckman requests that the defendant Thomas Harmensen, farmer, may be judicially dealt with in regard to the back three-monthly payment of the excise on wines and beers, as per pronounced judgment on Nov. 25, 1664. The hon. court orders the officer to proceed with the execution.

Thomas Chambers appeals from the above decision in regard to the answer to the petition of the guardians of the minor children of Mattys Jansen, deceased.

Ordinary Session, Tuesday, January 27, 1665.
Present: Willem Beeckman, Schout; Thomas Chambers, Gysbert Van Imbroch, Jan Willemsen Hoochteylingh, Henderick Jochemsen, Commissaries.

Willem Beeckman, Schout, Plaintiff
vs. Tjerck Claesen De Wit, Defendant. Absent. Default.

Roelof Swartwout, Plaintiff
vs. Albert Govertsen, Defendant

Plaintiff says that he finds that on the village account sent to him, he is debited for two years /contribution/ toward the preacher's salary, and whereas the lot at present possessed by him has been only one year in his possession, as per deed, he maintains not to owe any more than for the year 1664, and requests that he may be relieved of the payment of one year's /contribution to/ the salary. The hon. court, for cause, permits that plaintiff shall be relieved from contributing /said/ one year toward the salary.

The guardians of the minor children of the deceased Mattys Jansen, Plaintiff
vs. Thomas Chambers, Defendant

Plaintiffs demand from defendant, as per lease, the

rent for two years amounting to 640 gldrs., as also /payment/ for the palisades which defendant, with knowledge of plaintiff, has partially or wholly appropriated, amounting to 94 gldrs., and request that the hon. court will sustain them, and to guard the rights of orphans as their heads. Defendant denies having had the administration of the palisades and, concerning the lease, he says not to owe the full two years' rent, on account of the unexpected war against the savages during those two years, and supports /his denial/ in a written statement containing seven points: 1) that all during the summer he was obliged to go against the enemy with all his available horses; 2) that lessors did not furnish him horses with the farm, as is done to other lessees, for the purpose of using the same for the aforenamed services; 3) that he was obliged to harvest his crops, in part, under heavy expenses for convoy of 25 or 26 soldiers, he being at the expense of feeding them; 4) that he was obliged to leave about 20 morgens of grain standing on the land which he could not harvest; 5) that during the fall the little that he could sow had to be done under heavy convoy, and also that the same could not /illegible/ at the proper time; 6) that during the early part of 1664 the sowing of the summer grain also took place under convoy, and he was obliged to board the same; 7) that a few morgens still had to remain unsown, and on this account requests a reduction as has been granted to other lessees whose lands are situated close by the village, while these lands lie at a considerable distance from the village.

Plaintiff's request copy of defendant's written reply for the purpose of answering at the next session of the court.

The hon. court orders plaintiffs to prove at the next session of the court that defendant appropriated the palisades to his own use and they are, according to their request, furnished with a copy of defendant's reply for the purpose of answering the same at the next session of the court.

Thomas Chambers requests the hon. court to revise its answer to the guardians of the minor children of Mattys Jansen, deceased, given on Jan. 20, 1665, and further requests to be relieved from the leased farm of the aforesaid guardians, provided the standing crop be appraised, or that he may be permitted to harvest said crop and return to them the empty land the same as he has found it.

The hon. court, having revised the answer aforementioned, and having been informed that petitioner rents no more than 26 morgens, orders petitioner to contribute at the rate of ½ of said 26 morgens toward the salary.

In regard to the further petition to be relieved from the lease of the land, the hon. court refers the petitioner to the guardians for the purpose of arriving at an under-

standing with them.
Evert Pels, Plaintiff
vs. Juriaen Westphael, Defendant

Plaintiff demands from defendant a sum of 262 gldrs.
5 st. heavy money as per note, and also 20 gldrs. 4 st.
light money for expenses incurred. Defendant admits the
debt, but says having paid something on the same, viz.,
13 sch. of peas, 6 sch. of buckwheat and two half kegs of
small beer, amounting to a sum of 45 gldrs. 10 st. heavy
money, besides ten sch. of wheat furnished to the help,
and a pair of children's shoes, amounting to 33 gldrs.
heavy money. Plaintiff answers and says that the 11 sch.
of wheat had been liquidated for the making of the note
and claims the expenses incurred and yet to be incurred.
The hon. court orders that defendant shall prove that
he paid the 11 sch. of wheat after passing the note, and
defendant is further condemned to satisfy plaintiff's
aforementioned claim with the costs.
Evert Pels, Plaintiff
vs. Pieter Hillebrants, Defendant

Plaintiff demands from defendant 34 gldrs. in beavers
which he paid for defendant to Jan Bastiaansen in the year
1659. Defendant says not to owe more than 12 sch. of
wheat, and that he paid Jan Simonsen three sch. Plaintiff
replies, saying that defendant shall prove that he paid
Jan Simonsen three sch. of wheat for the plaintiff.
The hon. court orders defendant to prove that he has
paid the three sch. to Jan Simonsen, or if not, defendant
shall pay plaintiff aforesaid claim of 34 gldrs. in beavers.

Pieter Cornelissen sends in a petition by which he
requests that the mill house at Wildwyck, belonging to him
and his deceased friend and partner Pieter Jacobsen, may
be appraised as to the just value of the structure, that in
making repairs to the same petitioner afterward may not
suffer loss, and also that hereafter in what he pays more
to the creditors than the valuation will show it to be
worth, may be credited to his account in case the deceased's
friends should urge him. And takes it upon himself to pay
the creditors as opportunity will allow. Petitioner will
first have to produce an inventory of the effects having
belonged to him and his deceased partner, and thereupon the
hon. court will arrange matters.

Geertruyd Andriesen requests payment of the balance
of the room rent, and to transfer said balance to the hon.
Heer Beeckman. The hon. court grants petitioner's aforestated request.

The hon. court orders Jacob Burhans to hand his books
of the administration.of the excise to the secretary here,
that the accounts in the village book may be balanced.

Extraordinary Session, Saturday, Jan. 31, 1665.
Present: Willem Beeckman, Schout; Thomas Chambers,

Gysbert Van Imbroch, Jan Willemsen Hoochteylingh, Henderick Jochemsen, Commissaries; Christoffel Berrisfort, Commander of the Militia.

The hon. Schout Willem Beeckman, having yesterday arrested one Pieter Gillissen because said Pieter Gillissen, being drunk, wounded yesterday a savage with a knife in his behind, requests what shall be done with said Pieter Gillissen.

Pieter Gillissen, having been asked whether he knew what he had yesterday done to the savage, answers to know quite well that he stabbed the savage, because said savage called him a drunken dog. Pieter Gillissen, having been ordered to settle with the savage, answers, "If I had only stabbed the savage to death, he /the savage/ would now be forgotten."

The hon. schout advises that defendant Pieter Gillissen shall be obliged to fully satisfy the savage, and to pay the surgeon's fee, and that he shall also give bail till the spring, to appear before the court, if required, or else that he shall be kept under arrest till the spring. The abovementioned advice is approved by the whole court.

Burgher and War Council, held Wednesday, January 28, 1665.

Present: Willem Beeckman, Schout; Thomas Chambers, Commissary and Captain; Gysbert Van Imbroch, Jan Willemsen Hoochteylingh, Commissaries; Henderick Jochemsen, Commissary and Lieutenant; Christoffel Berrisfort, Commander of the Militia.

In consequence of the hurried dispatch of a letter from Fort Orange by Capt. Manningh to the hon. Lord Governor at New York, and the written information by the Capt. Manningh to Christoffel Berrisfort, Commander of the Militia here, that about 3,000 savages were to appear at Fort Orange, and also we having been informed that a savage has examined the palisades around the village or fortification, the following resolution was passed: that on tomorrow the 29th the burghers shall be called to arms, and shall then be instructed to provide the points of the palisading with breastworks, and also that in time of need the local English garrison shall be divided among the burghers, to which Christoffel Berrisfort consented, being four men for each of the three principal points. Further that the decree concerning the attachment of the company's effects and claims, issued by the Noble Lord Governor of the Manhatans to the local court, besides an order by the Noble Lord Governor to Capt. Thomas Chambers, shall be published. It was also approved, upon the advice of the Commissary Gysbert Van Imbroch, that John Charp, an English soldier, shall be employed as assistant-gunner for the cannon in the village, because aforenamed Charp is a fit person for said work, which aforesaid Charp has accepted with the permission of Berrisfort.

Ordinary Session, Tuesday, February 3, 1665.
Present: Willem Beeckman, Schout; Thomas Chambers, Gysbert Van Imbroch, Jan Willemsen Hoochteylingh, Henderick Jochemsen, Commissaries.

Henderick Cornelissen, Lyndrayer, Plaintiff
vs. Ariaen Gerretsen Van Vliet, Defendant
Plaintiff demands from defendant the rent for the barn as per lease, being 25 sch. of wheat, and due on Christmas of the year 1664. Defendant admits the debt, but says that he is not able to pay. The hon. court orders defendant to pay plaintiff the aforesaid amount.

Willem Beeckman, Plaintiff
vs. Tjerck Claesen De Wit, Defendant
Plaintiff demands from defendant 206 gldrs. 12 st. in sewan as per balance of account, as well for himself, as for the auction of Frederick Claesen's and other expenses as well as for the execution /legal sale/ of the horse as for other items. Defendant admits the debt but says not to be able to pay in wheat. The hon. court orders defendant to satisfy plaintiff's aforenamed claim.

Juriaen Westphael, Plaintiff
vs. Tjerk Claesen De Wit, Defendant. Absent. Default.

Gysbert Van Imbroch, Plaintiff
vs. Tjerck Claesen De Wit, Defendant. Absent. Default.
Whereas defendant has absented himself for the second time, plaintiff demands from defendant 31 gldrs. in sewan for expenses incurred at the sale of Henderick Looman's effects. He also demands interest for the aforesaid amount, because defendant himself also has taken some moneys from said estate on interest.

Thomas Chambers, Plaintiff
vs. Tjerck Claesen De Wit, Defendant. Absent. Default.

Thomas Chambers, Plaintiff
vs. Evert Pels, Curator of the estate of Jan Albertsen Van Steenwyck's, and Henderick Jochemsen, Guardian, Defendants.
Plaintiff demands from defendants 17 gldrs. 2 st. in sewan as per account. Defendants show their account book, in which it is found that plaintiff owes said book and estate 25 gldrs. 15 st. in sewan. Plaintiff replies that deceased Jan Albertsen's book cannot be admitted, because it neither contains day nor date and says not to know that he received brandy of the deceased Jan Albertsen, for which he would have remained indebted.
The hon. court orders plaintiff to prove that he is not indebted to deceased Jan Albertsen and that he paid him for the brandy, or he shall be obliged to satisfy plaintiffs for the balance.

Arent Jansen, Plaintiff
vs. Tjerck Claesen De Wit, Defendant. Absent. Default.
The guardians of the minor children of deceased Mattys Jansen, Zaele (meaning deceased), Plaintiffs,
vs. Thomas Chambers, Defendant

Plaintiffs bring in their reply, showing that defendant has no case in his answer to the demand made by them. Defendant requests that he may be allowed a reduction of rent because it is known that at the last war with the savages the whole village has suffered, and in consequence of which he himself also sustained much damage, as can be seen from his answers.

The hon. court decides whereas on account of the war much damage has been caused to the village, and defendant has also suffered, that in consideration of this, parties are referred to good men, being Evert Pels, Allert Heymans, Jan Joosten and Aert Jacobsen, for the purpose of bringing the parties together if possible, or else that parties shall again appear before the court.

Evert Pels, attorney for Jonas Rantsou, produces a certificate signed by Walran DuMont and Jan Cornelissen Van Gottenborsh dated Nov. 6, 1664, in proof that Thomas Harmensen owes Jonas Rantsou 36 gldrs. to be paid in sewan and requests that Thomas Harmensen, as per promise, shall pay the 36 gldrs. in sewan.

Whereas petitioner Evert Pels has shown proof about the 36 gldrs. in sewan in the difference between one Jonas Rantsou and Thomas Harmensen, petitioner is ordered to acquaint Thomas Harmensen with the same, and in case he is unwilling to pay him, that he shall summon the person of Thomas Harmensen to appear at the next session of the court.

Aert Martensen Doorn, Plaintiff
vs. Roelof Swartwout, Defendant

Plaintiff demands from defendant 76 gldrs. in corn, heavy money, as per note. Defendant admits the debt, but answers that plaintiff is obliged to break new land for him for four days, as is also shown by above note.

The hon. court decides that plaintiff shall carry out the conditions about four days' ploughing for defendant, and then defendant is ordered to satisfy plaintiff's aforesaid claim.

Walran DuMont, Plaintiff
vs. Arent Jansen, Defendant

Plaintiff demands from defendant 18 sch. of wheat for delivered goods, as per account. Defendant admits the debt and says he intends to pay plaintiff as soon as he shall receive payment himself. The hon. court orders defendant to pay plaintiff the abovenamed claim.

Walran DuMont, having been asked by the schout whether he intends to pay the village bill sent to him, answers not to be willing to pay more than four sch. of wheat for one year, and that he has paid the two sch. of wheat promised last yesr for the minister's salary. Further says not to intend to pay the 10 gldrs. owed by his predecessor, because he has publicly announced that those having claims against his predecessor should give them

in, or else should be denied their claims.
Jan Willemsen Hoochteylingh, Plaintiff
vs. Allert Heymans, Defendant
Plaintiff demands from defendant 42 sch. of wheat and
30 st. in sewan, for delivered merchandize and assignments
by others. Defendant admits the debt, but says not being
able to pay right away. The hon. court orders defendant
to satisfy plaintiff's aforenamed demand.
Jan Willemsen Hoochteylingh, Plaintiff
vs. Aert Martensen Doorn, Defendant
Plaintiff demands from defendant 14½ sch. of wheat for
delivered goods. Defendant admits the debt, but says not
to be able to pay right away. The hon. court orders defendant to satisfy plaintiff's abovementioned demand.
Jan Willemsen Hoochteylingh, Plaintiff
vs. Claes Claesen, Defendant
Plaintiff says that he has engaged defendant for a
year, and demands from him proper work, because defendant
neglects his work by getting drunk and gaming, and demands of defendant what he has to say against him. Defendant says not to have anything to say against food or
drink at plaintiff's, his master. The hon. court orders
defendant to properly attend to his duties in his service
with plaintiff, his employer.

Jacob Jansen Van Etten requests payment from the estate of Aert Pietersen Tack for wages, amounting to 388
gldrs. heavy money in wheat. The hon. court decides that
after the preferred creditors, plaintiff shall be paid
pro rata.

The hon. schout complains about Ariaen Gerretsen Van
Vliet, because aforesaid Ariaen Gerretsen has carried away
the inventoried effects which were to be legally sold in
behalf of Thomas Harmensen on Jan. 25, 1665, and requests
the hon. court to sustain him against aforesaid Ariaen
Gerretsen. The hon. court orders Ariaen Gerretsen Van
Vliet to again produce the inventoried effects he has carried away, under penalty of arrest.

Hermanus Blom, preacher, requests payment for his
past services, and also of his advanced money; and that
measures be taken for the requested payment, and complains
that in this manner he cannot keep house, because from the
congregation he has only received very little. The hon.
court will, as much as possible, do its duty in this regard, and urge the congregation to contribute.
Willem Beeckman, Schout, Plaintiff
vs. Tjerck Claesen DeWit, Defendant
Plaintiff demands from defendant toward the salary of
the preacher a sum of 101 gldrs. two st. four cents in
beavers, and also 39 gldrs. five st. in grain heavy money,
as per bill from the village book /which bill was/ handed
to him. Defendant refers to his answer given to schout
and commissaries, while they were speaking to him about

the preacher's salary, when he said, "To be willing to
carry out his given promise, but right away not to be
able to do more." The hon. court orders the officer to
proceed against defendant on account of the aforesaid village charges, because in presence of the hon. Ld. Dir.
Genl. it was decided that for the past three years one
gldr. per morgen was to be paid toward the preacher's
salary. Plaintiff, the schout, further demands 50 gldrs.
in sewan as per sentence on Jan. 20, 1665, because defendant showed contempt of court, upon being summoned to
appear before the same. Defendant says not to intend to
pay the 50 gldrs. as per sentence.

Examination of Tjerck Claesen, in the case between
Foppe Barents and Ridsert Keesye, English soldier;
Tjerck Claesen is asked whether he does not know that
Foppe Barents, on Jan. 3 last, said to Ridsert Keesy,
soldier, "You English have come here for the purpose of
troubling the farmers, and robbing the country." Answers,
"No," but that Foppe Barents has said, "You are here with
the farmers to get something to eat, and they themselves
haven't got anything to eat." Whether he did not hear
that Foppe Barents said to the aforesaid soldier; "I
don't care a snap for you, we shall kill all of you next
spring." Answers, "No," but that the aforesaid Foppe
should have said, "to receive other news about spring."
Whether Foppe Barents, while passing through the house,
snapped his nails against his teeth, saying, "So much
do I care for all the English and their King," answers
that he snapped with his nail against his teeth against
Keesy, but that he did not mention the King with it. And
is prepared, if necessary, to confirm the foregoing with
an oath.

Jacob Joosten, court messenger, requests payment for
his services, ecclesiastical as well as political, since
the year 1661. Petitioner, concerning his church service,
is referred to the consistory, and concerning his service
for the court, petitioner/'s name/ has been entered in the
village book.

Pieter Cornelissen requests in a petition that the
hon. court be pleased to appraise the mill house at Wildwyck with its appurtenances, for which purpose he has inventoried all the effects belonging to him and his
deceased partner, Pieter Jacobsen. The hon. court decides that petitioner may sell at public auction to the
highest bidder all the effects belonging to himself and
his deceased partner, Pieter Jacobsen.

Extraordinary Session, Wednesday, February 4, 1665.

Present: Willem Beeckman, Schout; Thomas Chambers,
Gysbert Van Imbroch, Jan Willemsen Hoochteylingh, Henderick Jochemsen, Commissaries.

Aert Jacobsen and his wife Annetje Gerrets complain

about violence committed against them in their house on
this day, by Christoffel Berrisfort and five English
soldiers who entered their house fully armed and took from
them by violence a ham, which the aforenamed wife wanted
to prevent and was wounded in the arm by Daniel Botterwout while he was cutting loose the ham in the presence
of the court-messenger Jacob Joosten. Said Botterwout
furthermore drew his sword for the purpose of resisting
those who would prevent him from taking the ham with him.
Aforesaid Aert Jacobsen declares that on Jan. 29 last he
provided his soldier, Tomas Marcham, with provisions for
a whole week, and that he asked him if he wanted more; he
said he had enough. Said soldier, the day before yesterday on Feb. 2, sent Samuel Olivier for bread which plaintiff gave him, and further asked him whether the aforenamed soldier wanted meat or pork, to which he answered,
not to have orders from him concerning the same. Thereupon, yesterday, another soldier, Tomas Elger, coming to
their house for meat and pork, they refused the same to
him because, before this, while their soldier was stationed at the redoubt, another also came, by his authority,
for meat and pork which was sent to him, and when he was
relieved from the redoubt and came back home, he said that
he had had enough food and had given no orders to get more.

Juriaen Westphael and his wife, having been asked
when they had given their soldier Eduard French provisions
for the redoubt, answer that on last Thursday, Jan. 29,
they gave their aforenamed soldier for the redoubt for
one week nine lbs. of meat and pork, a loaf of bread
weighing eight lbds. and two heads of cabbage in the
presence of Femmetje the baker and Magdelena Dirricks,
and asked him if he wanted more for one week; he said that
he had enough. He further says that his soldier aforenamed, on yesterday, Feb. 3, sent a soldier Tomas Elger
to his house for more meat and pork, but he refused him
the same. He makes a complaint that the soldier Daniel
Botterwout on this day entered his house fully armed and
wanted to forcibly take meat and pork if he would not send
the same to his soldier Eduard French.

Eeshie, the wife of Ariaen Gerretsen Van Vliet,
having been asked about what she has seen and heard at
Christoffel Davids', when he saw his wife home on Feb. 2,
answers that she called on said day at the house of
Christoffel Davids, and was by him invited to share their
meal and that Christoffel Davids said that he had bought
a loaf of bread for tobacco from the soldier, Mr. Paul.

Mr. Christoffel Berrisfort, having been handed the
instructions of the hon Ld. Governor Richard Nicolls to
the court, for the purpose of reading the same, and having
been asked if he had another and more binding instruction,
that he should inform the court about it, and that the
hon. court would submit to his instruction, answers that

he has no instruction of the hon. Ld. Governor of New
York.

Mr. Berrisfort was further talked to about the violence committed against Aert Jacobsen in his house, by
him and five soldiers, and at the same time shown the
evils which might ensue from similar violence. He is
therefore requested to conduct all the English soldiers
about 8:00 o'clock tomorrow before the hon. court for the
purpose of again reading to them the instructions given
to the hon. court here by the hon. Ld. Governor of New
York thus to prevent any disasters.

Extraordinary Session, Thursday, Feb. 5, 1665.

Present: Willem Beeckman, Schout; Thomas Chambers,
Gysbert Van Imbroch, Jan Willemsen Hoochteylingh, Henderick Jochemsen, Commissaries.

On this date the instruction by the hon. Ld. Governor
of New York was again read to the English soldiers, and
thereupon the following protest was drawn up against Mr.
Berrisfort and the aforenamed soldiers:

Protest

Whereas, to us Schout and Commissaries of the village of Wildwyck complaints have been made by some inhabitants here, concerning violence and outrage committed
by some English soldiers against some of our residents,
and we fear that, on account of further similar violence
and outrage which the soldiers hereafter may commit at
this place, many and fearful quarrels will arise among the
burghers and residents of this place, therefore we protest
to them and everybody before God and the world, if any
disasters and rebellion should arise on account of similar
bad conduct, that we, Schout and Commissaries, absolve
ourselves from all responsibility for possible calamities.
We therefore by the present advise any and all of them, if
any of our residents should be unreasonable to them, to
lodge a complaint with us concerning the same, and we
shall then sustain them in their just cause. Done at
Wildwyck, this Feb. 5, N. S. 1665.

Daniel Botterwout, having been questioned whether he
would have fought about it, because he entered Aert
Jacobsen's house armed, when on yesterday he took the ham
from the aforesaid house, in case said /ham/ was refused
him, answers that he would have fought for the same, in
case he had been prevented from taking it.

The hon. schout complains because this morning, after
the drummer had drummed off the guard, the entire corporal's guard which had had the watch last night came to
his house with one Pieter Gillissen who is under arrest,
and corporal Henderick Martensen and Jan Joosten asked
him, while he was at the time still in bed, what was to
be done with the aforesaid Pieter Gillissen, whether he
was not to be discharged. Hereupon the schout answered

that the magistrates had a meeting yesterday and that on
account of Mr. Berrisfort's absence nothing could be
done in this case, and that at about 9:00 o'clock there
would again be a meeting. Then they would consider this
case. Said Pieter Gillissen and the guard being in the
vestibule shook off the shackles and left them there, and
/the schout/ requests, in regard to the same, that justice
may be done.
  The hon. court, having sent the court messenger for
the arrested Pieter Gillissen, /said court messenger/ reports that he did not find aforesaid Pieter Gillissen in
arrest, but has heard it said that he went with Roelof
Swartwout into the woods.
  On this February 5, 1665, was handed to me, the undersigned Mattheus Capito, by the hon. Willem Beeckman,
schout, the following document for the purpose of being
recorded. Said document reads as follows:

  On August 14 the Lord General Stuyvesant arrived at
this place, and immediately convened the hon. court,
owing to the complaint by the preacher, Hermanus Blom,
that he could not receive his salary when due. And
whereas the village has not sufficient revenue for the
payment of the preacher's salary and other expenses, it
was at last, after many deliberations, ordered and de-
creed by the Lord General Stuyvesant that the tax of one
gldr. before levied on each morgen of land, for this purpose, should be continued until the end of the four years
during which Domine Blom had been engaged by the company,
the tax upon the lots the same as heretofore. Further for
the fifth and following years negotiations were pending
with Domine Blom, and his demand of 300 sch. of wheat was
met by an offer of 200 sch. and his Rev. at last came down
to 250 sch., but no further offer was made by commissaries
and they separated without coming to an agreement. Done
at Wildwyck, on the abovenamed date, Anno 1664, (signed)
in the absence of the Secretary. Willem Beeckman.
  Upon comparison, /this was/ found to accord with the
original in the office of the Secretary at Wildwyck, which
testifies (signed) Mattheus Capito, Secretary.

  On this Feb. 6, Henderick Cornelissen, ropemaker,
had judicially attached all the grain still being unthreshed in the barn and storehouse, belonging to Ariaen
Gerretson Van Vliet, for the purpose of receiving his
claim of 25 sch. of wheat, on account of which he had recorded this attachment.

Ordinary Session, Tuesday, February 10, 1665.
  Presdent: William Beeckman, Schout; Thomas Chambers,
Gysbert Van Imbroch, Jan Willemsen Hoochteylingh, Hen-
derick Jochemsen, Commissaries.

Gysbert Van Imbroch, Plaintiff
vs. Tjerck Claesen De Witt, Defendant. Absent. Default.

Plaintiff demands from defendant who has absented himself for the third time, as curator for the estate of Henderick Looman, 31 gldrs. in wheat, for liquor furnished at
the public auction of Looman's and Seba's effects, with
the interest of the same, and the expenses made and yet to
be made on account thereof, because defendant himself has
taken some money at interest from the estate of Looman,
and plaintiff, for more than a year, has been left unpaid.

The hon. court at the third default, for contempt by
having not appeared, sentences defendant to pay plaintiff
the aforementioned claim of 31 gldrs. in grain, wheat, besides the interest and the expenses made and yet to be
made, without any delay.

Thomas Chambers, Plaintiff
vs. Tjerck Claesen De Wit, Defendant. Absent. 2nd Default.

Hendrick Cornelissen, Lyndraejer, Plaintiff
vs. Christoffel Davids, Defendant. Absent. Default.

Juriaen Westphael, Plaintiff
vs. Tjerck Claesen De Wit, Defendant. Absent. 2nd Default.

Arent Jansen, Plaintiff
vs. Tjerck Claesen De Wit, Defendant. Absent. 2nd Default.

Plaintiff demands from defendant 91 sch. of wheat
which he has earned with him by working, and says that he
has nothing to dress himself, and not to be able to satisfy others, his creditors.

Henderick Jochemsen, attorney for
Geertruyd Vossenborch, Plaintiff
vs. Walran DuMont, Defendant

Plaintiff demands from defendant 11 sch. of wheat for
wages. Defendant, being absent, is represented by his
wife who says, if plaintiff or Geertruyd Vossenborch will
produce her deceased husband's handwriting, or if she is
willing to affirm under oath ⁄the debt having run for six
years, and she not having been here during this time, so
the debt is unknown to her⁄ that she ⁄Geertruyd⁄ is entitled to the 11 sch. of wheat, defendant is willing then
to pay. The hon. court decides that plaintiff shall produce valid proof of the claim.

Evert Pels, Plaintiff
vs. Tomas Harmensen, Defendant

Plaintiff says that in compliance with a previous
minute dated Feb. 3, 1665, he has informed defendant to
pay the 36 gldrs. in sewan and says that defendant refused him the payment, and requests satisfaction for the
aforenamed 36 gldrs. Defendant requests that the attestors
shall affirm under oath their attestation in behalf of
Jonas Rantsou, and then he is willing to pay. The hon.
court orders plaintiff to have the passed attestation confirmed by oath, or if at fault, that plaintiff shall be
refused any further claim against defendant.

Roelof Swartwout, Plaintiff
vs. Henderick Jochemsen, Defendant

Plaintiff says that he privately sold defendant a
plough under the same conditions as he sold by public
auction on Dec. 29, 1664, his other effects. Defendant
says that he first wants to balance accounts with plaintiff. The hon. court orders parties to liquidate their
accounts.

Roelof Swartwout, Plaintiff
vs. Tomas Harmensen, Defendant

Plaintiff says that he bought from defendant an anker
of brandy for 100 gldrs. in sewan, and that defendant has
neglected to deliver the same, because the time is passed.
Defendant says that yesterday he notified plaintiff
through the court messenger that his wine was ready and
had him ask plaintiff if his payment was also ready.
The hon. court orders plaintiff to prove that he can also
pay in grain, in place of sewan, for said brandy.

Henderick Jochemsen, guardian for the minors,
left by Jan Albertsen, Plaintiff
vs. Roelof Swartwout, Defendant

Plaintiff demands from defendant on account of public
auction of the effects of Jan Albertsen Van Steenwyck
139 gldrs. 15 st. and for debts as per account book 55
gldrs. 10 st. and still six gldrs. as per note. Defendant denies the 55 gldrs. 10 st. debt, as per the book,
and says he paid the same, and is able to prove it; the
remaining debts of 139 gldrs. 15 st. and the six gldrs.,
as per note, defendant admits, but says that he has a
counter bill. The hon. court orders defendant to prove
that he paid the debt in the book of 55 gldrs. 10 st. and
further orders parties to balance their accounts.

The hon. Willem Beeckman requests that in regard to
the demand on Feb. 3, 1665, against Tjerck Claesen De Wit,
defendant, Tjerck Claesen de Wit may be judicially proceeded against for the amount of 206 gldrs. 12 st. in
sewan. The hon. court orders the officer to proceed with
the execution.

The hon. Willem Beeckman requests that in regard to
the demand on Dec. 16, 1664, against Ariaen Gerretsen Van
Vliet, he may be judicially proceeded against to the
amount of 165 gldrs. three st. in sewan. The hon. court
orders the officer to proceed with the execution.

Roelof Swartwout, appearing in the name of other
guardians of the minor children of Mattys Jansen, deceased,
says that they have given out on interest to Evert Pels
1,000 gldrs. in beavers' value, and whereas the two years
have elapsed, they, petitioners (for the purpose of not
ruining him, if he was to return aforementioned 1000
gldrs. with interest) are willing to allow aforesaid
Evert Pels to keep the aforementioned /amount/ another
year, if he is willing to furnish, besides the mortgage,

two satisfactory bondsmen, which he has refused to do, for which reason they, petitioners, want to consult with the hon. court as head guardian, about what to do. The hon. court, having considered the above request, orders Evert Pels to furnish two bondsmen besides the mortgage, or otherwise he shall return the 1,000 gldrs. beavers' value besides the interest for the two past years without delay.

Tomas Harmensen, farmer /of the excise/, complains that Henderick Palingh furnishes another with beer for the purpose of retailing the same, notwithstanding that he has for himself personally /or privately/ agreed with him to brew and to retail, and has delivered to Joris Hael five half kegs of beer, and has exempted aforesaid Joris Hael from the excise.

Thomas Harmensen requests that he may receive full payment through judicial sale of the effects of Ariaen Gerretsen Van Vliet, and further points out a new wagon, plough and harrow, belonging to aforesaid Ariaen Gerretsen. The hon. court decides, if it is proven that aforesaid pointed-out effects belong to Ariaen Gerretsen, that they shall be sold by judicial sale.

The hon. Willem Beeckman and Jan Willemsen Hoochteylingh, as members of the consistory at Wildwyck, request that the preacher, Hermanus Blom, as well in answer to his previous request of Feb. 26, 1664, as to his daily solicitation may receive his due salary. The hon. court orders the officer to judicially proceed against the unwilling, as per village account sent to them, concerning the salary of the aforenamed preacher.

We, the undersigned, schepenen of the village of Wildwyck, Thomas Chambers and Jan Willemsen Hoochteylingh, make known and know that there appeared before us the worthy Tjerck Claesen De Wit, resident of Wildwyck, who declares to owe to Swerus Teunissen, inhabitant of the colony of Rentselaerswyck, a sum of 111 gldrs. in good merchantable winter wheat, the shepel reckoned at three gldrs., originating on account of a cow bought by appearer from the estate of Aert Pietersen Tack which aforesaid amount of 111 gldrs. appearer takes at interest, from the attorney of Swerus Teunissen, at ten percent. annually for the time of one current year, commencing on Nov. 18, 1664, and terminating on Nov. 18 of this underwritten year 1665. With promise to pay said principal with the interest on the same precisely on Nov. 18 of this underwritten year to Swerus Tuenissen or his attorney. For the purpose of carrying out the same, he, appearer, specially mortgages the crop of all the grains which, under God's blessing, shall in this year 1665 be harvested from his land. And further in general his person and other estate personal and real, present and future, submitting himself and them to the jurisdiction of all courts and judges.

And renounces by these presents all exceptions and defences which might in any manner be contrary to these
presents. For the purpose of legalising the same, he,
appearer, has subscribed to the same, besides ourselves,
at Wildwyck this Feb. 11, 1665. (signed) Tjerck
Clasen De Witt, Thomas Chambers, Jan Willemsen Hoochteylingh. In my presence, to which certifies, Mattheus
Capito, Secretary.

Extraordinary Session, Thursday, February 12, 1665.
Present: William Beeckman, Schout; Thomas Chambers,
Gysbert Van Imbroch, Jan Willemsen Hoochteylingh, Henderick Jochemsen, Commissaries.
Whereas complaint has been made to the hon. court
that Jacob Joosten, court messenger, has refused to summon
to appear before the hon. court Christoffel Davids, living
across the Kill at the redoubt, and then was notified for
the third time to appear before the court, where he was
asked if he would summon said Christoffel Davids to appear
before the hon. court, because the hon. schout and others
wanted said Davids summoned before the court, answers,
"No," unless he is provided with a guard of two soldiers,
but he personally and alone, did not intend to imperil
his life. Upon refusing abovenamed service, Jacob Joosten,
court messenger, is therefore by the hon. court discharged
from his office. In whose place is appointed Albert Jansen Van Steenwyck, who, in consequence, is authorised by
the present to hold the office of court messenger at Wildwyck, and for this purpose he is given the following act
of qualification:
Whereas to the service of the hon. court at Wildwyck
an able person is needed as court messenger, the previous
court messenger having been discharged, /therefore/ by us
Schout and Commissaries of this village of Wildwyck is appointed Albert Jansen Van Steenwyck who, by the present,
is qualified as such, in whose attentive services we put
confidence.
Thus given in our meeting at Wildwyck, February 12,
1665.

Ordinary Session, Tuesday, February 17, 1665.
Present: Willem Beeckman, Schout; Thomas Chambers,
Gysbert Van Imbroch, Jan Willemsen Hoochteylingh, Henderick Jochemsen, Commissaries.
Willem Beeckman, Schout, Plaintiff
vs. Christoffel Davids, Defendant. Absent. Default.
Willem Beeckman, Schout, Plaintiff
vs. Pieter Gillissen, Defendant
Plaintiff demands from defendant restitution of money,
amounting to 12 gldrs., advanced at the request of the
court to satisfy the savage whom defendant on Jan. 31
last wounded, on account of which he was also sentenced,

and requests payment as well of the advanced money mentioned before, as of the jail expenses four gldrs., surgeon's fee six gldrs., board six gldrs., amounting together to 28 gldrs. sewan. Defendant answers he is not
able to pay, because others do not pay him. Plaintiff
replies and requests that if defendant cannot pay he be
arrested again, the more so because he left his arrest in
an irregular manner without orders from the court. Plaintiff also demands from defendant an axe which he loaned
him for the common work and says that in place of the
loaned axe he returned him a strange axe and that the
owner of the returned axe demands the same from the plaintiff. Defendant says that he brought the loaned axe into
his house and it got lost.

The hon. court orders defendant to pay plaintiff
within the time of six days the money advanced to the
wounded savage, prison money, surgeon's fee and board,
together amounting to 28 gldrs. in sewan, and in case of
neglect defendant shall again be put under arrest. Concerning the axe, defendant is ordered to return the same
loaned axe to plaintif within 24 hours or in case of
neglect defendant shall pay plaintiff the value of the
loaned axe.

Gysbert Van Imbroch, Plaintiff
vs. Thomas Chambers, Defendant

Plaintiff says that he credited defendant on his account in the year 1663 in the name of Aert Pietersen
Tack with 294 gldrs. in corn, at 10 gldrs. per mudde, and
requests from defendant receipt for the same, because he
has been security for the aforesaid money. Defendant says
when plaintiff shall have paid him as per note he will
give plaintiff a receipt. The hon. court orders parties
at the next session of the court to produce their bond
and "schepen knowledge," and then the case will be further considered.

Henderick Jochemsen, Plaintiff
vs. Christoffel Davids, Defendant. Absent. Default.
Henderick Cornelissen Lyndraeyer, Plaintiff
vs. Christoffel Davids, Defendant. Absent. 2nd Default.
Thomas Chambers, Plaintiff
vs. Christoffel Davids, Defendant. Absent. Default.
Juriaen Westphael, Plaintiff
vs. Tjerck Claesen DeWit, Defendant

Plaintiff demands payment coming to him from the estate of Henderick Jansen Looman. Defendant says that at
Fort Orange there are yet some debts standing out and on
that account said estate cannot be liquidated. And once
more requests to be discharged from his office of curator
because he is alone and his partner Albert Gysbertsen has
died. Defendant's request to be relieved from the office
of curator of /the estates of/ Henderick Jansen Looman
and Willem Jansen Seba is granted on account of the death

of his partner and because the liquidation does not
properly take place and the estate is not administered
to the satisfaction of the creditors, and in his place
are appointed Jacob Burhans and Aert Jacobsen, and defendant is ordered to transfer the accounts, proofs and
that which is left to the aforenamed persons.

Arent Jansen, Plaintiff
vs. Tjerck Claesen De Wit, Defendant

Plaintiff demands from defendant as per previous demand on Feb. 10 91 sch. of wheat for earned wages. Defendant says he does not know what plaintiff can claim.
The hon. court orders defendant to satisfy plaintiff's
aforenamed demand, provided he may deduct what he can
satisfactorily prove having paid plaintiff on the same.

Tomas Harmensen, Farmer, Plaintiff
vs. Henderick Palingh, Defendant

Plaintiff says that he prosecutes defendant for
smuggling because he has made an agreement with him to be
permitted to brew and to sell at retail for himself in
particular, but that defendant also has his brewed beer
retailed by another, Joris Hael. Defendant says that on
Jan. 13 last, he contracted with plaintiff for as long as
plaintiff has farmed the excise for eight sch. of wheat,
one half to be paid within three months, the other half
at the expiration of the time, for the purpose of being
permitted to brew and to retail, and further says that
yesterday, Feb. 16, he again contracted with plaintiff in
the presence of several persons, provided he pay plaintiff seven sch. of wheat, or the value of the same, in
ready money, as he has done, that he was to be permitted
to have brewn, bought and sold, as much beer as he could
brew, if he wanted to employ 20 retailers. Plaintiff replies and denies defendant's statement. Defendant takes
it upon himself to prove the last condition. The hon.
court orders defendant to produce trustworthy evidence.

Walran DuMont, Plaintiff
vs. Allert Heymans, Defendant

Grietje the wife of Walran DuMont demands from defendant payment of the amount of 98 gldrs. 4 st. heavy
money in grain at three gldrs. the sch. of wheat. Defendant says there is still a difference about the bill
concerning a pair of scissors which John the Smith promised
to repair for the same money and would like to have it deducted from the aforesaid amount, and also says he paid a
mudde of wheat on the aforenamed debt which mudde has not
been entered in his book nor in plaintiff's book, though
defendant's wife delivered said mudde which was taken away
by the smith's helper. Plaintiff replies he is not willing to accept nor to have deducted the scissors, but requests that defendant shall adduce further evidence concerning the same. Concerning the mudde of wheat, plaintiff is not willing to admit, but says if defendant is

ready to swear that he paid the mudde of wheat on account of the claimed amount, she is willing to deduct the
mudde. The hon. court orders defendant to prove that Jan
the smith promised him to repair the scissors, for the
same money, up to the third time, as also the delivery of
the mudde of wheat in question, or in case he is unable to
do so, he is sentenced to pay the entire amount claimed.

The guardians of the minor children of Mattys
Jansen, deceased, Plaintiffs,
vs. Thomas Chambers, Defendant

Plaintiffs demand from defendant the balance of the
rent for the land. Defendant says he is not able to bring
together the money now, but requests time till the following harvest time. Plaintiffs reply, saying, if defendant
is willing to keep said money on interest, they will allow
it to remain with him, as soon as to give it to some body
else. Defendant answers that it has never been customary
here to immediately pay the rent, and especially during
such dangerous times the lessee is not expected to pay interest on the rent due. Parties having been heard, the
hon. court decides, especially since it concerns the
property of orphans, that defendant is obliged to pay
plaintiffs the rent due or to pay interest on said money.

The above named guardians, Plaintiffs
vs. Evert Pels, Defendant

When made acquainted with the decision of the hon.
court on Feb. 10, 1665, defendant answered that he cannot
produce any other sureties than by mortgaging his lands.
The guardians aforenamed request the judgment of the court.
Defendant says that he offered the aforenamed guardians to
privately sell them his house, barn and store-house for
the satisfaction of the mortgage and interest. Plaintiffs
reply, saying that they have not got the power to do so,
and further that they do not deem it advisable. The hon.
court decides that the guardians are justifiable in their
demand and it is not advisable to turn real into personal
estate, which is subject to fire and other accidents, and
also considering that some of the children, upon reaching
their majority, will want some money, the hon. court orders defendant to satisfy plaintiffs' aforementioned
claim or to satisfy them in some other manner.

The aforenamed guardians, Plaintiffs
vs. Walran DuMont, Defendant

Plaintiffs demand from defendant certain balance as
per account, being an amount of 63 gldrs. and some stivers
heavy money, among which are included 30 gldrs. 4 st. for
interest. Defendant answers (in his absence being represented by his wife) to be willing to pay the principal,
but refuses to pay the interest on the same, and says that
she was not made acquainted with it at her first arrival.
Plaintiffs reply, saying that her deceased husband Jan Arents,
during his life, promised them to pay interest on the balance
which he was unable to pay. The hon. court decides, after the

testimony of three persons, whereas her deceased husband
promised to pay interest, that she shall satisfy plaintiff's
demand, but may deduct the interest for nine months or 157
gldrs. 10 st. for reason that defendant, when coming here,
was not informed about the interest.

Evert Pels, Plaintiff
vs. Aert Martensen Doorn, Defendant

Plaintiff demands from defendant a sum of 119 gldrs.
17 st. heavy money as per note, besides the interest on
the same. Defendant admits the debt but says he is powerless to pay the same right away. The hon. court orders
defendant to satisfy plaintiff's above claim.

Aert Martensen Doorn, Plaintiff
vs. Juriaen Westphael, Defendant. Absent.   Default.

Thomas Chambers and Gysbert Van Imbroch ex-delegates
to the diet of last year request that the inhabitants may
be judicially proceeded against for such moneys as are
owing them for advances to said diet, besides the interest
on the same. The officer is ordered to judicially proceed
against the unwilling inhabitants for such money as
charged against them on the village account, sent to their
house, concerning the advanced money for the delegates to
the diet.

A petition was received from Jacob Joosten, wherein
petitioner complains about the court having discharged him
from office, and in which he further requests that his due
salary may be paid. The hon. court recommends petitioner
to properly express himself in his petition, or it will
have to punish him on account of the same.

Tomas Harmensen requests that the officer may judicially proceed against Ariaen Gerretsen Van Vliet so
that he may receive the money which is due him.

Oath administered to the court officer Albert Jansen Van
Steenwyck:

I, Albert Jansen Van Steenwyck, promise by the present
to faithfully attend to my duty as court messenger and not
to do anything contrary to the orders of the royal majesty
of England, his governor or his magistrates at this place,
promising also not to be partial in reporting one or the
other party. So help me God.

Instructions for the Court Messenger: To be obedient and
of service to the schout and the magistrates, especially
to the officer in the requirements of his office, as well
in judicial proceedings as in other affairs. Not to be
partial in reporting the answers of the one party and the
other. To carefully note down the answers and reports,
for the purpose of the better being able to produce them
when the occasion offers. Not to levy attachments or to
serve summons after sunset. Not to take more for a single
summons, attachment or warning than 12 stivers, but outside
the village or to the shore double money.

218

Letter to the Governor at New York:
    Very Noble, honorable, valiant, wise and very discreet Sir:
    By this offered opportunity this is /sent/ to your
honor for the purpose of sending us as per promise, meat
and pork for the soldiers quartered here, because we find
that among the inhabitants here there is great scarcity
of meat and pork. /We/ therebesides request that it may
please your honor to provide us also with more powder for
the security of this place, because the powder, sent before, has been partially distributed and divided. /We/
hope and expect your honor's arrival to be here as soon
as the water shall be open, for the purpose of further and
better arranging matters here, the more so because the
residents here complain that owing to past disasters they
are unable to further provide the soldiers with food and
drink. Closing these presents, we recommend your honor,
after greetings, into God's protection. Done at Wildwyck,
this February 10/20, 1665.
    Your honor's obedient servants, the magistrates of
the village of Wildwyck in the Esopus, (signed) Willem
Beeckman.

    We, the undersigned Gysbert Van Imbroch and Henderick
Jochemsen, Commissaries of the village of Wildwyck, make
known that before us has appeared the worthy Evert Pels,
inhabitant of Wildwyck, who declares that, at the request
of the guardians of the minor children of the deceased
Mattys Jansen, and their consent to keep at interest the
1,000 gldrs. in grain beaver's value, desires and accepts,
as he is accepting, to hold from the aforesaid guardians
the aforementioned 1,000 gldrs. at interest at 12 percent,
annually, in obedience to previous "schepen knowledge,"
dated Feb. 15, 1663, for the period of one more current
year, commencing Feb. 15, 1665, and terminating Feb. 15,
1666, under promise of returning and paying said principal
of 1,000 gldrs. besides the interest on the same, precisely on Feb. 15 of the coming year 1666, but under the
following exception, that if any other creditors, whatever
power they may possess, and unknown to aforesaid guardians
by subsequent confession of the appearer, might judicially
force within the aforesaid time the appearer to satisfy
them for their money, the aforesaid guardians are entitled
to also claim the above principal with interest of the
same, wherefore he, appearer, as per foregoing "schepen
knowledge" binds and specially mortgages his lands situated under the village of Wildwyck and his house in the same
village which appearer declares to be unburdened and unencumbered and further generally his person and further
estate,personal and real, present and future, none excepted, submitting himself and them to the jurisdiction of
all judges and courts. And produces, besides, the afore-

said mortgage, as bondsmen and fellow-principals Cornelis
Barentsen Slecht and Aert Martensen Doorn, both residents
of Wildwyck who besides the appearer also bind their persons and estates, personal and real, present and future,
none excepted, with the expenses herefore made and to be
made, renouncing for this purpose all exceptions and defences which, in any manner might be contrary to the
present. For the purpose of legalizing the same the appearer, besides Cornelis Barentsen Slecht and Aert Martensen Doorn, as bondsmen and fellow-principals, have subscribed to the present, besides ourselves, at Wildwyck
this Feb. 21, N. S. 1665.

                        Evert Pels
                        Cornelis Barents Slecht
(signed)   the mark AMD of Aert Martensen Doorn
Gysbert Van Imbroch
Hendrick Jochemsen

                        In my presence,
             (signed) Mattheus Capito, Secretary

Ordinary Meeting, Tuesday, February 24, 1665.
    Present: Willem Beeckman, Schout; Thomas Chambers,
Gysbert Van Imbroch, Jan Willemsen Hoochteylingh, Henderick Jochemsen, Commissaries.
             Henderick Jochemsen, Plaintiff
             vs. Ariaen Gerretsen, Defendant
    Plaintiff says that on Feb. 16 past defendant called
his wife a "Mangelstok" (Manglestick) and threatened to
strike her, and to push her through the door of his
house. He also shows two declarations against defendant
and requests defendant to explain what it means to say,
"Manglestick." Defendant says he is not able to explain
what saying "Manglestick" means. The hon. court orders
parties to hold their children under better discipline, so
as to call people by their proper names.
             Evert Pels, Plaintiff
             vs. Thomas Chambers, Defendant
    Plaintiff says that defendant promised to assist him
in paying the semiannual interest on 1,000 gldrs., being
60 gldrs. in grain, beaver's price. Defendant says he
does not remember having promised plaintiff the same.
Plaintiff introduces Cornelis Barentsen Slecht, who declares having heard that plaintiff wanted to have said
promise of one-half year's interest mentioned in the
"schepen knowledge," but that defendant, Thomas Chambers,
answered, "it is not necessary." The hon. court orders
plaintiff to produce nearer and clearer proof concerning
this affair.
             Cornelis Barentsen Slecht, Plaintiff
             vs. Aert Jacobsen, Defendant
    Plaintiff demands from defendant five sch. of wheat
for earned wages, in brewing. Defendant denies the above

debt, but says he brewed 12 times and contracted for
every brew, for 10 gldrs. in sewan. Plaintiff replies that
after he had brewed once or twice he demanded 10 gldrs. in
sewan or two sch. of wheat. The hon. court decides and
orders plaintiff to prove that he contracted for 10 gldrs.
in sewan or two sch. of wheat for every brew, and if not,
that defendant shall pay plaintiff in sewan inside of six
days, and that plaintiff then shall be obliged to return
to defendant the received grain. The same plaintiff says
and complains about defendant's wife, she having said plaintiff requires from the people eight lbs. of hops for every
brew, and that he cheats the people with the same. Defendant's wife answers having said the same from hearsay,
and having again been called inside, and being asked what
she has heard others say, answers that plaintiff shall
prove what she should have said. The hon. court orders
plaintiff to adduce proof in this affair.

Walran DuMont, Plaintiff
vs. Warnaer Hoornbeeck, Defendant

Plaintiff demands from defendant 19 sch. of wheat as
per note for delivered goods. Defendant admits the debt,
but says that he, himself, cannot collect it from another.
The hon. court orders defendant to satisfy plaintiff's
aforementioned claim.

Aert Martensen Doorn, Plaintiff
vs. Juriaen Westphael, Defendant. Absent. 2nd Default.

Plaintiff demands of defendant a plough-chain belonging to plaintiff.

Joris Porter, Plaintiff
vs. Allert Heymans, Defendant

Plaintiff demands of defendant payment for three
days' threshing, 1½ days' labor on the cellar, for assist-
ing in grinding 16 sch. of malt. Defendant says they
threshed 2½ days, and that plaintiff began to work about
dinnertime, worked one-half day on the cellar, and that he
helped some at grinding 16 sch. of malt. Defendant also
says that his wife washed for plaintiff and that he bought
some woolen yarn of her, amounting, both together, to 45
stivers in sewan. The hon. court orders defendant to pay
plaintiff for his work, as per balance, the amount of
five sch. of oats.

Roelof Swartwout, Plaintiff
vs. Henderick Jochemsen, Defendant

Plaintiff says that Gommert Paulussen is pressing
him for payment on which account he has sold defendant a
plough for the amount of 22 sch. of wheat, and requests
that defendant shall pay him. He also petitions that the
hon. court will be pleased to revise its former judgment
in this affair. Defendant, having been asked whether he
specially bought the plough at auction on Dec. 29, 1664,
upon said condition, answers that it is quite possible,
because he was drunk, but says, "No." And having been

asked a second time whether he would declare that he did
not buy the same under said condition, answers, "No."
The hon. court orders defendant, because he refuses to
affirm under oath that he did not buy the plough under
the aforementioned condition, to pay plaintiff the plough
according to the condition, and parties are ordered to
liquidate their respective accounts in the meantime.

Jacob Burhans, attorney for Thomas Hal, Plaintiff
vs. Cornelis Barentsen Slecht, Defendant

Plaintiff demands of defendant an amount of 70 and
90 gldrs. in beavers' value as per note. Defendant admits the debt, but says he is not able to pay, owing to
the troublesome times and requests time till next fall.
The hon. court orders defendant to satisfy plaintiff's
aforestated demand.

Jacob Burhans, attorney for Thomas Hal, Plaintiff
vs. Geertruyd Andriesen, Defendant

Plaintiff demands of defendant an amount of 172
gldrs. in beavers' value, as per note. Defendant admits
the debt, but says she is unable just now to pay and requests time. The hon. court orders defendant to satisfy
plaintiff's above demand.

The same, Plaintiff
vs. Geertruyd Andriessen, Defendant

Plaintiff, attorney for Jacobus Vis, demands of defendant 168 gldrs. 1 st. in grain at 3 gldrs. 4 st. per
sch. Defendant admits the debt, but says she is not able
just now to pay, and requests time. The hon. court orders defendant to satisfy plaintiff's above claim.

The same, attorney for Tomas Hal, Plaintiff
vs. Allert Heymans, Defendant

Plaintiff demands of defendant an amount of seven
sch. of wheat. Defendant says he does not owe more than
five sch. of wheat for six pairs of stockings. The hon.
court orders defendant, as per his admission, to pay
plaintiff five sch. of wheat, and plaintiff to adduce
proof for the balance of two sch. of wheat.

The same, attorney for Tomas Hal, Plaintiff
vs. Ariaen Gerretsen, Defendant

Plaintiff demands of defendant 18 sch. of oats as
per note and an assignment passed by Joris Jacobsen to
Thomas Hal. Defendant, being absent, is represented by
his wife who admits the debt, saying that Joris Jacobsen
has told her when she was at the Manhatans to pay him the
18 sch. of oats, not Thomas Hal. The hon. court orders
defendant to satisfy plaintiff's above claim.

Evert Pels requests that the claim against Juriaen
Westphael for the amount of 262 gldrs. 5 st. heavy money
and of 20 gldrs. 4 st. light money may be collected by
the court. The hon. court orders the officer to proceed
with the execution.

Evert Pels requests that the claim against Pieter

Hillebrants for the amount of 39 gldrs. in beavers may be collected by the court. The hon. court orders the officer to proceed with the execution.

The baseless writing of Jacob Joosten having been received by which, under threats, he demands his earned salary for his services as village messenger, is replied to in this manner: "That aforesaid Jacob Joosten may summon the hon. court before /an/ impartial /tribunal/ where he shall be answered."

Walran DuMont requests that the claim against Allert Heymans Roose for the amount of 98 gldrs. 4 st. heavy money in wheat may be collected through the court. The hon. court orders the officer to proceed with the execution.

Aert Otterspoor shows in a petition that he has caught ten wolves and received for the same 23 gldrs. in sewan, leaving a balance in his favor of 101 gldrs. and requests that said money may be found by the commonality. The hon. court orders that the late court messenger Jacob Joosten render an exact accounting to petitioner of how much money he received of the village; measures are further taken to have petitioner receive the balance of the money.

In obedience to an order at the last session on Feb. 17, 1665, was shown the bond and "schepen knowledge" between parties Gysbert Van Imbroch, plaintiff, and Thomas Chambers, defendant, the more so because plaintiff demands from defendant to affirm the settlement of accounts made in the year 1663, as well in regard to the bond as to other accounts, to which defendant answers not to be disposed to do so, and plaintiff further says, if he, plaintiff, is ordered by the court, he is willing to affirm the liquidation of accounts as per his book, and what has been entered in the same. The hon. court decides whereas it appears from the liquidation of accounts in plaintiff's book that defendant did not oppose the same at the time the settlement between them took place, and defendant is not willing to swear that he was not satisfied with said account in December 1663, therefore defendant is ordered to grant plaintiff receipt in accordance with the settlement made and to destroy the bond.

Henderick Jochemsen and Mattheus Capito, attorneys for Swerus Teunissen, send in a petition and request the hon. court to be pleased to revise the preference granted to Gysbert Van Imbroch, before the preference of Jan Barentsen Wemp, and that Jan Barentsen Wemp's successor, Swerus Teunissen, may be preferred before said Imbroch because the "schepen knowledge" of Gysbert Van Imbroch contains only the crop of grain, and the "Lord's knowledge" of Wemp /contains/ land, house, barn, store house, etc. The hon. court decides whereas the "Lord's knowledge" of Wemp has been made known here before the court after the

"schepen knowledge" of Gysbert Van Imbroch, that the
"schepen knowledge" of Gysbert Van Imbroch is granted
precedence.

Ordinary Session, Tuesday, March 3, 1665.
    Present: Willem Beeckman, Schout; Thomas Chambers,
Gysbert Van Imbroch, Jan Willemsen Hoochteylingh, Henderick Jochemsen, Commissaries.
        Willem Beeckman, Schout, Plaintiff
    vs. Walran DuMont, Defendant. Absent. Default.
        Henderick Jochemsen, Plaintiff
    vs. Roelof Swartwout, Defendant. Absent. Default.
        Henderick Jochemsen, Plaintiff
        vs. Aert Martensen Doorn, Defendant
    Plaintiff demands of defendant, as per settlement of
accounts, 43½ sch. of wheat. Defendant admits the debt
and requests time because he is not able to pay right
away. The hon. court orders defendant to satisfy plaintiff's aforementioned claim.
        Henderick Jochemsen, Plaintiff
        vs. Aert Martensen Doorn, Defendant
    Plaintiff, as attorney for Catalyntje Andriesen, de-
mands of defendant an amount of 251 gldrs. in sewan and
one beaver, as per note dated 1653, signed by Jacob Jansen
Stol, his predecessor. Defendant says that his predecessor
contracted said debt, and consequently he knows nothing
about it. The hon. court orders defendant to satisfy
plaintiff's above claim, if he cannot adduce further
proof that the same has been paid.
        Aert Martensen Doorn, Plaintiff
        vs. Juriaen Westphael, Defendant
    Plaintiff demands of defendant a plough-chain belong-
ing to him which he has lost in the last war with the
savages. Defendant said he bought said chain, and that he
again returned the same to the miller of whom he had
bought it. The hon. court orders plaintiff to summon the
miller concerning this affair to appear at the next session.
        Walran DuMont, Plaintiff
        vs. Allert Heymans, Defendant
    Plaintiff demands of defendant a mudde of wheat and
on account of the scissors as per previous demand on Feb.
17 last requests that defendant shall be sworn concerning
the mudde of wheat /which he said/ having paid him for his
personal debt. Defendant says that said mudde of wheat
was delivered during the period in the year 1664 when the
people had proceeded against the savages, and on account
of this trouble it had been forgotten to mark it down and
he and his wife refuse to swear concerning the same; in
regard to the scissors, he is willing to swear. The hon.
court decides that defendant shall pay plaintiff the mudde
of wheat, and that defendant shall deduct what plaintiff

says he owes for the repairing of the scissors, because he
has taken an oath in regard to the same.

Evert Pels, curator of the estate of Jan Albertsen
Van Steenwyck, and Henderick Jochemsen, guardian, Plaintiffs
vs. Roelof Swartwout, Defendant

Plaintiffs demand of defendant 145 gldrs. 15 st. in
sewan for received and purchased goods from the estate,
with the interest and costs of the same. Defendant admits
the debt, but refuses the interest, because he never refused to pay the principal, and says he is not able to pay
right away. The hon. court orders defendant to satisfy
plaintiffs for the above demand, besides the costs; the
demand concerning the interest by plaintiffs is refused
them becuase they did not notify defendant.

The same, Plaintiffs
vs. Evert Prys, Defendant

Plaintiffs demand of defendant an amount of 64 gldrs.
10 st. light money, debt as per book, with the costs. Defendant says that Tjerck Claesen paid per his order. The
hon. court orders defendant to pay plaintiff the above
debt with the costs, and /decides/ that defendant shall
seek satisfaction of Tjerck Claesen.

The same, Plaintiffs
vs. Aeltje Wygerts, Defendant

Plaintiffs demand of defendant 36 gldrs. light money,
book debt, with the interest and costs of the same. Defendant admits the debts and says that she will do her
best to pay. The hon. court orders defendant to satisfy
plaintiffs for the above demand with the interest and the
costs of the same.

The same, Plaintiffs
vs. Aert Martensen Doorn, Defendant

Plaintiffs demand of defendant 72 gldrs. light money,
book debt, with the interest and costs of the same. Defendant admits the debt, but says he is not able to pay
just now. The hon. court orders defendant to satisfy
plaintiffs in regard to the above claim with the interest
and the costs of the same.

Henderick Palingh, Plaintiff
vs. Jan Jansen Van Amersfoort, Defendant. Absent. Default.

A petition having been received of Cornelis Barentsen Slecht, the hon. court decides that in consideration
of petitioner's statement as to his claimed land, 14 morgens shall be deducted from the village account.

The unmeasured meadow land of Juffr. Ebbingh esti-
mated at 25 morgens remains on said account; for Jacob
Jansen Stoutenborch to be deducted on said account, 10
gldrs.; for Willem Jansen Seba, to be deducted,two gldrs.
10 st.; for Henderick Aertsen, to be deducted, two gldrs.
10 st.; for Pieter Bruynsen, to be deducted, two gldrs.
12 st. The preacher's salary for the year 1663 remains on
said account in full. For the lot which petitioner at

present possesses, he shall contribute towards the salary of the preacher for the year 1664, for four months.

Jacob Burhans, having been appointed curator for the estates of Henderick Jansen Looman and Willem Jansen Seba, excuses himself on account of his age, and the hon. court, on this account, also excuses petitioner, and appoints in his place Roelof Swartwout besides Aert Jacobsen as curators of the aforesaid estates.

Gysbert Van Imbroch requests that Tjerck Claesen De Wit may be judicially proceeded against for the amount of 31 gldrs. with the interest and costs, as per the minute dated Feb. 10, 1665. The hon. court orders the officer to proceed with the execution.

Whereas the hon. court finds that notwithstanding the continual warning and notification, as well to pay toward the preacher's salary as also the expenses for the general diet of the year 1664, many of the residents are negligent in paying their share, as per the village account sent to them; therefore, it is resolved that the officer shall proceed with the execution.

In accordance with the petition of Mattheus Capito, secretary, for some salary for his services as secretary, he is allowed by the hon. court, till May next, a remuneration of 100 gldrs.

In regard to the received petition of Cornelis Barentsen Slecht, the hon. court decides that petitioner shall be allowed on the village account for his claimed land in dispute with Thomas Chambers, 14 morgens at 50 st. in grain-money per morgen; item, for Jacob Jansen Stoutenborch, 10 gldrs.; for Willem Jansen Seba, two gldrs. 10 st.; for Henderick Aertsen, two gldrs. 10 st.; for Pieter Bruynsen, two gldrs. 12 st., all in corn-money.

Henderick Cornelissen, ropemaker, complains about his village account, in which he has been charged for the preacher's salary for the year 1661, 25 gldrs. in beavers, and says that for said year he promised to contribute toward said salary 25 gldrs. in sewan. The hon. court orders the secretary to change the item on petitioner's village bill and to reduce from 25 gldrs. beavers value to 25 gldrs. in sewan, because he did not promise anything else to the preacher's salary than 25 gldrs. in sewan.

Henderick Cornelissen, ropemaker, requests that the judgment pronounced on March 10 against Christoffel Davids may be executed. The hon. court orders the officer to proceed with the execution.

Extraordinary Session, Thursday, April 2, 1665.

Present: Willem Beeckman, Schout; Thomas Chambers, Gysbert Van Imbroch, Jan Willemsen Hoochteylingh, Henderick Jochemsen, Commissaries.

Whereas a savage has warned us that the Esopus savages are planning mischief against our village, it is

on this account resolved, and the captain of the burghers
is ordered, that he shall cause a strict daily watch to
be held and in case any savages should come into our village, that we may know how numerous the entered savages may
be. It is also resolved that the large and small gates
shall be properly provided, for the purpose of being
closed.

Ordinary Session, Tuesday, April 10, 1665.
    Present: Willem Beeckman, Schout; Thomas Chambers,
Gysbert Van Imbroch, Jan Willemsen Hoochteylingh, Henderick Jochemsen, Commissaries.
        The Hon. Heer Petrus Stuyvesant, Plaintiff
            vs. Tjerck Claesen De Wit, Defendant
    Plaintiff requests satisfaction as per sentence pro-
nounced on Nov. 18, 1664, being the balance 82 sch. of
oats, or sewan 164 gldrs. and the costs of the same. Defendant admits above 82 sch. of oats, and requests time
for the same. Plaintiff replies saying not to be able to
grant time, and either asks back the cow or execution as
per foregoing demand. Defendant requests that a cow from
his stable may be appraised by two impartial, good men, in
satisfaction of the above claim. The hon. court appoints
as good men Allert Heymans Roose and Evert Pels for the
purpose of appraising, for ready money, a cow from defendant's stable, in satisfaction of plaintiff's above claim.
        The Hon. Heer Petrus Stuyvesant, Plaintiff
            vs. Ariaen Gerretsen Van Vliet, Defendant
    Plaintiff demands again as per previous judgment
dated Nov. 18, 1664, payment, or execution, or bond by
neglect of payment, and if not that defendant may be dispossessed of the leased land, as per custom of our fatherland. Defendant requests reduction of rent on account of
the passed unexpected assaults of the savages, and the
damage suffered by him during that time, and further payment for erecting the curtains in front of the Heer lessor's
lot. The hon. court decides that defendant shall pay
plaintiff as per previous judgment or give surety for the
same as per plaintiff's request, or by neglect that defendant shall return the lease of the land and /also/ return
the received cattle and other received effects inside of
24 hours, provided the Heer plaintiff shall compensate him
upon the appraisal of impartial /men/ for what has been
sowed and ploughed and for the palisades which defendant
has erected before the Heer plaintiff's lot in the curtains, and that defendant may request a reduction of the
Heer plaintiff, and further, in regard to defendant's
further demand, the hon. court refers to the previous
judgment pronounced on Nov. 18, 1664.
        The Hon. Heer Petrus Stuyvesant, Plaintiff
            vs. Juriaen Westphael, Defendant
    Plaintiff demands satisfaction as per the "schout

and schepen knowledge" dated Nov. 29, 1664, and whereas
plaintiff has been continually having differences with defendant concerning the aforesaid lease and never, as per
lease, was able to obtain payment at the proper time, he
requests for the sake of preventing further difficulties
and loss, sufficient sureties for the future, or by neglect
that his horses, cattle, house, land and farming implements may be returned to plaintiff as per law, and the expenses may be paid.

Defendant says that he paid the Heer plaintiff on the
aforesaid "schout and schepen knowledge" a sum of about
300 gldrs. and that now he will pay 50 or 60 sch. of wheat
on account of said "schout and schepen knowledge" and
agrees as soon as he shall have harvested his crops to
satisfy plaintiff's entire claim.

The hon. court decides that defendant is obliged, as
per his own obligation in the aforenamed "schout and
schepen knowledge" in case of nonpayment, to produce sufficient sureties for the future, inside of 24 hours, or in
case of default, that defendant shall return to the Heer
plaintiff the leased farm and there besides deliver up to
the Heer plaintiff, all he has received as per the lease.

The hon. Heer Petrus Stuyvesant requests that the
judgment, dated Nov. 18, 1664, against Jan Joosten, may be
judicially enforced. The hon. court orders the officer to
proceed with the execution.

Evert Prys, Plaintiff
vs. Evert Pels, curator of the estate of
Jan Albertsen Van Steenwyck, Defendant

Plaintiff demands of defendant restitution of such
moneys as defendant heretofore, on Mar. 3, 1665, demanded
of him. Defendant says that before this he was plaintiff
for the amount of 64 gldrs. in sewan, against plaintiff,
and that he still is and remains plaintiff for the aforesaid amount. He further says, if Tjerck Claesen will
swear that he, Tjerck Claesen, paid on the account of
plaintiff to Jan Albertsen Van Steenwyck 20 sch. of wheat,
that he is then willing to reimburse plaintiff out of the
said estate. The hon. court refers to the previous judgment, pronounced on Mar. 3,* 1665.

Evert Pels, curator of the estate of
Jan Albertsen Van Steenwyck, Plaintiff
vs. Tjerck Claesen De Wit, Defendant

Plaintiff demands from defendant declaration that he
has paid on the account of Evert Prys to Jan Albertsen Van
Steenwyck 20 sch. of wheat, because it is not shown by the
papers of Jan Albertsen, deceased, that he, defendant, has
made above payment of 20 sch. of wheat on the account of
Evert Prys to Jan Albertsen. Defendant answers having
made the payment, and says not to be obliged and neither
to be willing to swear to the aforesaid, but says that he
is able to prove, through his brother, that he took the wheat

to Jan Albertsen's. Defendant Tjerck Claesen, having been
asked by the hon. court to swear that he paid on the account of Evert Prys 20 sch. of wheat to Jan Albertsen Van
Steenwyck, on account of refusing the oath, is ordered to
pay the said 20 sch. of wheat to plaintiff, the curator.

Dievertje Volckerts, wife of
Pieter Jansen Van Hoorn, Plaintiff
vs. Tjerck Claesen and Evert Pels, curators of the
estate of Jan Albertsen Van Steenwyck, Defendant
Plaintiff demands of defendants 80 gldrs. Dutch money
on account of Jan Albertsen Van Steenwyck (being the
balance of 250 gldrs. Dutch money) and the costs of the
same, and shows a notarial receipt that Jan Albertsen has
received said 250 gldrs. of Douwe Meyndertsen. The curators and heirs say that Jan Albertsen Van Steenwyck has
not received any more for the 250 gldrs. Dutch money than
200 gldrs., and that there is a balance of 50 gldrs., and
say that they have a receipt for the same. The hon. court
orders defendants to pay plaintiff the aforesaid claim with
the costs of the same, or prove the contrary within three
weeks.

Marten Hofman, Plaintiff
vs. Evert Pels, curator of the estate of Jan Albertsen Van
Steenwyck, and Henderick Jochemsen, guardian, Defendants
Plaintiff as heir of the estate of Jan Albertsen Van
Steenwyck, demands of defendants proofs, an accounting and
that which remains of the administration of the aforesaid
estate. Defendants consent to render plaintiff concerning
their administration proof, account, and what remains, and
request that the same may be done in the presence of two
commissaries from the bench. The hon. court appoints for
the purpose of examining and settling the accounts of the
estate of Jan Albertsen Van Steenwyck, with the curators
and the guardian, the hon. Schout Willem Beeckman and the
Commissary Gysbert Van Imbroch.

The hon. Heer Petrus Stuyvesant, having requested that
from among the court two commissioners may be appointed for
the aforementioned affairs between him and Ariaen Gerretsen and Juriaen Westphael, there are appointed from among
the hon. court the Commissaries Tomas Chambers and Jan Willemsen Hoochteylingh, for the purpose of appraising and of
adjusting matters between parties.

The aforementioned decision having been judicially
communicated to defendant Ariaen Gerretsen, and he being
unwilling to appear, but is continually fulminating, calling names, and thumb snapping even in the presence of the
Heer Officer and the Commissary who were yesterday appointed
and authorized by the hon. court as appraisers and adjusters
and was today once more legally and judicially notified by
the secretary Capito in the absence of the court messenger
to appoint somebody, in accordance with the judgment, for
the purpose of appraising what was sowed and ploughed and

the erected palisades, for which purpose Allert Heymans
had been requested by the Hon. Heer plaintiff, but defendant remaining contumacious and refractory, and the hon.
Heer plaintiff requesting to expedite matters, therefore
we the undersigned decide that the Heer plaintiff shall
allow a reduction of debt or pay to defendant for every
morgen of land that has been twice plowed and sowed, and
upon proof of the same, 60 gldrs. in grain beavers' value,
and for every morgen that has been once plowed and sowed
50 equal gldrs., and for every morgen that was last fall
plowed but not sowed 12 equal gldrs., and for erecting and
carting the palisades in the curtains 22 sch. of wheat.
Thus given at Wildwyck, this April 5/15, 1665. (Signed)
Thomas Chambers, Jan Willemsen Hoochteylingh, Alaerdt
Heymans Roose.

Extraordinary Session, Monday, April 20, 1665.
     Present: Willem Beeckman, Schout; Thomas Chambers,
Gysbert Van Imbroch, Jan Willemsen Hoochteylingh, Henderick Jochemsen, Commissaries.
     On this day the hon. court, having examined the let-
ters from the hon. Lord Governor, dated 31 Mar., it was
thereupon ordered to firmly close the small gates in the
village, to examine the palisades of the fortification for
the purpose of renewing the old or decayed ones, and that
the burghers shall keep a daily guard at one of the gates.
And further, the instructions given by said hon. governor
to Mr. Berrisfort were shown by said Berrisfort to the hon.
court. And there besides the court commissioned a savage
to notify the chiefs (Sakimaas) to come here, for the
purpose of making known what claims they may have on some
land, for which the said hon. Lord Governor, upon his arrival, shall satisfy them.
     Whereas it is deemed necessary to authorize some
/person/ to farm out the caretaking of the cattle to the
lowest bidder, for this purpose are appointed and authorized Allert Heymans Roos and Aert Jacobsen, to draw up
the conditions, as is customary, with the lowest bidder.

Ordinary Session, Tuesday, April 28, 1665.
     Present: Willem Beeckman, Schout; Thomas Chambers,
Jan Willemsen Hoochteylingh, Henderick Jochemsen, Com-
misaries.
                 Christoffel Davids, Plaintiff
                 vs. Juriaen Westphael, Defendant
     Plaintiff says that about nine years ago he bought a
demolished house of defendant, and that in the mean time
the war against the savages at the Manhattans broke out,
on accout whereof /the people/ here were also obliged to
flee, in consequence of which defendant has never delivered the house, of which plaintiff still demands delivery or restitution of the money to the amount of 180

gldrs. Defendant says that he bought the aforesaid demolished house of Thomas Chambers, under condition that
Thomas Chambers was to rebuild the aforesaid house, and to
surrender it under roof and that he, defendant, was to cut,
shorten, and split the woodwork which should be further
necessary to the same, and that he, defendant, should assist him, Chambers, in loading, unloading and carting the
said house. And defendant further says that he sold and
transferred the aforesaid demolished house in the aforementioned state which plaintiff, replying, acknowledges
having thus bought the same of defendant.

Defendant having again been questioned if he has ever
been pressed by Christoffel Davids after the troubles with
the savages, to have the house erected, answers, "No," and
that Christoffel Davids, in the mean time, has sold the
land to Jacob Jansen Stol, where the house should have
stood, and the house, in the meanwhile, has been left
neglected, so that it is entirely decayed.

The hon. court decides whereas it appears from plaintiff's answers that plaintiff has been negligent in pre-
paring the required woodwork for said house, in trans-
porting, and even in pressing defendant after the troubles
with the savages, and furthermore it is shown that he sold
the land on which the house was to be erected, and the
woodwork of the demolished house, consequently, has been
left laying until it has decayed, therefore, plaintiff's
demand against defendant is denied.

Aert Jacobsen, Plaintiff
vs. Aert Otterspoor, Defendant

Plaintiff says that defendant works the patch of
/strawberry/ land situated outside the curtains and which
was granted to him. He had defendant notified by the
court messenger not to continue cultivating the same,
which defendant did not obey, and plaintiff therefore requests that defendant may be once more restrained from
working his patch and shows the minute /of the judgment/
of May 6, 1664, pronounced by the court in his favor. Defendant says that he also has been permitted by the hon.
court on Dec. 9, 1664, to cultivate the patch of land
which is situated outside the curtains, opposite the house
of Aert Jacobsen. The hon. court decides whereas Aert
Jacobsen has neglected to receive the approbation of the
hon. Lord Dir. Genl. in regard to the grant of the patch
of land, that he is again refused the same. And the hon.
court, also having perceived the labor and the sowing done
on said patch of land by Aert Otterspoor, he is for this
present year granted the use of said patch of land, for the
purpose of enjoying the fruits thereof, and after said time
Aert Otterspoor shall remove the palisades, because,
though he has said that the aforesaid /strawberry/ patch
has been granted him by the hon. Lord Dir. Genl. Petrus
Stuyvesant, he cannot show proof of the same.

Joris Porter and Roelof Swartwout appear on account of their quarrel, because Roelof Swartwout suddenly broke Joris Porter's sword in his house, taking hold of the same for the purpose of striking his boy* with the same. On which account he, Roelof Swartwout, offered Joris Porter to furnish him with another sword or blade which Joris Porter refused to accept, but wanted to have the case delayed till the arrival of the hon. Lord Governor Ridsert Nicolls. The hon. court decides that Roelof Swartwout, in offering Joris Porter to present him with another sword, said Roelof Swartwout has done enough in this affair, and if the other remains obdurate in his refusal to accept the same, that the hon. Lord Governor's arrival shall be awaited.

The schout complains about the offensive conduct by Jan Jansen Van Amersfoort on Mar. 13, 1665, before the hon. court, on account of which he has also been summoned by the hon. schout on Mar. 24 next, but has remained absent and committed default, and requests that defendant may be punished for the same, or sent to the hon. Lord Governor of New York. Defendant says that he consents to being sent, on account of the same, to the Manhatans to the hon. governor. The hon. court orders defendant's arrest, and, owing to his stubbornness, that, with the first yacht, he shall be sent to the Manhatans.

The hon. schout proposes that the old, decayed palisades in the points shall be renewed and repaired. The hon. court decides that the points shall be properly repaired with new palisades, and for this purpose one man out of every family, besides the carters, is ordered to cut the wood and to set it up.

The hon. Willem Beeckman requests payment of the back room rent. Petitioner will, as soon as the condition of the treasury permits, receive payment of due room rent.

Ordinary Session, Tuesday, May 5, 1665.
    Present: Willem Beeckman, Schout; Thomas Chambers, Gysbert Van Imbroch, Jan Willemson Hoochteylingh, Henderick Jochemsen, Evert Pels, Jan Joosten, Commissaries.

On this day the elected persons (having been elected in accordance with a missive of the hon. Lord Gov. Genl. Ridsert Nicolls) Evert Pels and Jan Joosten were qualified as commissioners in place of the retiring commissaries Thomas Chambers and Gysbert Van Imbroch, and took the following oath:

We promise and swear that we shall be true and faithful to his Majesty of England and the Duke of York, and to the Lord Gov. Genl. appointed by them, and to duly obey them; and to observe the stipulations and articles in the instructions given and yet to be given, and to administer good right and justice to the best of our knowledge and without partiality, and further to act as an honest magistrate must be expected to act. So really help me God.

The captain of the civil guard, Thomas Chambers, as per previous orders dated Apr. 2 and 20, 1665, given him to keep a daily guard at one of the gates, requests backing, because he finds that some are unwilling to obey and observe said /orders/, and if not, that he may be held blameless for all possible and future damage and perils which might ensue on account of /said disobedience/.

On account of which aforesaid complaints by the aforenamed captain, Joost Ariaens was called, and he was asked for what reason he did not, yesterday, as per the order of his corporal, mount guard, to which he answered that he had neglected to do so because on the evening before there had been dissatisfaction among the guard, owing to the annoyance caused them, the guard, by the English soldiers; on which account he, Joost Ariaens, having been reprimanded by the hon. court, promises to do his duty the same as the other residents.

Mr. Berrisfort, having been acquainted with the reasons of the aforenamed Joost Ariaens, says that they heard some noise between the guardsmen and the aforenamed captain, and therefore they entered the guard house for the purpose of preventing any mishaps between the guardsmen and the captain.

Extraordinary Session, Monday, May 18, 1665.

Present: Willem Beeckman, Schout; Jan Willemsen Hoochteylingh, Henderick Jochemsen, Evert Pels, Jan Joosten, Commissaries.

The hon. schout presents the complaints of Mr. Berrisfort in regard to the quarters of his soldiers, and in which he requests that the soldiers shall be taken away from the common people who have no food for the soldiers, and quartered among the farmers who are provided with more food. On which account were summoned those farmers having double farms, and having been acquainted with the above complaint, most of them complain also, saying that at the present time they have little meat and pork, and therefore cannot be burdened with more soldiers. It is, notwithstanding, resolved, that those having some wealth shall be burdened with a second soldier till further orders or till the arrival of the hon. Gov. Genl. It is further proposed that the small gates shall be closed as per the order of the Hon. Ld. Gov. Genl. In consequence, it is resolved, Whereas said order has not been obeyed, that the aforesaid small gates shall, by the proprietors, be closed with palisades exactly on tomorrow under penalty of a fine of 25 gldrs.

Extraordinary Session, Wednesday, May 27, 1665.

Present: Willem Beeckman, Schout; Jan Willemsen
Hoochteylingh, Henderick Jochemsen, Evert Pels, Jan
Joosten, Commissaries.

In regard to the quarrel which broke out yesterday
between Allert Heymans Roose and Daniel Botterwout, the
soldier quartered with him, appeared Mr. Berrisfort, who
requests that the Heer Officer shall deposit in the store-
house the gun which he /Berrisfort/ took last night from
some free people who, though not being on guard, carried
the same through the street.

It is proposed to the hon. court that said gun may
be returned to said persons, out of consideration that in
case of alarm on account of the savages or other cause,
they may immediately be able to use their gun, and also
because they have to mount guard, and further that owing
to the dangerous times, they may be provided with a gun,
when working on the land. And in consequence said persons were called and reprimanded for what had happened.
They promised that it would not occur again, and the hon.
court becomes surety for the gun of said persons, so that,
at the order of the Gov. Genl. it will be surrendered.

The wife of Allert Heymans requests that Mr. Berrisfort be pleased to relieve her of the people he brought
into her house. To which Mr. Berrisfort answers, saying,
as soon as her husband Allert Heymans will again allow himself to be found at home, he will then relieve her of this
trouble. And he intends to arrest her husband and to take
him to the redoubt until the arrival of a yacht then to
send him to the Manhatans to the Governor General, for the
purpose of there answering any accusation which they, the
soldiers, may make against him.

The hon. court proposes to adjust the affair between
Allert Heymans and his soldier here before the court, as
per instructions, and in the mean time, to keep him under
arrest in his own house, with orders for him to keep si-
lent and quiet until the arrival of a vessel, then to go
to the Manhatans to answer there, in case the difference
cannot be adjusted here, and in case he does not keep
still and quiet during his arrest, that he shall be hand-
cuffed and sent to the redoubt.

Mr. Berrisfort permits that Allert Heymans shall,
during his arrest in his own house, keep still and quiet
until the arrival of a vessel. The aforesaid wife, having
been called in, was acquainted with the foregoing, and
/advised/ to see her husband in regard to the same.

Cornelis Barentsen Slecht, appearing, complains about
his soldier, that sometimes he takes in three or four
soldiers, and forces plaintiff to draw for them the good
beer, and fears, in case he should refuse him in the
future, that he might get into difficulties. The hon.
court has acquainted Mr. Berrisfort with the above complaint, who will forbid the aforesaid soldier doing so again.

Extraordinary Session, Thursday, May 28, 1665.

Present: Willem Beeckman, Schout; Jan Willemsen Hoochteylingh, Henderick Jochemsen, Evert Pels, Jan Joosten, Commissaries; Christoffel Berrisfort, Commander of the Troops.

Examination concerning the question and the differences between Daniel Botterwout, soldier, and Allert Heymans Roose. Daniel Botterwout says that Allert Heymans, during the morning of last Tuesday, challenged him, and at the first challenge he would not come, and at the second challenge he jumped outside, and drew his sword against Allert Heymans.

Allert Heymans denies having thrice challenged Daniel Botterwout last Tuesday morning, and says that said Botterwout last Monday evening came drunk to his house, and that he noisely demanded pork and meat which Allert Heymans said not to have, whereupon aforesaid Botterwout tried to get up a quarrel, and wanted to fight everybody that was willing, on account whereof Dirrick Hendericksen and Henderick Albertsen went into his house, and made the following declaration:

"Dirrick Hendericksen and Henderick Albertsen declare that last Monday evening, both passing along the street, they came to the house of Allert Heymans, and arriving there, one of Allert Heymans' sons said to them, 'Daniel, our soldier, wants to fight,' and the aforesaid son said to Daniel Botterwout, 'Here is a man who wants to fight,' whereupon the aforesaid Daniel took his sword and went outside, but nobody followed him, and seeing this he again entered, and was then advised by Allert Heymans to sheathe his sword, and to go to sleep, and say not to know any more."

The aforementioned case is adjourned till Mr. Laval's arrival.

At the request of the hon. Heer Pieter Stuyvesant the following "schout and schepen knowledge" was recorded, the original remaining in the possession of his honor, and reads as follows:

"We, the undersigned, schout and commissaries of the village of Wildwyck, make known and know that before us has appeared Adriaen Gerretsen Van Vliet ex-lessee of the farm of the hon. Heer Petro Stuyvesant /which appearer/ acknowledged and declared that he felt sorry having so badly treated the aforenamed Heer leesor on account of his requesting and obtaining judgment against him /appearer/, further promising /in case the aforesaid Heer lessor for the sake of his wife and children should permit him to stay on said farm/, that, by the present, he voluntarily and without any constraint, and renouncing all former pretence, is willing to actually and honestly pay and satisfy the debt expressed in the judgment beside the current rent for this year and on such terms as the aforesaid Heer lessor

shall be pleased to favorably prescribe and permit him.
Mortgaging on this account all winter and summer crops to
be grown on the land, whether the same are standing on the
field or may hereafter be harvested and brought indoors,
to deliver them, without any opposition or recourse to
law, into the hands of the Lord Officer Willem Beeckman
and Capt. Thomas Chambers, the aforesaid Heer lessor's
attorneys in this affair, for the purpose of being by them
sent to the Heer lessor's wife, after having been threshed
by them or upon their order at the expense and charge of
the appearer, on account of the debt, without appearer being allowed to have any of them, whether summer or winter
crops, threshed beforehand much less to alienate or
transfer the same without special permission of the aforesaid attorneys, and voluntarily consenting to be immediately dispossessed of the farm by aforesaid attorneys, and to
be deprived of the surplus of the crops, if there should be
more of them than the debt and rent amounts to, and to immediately, without recourse to law, leave the farm /in
case he should violate any of the above stipulations/.
Further, after the Heer lessor shall have sent boards and
nails and employed a carpenter to repair the fallen down
barn and house, appearer takes upon himself to furnish and
transport for the same, the other necessary woodwork and
the reed necessary for completing the barn, the carting to
be at the appearer's expense, the wages for cutting wood,
mowing reed and thatching, upon appraisal by impartial
/men/ at the expense of Heer lessor. Appearer further
promises to properly fence in the lot, and to keep the
dwelling, after it shall be completed, in good repair, as
is proper. For legalizing the present, we the undersigned,
besides the appearer, have subscribed to the same at Wildwyck, in the Esopus, this 18/28 May, 1665.
    The aforesaid lessee is by the present, upon his re-
quest, allowed and rebated a year's rent by the attorney's
of the Heer Petrus Stuyvesant, for the surrender of all
claims which the lessee has had against his honor, in accordance with the promise made by the hon. Heer lessor in
the spring of 1665. And the lessee is again on this day
furnished with a cow and a grown calf by the aforesaid attorneys, as per lease. Lessee also gives up a cow and a
bull calf of his own, in the place of the Heer lessor's
cow, which the lessee has killed. Thus done at Wildwyck
this 18/28 May, Anno 1665. (signed) The mark of Ariaen
Gerretsen Van Vliet + thus made, Jan Willemsen Hoochteylingh, Evert Pels. After comparison, the present has been
found to be an exact copy of the original, which testifies,
(signed) Mattheus Capito, Secretary.

Extraordinary Session, Monday, June 1, 1665.
    Present: Capt. DelaVal; Willem Beeckman, Schout;
Jan Willemsen Hoochteylingh, Henderick Jochemsen, Evert

Pels, Commissaries; Christoffel Berresfort, Commander of
the Troops.
The affairs and differences between Allert Heymans
Roose and Daniel Botterwout, soldier, having been presented by the hon. court to Capt. DelaVal, according to
the decision on May 28 last, who, having heard the same,
excuses himself from pronouncing sentence about the same,
much less from hearing the examination concerning the
same, and postpones the same till the hon. Gov. Genl's
arrival, but desires, as also he would be pleased to see
and hear, that the aforementioned affairs, in the mean
while, might be amicably settled, so that, upon the hon.
Gov. Genl's arrival, he may not then find any differences,
existing here between soldiers and inhabitants.

Extraordinary Session, Tuesday, June 2, 1665, of the hon.
Court and the Burgher Council of War at Wildwyck.
Present: Willem Beeckman, Schout; Jan Willemsen
Hoochteylingh, Henderick Jochemsen, Evert Pels, Jan
Joosten, Commissaries; Thomas Chambers, Captain; Cornelis
Barentsen Slecht, Tjerck Claesen De Wit, Sergeants.
Examination of the below-mentioned persons, in regard
to the turmoil on May 26 last. Aert Jacobsen, Corporal,
having been asked why he did not mount guard on May 26
last, said, having been indisposed, and having sent his
son to go on watch, /and to request/ in the mean time the
cadets to take his watch. Harmen Hendericks, cadet, having
been asked whether Aert Jacobsen requested him to take his
watch during his absence on May 26 last, says, not having
been requested to do so by the corporal, but by the corporal's son. Whether he gave the word to nobody else but
his watch, says, that he gave the word to his watch only.
Jan Cornelissen, drummer, having been asked why, on
May 26 last, he carried his gun by night in the street,
says, that he did as any other. How he received the sign?
says, having received the word of Gerret Aertsen, and at
Gerret Aertsen's request made the rounds with him.
Tomas Teunissen Quick, having been asked what induced him on May 26 last to take hold of the gun, when he
did not have the watch? says that he did as any other, and
that he was very drunk. Neither does he know who took his
gun from him.
Who persuaded him to do so? says that he was in company with a number of young fellows drinking and bowling,
and then went out with the others. Of whom he received
the word? says not being able to remember whether he had
the word, because he was very drunk.
Henderick Cornelissen, ropemaker, being asked what induced him to carry his gun along the street on last Tuesday evening? says, that it was rumored that the soldiers
had chased Allert Heymans' wife and children out of the
house, on account of which he went to the captain and told

him about it, whereupon the captain said that it was not as bad as all that, and that they should go home and not bother with it, and that it was the magistrate's business to enquire into the same.

Who gave him the word? says, he has forgotten, but thinks or knows no better than having received the same of Gerret Aertsen, and received it while on his way, on the street.

Walran DuMont, having been asked what induced him to appear with his gun last Tuesday evening at the watch, says that he returned with his gun from the land, and while entering the village saw a turmoil, and therefore went to the guardhouse to inquire what was the matter, and having lit a pipe of tobacco in the guardhouse, went immediately home.

Jan Broersen asked whether last Tuesday he had the night watch, says "No." What, then, he had to do there said evening with his gun? says because he saw the soldiers carrying their guns along the street, and did not know what they intended to do. Of whom he received the word? says not having had the word.

Jan Jansen Van Oosterhout asked, what he did last Tuesday evening with his gun in the guard house, says, having gone with his gun to the guard house, for the purpose of enquiring what was the matter, and left his gun in the guard house, and meeting Mr. Berrisfort, without his gun, on the street, asked him what was the matter, whereupon Mr. Berrisfort told him to go home and that nobody would be molested, whereupon taking his gun out of the guard house, he immediately returned home.

Jan Hendericksen, alias Jan Buyr, asked whether his watch fell on last Tuesday evening, says, "Yes, because Warnaer Hoorenbeeck on the previous night took his watch," and that on said evening he mounted guard for Warnaer. The corporal, having been asked about the same, says, "Yes."

Antoni Delva asked, what he did with his gun last Tuesday in the guardhouse?, says that he did as any body else, having heard some tumult, and thereupon not hearing any more, immediately went home.

Aert Otterspoor asked, whether he had the watch last Tuesday, says, "Yes," which having been asked the corporal, also says, "Yes."

Why he pulled the trigger of his gun? says, not having done so, but that the trigger has to be pulled very deep when it is to be drawn, which makes it appear, when not pulled, as if /the trigger/ were pulled.

Gerret Aertsen asked, whether his watch fell on last Tuesday, says, no, but he took his father's turn. Who ordered him to make the rounds? says the corporal. Why he imparted the word to the drummer who made the rounds with him? says having had scruples about giving the word to the English guard in case they should meet him.

Henderick Albertsen asked, whether he had the watch on Tuesday last, says, "No." What he did with his gun in the guard house? says having personally been there, but without gun.

Ariaen Huybertsen asked, What he did with his gun last Tuesday in the guardhouse? says, not having been there, but that, late at night, he went to see Allert Heymans' wife on the land, and returned to the village at about 2 o'clock at night.

Ariaen Allertsen Roos asked, whether he had the watch last Tuesday? says, "No." What he did at the guard house? says that he had something to do at the minister's, and seeing some people at the guardhouse also went there, and after having delivered his message to the domine, he returned home.

This examination of the aforesaid persons by the hon. court and Burgher Council of War is adjourned till the arrival of the hon. Ld. Gov. Genl. or his order, just as the different between Allert Heymans and Daniel Botterwout was, yesterday, also adjourned till the arrival of the said Ld. Gov. Genl.

Ordinary Session, Tuesday, June 23, 1665.
Present: Willem Beeckman, Schout; Jan Willemsen Hoochteylingh, Henderick Jochemsen, Evert Pels, Jan Joosten, Commissaries.
Jan Willemsen Hoochteylingh, Plaintiff
vs. Ariaen Gerretsen, Defendant
Plaintiff says that defendant has plowed and sowed a corner of his, plaintiff's, leased land, and asks for what reasons has he done so? Defendant says not to know how far his land extends. The hon. court decides that the separation or boundary of the land shall be again examined and determined by those who prior to this determined the same, viz., by Cornelis Barentsen Slecht, Juriaen Westphael and Walran DuMont.
Tomas Harmensen, farmer /of the excise/, Plaintiff
vs. Jan Willemsen Hoochteylingh, Defendant
Plaintiff says that defendant took out of the brewery a brew of beer without his knowledge, and says that defendant smuggled said brew of beer. Defendant denies having smuggled but says that he has agreed with plaintiff to pay six gldrs. for each brew, and that he also agreed to notify plaintiff when he has brewed, so that it shall be noted down by each of them, and that he gave notice of the same, before he took the aforesaid brew at all out of the brewery.
Plaintiff, replying, denies that he agreed with defendant to allow him to fetch in the beer without defendant's having previously notified him of the same, but says that defendant is obliged to declare the beer before being permitted to take it from the brewery.
Defendant says, after the hon. court demanded the same

from him, to be prepared to affirm under oath that he has an agreement with plaintiff in the manner as heretofore stated. The hon. court decides that plaintiff shall prove his reply or otherwise that plaintiff's demand against defendant shall be denied him, the more so because defendant, being worthy of belief, is prepared to take the oath.

The missive of schout, burgomasters and scheepenen of the city of N. York, as also the sentence of said court against Thomas Harmensen having been communicated to this court, he ⟨Harmensen⟩ brings in that he did not absolutely buy the two accounts of Aeltje Constapels, but only accepted them, in such a manner that he would receive them if he could obtain payment of the bills, and further that he assigned Cornelis Plavier on the hon. Company, and that said Cornelis Plavier must still claim the money of the hon. company.

The hon. court, having seen the three warnings by the court messenger of N. York, Claes Van Usland, to Thomas Harmensen, which he did not oppose with the abovenamed exceptions, therefore it is decided that he is obliged to pay, and consequently the officer is ordered to execute the judgment pronounced by schout, buromasters and schepenen of the city of N. York, in case of nonpayment.

Jan Cornelissen, Plaintiff
vs. Henderick Cornelissen Slecht, Defendant

Plaintiff demands of defendant payment of 12 sch. of wheat for making a large auger. Defendant says that he cannot use the auger, and also that the auger is no good, and that plaintiff contracted to make the same good for said 12 sch. of wheat. Defendant also shows by written statements that said auger has already cost him for materials and expenses incurred 15½ sch. of wheat, and desires that plaintiff shall make said auger serviceable, so that he can make use of the same. Plaintiff answers, saying, not to have contracted to make said auger good, but that he would do his best, because he never did a similar job. The hon. court, having heard parties, refer the same to impartial good men, viz., to Capt. Thomas Chambers and Albert Gerretsen, for the purpose of, if possible, settling their differences, and if not, to again address themselves to the court.

Severyn Tenhout, Plaintiff
vs. Tjerck Claesen De Wit, Defendant

Plaintiff says that defendant has beaten and pushed him, as well on his work as in the guard house, and requests his payment for his earned services and to be released of his contracted time. Defendant says that he ordered plaintiff to drill holes in the railing of the hill and that he left his work and went to the barn, on which account defendant followed him, in order to make him return to the work which plaintiff not being willing to do; defendant slapped him two or three times about the ears.

Defendant further says that he ordered plaintiff to peel
the firs and while defendant was absent, he left his work,
and went to have a talk with Pieter Hillebrants, whence
either defendant's servant girl or wife went to fetch him,
and requests that plaintiff shall serve out with him his
legal time. Plaintiff replies and says that defendant
first struck him while he was drilling holes in the railing
of the hill, because he did not understand boring very
well, not being a carpenter. Defendant said he would give
him other work; he requests once more to be relieved of his
further legal time, on account of the bad treatment by his
master.

The hon. court orders plaintiff to serve out his legal
time with defendant, and orders defendant Tjerck Claesen
to decently treat plaintiff, as a helper ought to be
treated, and if it shall be found that defendant, after
this, shall again improperly treat plaintiff, defendant
shall be obliged to pay plaintiff's full wages and further
plaintiff shall then be at liberty to leave his service.

Tjerck Claesen De Wit, sergeant of the civic guard,
requests that the cattle, at night, may be kept off the
street, that the round may pass freely and without obstructions, and also that, in time of need or alarm, there
may not be obstacles along or on the street. The hon.
court decides that in this matter the inhabitants shall be
ordered by decree; that each one shall keep his cattle,
during the night, inside his enclosure, and not on or about
the street, under penalty of a fine of one daalder each
time for every head of cattle thus found. Also that the
streets shall be cleared of lumber, firewood, wagons,
etc., under penalty to the violator of one pound Flemish
for every violation. Whereupon the following decree was
issued and published:

Decree that each one shall keep his cattle, by night,
on his farm, and to clear the streets.

Whereas Schout and Scheepenen at Wildwyck have heard
complaints that the round cannot, by night, freely and
without obstructions pass along the streets, because the
cattle are lying here and there in and about the streets,
on account whereof not only by an unexpected alarm or other
dangers, the guard and other burghers who might assemble,
could not on account of said cattle occupying the streets,
make a free use of the same, for fear of stumbling and
falling over said cattle lying down during dark nights, but
also that, on account of the obstruction caused by said
animals, they could not quickly and speedily enough come
together at the spot where the danger would require them,
therefore, Schout and schepenen of this village aforenamed
have resolved and therefore order and command everyone to
keep his cattle, at night, on his farm but not allow them
to lie on and about the streets during the night, under
penalty of a fine of one daelder every time for each head

of cattle.

The aforesaid schout and schepenen, also, finding that
some residents, here, do not scruple to obstruct the streets
with firewood, lumber, wagons, etc., even keeping and putting them in the middle of the street, which also greatly
obstructs the round, and in time of alarm or distress the
burghers, which should come together, and for the purpose
of preventing all such improprieties, the aforesaid schout
and schepenen order and direct all those leaving firewood,
lumber, or wagons, etc., at night on the streets, to clear
the street of the aforementioned obstructions inside of
two times 24 hours after date, for the purposes of being
in a condition to be more safely and securely used at
night and in times of danger, under penalty to the violator
of a pound Flemish for every time. Let everyone look out
for himself. Thus given at the session of schout and
schepenen at Wildwyck, June 23, N. S. of the year 1665.

At the further verbal complaint of the Capt. Thomas
Chambers concerning some refractory individuals, unwilling
to mount the daily guard, the aforesaid Capt. Thomas
Chambers, besides the other burgher officers, are authorized and requested to pay close attention to the daily
watch, and to have the unwilling individuals disciplined
on account of the same by the burgher council of war.

Extraordinary Session of the Hon. Court and Burgher Council of War, besides the Commander of the Troops Christoffel
Berrisfort, Tuesday, July 7, 1665.

Present: Willem Beeckman, Schout; Jan Willemsen
Hoochteylingh, Evert Pels, Jan Joosten, Commissaries;
Thomas Chambers, Captain; Henderick Jochemsen, Commissary
and Lieutenant; Christoffel Berrisfort, Commander of the
Troops.

Having been warned yesterday by Christoffel Davids,
through Joris Bolus, a soldier, that the savages are planning mischief against our village, and intend to fight and
make war against us, which said Mr. Bolus, besides four
other residents here have also experienced yesterday on
their way to the bank, because said persons were assailed
by some drunken savages, and some of them were threatened
by said savages with bare knives, and one of our residents,
therebesides, was prohibited by the savages from mowing
grass on the land of the burnt down new village, and the
more so because, today, while we were in session, a savage
had the boldness to scale the palisades and to enter the
village, it is therefore resolved by the Magistrates,
Burgher Council of War and Mr. Berrisfort, commander of
the troops, until further orders and approbation by the
hon. Ld. Gov. Genl. at New York, that from now on no more
savages shall be permitted to enter the village, but that
they shall be kept outseide, and that their chiefs shall
be acquainted with our reasons for this resolve. And in

case they should have anything for sale that they shall
sell the same outside the strand-gate only, in order to
prevent them by this means from further spying on our
village, because we have seen through daily experience
that the savages who have everyday entered our village
belong to various nations and enter in large numbers and
the greater portion among them offer nothing for sale
and don't do anything but spy on our village and visit
everybody's house in the village.

Ordinary Session, Tuesday, July 7, 1665.
    Present: Willem Beeckman, Schout; Jan Willemsen
Hoochteylingh, Henderick Jochemsen, Evert Pels, Jan
Joosten, Commissaries.
        Tomas Harmensen, Farmer, Plaintiff
        vs. Jan Willemsen Hoochteylingh, Defendant
    Plaintiff requests per petition, revision of the
sentence previously pronounced on June 23 last, on account
of the smuggling by defendant of a brew of beer. Defendant says that when plaintiff, last spring, started for the
Manhatans, he asked him whether, if in the meantime he
should want to brew, he would have to get a permit from
the collector Jacob Joosten, whereupon plaintiff answered,
"No," but that he, defendant, should mark it down and acquaint him, plaintiff, upon his return. Plaintiff replies
and denies defendant's answer, saying that he did not agree
with defendant in said manner, and says having demanded
the fine, etc., against defendant for the last brew of
beer, he /plaintiff/ being at the time present and visible.
The hon. court, considering plaintiff's petition, refers
parties to two impartial good men, viz., the Capt. Thomas
Chambers and Roelof Swartwout, for the purpose of, if possible, settling the differences between parties, provided
the justice of the officer and, if not, to again address
the court.
        Christoffel Davids, Plaintiff
vs. Jan Jansen Van Amersfoort, Defendant. Absent. Default.
      Henderick Cornelissen Lyndraeyer, Plaintiff
    vs. Ariaen Gerretsen, Defendant. Absent. Default.
      Henderick Jochemsen and Mattheus Capito,
    attorneys of Johannes Withart, Plaintiff
        vs. Aert Martensen Doorn, Defendant
    Plaintiffs demand, as having procuration of Johannes
Withart, as per obligation dated Mar. 23, 1656, amounting
to 44 whole beavers, also as per bill dated Nov. 22, 1657,
seven beavers with the interest and costs of the same, or
else a written surety or mortgage. Defendant answers that
for the present he is unable to pay, but that last spring
he agreed with Jan Jansen Bleeck, Jan Withart's attorney
at Fort Orange, to give security for the payment in case or
at the coming harvest he could not pay. The hon. court,
having seen proof of debt, orders defendant, as per ob-

ligation and account, to pay the same, besides the expenses
and also the interest, if plaintiffs can show that the same
was promised, and by default of payment, security or
mortgage.

Evert Pels, Plaintiff
vs. Aert Martensen Doorn, Defendant

Plaintiff protests against defendant on account of
damage and expense suffered and yet to be suffered through
the pigs which came through defendant's fence, because
plaintiff on last Friday chased 23 pigs off his land, of
which he notified defendant, and yesterday, being Monday,
he chased more than 30 pigs off his sowed land, and requests compensation for the suffered damage to his grain,
and that his grain may be examined and the damages to the
same appraised. Defendant denies that plaintiff can suffer damage by pigs through his fence, saying that in this
respect, his fence can bear examination. The hon. court
commissions Aert Jacobsen, Tjerck Claesen De Wit, and
Juriaen Westphael besides the officer to examine, tomorrow, the fences of both parties, where the pigs can pass
through to the sowed land, and the aforesaid three examiners shall appraise the damage caused plaintiff's wheat,
and announce the same to the court.

Whereas it becomes necessary to examine the fences
around the lands under Wildwyck, so that no damage be
caused to the sown crops by pigs or cattle, for this purpose schout and schepenen at Wildwyck qualify and elect
as examiners of the fences Aert Jacobsen, Tjerck Claesen
De Wit, and Juriaen Westphael, in order to examine the same
every 14 days or three weeks, and to fine the negligent,
after having warned them once, as they shall find them to
deserve.

Owing to meeting the savages, the burgher Captain
Thomas Chambers is ordered by the hon. court at Wildwyck
to keep watch at nighttime with a full corporal's guard in
both guardhouses till further orders.

Walran DuMont, appearing, delivers an inventory of
the effects, left by his predecessor Jan Aertsen, deceased,
and requests that guardians may be appointed for his wife's
and /Jan Aertsen's/ child. In accordance with petitioner's
request, the hon. court here appoints as guardians of the
child of his wife and her deceased first husband, Gysbert
Van Imbroch and Jacob Joosten.

Extraordinary Session of the Hon. Court, Burgher Council
of War and the Commander of the Troops Christoffel Berrisfort, Thursday, July 16, 1665.

Present: Willem Beeckman, Schout; Jan Willemsen
Hoochteylingh, Henderick Jochemsen, Evert Pels, Jan
Joosten, Commissaries; Thomas Chambers, Burgher Captain;
Cornelis Barentsen Slecht, Tjerck Claesen De Wit, Burgher
Sergeants. Christoffel Berrisfort, Commander of the Troops.

Whereas on July 7 last it was resolved by the hon.
court, the Burgher Council of War and Christoffel Berrisfort, commander of the troops, that from now on no more
savages shall be admitted into the village, but shall be
kept outside, for reasons shown in the said resolution,
which resolution on the next day July 8 was violated by
some soldiers quartered here, and who again admitted the
savages into the village because they had heard that it
was said to be their fault that the savages shall no longer
be permitted to enter the village, therefore said resolution is limited by the said hon. court, burgher council
of war and Christoffel Berrisfort, commander of the troops,
besides the for that purpose invited soldiers by said
Berrisfort, viz., Mr. Bolus, Henderick Palingh, and Ridsert Cage, and therefore resolved and decided under further approbation and order of the hon. Ld. Gov. Genl.,
the more so because harvest time is approaching, and the
greater portion of the population are obliged to attend to
the labor on the fields that no male savage shall from now
on be any longer admitted into the village, but be kept
outside, and only the women and children of the savages,
for the purpose of buying necessaries /shall be permitted
to enter/ in consideration of the aforementioned resolution dated July 7 last.

Aeltje Claesen, wife of Henderick Aertsen, having
been summoned before the court, and asked what reason she
gave the savages on July 8 last, says that the savage
asked her why they were not allowed to come into the village, whereupon she answered him, "Because yesterday the
savages had maltreated Mr. Bolus near the Twaalfs Kil,"
which she had heard thus told by others.

The hon. court orders the Burgher-captain Thomas
Chambers, besides his council of war, to charge the sentinels not to admit, until further orders, any more male
savages into the village, but only women and children.

In regard to the complaint to the hon. court at Wildwyck by the commander of the troops Christoffel Berrisfort and the soldiers quartered here, that the inhabitants
here accuse them /the soldiers/ of being the cause that
the savages are not permitted to enter the village, therefore schout and schepenen of Wildwyck order and command
each and every inhabitant here that nobody shall undertake
to tell the savages the "wherefore," much less accuse the
soldiers or any other persons of being the cause why this
or that has been ordered and commanded, this being a
specimen of treason, but that they shall bridle their
tongue and upon the questions of the savages answer "not
to know about this affair or affairs" under penalty for
those who shall be found to violate the present, of punishment in accordance with the deed. Thus given at the session of schout and schepenen at Wildwyck this July 16,
1665.

Extraordinary Session, Monday, July 27, 1665.
Present: Willem Beeckman, Schout; Jan Willemsen
Hoochteylingh, Henderick Jochemsen, Evert Pels, Jan
Joosten, Commissaries.
In regard to the missive by the hon. Lrd. Gov. Genl.
at New York, dated July 12, O. S., containing the order
that during the harvest only one gate in the village shall
be open, and the others remain closed, the commander of
the troops here, Mr. Berresfort, was for this purpose invited to come to court, and he was requested to close the
Strand gate and to keep the Millgate open, because through
the same most of the crops will have to be brought in. He
answers that he will not withdraw his troops from the
Strandgate on account of the road leading to the Strand,
and that the Millgate (notwithstanding through the same
most of the crops from the fields will have to be brought,
and thus, of necessity, ought to be kept open, owing to
the fact that near and about said gate all the farmers,
Thomas Chambers only excepted, have their crops) shall be
closed during the harvest. This being not at all feasible,
he was further requested to close both gates, and to make
a new gate near the Walepoint on the southwest side, where
there has long since been a guardhouse, and where even yet
the burghers keep a night watch, in order thus to prevent
all jealousy among the farmers. Answers not at all to intend to remove his sentinels. For this reason the hon.
court has been obliged to follow said commander's orders,
and for the purpose of executing said hon. Ld. Gov. Genl's
command, it was resolved by a majority vote to keep the
Millgate closed during harvest time and to open the
Strand gate.
Whereas the inhabitants, here, have petitioned the
hon. court to be relieved from the night watch, because on
account of harvesting they are considerably tired and ex-
hausted, therefore the captain of the Burghers, Thomas
Chambers, in consideration of this circumstance, is requested and ordered by the hon. court to divide the watch
and to have the inhabitants mount guard with half-corporal
guards, as was done before this.

Extraordinary Session, Saturday, August 15, 1665.
Present: Willem Beeckman, Schout; Henderick Jochemsen, Evert Pels, Commissaries.
Whereas the period of the farm of the innkeeper's and
burgher excise here in the village of Wildwyck expires on
the 6/16 of the present month of August, therefore everybody is informed by the present that in accordance with the
order of the hon. Lord Cov. Genl. Ridsert Nicolls the excise shall be collected until further orders, and is appointed collector the hon. Heer Willem Beeckman, Schout,
to whom from now on all wines and beers shall have to be
declared, and of whom a permit shall have to be received

before the beers shall be allowed to be taken out of the
breweries, and the wines will be permitted to be stored in
their houses and cellars by the merchants. And to pay for
the same, as per previous valuation, the excise for the
wines and beers of innkeepers as well as burghers. And
for the purpose of preventing all smuggling, the brewers
are ordered not to transport any beers, before it shall appear to them, from a permit, that the same was duly declared. Thus enacted at the session of the hon. court at
Wildwyck, this August 5/15, 1665.

Against those accommodating the savages through the
curtains of the villa   Whereas experience shows us that
the Indians or savages are offered opportunities to enter
from the outside over the palisades, and through this are
accommodated and provided with what they want, on account
of which practice the savages are induced to approach and
visit the palisades, a practice which may have evil consequences, therefore schout and schepenen at Wildwyck prohibit the inhabitants, either themselves, their wives,
children or servants from providing, through the palisades,
the savages with any more drink, food or whatever else it
might be, under penalty of a fine of 25 gldrs. for every
violation. Thus enacted at the session of the hon. court
at Wildwyck, this August 5/15, 1665.

Extraordinary Session, Monday, September 7, 1665.
Present: Willem Beeckman, Schout; Jan Willemsen
Hoochteylingh, Henderick Jochemsen, Eveert Pels, Jan
Joosten, Commissaries.

Jacob Kip, brother-in-law of Mr. Gysbert Van Imbroch,
deceased, shows the hon. court the last desire of the aforenamed deceased Van Imbroch, signed by said deceased himself,
and also an authorization of the hon. Heer Johannes La
Montange Sr., deceased's father-in-law, containing that he,
besides Willem LaMontange (both being brothers-in-law of
said deceased) have been expressly sent thither, for the
purpose of supervising deceased Van Imbroch's left estate
and effects, because he left three minor children, and
there besides requests that the hon. court be pleased to
commission and appoint legal guardians for the same, for
which reason the hon. court appoints the following guardians in accordance with the authorization, appearing below
and reading thus:

"Whereas the person of Mr. Gysbert Van Imbroch, surgeon in this village of Wildwyck and widower of Rachel
Monjeur DelaMontange (who in the month of October of the
past year 1664 in the aforenamed village died in the Lord)
also died in the Lord on Aug. 19/29 last, leaving three
minor children, a daughter named Lysbet now about six
years old, two little sons, the eldest named Johannes
about four years old, and the youngest named Gysbert about
one year old, who necessarily ought to be taken care of

and kept, out of the means and effects left by their
parents. And whereas the deceased Mr. Van Imbroch on the
same day of his death requested verbally and in writing
that his left estate should be inventoried and sealed up
until the same time when the friends from the Manhatans
should arrive for the purpose of then being done with by
them, for the best interest of the minor children, as they
should find to be necessary, therefore for this purpose
were expressly sent off and have arrived here Jacob Kip
and Willem Monjeur DelaMontange, both brothers-in-law of
the said deceased who requested our court that legal
guardians /might be appointed/ over the aforesaid minor
children left by deceased, /and said children/ may be decently taken care of and kept, out of the means left; and
also that said means may be most faithfully administered,
the credits and debits settled, and further that everything
may be done necessary for the settlement of the estate.
And whereas we deem it highly necessary, have after mature
deliberation /whereas in these regions there are no nearer
friends or acquaintances/ in accordance with the aforesaid
deceased's last desire, commissioned and appointed as
guardians, as, by the present, we do commission and appoint, the persons of Jacob Kip, Willem Monjeur DeLaMontange and the hon. Heer Willem Beeckman who are also authorized by the present /to act/ as guardians over the aforenamed minor children, and they, guardians, may take possession of the aforenamed deceased's goods, estate and effects as well here as in other sections of the world, sell,
keep, distribute, administer the same, as they shall think
to be to the best interests of the minors, and further receive, demand and also pay all debits and credits, and for
that purpose use all means necessary for the same, and
further, in general, do and leave undone everything as is
proper, provided they, the guardians (having been legally
and properly invited for the purpose) shall render a proper
accounting and proof of their administration and of the
relics. Thus enacted at the session of the hon. court at
Wildwyck on the day and in the year as above.

Ordinary Session, Tuesday, September 8, 1665.
    Present: Willem Beeckman, Schout; Jan Willemsen
Hoochteylingh, Henderick Jochemsen, Evert Pels, Jan
Joosten, Commissaries.
            Thomas Chambers, Plaintiff
    vs. Henderick Cornelissen Lyndraeyer, Defendant
    Plaintiff says that he contracted with defendant for
cordage in behalf of his lands for the period of four
years, and that three years expired, and that defendant
has now refused him cordage. Defendant answers that during the first year he made cordage for plaintiff from his
own hemp, and that further they contracted whatever more
hemp plaintiff should cultivate than was necessary for

his own cordage, defendant should be permitted to use for
himself, and that he, defendant, would not object to working half a year on plaintiff's land for the latter's benefit.   Plaintiff replies, saying that in case defendant is
willing to declare that he was in need of plaintiff's furnished hemp for making cordage, he has no further claim
against him for the furnishing of cordage for the three
years and, if not, that he, plaintiff, will demand from
defendant the damages suffered on account of it.   Defendant, replying to the same, says to be able to declare with
a good conscience that he has been in need of hemp for the
furnishing of cordage to plaintiff during the preceding
three years.   In accordance with the foregoing defendant
made a proper declaration before the hon. court, and plaintiff's demand for damage on account of the nondelivery of
cordage is refused, and parties are thereby further ordered to live up to their contract in regard to the cordage.

       Mattheu Blanchan requests that the sentence pro-
nounced on Mar. 24, 1665, against Allert Heymans may be
executed.   A special injunction and order of the late Ld.
Dir. Genl. Petrus Stuyvesant with the attestation mentioned below, signed by the said Hon. Ld. Petrus Stuyvesant, dated 3/13 Apr. 1665, having been shown at the session, therefore the plaintiff Mattheu Blanchan is refused
his demand against Allert Heymans.

       Copy of the attestation of the hon. Heer Petrus Stuy-
vesant:

       Whereas we are in duty bound to testify as to the
truth, much more so if judicially requested to do so,
therefore I, the undersigned, certify and declare by the
present that at the time of the distribution and drawing
of the lots on both the large pieces, it was found that
there was one lot less than the number of subscribers and
consequently of tickets, which came to pass because from
Mattheu Blanchan's family there appeared three signers and
drawers, viz. Mattys Blanchan, Louwys DuBois and Antoni
Crupel, the two last named having each married a daughter
of the aforesaid Mattys Blanchan.   On this account it was
then resolved, and communicated and ordered to Allert Heymans that two lots /tickets/ should be put in and drawn
for Matthys Blanchan and his two sons-in-law together and
in company with each other which by these presents /I/
declare to be the truth.   Done at Wildwyck, this 3/13
April 1665. (was signed) P. Stuyvesant.

                Tomas Harmensen, Plaintiff
         vs. Jan Willemsen Hoochteylingh, Defendant
       Plaintiff demands judgment against defendant on ac-
count of the sentence pronounced July 7, 1665, because defendant refused to settle the suit between them by good
men as per order by the hon.court.   Defendant answers as

before that he had agreed with plaintiff to make known to
him when he had brewed, so that both could mark it down.
The hon. court decides and orders, whereas defendant has
been unwilling to call in the decision of the appointed
good men, that he shall be bound to purge himself under
oath, in such a manner that he had contracted with the
farmer to be allowed to remove his brewed beer and to put
it in his cellar, before he had declared the same to him,
the farmer, and if not, that he, defendant, be then made
amenable to plaintiff's demand of the full fine for smuggling, as having put the beers in his cellar two days
previously, after the judicial warning.

Extraordinary Session, Monday, September 21, 1665.
    Present: Willem Beeckman, Schout; Jan Willemsen
Hoochteylingh, Henderick Jochemsen, Evert Pels, Jan
Joosten, Commissaries.
    Frederick Hossy appearing before the Magistrates
says that last night he lay down on the bench in the
burgher head watch, and in the mean time one Henderick
Hendericksen Van Reyn who also had the watch came in.
He heard that said Henderick Hendericksen, upon entering,
said that the English soldiers had gone to Swartwout to
fetch a pail of beer, to defraud him, and those were rascally tricks. He further said, "I sat down among the
English and heard everything they said, and they thought I
could not understand them," and as having said, "We behave badly in our lodgings, then we get good ones," and
further said, "They ⁄the English⁄ are all together sneak
thieves," then the aforenamed deposer rose, taking hold
of his, Henderick Hendericksen's, coat, and asking him
who, among the English, had committed rascalities. And
then he, deposer, called upon Juriaen Westphael and Pieter
Hillebrants as witnesses.
    Juriaen Westphael, having been questioned by the
magistrates, answers concerning the foregoing that he has
heard that Henderick Hendericksen said, "The English intended to get a pail of beer of Swartwout on the hon. Ld.
Gov. Genl's name, that this was a thievish trick" and
that he further heard Henderick Hendericksen say, "They
⁄the English⁄ are sitting down and telling each other
sneak thieving tricks." Pieter Hillebrants declares that
he was asleep, and that Frederick Hossy woke him up, and
said, "bear knowledge of what is being said here" and he,
deposer, did not then hear any more that was said by Henderick Hendericksen than, "They are sneak thieving tricks,"
not knowing about whom he, Henderick Hendericksen, said,
because he awoke out of his sleep.
    Henderick Hendericksen Van Reyn, having been in-
formed of the aforenamed complaint, says and admits having
said, after the English had gone for the beer, "They are
sneak thieving tricks," and also said, "I sat down among

the English, and heard all they said, and they thought I
could not understand them when saying, 'We behave badly in
our lodgings, then we get good ones,' and further says
that he did not well understand their talk in regard to
the foregoing, and further denies having said that all
the English were sneak thieves, and further adds that he
spoke all the aforesaid words without any afterthought of
evil.

The hon. schout in regard to the above complaint of
slandering the English nation by Henderick Hendericksen, he
having said according to his own admission that they intended to get beer in a fraudulent manner, and further
said that these are sneak thieving tricks, therefore demands that he shall be sentenced to pay 50 gldrs. fine.
The hon. court, having heard the schout's aforenamed demand, and also the answer of the plaintiff Henderick Hendericksen, besides taking into consideration his guilelessness, he being a person about whom, up to now, never
any evil has been reported, sentences defendant to pay a
fine of 24 gldrs. and six gldrs. for the guard as arrest
money to be paid inside 24 hours, being as an example for
others, to keep his mouth shut at other times.

Extraordinary Session, Friday, October 2, 1665.
Present: Willem Beeckman, Schout; Jan Willemsen
Hoochteylingh, Henderick Jochemsen, Evert Pels, Jan
Joosten, Commissaries.
Thomas Chambers, Plaintiff
vs. Jan Jansen Van Amersfoort, Defendant
Plaintiff says that he loaned defendant two handmill-
stones and requests that defendant shall return the same
to him, because he cannot, besides another, be accommodated with said handmill. Defendant answers that plaintiff gave him the aforesaid two handmill-stones. Plaintiff replies, saying that defendant shall prove him his
assertion. Defendant again replies that plaintiff gave him
said millstones, except the iron work on the stones.
Plaintiff demands of defendant to affirm the same under
oath. Defendant answers that he will think about taking
the oath, till the next session. The hon. court orders
defendant and allows him for the purpose of taking the
oath that the aforesaid millstones were given him by
plaintiff 24 hours time, and that, in the mean time, defendant shall not use said millstones, and by default of
the oath, that defendant shall return the aforesaid millstones to plaintiff at the place whence he fetched them.

Plaintiff further says that he has seen from a deposition that defendant the day before yesterday called his,
plaintiff's, wife, in public on the street in the presence
of the hon. schout and some of the local court, a whore, a
hog and a beast, and requests that defendant shall prove
the same, or else that he shall be commanded to keep his

mouth bridled. Defendant denies having called plaintiff's
wife said names. The hon. court is busy enquiring further
into this matter, and will punish defendant, as the case
will require.

Willem Beeckman, Schout, Plaintiff
vs. Jan Jansen Van Amersfoort, Defendant

The schout says that Margarita Hendericks, wife of
Thomas Chambers, has sent in a written complaint on Sept.
30 last, against her son-in-law, Jan Jansen Van Amersfoort, that her aforenamed son-in-law has badly treated
her daughter, the aforesaid son-in-law's wife, and even
has called her an old whore, hog and beast, pushing her
from his farm by the arm. On account of which aforesaid
complaint, he /schout/ has arrested defendant and summoned
him before the court, accusing him, as is also shown by
attestation of the following deeds: maltreating his wife
and threatening to shoot her, and calling his mother-in-
law, aforenamed, an old hog and a beast. Defendant denies
the whole of the aforesaid complaint, saying not to know
anything at all about it.

The hon. Schout Willem Beeckman sums up the misdeeds
committed by Jan Jansen Van Amersfoort on September 20/30
and at diverse other times against his wife, that he has
badly beaten, pushed, and threatened her, as per the attestations and proofs, to shoot her, on account whereof
she fled to the street; also that, about ten or 12 weeks
ago, when his wife was in the last stage of pregnancy, he
cruelly beat her and threw her out of the house, so that
she was taken up for dead and was taken to her mother's
house where she was again nursed like a child, and further
the evil and indecent treatment done by him to his mother-
in-law, how on September 20/30 he took her by the arm, and
without reasons, pushed her out of his house, while calling her an old hog and beast, and further, even before
this, jumping on his mother-in-law in her own house for the
purpose of stabbing her with some sharp object in his hand.
Further that, Mar. 3/13 last, having been cited by the
local magistrates to testify about the truth, he treated
them very shamefully; first, after he had been sent for
three times gave as answer that the magistrates should
first come and treat him to a drink (dat den Magistraet
eerst syn gelach soude coomen afbetaelen - which may also
mean "that the Magistrates should first come and pay for
their drinks"); at last, after the threat that he would be
fetched, he appeared, entering with his head covered,
though warned to uncover himself, speaking very roughly
and indecently /saying/ not to be willing to testify.
Which disobedience, dirty, contemptible, despicable treatment and other committed misdeeds and perpetrated offences
cannot remain unpunished, so that the schout demands, in
the name and by the authority of his Royal Majesty of
Great Britain, and of the hon. Ld. Gov. Genl. that he, Jan

Jansen Van Amersfoort shall be punished as a tumultuous and seditious person, viz. to be banished during three years out of the boundaries of this village, and therebesides to pay a fine of 500 gldrs. others as an example.

The hon. court, having seen the written complaint of Margarita Hendericks, wife of Thomas Chambers, dated Sept. 20/30 last, besides the attestations and proofs by the same, against Jan Jansen Van Amersfoort, her son-in-law, the aforesaid Jan Jansen having called said Margarita Hendericks an old hog and beast, and further that aforenamed son-in-law has hadly treated his wife, and threatened to shoot her, and heeding the demand of the schout in regard to these and previous misdeeds committed by the aforesaid Jan Jansen Van Amersfoort, viz. that Jan Jansen Van Amersfoort shall be banished outside the limits of this village for the period of three years and pay a fine of 500 gldrs., therefore the hon. court, wanting to do right in the name and by the authority of his Royal Majesty of Great Britain, noting that Jan Jansen Van Amersfoort has behaved badly, as well before this as even up to the present in all kinds of committed misdeeds against his wife by calling her names, beating and threatening to shoot her, and against his mother-in-law Margarita Hendericks as well before this as up to the present in calling her an old hog and beast; and further that he, Jan Jansen, on Mar. 3/13 last has contemptibly treated the hon. local court, therefore condemns Jan Jansen Van Amersfoort to pay a fine of 200 gldrs. for the schout and 50 gldrs. for the local poor, both within the time of 14 days, and there besides the arrest money to the soldiers to be paid immediately. And further orders Jan Jansen Van Amersfoort to quietly and decently hold and behave himself against his wife and mother-in-law, so that no further complaints for heavier punishment may be brought against him.

Ordinary Session, Tuesday, October 6, 1665.
Present: Willem Beeckman, Schout; Jan Willemsen Hoochteylingh, Henderick Jochemsen, Evert Pels, Commissaries.

Willem Beeckman, Schout, Plaintiff
vs. Albert Gerretsen, Defendant

Plaintiff says that yesterday, when coming out on the street, he saw that defendant lit, on the street, a fire of straw and rubbish. On this account he demands, as per a previous decree, a fine amounting to 50 gldrs. Defendant answers having taken her bedstraw which was full of bed bugs out of her bedstead, and having set fire to it, says not having known that there existed an order against it. The hon. court, having noted plaintiff's demand, and heard defendant's answer, and also having noted defendant's guilelessness and simplicity, not having known that in this regard an order had been issued by the hon.

court, sentences defendant to pay the half fine, being 25
gldrs.,to plaintiff.

                Mattheus Capito, Plaintiff
            vs. Gerret Fooken, Defendant

Plaintiff demands, on account of Henderick Jansen
Looman's estate, three sch. of wheat for a brew of beer
which Looman brewed for Jan Gerretsen, defendant's partner. Defendant says being willing to pay one half, and
that he has nothing to do with the balance. The hon.
court, considering that in the murders by the savages, defendant's partner has been killed and all his effects were
burned, as also those of the defendant, therefore sentences defendant to pay his share, being one half, which is
sufficient.

                Tomas Harmensen, Plaintiff
        vs. Joris Hael, Defendant. Absent. Default.

                Henderick Palingh, Plaintiff
            vs. Evert Pels, Defendant

Plaintiff demands of defendant 166 gldrs. 10 st. in
sewan, on which has been paid 50 gldrs. Defendant admits
the debt and agrees to pay the same next week. The hon.
court orders defendant as per his own promise (plaintiff
being satisfied with the same) to satisfy the aforesaid
claim of plaintiff by next week.

                Henderick Palingh, Plaintiff
    vs. Aert Martensen Doorn, Defendant. Absent. Default.

                Henderick Palingh, Plaintiff
    vs. Arian Gerretsen, Defendant. Absent. Default.

        Henderick Cornelissen, Lyndraeyer, Plaintiff
    vs. Ariaen Gerretsen, Defendant. Absent. 2nd Default.

Plaintiff says that defendant, in accordance with
the lease, is obliged to clear the barn of straw and rubbish, to repair the roof, bringing two layers above in
the ridge of the barn, and to lay a new earthen floor, as
far as the old floor has lain; also demands the costs of
the same.

Decree concerning the carrying of dead bodies of
animals outside the village:

Whereas daily experience shows that the residents of
this village, prior to this, did not only leave the dead
bodies of their large and small cattle in the streets of
this village, but that some even have brought the said
dead bodies close by the curtains outside of this community directly upon and near the common roads, which de-
composing bodies, on account of their stench, not only
much inconvenience passers by, but may also be the cause
of bad diseases, owing to said nasty stench, for the purpose of remedying and preventing which in the future, the
hon. schout and schepenen of this village of Wildwyck, in
the name and by the authroity of his Royal Majesty of
Great Britain and the hon. Lord Ridsert Nicolls, gov. genl.

at New York by the present order and command each and
every resident of this place that, after this date, nobody shall further venture neither to leave his dead
bodies of the cattle, however named, on the street of this
village or to bring them near or about the curtains of
this community on or about the common roads, but that said
dead bodies shall be carried the distance of the two
/rifle/ shots outside of the village, away from the common
roads, under penalty to the violator of 25 gldrs. for
every violation. Let everybody look out for himself.
Thus enacted at the session of the hon. schout and schepenen of Wildwyck Sept. 26/Oct. 6, 1665.

Ordinary Session, Tuesday, October 13, 1665.
        Present: Willem Beeckman, Schout; Henderick Jochem-
sen, Evert Pels, Jan Joosten, Commissaries.
                Henderick Palingh, Plaintiff
            vs. Aert Martensen Doorn, Defendant
        Plaintiff demands of defendant an amount of 118 gldrs.
12 st. light money for delivered merchandise. Defendant
admits the above debt. The hon. court sentences defendant
to satisfy plaintiff's above claim.
                Henderick Palingh, Plaintiff
            vs. Ariaen Gerretsen, Defendant
        Plaintiff demands of defendant a sum of 229 gldrs.
light money for delivered merchandise. Defendant admits
the above debt. The hon. court orders defendant to satisfy plaintiff's above demand.
                Henderick Palingh, Plaintiff
vs. Warnaer Hoorenbeeck, Defendant. Absent. Default.
                Henderick Palingh, Plaintiff
            vs. Pieter Pietersen, Defendant
        Plaintiff demands of defendant a sum of 36 gldrs. for
delivered goods. Defendant admits the debt. The hon.
court orders defendant to satisfy plaintiff's above demand.
            Henderick Cornelissen,Lyndraejer, Plaintiff
            vs. Ariaen Gerretsen, Defendant
        Plaintiff demands that defendant, as per the lease,
shall clear the barn of straw and rubbish, lay two layers
of reed on each side of the barn, and lay a new earthen
floor as far as the old floor has laid; and demands the
costs incurred and yet to be incurred for the same. Defendant admits the foregoing. The hon. court, having seen
the lease between parties, orders defendant, in accordance
with his admission, to satisfy plaintiff's demand as per
lease, within 14 days, and in case of neglect by defendant,
plaintiff is authorised to have himself fixed the aforesaid at defendant's expense. And defendant is also ordered to pay the expenses made.
                Thomas Harmensen, Plaintiff
                vs. Joris Hael, Defendant
        Plaintiff enters a complaint against defendant, about

255

smuggling two ankers of brandy which defendant retailed
during plaintiff's farm and which he did not declare.
Defendant says that not until the hon. Ld. Gov. Genl. had
been here did plaintiff claim the excise for the wine.
Plaintiff also demands of defendant 45 gldrs. for delivered three half kegs of beer; also 36 gldrs. for contracted for excise of beers. Defendant answers having
received two half kegs of beer and another half keg containing five or six cans less, and says having some
claim against plaintiff about contract of beers which he
will have brought against plaintiff at the next session.
The hon. court, having heard parties, decides, whereas
plaintiff did not at the proper time summon defendant before the court in regard to the muggled wines, three or
four months having elapsed since defendant received the
wines, therefore plaintiff is refused the further claim
for smuggling against defendant, and defendant is sentenced to simply pay plaintiff the legal excise of the
wines.

Ordinary Session, Tuesday, October 27, 1665.
    Present: Willem Beeckman, Schout; Jan Willemsen
Hoochteylingh, Henderick Jochemsen, Evert Pels, Jan
Joosten, Commissaries.
              Willem Beeckman, Plaintiff
    vs. Henderick Cornelissen, Lyndrayer, Defendant
    Plaintiff demands of defendant 36 gldrs. 12 st. in
sewan, as per bill sent in. Defendant admits the debt.
The hon. court sentences defendant to satisfy plaintiff's
above demand.
        Henderick Cornelissen, Lyndrayer, Plaintiff
              vs. Willem Beeckman, Defendant
    Plaintiff says that defendant called him, at the
house of Jan Willemsen, a whoremaster, and demands proof
for the same. Defendant admits having said the same,
originating in the difficulty caused him by plaintiff at
the aforesaid house, accusing the hon. court of having
dealt unjustly with him in the quartering of soldiers,
/plaintiff/ having said, "You always send us one soldier
more to our house, than to any body else" and requests
that plaintiff may be disciplined for same. Plaintiff
admits having said that one burgher is more burdened with
soldiers than another, and that he, plaintiff, is obliged
to pay half of the board of the soldier, quartered in his
boarding-house. The hon. court orders plaintiff to prove
at the next session of the court that it (the court) burdens one burgher heavier than another in the quartering
of soldiers, and if not that plaintiff, in accordance with
defendant's request, shall be disciplined on account of
the same, as an example for others.
              Thomas Harmensen, Plaintiff
        vs. Dirrick Hendericksen, Defendant

Plaintiff demands of defendant 12 sch. of wheat as per assignment of Aeltje Sybrants. Defendant says owing Aeltje Sybrants, and also that aforenamed Aeltje owes him, and consequently he has a counter bill, and promises to pay the balance he will be shown to owe after liquidation. The hon. court decides that defendant shall balance accounts with Aeltje Sybrants in regard to the aforenamed demand per assignment, and that defendant shall be obliged to pay the balance to plaintiff.

Thomas Harmensen, Plaintiff
vs. Roelof Swartwout, Defendant

Plaintiff demands of defendant 75 gldrs. in sewan on account of a contract about the excise of wine. Also two sch. of wheat for beer excise. Defendant replies and denies the debt of the wine excise, and requests time to prepare his answer, and claims expenses which may be incurred on account of this case. The hon. court orders defendant to file his answer at the next session of the court.

Thomas Harmensen, Plaintiff
vs. Joris Hael, Defendant

Plaintiff demands of defendant payment of two half kegs of beer and one half aem of beer, amounting to 45 gldrs. sewan, provided a reduction on account of waste of the half aem, reckoned at a half keg. Defendant admits the debt, but answers having a claim of 500 gldrs. for damages sustained on account of a contract between him and plaintiff for the furnishing of beers, the condition being as follows: As long as Thomas Harmensen had any brew corn, he was bound to furnish him, Joris Hael, with one half of the brewed beer, at 15 gldrs. the half barrel. And to the further demand of Thomas Harmensen on Oct. 13 last for the 36 gldrs. on account of the beer excise, defendant answers that he promised the same at the delivery of beers, but that he did not receive any more beers as per contract, and therefore defendant has demanded, as above, for interest and damage 500 gldrs. Samuel Olivier, called in as a witness by Joris Hael in this affair, says and admits having heard that the above contract was thus entered into between parties. Thomas Harmensen, also, does not deny having made the above contract with Joris Hael, but says that after Joris Hael should have retailed the one half of the first delivery of the beers, the payment of the same was to follow, before he was to deliver him more and other beers. Joris Hael answers, and denies that mention had been made concerning the immediate payment of the first retailed beers, because the time of the year did not allow to pay cash.

The hon. court orders Thomas Harmensen to prove at the next session of the court that Joris Hael was obliged to pay as soon as the first delivered beer had been retailed before being obliged to deliver more beer to Joris Hael,

and if not that parties again shall address the court.
                    Bastiaen Pietersen, Plaintiff
                       vs. Evert Pels, Defendant
    Plaintiff demands of defendant payment of 12 sch. of
wheat for wages for six days, working on the land, and for
12 days threshing, and requests to receive his pay right
away because he wants to leave. Defendant answers that
plaintiff worked six days on the land and threshed nine
days only, and defendant called on him for the purpose of
himself earning /plaintiff's/ wages by threshing for him,
and consequently did not refuse plaintiff his payment, but
plaintiff detained him 14 days with promises of threshing.
Plaintiff replies and denies having put off defendant 14
days in regard to threshing. The hon. court orders defendant to pay plaintiff for six days for field work and nine
days for threshing.
        Mattheus Capito, auctioneer of the estate of
           Gysbert Van Imbroch, deceased, Plaintiff
    vs. Henderick Palingh, Defendant. Absent. Default.
    Henderick Palingh requests that the judgment pro-
nounced against Aert Martensen Doorn on Oct. 13, 1665, may
be executed. The hon. court orders the officer to proceed
with the execution.

Ordinary Session, Tuesday, November 3, 1665.
    Present: Willem Beeckman, Schout; Jan Willemsen
Hoochteylingh, Henderick Jochemsen, Evert Pels, Jan
Joosten, Commissaries.
        Jan Willemsen Hoochteylingh, Plaintiff
             vs. Ariaen Gerretsen, Defendant
    Plaintiff says that defendant has, the other day,
ploughed and sowed on plaintiff's land, and thereupon he
attached the crop, and that defendant notwithstanding the
attachment, harvested said crop. Defendant answers that
he did not sow more of the land than was leased to him,
and consequently mowed and harvested his grain off his own
leased land. The hon. court orders plaintiff to prove
that defendant poughed and sowed on his, plaintiff's,
leased land, and upon proof he will be awarded damages
against defendant.
            Ariaen Gerretsen, Plaintiff
      vs. Jan Willemsen Hoochteylingh, Defendant
    Plaintiff says that during harvest time defendant's
horses caused damage to his buckwheat, and consequently
had appraised said damage by two impartial /appraisers/
which has been done by them and was valued at 20 sch. of
buckwheat. Defendant answers that plaintiff did not judicially and immediately have the caused damage to his
buckwheat appraised, but, as per admission by Allert Heymans, one of the impartial appraisers, said appraisement
was done by them three or four days later. The hon. court
decides, whereas plaintiff did not, as per custom, at the
proper time and immediately have the sustained damage to

the buckwheat appraised, but allowed three or four days
to intervene, and in the meanwhile somebody else's besides defendant's cattle might have caused some damage;
therefore, plaintiff's demand against defendant is refused.

Thomas Chambers, Plaintiff
vs. Teunis Jacobsen and Andries Pietersen, Defendants.

Plaintiff complains about defendants' having taken the
reed off plaintiff's land without his knowledge, and which
he himself needed, and requests justice about the same.
Defendants admit having taken the reed off plaintiff's
land, and that said reed was mowed by Jan Gerretsen and
Henderick Hendericks Van Wye, which these owed to defendants, and that they ordered defendants to punctually on
the following day take the aforenamed reed away. Plaintiff
further says that, on the day before, he spoke to the
aforenamed persons, Jan Gerretsen and Henderick Hendericksen about mowing the reed on his land for himself, which
they refused him to do, saying that they had other work,
but notwithstanding they asked plaintiff where they should
mow the reed and /he/ answered them, "I shall drive to
Pisseman's Corner to see whether there is reed there," and
upon his return told them there was reed there, and they
nevertheless refused to mow the same, and shortly afterward mowed the reed for themselves, and had it carted away
by defendants, on account of which plaintiff enters a complaint against the aforesaid persons as thieves, and requests justice for the same.

Henderick Palingh, Plaintiff
vs. Teunis Tomassen Quick, Defendant

Plaintiff demands of defendant 30 gldrs. in sewan.
Defendant admits the debt and promises to satisfy plaintiff
in five or six days. The hon. court orders defendant to
satisfy plaintiff's demands, as per his promise, in the
above stated time.

Tomas Harmensen, Plaintiff
vs. Roelof Swartwout, Defendant. Absent. Default.

Plaintiff demands, as per a previous demand on Oct.
27 last, of defendant a sum of 75 gldrs. in sewan as per
contract for wine excise and two sch. of wheat for beer
excise. Defendant absent.

The hon. court once more orders defendant to file his
answer at the next session of the court or by default he
will be sentenced to satisfy plaintiff's demand.

Tomas Harmensen, Plaintiff
vs. Aert Martensen Doorn, Defendant. Absent. Default.

Tomas Harmensen, Plaintiff
vs. Juriaen Westphael, Defendant

Plaintiff demands of defendant five sch. of wheat for
excise, and two sch. of wheat for small beer. Defendant
admits the debt, and says having offered plaintiff to
satisfy him by next week. The hon. court orders defendant
to satisfy plaintiff, as per his own promise.

Thomas Harmenson, Plaintiff
vs. Arent Teunissen, Defendant
Plaintiff demands of defendant six sch. of wheat. Defendant admits the debt and says that plaintiff without his
knowledge has taken 50 palisades from his batch of palisades, and desires to deduct the same from plaintiff's
claim. Plaintiff agrees to pay for the palisades. The
hon. court orders defendant to satisfy plaintiff's demand,
provided he may deduct the 50 palisades.
Christoffel Davids, Plaintiff
vs. Juriaen Westphael, Defendant
Plaintiff demands of defendant an amount of 37 gldrs.
four st. as per bill produced. Defendant admits the debt
and claims a can of plaintiff, which plaintiff broke last
year. The hon. court orders defendant, in accordance with
his admission, to satisfy plaintiff, provided he may deduct the value of the can claimed.
Christoffel Davids, Plaintiff
vs. Juriaen Westphael, Defendant
Plaintiff demands of defendant restitution of 180
gldrs. for a demolished, not delivered house. Defendant
answers that defendant had been summoned by plaintiff on
this account before the hon. court, and that, at the time,
the hon. court refused plaintiff's demand, because it was
not defendant's fault. The hon. court refers to the
previous judgment, pronounced on Apr. 28, 1665.

Ordinary Session, Tuesday, November 24, 1665.
Present: Willem Beeckman, Schout; Jan Willemsen
Hoochteylingh, Henderick Jochemsen, Evert Pels, Jan
Joosten, Commissaries.
Willem Beeckman, Schout, Plaintiff
vs. Jan Jansen Van Amersfoort, Defendant. Absent. Default.
Nicolaes De Meyer, Plaintiff
vs. Roelof Swartwout, Defendant
Plaintiff demands of defendant 35 sch. of wheat as
per mortgage and seven sch. for interest, and one sch.
for writing, with the costs of the same. Plaintiff further requests that defendant, by virtue of his signature,
shall give him a mortgage amounting to 423 gldrs. in
beaver at eight gldrs. a piece, and of 18 sch. of wheat.
Defendant admits the debt, and says not to be able to immediately satisfy him. The hon. court, having heard both
parties, orders defendant to satisfy plaintiff's above
demand, and in regard to plaintiff's further request, defendant is ordered to give plaintiff a mortgage for the
aforesaid amounts as per the passed signature.
Tjerck Claesen De Wit, Plaintiff
vs. Evert Prys, Defendant
Plaintiff says that in regard to defendant's claim for
20 sch. of wheat, defendant has received some cans of
brandy of his brother-in-law Jan Albertsen Van Steenwyck,

deceased, which 20 sch. of wheat he, plaintiff, paid to
his aforesaid brother-in-law for defendant. Defendant answers and says that it is true that he has received wine,
but knows not how much, and says that he settled with Jan
Albertsen, deceased, according to his book, and that he
will not pay more than is shown by the book, and defendant
demands proof of plaintiff that he received more wine than
is shown by deceased Jan Albertsen's book. Plaintiff
agrees to show proof at the next session. The hon. court
orders plaintiff to produce proof at the next session that
defendant has received more wine of Jan Albertsen, deceased, than is shown by aforenamed Jan Albertsen's book;
otherwise, the hon. court refers to the previous judgment
on Mar. 10, 1665.

Andries Pietersen Noorman, Plaintiff
vs. Warnaer Hoorenbeeck, Defendant. Absent. Default.

Arent Jansen requests that the sentence against Tjerck
Claesen prounounced on Feb. 17, 1665, to the amount of 54
sch. of wheat, may be executed. The hon. court orders the
officer at the request of Arent Jansen, aforenamed, to
proceed with the execution.

Henderick Jochemsen requests that the sentence pronounced against Aert Martensen Doorn on Mar. 3, 1665, for
the amount of 43½ sch. of wheat may be executed. The hon.
court orders the officer to proceed with the execution.

Extraordinary Session, Wednesday, November 25, 1665.
Present: Willem Beeckman, Schout; Jan Willemsen
Hoochteylingh, Henderick Jochemsen, Evert Pels, Jan
Joosten, Commissaries.

Nicolaes Meyer, Plaintiff
vs. Roelof Swartwout, Defendant

Plaintiff requests that he may receive satisfaction
of defendant for his mortgage, in accordance with the
obligation passed on Apr. 8, N. S. 1665, for the amount of
423 gldrs. in beavers, and 18 sch. of wheat, being specially a house and lot in the colony of Renselaerswyck, a house
and lot in the village of Wildwyck, the lands under*the new
village in the Esopus, and three milch-cows with their
natural increase, with expenses.

Defendant answers being willing to mortgage said real
estates to plaintiff, and does not intend to furnish an
inventory in this business. Plaintiff replies, saying not
to be satisfied with defendant's answer, and requests
satisfaction of defendant as per the passed obligation.

The hon. court, having seen defendant's bond in his
obligation, to give plaintiff at his request a satisfactory
mortgage for securing the demanded 423 gldrs. in beavers
and 18 sch. of wheat, decides that defendant is obliged to
specially bind in plaintiff's behalf within the time of 24
hours the house and lot in the colony of Rentselaerswyck,
the house and lot in Wildwyck, the lands situated under

the new village in the Esopus, and the three milch-cows
with their natural increase, and sentences defendant to
pay the expenses incurred on account of the same.

Ordinary Session, Tuesday, December 1, 1665.
    Present: Willem Beeckman, Schout; Jan Willemsen
Hoochteylingh, Henderick Jochemsen, Evert Pels, Jan
Joosten, Commissaries.
            Willem Beeckman, Schout, Plaintiff
vs. Jan Gerretsen and Henderick Hendericks Van Wye, De-
                        fendants
    Plaintiff says that on Nov. 3 last Thomas Chambers
made a complaint against defendants on account of theft,
and that they mowed the reed off his land without his
knowledge, and as soon as it had been mowed, had it removed by others, on which account the schout, as per
aforesaid complaint, prosecutes defendants before the
court, to punish the same as the case may be found. Defendants answer, saying not having stolen the reed, because Thomas Chambers had not fenced in the said piece of
land where they mowed the reed, and also that Thomas
Chambers had already had his reed mowed, before they mowed
the reed for themselves.
    Thomas Chambers, having been further heard on this
account, denies defendants' answers in their presence, saying that they, defendants, have knowingly and with intent
to steal, mowed the reed from his land, because, forsooth,
they knew that he had put a mower on the said land for the
purpose of mowing the reed for him, and while he needed
said mower at home, they, defendants, in the meanwhile,
took the liberty of mowing the reed off his land and to
have it removed.
    The hon. schout replies, because it is plain that de-
fendants as per Thomas Chambers' complaint, have thievish-
ly taken the reed off his land, therefore he demands, that
in the future everybody may the more securely possess his
property, and similar deeds may not be further committed,
that they shall be obliged to indemnify Thomas Chambers for
the damage or injury caused on account of said reed, and
/be sentenced to pay/ a fine of 100 gldrs. each. The hon.
court, having considered the aforesaid case, decides that
defendants have misbehaved, and appropriated another's
property in mowing the reed without the owner's knowledge.
Wherefore, for the purpose of preventing similar /actions/
the defendants are condemned to return to said Thomas
Chambers the reed they mowed off Thomas Chambers' land and
therebesides are sentenced each to pay in behalf of the
hon. schout a fine of 25 gldrs.
            Joost Ariaens, Plaintiff
        vs. Pieter Hillebrants, Defendant
    Plaintiff demands of defendant four sch. of wheat.
Defendant admits the debt. The hon. court orders defendant

to satisfy plaintiff's aforesaid demand.

Thomas Hal, Plaintiff
vs. Aert Martensen Doorn, Defendant

Plaintiff says that, in accordance with the sentence on Feb. 24, 1665, defendant was ordered to pay a sum of 172 gldrs. beavers' value, and that defendant, in payment of said claim, has already paid him 100 sch. of oats and requests that defendant shall give him security for the balance. Defendant says not being willing to give further security, because he has signed an obligation. Plaintiff replies saying being willing to take security for the balance in cattle, or that the said sentence must be executed. The hon. court, having heard the parties, decides that defendant shall be obliged to furnish security to plaintiff for the balance, or in case of default, that defendant, as per plaintiff's demand, is ordered to immediately pay the balance, under penalty of execution, because plaintiff is a stranger.

Thomas Harmensen, Plaintiff
vs. Roelof Swartwout, Defendant

Plaintiff demands, as per a previous demand, 75 gldrs. for the excise on wine, and two sch. of wheat for beer excise. Defendant answers not to owe in regard to the excise on wine, because he has contracted with plaintiff about the delivery of an anker of distilled waters, and did not receive said waters of plaintiff, and owing to failure of delivery concludes as before. Plaintiff replies saying that his wine was ready, and consequently he notified defendant through the court messenger, and had him asked, if his, defendant's, payment was also ready. Defendant admits that plaintiff has notified him about the same, but says that notwithstanding plaintiff's wine was not ready. The hon. court refers parties to good men, viz., Thomas Chambers and Tjerck Claesen De Wit, for the purpose of settling, if possible, the above affair with parties, and if not, that parties shall again address the court with the report of the aforesaid good men.

Willem Beeckman, Schout, Plaintiff
vs. Jan Jansen Van Amersfoort, Defendant

The hon. schout says that on Oct. 31 last five half barrels of good beer were brought to his house which has been confiscated by the farmer and the court messenger, on account of which the farmer had also cited defendant about this affair, and in the meanwhile he, defendant, has settled this case with the farmer, and further says that defendant's wife invited him, plaintiff, on Nov. 2 to the house of the secretary for the purpose of settling this case with defendant on account whereof the hon. schout requests the payment of his third part, nomine officy. Defendant answers saying that the beer was not confiscated but was only seized by the farmer, and further that he sold said five half barrels of beer to the farmer. The

hon. court orders defendant to prove at the next session
of the court that his seized beers were not confisacted
by the farmer, and if not, that defendant is sentenced to
pay the claim of the demanded third part of the schout.

Willem Beeckman, Schout, Plaintiff
vs. Jan Jansen Van Amersfoort, Defendant

The hon. schout requests that defendant, in accordance
with the judgment on Oct. 2 last, shall satisfy him within
two times 24 hours, or otherwise defendant may be legally
forced to do so, because the time for payment has appeared
more than six weeks ago. The hon. court orders defendant
to satisfy to the schout the above judgment inside of
four times 24 hours, or by default that defendant shall
be legally forced to do so.

Henderick Cornelissen, Lyndrayer, Plaintiff
vs. Ariaen Gerretsen, Defendant

Plaintiff demands of defendant payment of the incurred
expense, as per schepen sentence on Oct. 13, 1665, being
to remove the manure to lay the floor in the barn and to
cover the roof of the barn with two layers of reed on both
sides, which he /plaintiff/ has been obliged to do himself
at defendant's expense, as also other expenses amounting
to 108 gldrs. six st. in sewan. He also demands of plaintiff, as per obligation, 55 gldrs. in sewan. Defendant answers that, from the conditions in the lease he is not yet
obliged, as plaintiff demands, to lay the floor and to
cover /the roof/ and in regard to carting the dung, he had
contracted with Teunis Jacobsen that the latter was to
take away the dung for him, in return /for which service/
he would, next spring, loan him two horses, with his son,
to plough. Defendant does not deny the obligation. Plaintiff replies that defendant has never acquainted him with
the same, and consequently he, plaintiff, has had others
do said work for him. The hon. court orders defendant to
satisfy the obligation to plaintiff. In regard to the expenses incurred, whereas defendant as per a previous sentence had been allowed 14 days in which to do the work
himself, and plaintiff was permitted, in case of neglect,
to have the same done at defendant's expense, therefore
defendant is, on account hereof, condemned to pay the expenses made, as per appraisal of good men, and further also
to satisfy plaintiff for the expenses for secretary and
messenger, excepting the carting of the dung, if defendant
proves that he had the same done by Teunis Jacobsen.

Albert Jansen, court messenger, requests increase for
the summons money. And in regard to this he is empowered
by the hon. court to demand for every summons 18 st., being six st. for the secretary and 12 st. for himself. He
also requests that he may receive the same salary as was
paid to his predecessor Jacob Joosten, which request is
granted to petitioner.

Mattheus Capito, secretary, requests that he may be

allowed an annual salary. The hon. court allows petitioner
an annual salary of 150 gldrs., commencing May 1 last.

Ordinary Session, Tuesday, December 8, 1665.
    Present: Willem Beeckman, Schout; Jan Willemsen
Hoochteylingh, Henderick Jochemsen, Evert Pels, Jan
Joosten, Commissaries.
                Willem Beeckman, Schout, Plaintiff
vs. Jan Jansen Van Amersfoort, Defendant. Absent. Default.
                Jacob Joosten, Plaintiff
    vs. Pieter Hillebrants, Defendant. Absent. Default.
                Louys Dubois, Plaintiff
        vs. Henderick Palingh, Farmer, Defendant
    Plaintiff makes a complaint against defendant as far-
mer, because he took an anker of distilled water out of
his house, notwithstanding two days before he paid the excise on said anker, and obtained a permit for the same of
the farmer. Defendant answers, saying, that he took an
anker of wine out of plaintiff's house, which was taken in
at night after sunset, and concludes that said anker is
confiscated. Plaintiff replies, saying that he took in
said anker by evening while it was yet light, and offers
to prove the same, thereby refusing to allow Onfre Fergeson
to testify against him, saying that said testimony cannot
be legally accepted, because said Onfre Fergeson was informer. The hon. court orders parties, at the next session, to produce clearer evidence and further proof.
            Henderick Palingh, Farmer, Plaintiff
            vs. Mattheu Blanchan, Defendant
    Plaintiff says that defendant sold and transported
his wine at an improper time, and sustains that he, plaintiff, on account of similar sale and transport might be
defrauded by defendant, and that, therefore, defendant
should be fined. Defendant answers that he has seen from
a permit that the wine had been declared, and consequently
he permitted the wine to follow and though this took
place while it was yet daylight, he maintains not having
violated anything, if he had done so at about eight or
nine o'clock at night. The hon. court orders parties to
both produce clearer evidence and further proof concerning
their affair at the next session.
            Henderick Palingh, Plaintiff
    vs. Christoffel Davids, Defendant. Absent. Default.
            Tjerck Claesen De Wit, Plaintiff
            vs. Evert Prys, Defendant
    Plaintiff shows a certificate signed by Ariaen Ger-
retsen and Jan Jansen Van Oosterhout, upon the order of
the court dated Nov. 24 last, by which it is shown that
Evert Prys got one day, between morning and night, at
several times, in an earthen can made to contain two pints
of beer, brandy of Jan Albertsen Van Steenwyck, deceased.
Defendant admits having fetched brandy in said can of Jan

Albertsen Van Steenwyck, deceased, and refers in regard to
the quantity to aforesaid deceased Jan Albertsen's book
which book has been shown by the curators of said estate
to the hon. court, by which it appears that defendant has
received such wine as is mentioned in the certificate. The
hon. court decides, whereas the certificate does not show
that defendant received more wine of Jan Albertsen, deceased, therefore refers to the previous judgments of Nov.
24 and Mar. 10 last.

Marietje Simons, Plaintiff
vs. Pieter Pietersen, Defendant

Plaintiff demands of defendant three sch. of wheat,
wages for washing. Defendant answers that plaintiff did
not fulfil her promise concerning the washing, it having
been contracted for for the period of one year, commencing
in the month of April, last. The hon. court orders defendant to immediately pay one half of the wages for washing
to plaintiff, and further orders plaintiff to wash for defendant during the period contracted for, and at the expiration of said period /defendant/ shall also pay the
second half of the wages for washing to plaintiff.

Thomas Harmensen, Plaintiff
vs. Roelof Swartwout, Defendant

Plaintiff demands of defendant, as per a former demand on Dec. 1, 75 gldrs. for excise of wine and two sch.
of wheat for the excise on beer, with the cost of the
same. Defendant admits the beer excise, but maintains that
he does not owe the wine excise, and shows by a contract
that plaintiff ought to have delivered the wine to him on
Feb. 6 last, on account whereof he also prosecuted plaintiff on Feb. 10 last before the hon. court, and therefore
requests that plaintiff may indemnify him for the expense
made and trouble caused him.

The hon. court, having seen the contract between parties in regard to the delivery of an anker of brandy
which anker was to be delivered by plaintiff to defendant
within one month, and whereas plaintiff did not effect the
delivery in the stipulated time, therefore plaintiff's demand in regard to the wine excise is refused, and he is
condemned to pay the costs. Defendant also is ordered to
pay plaintiff the two sch. of wheat for the beer excise.

Cornelis Slecht, Plaintiff
vs. Joris Hael, Defendant. Absent. Default.

Henderick Cornelissen, Lyndrayer, requests that the
judgment, pronounced on Dec. 1, 1665, against Ariaen Gerretsen Van Vliet may be judicially enforced. The hon.
court orders the officer to proceed with the execution.

Ordinary Session, Tuesday, December 29, 1665.
    Present: Willem Beeckman, Schout; Jan Willemsen
Hoochteylingh, Henderick Jochemsen, Evert Pels, Jan
Joosten, Commissaries.

Willem Beeckman, Schout, Plaintiff
vs. Jan Jansen Van Amersfoort, Defendant. Absent. 2nd
Default

The hon. schout requests that defendant Jan Jansen,
as per a previous sentence on Dec. 1 last, shall prove
that the beers taken from him by the farmer have not been
declared confiscated, and that defendant shall make known
at what price he settled said case with the farmer, because the same is a violation of the rules of the farming.
The hon. court orders defendant once more, in conformity with the hon. schout's request, to prove at the
next session of the court that the beers taken from him by
the farmer have not been declared confiscated, and also
that defendant shall make known the amount at which he
settled said case with the farmer.

Willem Beeckman, Schout, Plaintiff
vs. Jan Jansen Van Amersfoort, Defendant. 2nd Default.

Jacob Joosten, Plaintiff
vs. Pieter Hillebrants, Defendant

Plaintiff demands of defendant 21 sch. of wheat and
two sch. of gray peas, originating mostly from the school-
money. Defendant admits the debt, and says being quite
willing to pay the same, if plaintiff will be pleased to
grant him some time. The hon. court orders defendant to
satisfy plaintiff's demand.

Louwies DuBois, Plaintiff
vs. Pieter Hillebrants, Defendant

Plaintiff demands of defendant 13 sch. of wheat,
partly for goods received, partly for taking care of his
cows. Defendant admits the debt, but excepts ½ sch. of
wheat for a dry cow. Plaintiff replies, saying that defendant milked said cow till harvest time. The hon. court
orders defendant to satisfy plaintiff's demand, provided
plaintiff shall prove that defendant milked the same till
harvest time.

Michiel Verbrugge, Plaintiff
vs. Pieter Hillebrants, Defendant

Plaintiff demands of defendant three sch. of wheat
with the costs of the same. Defendant admits the debt.
The hon. court orders defendant to satisfy plaintiff's demand, and to pay the costs.

Henderick Palingh, Farmer, Plaintiff
vs. Louwies DuBois, Defendant

In regard to the suit of Henderick Palingh, plaintiff,
Louwies DuBois produces witnesses on account of the anker
of distilled waters seized by the farmer, Henderick
Palingh, on Nov. 4 last, viz., Henderick Hendericksen Van
Wye and Elsje Barents, young daughter, both of proper age,
who declare that it was yet day when Louwies DuBois carried
in the aforesaid anker of distilled waters, but not knowing whether the sun had set or not, because the day was
mostly cloudy, he Henderick Hendericksen being still at

work for Mattheu Blanchan, and she, Elsje Barents, having
at the time fetched straw for the purpose of covering the
rosemary in the garden. And said deposers have judicially
sworn their aforenamed depositions. In consequence of the
aforesaid deposition of the aforenamed persons, affirmed
under oath, the hon. court, in the name and by the authority of the Royal Majesty of Great Britain, etc., orders
Henderick Palingh, farmer, to return, without expense or
charge, except the claim of the officer, to Louwies DuBois
the anker of distilled waters seized by him on Nov. 4/11
last at defendant's house.

Henderick Palingh, Farmer, Plaintiff
vs. Louwies DuBois, Defendant

Plaintiff says that defendant has become liable to a
fine of 10 gldrs. each time for the nonreturn of the ex-
cise-permits taken out by him, as per the 14th article of
the farming regulations, and requests that defendant may
be sentenced in conformity with the same. Defendant answers that plaintiff's demand has never been made here and
that the 14th article of the farming regulations has been
made for the wine-workers, not for the tapsters. The hon.
court understands that said permits mentioned in the aforesaid regulations concern enclosed towns and not the open
country and the duty of sworn wine-workers and consequently plaintiff's demand is refused.

Henderick Palingh, Plaintiff
vs. Allert Heymans Roos, Defendant

Plaintiff demands of defendant a sum of 60 gldrs. 12
st., being for a grindstone, soap, excise and a day's
work. Defendant denies it, and says having paid on the
same 40 gldrs. and shows also a note of Ariaen Gerretsen
of 20 gldrs. containing that Ariaen Gerretsen promised to
pay the same to Palingh. Plaintiff replies saying, not
having been satisfied with Ariaen Gerretsen's note of the
20 gldrs., as he is not yet satisfied. The hon. court,
having heard parties, orders defendant to pay plaintiff
the balance of 20 gldrs. 12 st.

Tjerck Claeson and Walran DuMont, Plaintiffs
vs. Tomas Harmensen, Defendant

Plaintiffs say that they have become defendant's
sureties for the former farm, and request to be relieved
of their responsibility. Defendant answers to intent to
pay the farm in the time of three or four weeks. The hon.
court orders plaintifs to urge defendant to precisely and
fully pay the amount of his expired farm in the time of
four weeks, and then the plaintiffs will be relieved of
their responsibility.

Grietie Henderiks Westercamp, Plaintiff
vs. Pieter Cornelissen, Defendant

Plaintiff demands of defendant a sum of 200 gldrs.,
as per copy from the minutes dated Feb. 6, 1663, against
Pieter Jacobsen, defendant's partner. Defendant answers

that plaintiff ought to have attended to said claim during
the life-time of his partner, Pieter Jacobsen, and therefore concludes not to owe her anything. Plaintiff answers
whereas defendant possesses deceased Pieter Jacobsen's
goods and effects, he is also obliged to pay his debts.
Defendant answers that he did not agree with his partner
concerning this affair, and further says that plaintiff
kept his partner from working, so that /he/ was very much
inconvenienced through the same. The hon. court decides,
whereas plaintiff has been negligent in attending to said
business during Pieter Jacobsen's life-time, therefore she
is referred with her claim to the left own estate* of the
deceased Pieter Jacobsen.

Femmetie Alberts, Plaintiff
vs. Willemtie Alberts, Defendant

Plaintiff says that some time ago she bought a hood
of her daughter Grietje and did not receive the same of
her daughter, and in the meantime her aforesaid daughter
again sold and delivered said hood to Willemtje Alberts,
and requests that Willemtie Alberts shall return said hood
to her, plaintiff. Defendant answers having bought said
hood of plaintiff's daughter Grietje, and /that she/ partially paid for the same, the balance of the purchase
money is ready with her. Plaintiff replies not being
satisfied, but desires to have said hood for herself because she bought it first. The hon. court refers plaintiff
to her daughter, to look to her for securing the hood and
denies plaintiff's claim against defendant.

Frederick Hussey requests that the hon. court be
pleased to measure out for him a lot for a house and garden, according to the promise of the Hon. Ld. Dir. Genl.
The hon. court allows petitioner a lot for a house and
garden, as soon as the opportunity shall offer.

Albert Jansen Van Steenwyck, as attorney for Pieter
Jansen Van Hoorn, demands the 30 sch. of wheat of the curators of the estate of Jan Albertsen Van Steenwyck, deceased, with the interest of the same for the time of two
past years, on account of the inability of Jan Alberts, deceased, and the costs of the same, as per previous judgment dated Apr. 14, 1665. The hon. court refers to the
previous judgment, dated Apr. 14, 1665.

Ordinary Session, Tuesday, January 19, 1666.
Present: Willem Beeckman, Schout; Jan Willemsen
Hoochteylingh, Henderick Jochemsen, Evert Pels, Jan
Joosten, Commissaries.

Willem Beeckman, Schout, Plaintiff
vs. Jan Jansen Van Amersfoort, Defendant

Plaintiff says that defendant has been summoned
several times before the court for the purpose of asking
him what agreement he made with the farmer in regard to
his seized beers, and once more requests that defendant

shall impart information concerning the amount and how he
settled said affair with the farmer, under penalty of a
fine for defendant in case he remains obdurate concerning
the giving of information in said matter. Defendant answers, saying that he sold the farmer said seized beers,
and says not being obliged to state how, and upon what conditions he sold said beers to the farmer. The hon. court
once more orders defendant to give information concerning
this matter, viz., upon what condition he settled for the
beers seized by the farmer and brought into the officer's
house with the aforesaid farmer, under penalty of the fine
threatened against it, as per previous judgment on Dec.
1, 1665.

Willem Beeckman, Schout, Plaintiff
vs. Jan Jansen Van Amersfoort, Defendant

Plaintiff demands of defendant an amount of 22 gldrs.
four st. for expenses made for satisfying the savage whom
defendant hit with a knife in the chest. Further six
gldrs. for doctor's fee, and therebesides the fine for
wounding the **savage,** being 300 gldrs. Defendant answers
that he wounded the savage accidentally and involuntarily
and therefore asserts that he does not owe the fine. Regarding the expenses incurred, he, defendant, is willing
to pay them. The hon. court sentences defendant in regard to wounding a savage with a knife, to pay a fine of
36 gldrs., and to pay the expenses incurred for settling
with and satisfying the savage besides the doctor's fee.

Arent Cornelissen Vogel, Plaintiff
vs. Aeltje Claesen, Defendant

Plaintiff says that he sold to defendant's first,
deceased, husband 18 pieces of plank, the piece for 30
stivers, and received for the same a shirt to the value of
six gldrs. and a schepel of peas valued at two gldrs. 10
st. and the washing of two shirts. He further demands for
a child's coffin 10 pounds of butter and demands of defendant payment for the same. Defendant answers having
received 12 oak planks, but knows nothing about the six
deal boards; concerning the coffin, she says that he presented the same to her and that, on account thereof, she
twice made a present of butter to his son. The hon. court
decides that defendant shall pay plaintiff, as per his
demand, for the 18 planks or shall prove that she did not
receive the six deal boards; concerning the coffin, plaintiff is refused his demand out of consideration of rendered friendship.

Arent Cornelissen Vogel, Plaintiff
vs. Henderick Cornelissen, Lyndrayer, Defendant

Plaintiff says that he sold and delivered to defendant 40 deal boards for 20 sch. of Indian corn and demands
payment for same. Defendant says that plaintiff did not
deliver said planks as per contract, but eight days afterward, it being at the time the commencement of the first

war with the savages, and asserts not to be obliged to pay
for the aforesaid planks. Plaintiff replies, saying that
on one Saturday he sold the planks and on the following
Saturday delivered them, and notified defendant in regard
to this, whereupon defendant said, "'Tis well." Defendant
says that more time, 12 days, intervened between the sale
and the delivery. The hon. court refers parties to two
good men, viz., Cornelis Barentsen Slecht and Juriaen
Westphael, for the purpose of settling, if possible, said
affair between parties, and if not, parties will again address the court.

Arent Cornelissen Vogel, Plaintiff
vs. Walran DuMont, Defendant

Plaintiff said that he delivered to defendant's predecessor Jan Arentsen 14 planks at one gldr. heavy money.
Defendant answers, saying that plaintiff shall produce
writing of his predecessor or else prove that his predecessor received said boards. The hon. court orders plaintiff
to produce either proof or writing that he delivered said
boards to his predecessor.

Joris Hael, Plaintiff
vs. Warnaer Hoorenbeeck, Defendant. Absent. Default.

Joris Hael, Plaintiff
vs. Severyn Tenhout, Defendant. Absent. Default.

Walran DuMont, Plaintiff
vs. Pieter Hillebrants, Defendant. Absent, is sick

Evert Prys, Plaintiff
vs. Ariaen Gerretsen, Defendant. Absent. Default.

Samuel Olivier, Plaintiff
vs. Louwies Dubois, Defendant

Plaintiff says that defendant has slandered him and
has called him a thief, saying that he took a fox-skin out
of defendant's house and requests vindication of his honor.
Defendant denies the same and says that he does not know
having said such a thing, and declares not to have anything to say against plaintiff's reputation.

Andries Pietersen Noorman, Plaintiff
vs. Roelof Swartwout, Defendant. Absent. Default.

Henderick Palingh, Farmer, Plaintiff
vs. Willem Beeckman, Schout, Defendant

Plaintiff says that defendant received ½ aem of wine
of Willem Montagnie and that defendant did not pay the
king's excise for the same. Also that defendant has been
at the same time schout, tapster and excise master. Defendant answers that he bought said wine in August last
of Montagnie for which the excise had been declared to
the former farmer and, there being no farmer at the time,
he has been permitted by the court, by the order and written instructions of the hon. Ld. Gov. Genl., to put down
the excise, and that the payment should take place at his
honor's arrival, as has been done, on account of which defendant maintains that he cannot be prosecuted by plain-

tiff for /not/ getting a permit from plaintiff. Defendant
further answers that he is schout, as per his commission
of the hon. Ld. Gov. Genl., and that he retailed said ½
aem of wine, but that he did not sell the same to be drunk
on his premises; and /in regard to the assertion/ that at
the same time he should have been excise-master, says not
having been excise master, but that he only took notice of
the excise until the hon. Ld. Gov. Genl's arrival. The
hon. court decides whereas the ½ aem of wine was received
by defendant before plaintiff's time as farmer /of the ex-
cise/, the excise of the same having been declared and
paid to the former farmer and also whereas defendant kept
book of the excise as per instructions of the hon. Ld.
Gov. Genl., therefore plaintiff may issue to himself a
permit for removal, Willem Montagnie being absent at the
time of whom he bought said ½ aem of wine. It is also decided whereas in the fatherland a country-schout is permitted to retail liquors, therefore a country-schout here
is at liberty to follow the same business. Further,
plaintiff asks whether the anker of wine lately removed
from his house and delivered to Louwies Dubois was /thus
removed/ by the order of the hon. court. The hon. court
answers "Yes," because he, plaintiff, notwithstanding the
pronounced judgment, was backward, and unwilling to deliver said anker to Louwies DuBois, and therefore the
schout, with captain Brodhead's knowledge, had said anker
of wine removed.

            Henderick Palingh, Farmer, Plaintiff
      vs. Pieter Pietersen and Joris Hael, Defendants.
    Plaintiff says that Pieter Pieters got ½ keg of beer
of Joris Hael and did not pay the legal excise, and consequently plaintiff asks the fivefold fine. Defendant admits having removed ½ keg of beer without declaring the
same, but says that Joris Hael, of whom he bought, told
him that he did not need to declare it, because he /Hael/
had previously declared the beer and paid the excise,
which Joris Hael declares having told him, Pieter Pietersen. The hon. court decides that the half keg of beer,
seized by plaintiff, is confiscated, and that its value
shall be paid by defendants to plaintiff.

    Jacob Joosten requests to be paid the balance of ac-
count of 40 gldrs. heavy money, sent in by him, and also
requests satisfaction for the time since the court com-
menced to sit, up to July 12, 1662. Petitioner shall be
satisfied for the aforenamed balance, as soon as the condition of the treasury will allow, and the second request
shall be attended to after he shall have more fully explained.

Ordinary Session, Tuesday, January 26, 1666.
    Present: Willem Beeckman, Schout; Jan Willemse
Hoochteylingh, Henderick Jochemsen, Evert Pels, Jan

Joosten, Commissaries.
          Willem Beeckman, Schout, Plaintiff
              vs. Henderick Palingh, Defendant
     Plaintiff says that defendant as farmer settled with
Jan Jansen Van Amersfoort in regard to the seizure of
some beers, for the amount of 20 sch. of wheat, and the
seized beers, according to the declaration of the aforenamed Jan Jansen. And therefore plaintiff, in accordance
with art. 12 of the farming /conditions/, "that the farmer is not permitted to settle" demands of defendant 200
gldrs. over and above the agreement with Jan Jansen aforementioned. Defendant answers and denies having settled
with Jan Jansen in regard to the seized beers, but says
that Thomas Chambers approached him saying, "Countryman,
render me a friendship. I shall give you 20 sch. of
wheat," and produces as witness Ridsert Hamer who declares
having heard that Thomas Chambers offered to give defendant the 20 sch. of wheat for a friendship, but in case the
affair should become public, that the condition of the 20
sch. of wheat should be void.
     Plaintiff replies, saying that the case is notorious,
because defendant had seized the beers, summoned Jan Jansen Van Amersfoort on account of the same, and also the
witnesses necessary in this case, and when the bench was
about to sit in regard to this affair, defendant had the
case taken off the roll, saying that he was negotiating
concerning the same with Jan Jansen, and further says that
defendant's answer in the same tends to delay. The hon.
court, having heard parties, decides whereas defendant
denies having settled with Jan Jansen Van Amersfoort in
regard to the seized beers, therefore plaintiff is ordered
at the next session of the court to prove that defendant
has settled in regard to the seized beers with Jan Jansen
Van Amersfoort or with another in the name of said Jan
Jansen, for the amount of 20 sch. of wheat, and the said
seized beers.
     Defendant is also ordered to explain, at the next
session, for which "friendship" Thomas Chambers promised
him the 20 sch. of wheat, because such a promise of
friendship might be an affair of evil consequences.
          Willem Beeckman, Schout, Plaintiff
              vs. Allert Heymans Roos, Defendant
     Plaintiff says that defendant was negligent in clean-
ing his chimney and consequently on the 18th inst. said
chimney took fire and as a result there was a crowd, owing
to the fire. Therefore demands of defendant a fine of 100
gldrs. Defendant answers not to owe the fine, because the
bell was not rung, nor the drum beaten in the place of the
bell here, on account of the same. The hon. court sentences defendant to pay a fine of one Flemish pound because he did not keep his chimney clean, and on account of
the same took fire.

Walran DuMont, Plaintiff
vs. Pieter Hillebrants, Defendant

Plaintiff demands of defendant 41 sch. of wheat for
received merchandise. Defendant admits the debt but says
that five sch. of wheat must be deducted for rendered
services. Plaintiff replies, saying that defendant demands three sch. of wheat for carting three loads, and
that he will pay for said three loads what is reasonable.
The hon. court orders defendant to satisfy plaintiff's
claim and to settle for that which is in dispute.

Willem Montagnie, Plaintiff
vs. Pieter Hillebrants, Defendant

Plaintiff as guardian of the minor children of the
deceased Mr. Gysbert Van Imbroch demands of defendant 12
sch. of wheat as per obligation dated Nov. 27, 1664, to
be paid in the month of October 1665. Defendant admits
the debt and requests to keep said money at interest. The
hon. court orders defendant to satisfy plaintiff's demand.

Willem Montagnie, Plaintiff
vs. Henderick Cornelissen, Lyndrayer, Defendant. Absent.
Default.

Willem Montagnie, Plaintiff
vs. Aert Martensen Doorn, Defendant. Absent. Default.

Evert Prys, Plaintiff
vs. Michiael DeMot, Defendant

Plaintiff demands of defendant the doctor's fee for
the received wound, being five sch. of wheat. Defendant
answers that plaintiff was causa movens in regard to his
wound and therefore holds that he is not obliged to pay
the doctor's fee on account of his wound. The hon. court
orders defendant to prove that plaintiff was causa movens
in regard to his wound, and if not that defendant shall
also pay half the doctor's fee.

Evert Prys, Plaintiff
vs. Ariaen Gerretsen, Defendant. Absent. 2nd Default.

Albert Jansen Van Steenwyck, Plaintiff
vs. Tjerck Claesen and Marten Hofman, Defendants

Plaintiff as attorney for Pieter Jansen Van Hoorn demands of defendants 30 sch. of wheat, on account of Jan
Albertsen Van Steenwyck, deceased, besides interest for
two years and the expenses incurred. Defendants answer
whereas Pieter Jansen Van Hoorn has drawn an obligation of
Jan Albertsen Van Steenwyck, deceased, on Cornelis Barentsen Slecht that aforesaid Pieter Jansen must claim the
aforenamed amount of 30 sch. of wheat from Cornelis
Barentsen Slecht, and also hold that they do not owe the
expenses incurred because Jan Albertsen Van Steenwyck, deceased, did not receive his full money in Holland on account of said Pieter Jansen. The hon. court decides
whereas Jan Albertsen Van Steenwyck, during his life,
caused inconvenience to Pieter Jansen Van Hoorn by attaching the 30 sch. of wheat at Cornelis Barentsen Slecht's,

therefore the heirs and curators of the estate of the
aforenamed Jan Albertsen, deceased, are obliged to satisfy Pieter Jansen Van Hoorn for the expenses made. The
demand of two years' interest is refused plaintiff because
the deceased Jan Albertsen had to deduct in Holland 70
gldrs. for cash payment. The 30 sch. of wheat Pieter Jansen, aforenamed, will have to claim of Cornelis Barentsen
Slecht, as per accepted obligation.

Henderick Palingh, Plaintiff
vs. Jan Jansen Van Amersfoort, Defendant

Plaintiff demands of defendant 123 gldrs. 13 st. in
sewan for received liquor and excise. Defendant admits
the debt. The hon. court orders defendant to satisfy
plaintiff's demand.

Henderick Palingh, Plaintiff
vs. Evert Prys, Defendant

Plaintiff demands of defendant 130 gldrs. in sewan
for received liquor. Defendant admits the debt. The hon.
court orders defendant to satisfy plaintiff's demand.

Jan Jansen Van Amersfoort, appearing before the hon.
court, asks how to act in regard to the attachment by the
hon. schout Willem Beeckman of the 20 sch. of wheat on account of the settlement between him and Henderick Palingh,
farmer, concerning the seized beers. The hon. court decides that the attachment by the hon. schout Willem Beeckman, of the 20 sch. of wheat, provisionally, shall be
deemed valid.

Joris Poorter, Plaintiff
vs. Warnaer Hoorenbeeck, Defendant

Plaintiff demands of defendant three sch. of wheat,
besides the costs. Defendant admits the debt and says not
having refused him the same. The hon. court orders defendant to satisfy plaintiff's demand, with costs.

Joris Hael, Plaintiff
vs. Severyn Tenhout, Defendant. Absent. 2nd Default.

Plaintiff demands of defendant one sch. of wheat,
besides the costs.

Andries Pietersen Noorman, Plaintiff
vs. Roelof Swartwout, Defendant

Plaintiff as attorney for Hans Carolusen demands of
defendant three sch. of wheat and costs. Defendant answers, saying, that he passed an obligation to Hans
Carolusen, and requests the return of his obligation or
else not to intend to pay plaintiff. The hon. court refuses plaintiff's demand, because he cannot show defendant
his obligation.

Louwies DuBois requests that the sentence, dated Dec.
29, 1665, against Pieter Hillebrants may be judicially enforced. The hon. court orders the officer to proceed with
the execution.

Evert Pels requests that the judgment, dated Feb. 17,
1665, against Aert Martensen Doorn, may be judicially en-

forced. The hon. court orders the officer to proceed with
the execution.

The hon. schout proposes the necessity for this village that every house, covered with reed, straw or boards
shall keep a fire-ladder near its chimney.

The hon. court also decides that it is necessary for
every house covered with straw, reed or boards to continually have a fire-ladder near its chimney upon penalty of
25 gldrs. fine, and that every one shall be obliged to have
said fire-ladder made in the time of 14 days after date.
It is further ordered that every inhabitant here shall
properly clean his chimney, under penalty, if any accident
of fire (which God forbid) should occur, and the fire
should escape from the chimney, of equal 25 gldrs., whereupon the following decree was issued.

Whereas on June 10 of the year 1664 schout and commissaries appointed, on account of fires, two fire-wardens
for the purpose of examining with the officer every 14
days or three weeks or at least every month all chimneys
in this village to see that they are properly cleaned and
swept, and that the negligent should be fined one Flemish
pound for the first and double for the second time, and
for the third time four times as much, and also every resident having reed, straw or board roofs on his house was,
at the time, ordered to keep in readiness near his house a
good fire ladder which is sufficiently high to reach to
the chimney which order was not obeyed by many of the
residents here, therefore schout and commissaries renewing said order, command by the present in the name and by
the authority of his Royal Majesty of Great Britain, etc.,
each and every resident of this village of Wildwyck, for
the purpose of preventing fire (which God forbid) to keep
their chimneys clean under the penalty mentioned in the
previous decree, and the negligent in whose house the fire
comes out above the chimney, and in consequence causes a
concourse of people, shall be fined to the amount of 25
gldrs. for every time. And further, also, each and every
resident here, having reed, straw or board house roofs, is
once more ordered to continually keep within the time of
14 days near the house an efficient fire-ladder which can
reach up to the chimney, under penalty to the negligent in
this regard, of 25 gldrs. fine. Let each one guard against
damage. Thus enacted at the session of the hon. schout
and commissaries of this village of Wildwyck, 16/26 January, 1666.

Ordinary Session, Tuesday, March 2, 1666.
Present: Willem Beeckman, Schout; Jan Willemsen
Hoochteylingh, Henderick Jochemsen, Evert Pels, Jan
Joosten, Commissaries.

Willem Beeckman, Plaintiff
vs. Jan Willemsen Hoochteylingh, Defendant

Plaintiff says that the hon. Lord Gov. Genl., at the last harvest, ordered to keep one gate open in the village and to close the other, on account of which the hon. court resolved to keep the Strand gate open, and that the Mill gate should remain closed. And whereas most farmers were much inconvenineced on account of the closing of the Mill gate, in the direction of which most fields of the farmers are situated, therefore Jan Willemsen, defendant, accosted plaintiff in regard to the same and proposed that the Mill gate should be opened for their convenience, and said, that they had agreed among each other to be willing to give the English sentinel a schepel of wheat per day for this. About this proposition plaintiff saw Mr. Berrisfort, and brought about /the opening of said gate, under condition/ that plaintiff should become surety for the promised sch. of wheat per day, and also paid the largest portion of said sentinel-money, and requests to be reimbursed by Jan Willemsen, defendant, with whom plaintiff made the agreement in this affair.

Defendant answers and denies, saying that he did not speak about giving a sch. daily or a total of 42 sch. of wheat for the guard, but says that he and Tjerck and Palingh went to see the farmers and the double farmers promised to give six and the small farmers three sch. of wheat, and further says that he met plaintiff at the Mill gate when the same was again closed, and asked him, why the same was again closed, because they, nevertheless had to pay the money for keeping it open, and that they should not be prevented from harvesting.

Plaintiff replies, saying that, then, he answered defendant that Mr. Berrisfort had closed the gate because Tjerck Claesen did not give food to the soldier, quartered upon him, to go to the redoubt.

Defendant thereupon replies, having at the time asked plaintiff why close the gate, because they had to pay for keeping open, as had been agreed with Palingh, and that, in case Mr. Berrisfort had a case against Tjerck, he ought to have seen Tjerck Claesen about it, and that, on this account, Berrisfort had no right to trouble them.

Plaintiff further says that, upon defendant's complaint, he called on Mr. Berrisfort for the purpose of again opening the gate, which was done the following day, and a sentinel was again posted there, and again demands reimbursement of the money, with the expenses incurred, and yet to be incurred on account hereof.

Defendant answers that his personal contribution is ready, and again complains about the damage, because he was prevented from harvesting, on account of the gate's having been closed for one day.

The hon. court, having heard plaintiff's demand and

defendant's answer, decides that defendant Jan Willemsen
shall reimburse plaintiff the advanced money besides
costs, because defendant himself admits that he agreed
with Henderick Palingh to pay the sentinel for the purpose of keeping the Mill gate open, and that defendant
shall claim the full amount of 42 sch. of wheat from the
other farmers.

    Roelof Swartwout and Cornelis Barentsen Slecht,
guardians of the minor children of Mattys Jansen, deceased, Plaintiff
vs. Thomas Chambers, Defendant. Absent. Default.

Evert Prys, Plaintiff
vs. Ariaen Gerretsen, Defendant

    Plaintiff demands of defendant a sum of 374 gldrs.
in sewan, as per account sent in. Defendant brings a
counter bill of an uncertain amount. The hon. court refers parties to good men, viz., Allert Heymans Roos and
Henderick Aertsen, for the purpose of (if possible) settling the differences between parties, and if not, that
parties shall again address the court with the report of
the aforenamed good men.

Arent Teunissen, Plaintiff
vs. Aert Martensen Doorn, Defendant

    Plaintiff demands of defendant 8 sch. of wheat for
wages earned by his wife during the last harvest, with costs,
and requests payment. Defendant answers, saying that plaintiff's wife worked three days on the "balck" and pretends
that she did not earn as much on the "balck" as in the field,
and therefore is willing to pay for the work on the "balck"
half a sch. of wheat per day. Plaintiff says that his wife
could have found work with others, but did not want to take
her away from defendant's work, because he also needed her.
The hon. court orders defendant to satisfy plaintiff's demand
with the costs of the same.

Jan Hendericks, Plaintiff
vs. Pieter Hillebrants, Defendant. Absent. Default.

Henderick Alberts, Plaintiff
vs. Pieter Hillebrants, Defendant. Absent. Default.

Joris Hael, Plaintiff
vs. Pieter Hillebrants, Defendant. Absent. Default.

Henderick Cornelissen, Lyndrayer, Plaintiff
vs. Dirrickie Wevers, Defendant

    Plaintiff demands of defendant 3½ beavers for a
brandy-cellar, and shows a bill /from which it appears/
that he had to pay for said cellar with bottles, four
beavers to Jan Van Bremen; Albert Jansen Van Steenwyck,
attorney for Dirrickie Wevers, answers that plaintiff,
about nine years ago, put the brandy cellar in defendant's
house, and that plaintiff did not warn her concerning the
same until a year ago last summer, and that, in the mean
time, she used the bottles, and the bottles, belonging
with the cellar, were broken. The hon. court orders de-

fendant to again equip the cellar with similar bottles as
she received from plaintiff, and then deliver to the party
that shall come to claim said cellar for plaintiff.

Marten Hofman, Plaintiff
vs. Evert Pels and Henderick Jochemsen, Defendants

Plaintiff says that last year the guardians sent him
notice to come hither for the purpose of receiving his
share from the estate of Jan Albertsen Van Steenwyck, deceased, or to send a power of attorney, whereupon he answered in writing that he would personally come, and that,
in the mean time, they should keep the estate under themselves, and not alienate the same, and if they acted contrary to this, he would sue them for costs and damages.

Defendant Evert Pels, as curator, answers that he is
ready to render an accounting concerning his administration of Jan Albertsen Van Steenwyck's, deceased, estate,
and requests that the partitioning of the estate may be
done judicially, and further requests a reasonable salary
for his administration. The hon. court grants curator
Evert Pels' request to partition the estate aforementioned
at a proper place. And the hon. court awards them five
percent as their salary for administering said estate.

Michiel Mot, appearing, produces two witnesses in the
suit between him and Evert Prys, viz., Jan Tyssen and
Mattys Tyssen, who declare that Evert Prys first cut
against Michiel Mot three times before Michiel Mot
wounded Evert Prys. The hon. court decides whereas
Michiel Mot has had judicially examined his witnesses who
declare that Evert Prys was causa movens in being wounded,
therefore Michiel Mot shall be relieved from paying the
doctor's fee of five sch. of wheat.

Harmen Hendericks requests in a petition, whereas in
the village account he is charged 20 gldrs. in beavers
for the first annual salary of the preacher, and says
having promised 20 gldrs. in sewan that said 20 gldrs. in
beavers may be reduced to 20 gldrs. in sewan. Also that
Francois Le Cheer may also for the last two years assist
in contributing towards the preacher's salary, and also
calls the attention of the hon. court to this; further
that four days' wages for labor on the parsonage may be
put to his credit on his account.

To which is replied: that the 20 gldrs. in beavers
shall be reduced to 20 gldrs. in sewan; also that Francois Le Cheer shall assist in contributing one-third of
the last two years; the four days' wages shall be put to
petitioner's credit on the village account.

Harmen Hendericks complains, saying that he contracted
for the cutting of the wood for the watch, and that, in
the mean time, Joris Hael, tapster, used said fire wood,
and therefore requests to receive one sch. of wheat more
per month, because Captain Broodhead promised him the
same. The hon. court decides that petitioner is not

obliged to chop wood for the tapster Joris Hael, unless
he be paid for the same by said Horis Hael, notwithstanding, before this, no attention was paid to Joris Hael's
carting away fire wood.

Albert Jansen, court messenger, requests because he
already served one year, that he may receive some bread
corn, which request is granted petitioner, and he shall
be provided with the same.

Marten Hofman, husband and guardian of Amarens
Claesen De Wit, requests that from the estate of Jan Albertsen Van Steenwyck, deceased, he may receive 64 gldrs.
Holland money with the interest of the same, coming to him
from a cow which his brother-in-law Jan Albertsen, deceased, sold for Amarens, and received the money for the
same, with two years' rent for the said cow. The hon.
court, having considered petitioner's request, decides
that petitioner shall receive said money from the estate
of the deceased Jan Albertsen Van Steenwyck, provided that
petitioner shall furnish ample security for said money for
the purpose of returning said money, if hereafter it should
be found not to be so. And the aforesaid Holland money
shall be valued in sewan fourfold, out of consideration
that he shall not receive interest for the money of the
cow.

Ordinary Session, Tuesday, March 9, 1666.

Present: Willem Beeckman, Schout; Jan Willemsen
Hoochteylingh, Henderick Jochemsen, Jan Joosten, Commissaries.

Roelof Swartwout and Cornelis Barentsen Slecht,
guardians of the minor children of Mattys Jansen,
deceased, Plaintiffs
vs. Thomas Chambers, Defendant. Absent. 2nd Default.

Plaintiffs demand of defendant a sum of 703 gldrs.
six st. 14--heavy money in corn, four sch. of wheat at 50
st. for rent of the land of the children of Mattys Jansen, deceased, and interest as per account. Plaintiffs
further demand of defendant the deed of the land of the
children of Mattys Jansen, deceased, which deed the plaintiffs, as guardians, delivered to him. Plaintiffs, as
guardians, ask the hon. court as supreme guardians, what
to do in this case of the minor children of the deceased
Mattys Jansen, whether the loaned out money, bearing interest,shall be called in, to be used in cultivating the
still uncultivated land of the minor children, aforenamed.
This proposition shall be considered at the next session.

Henderick Palingh, Plaintiff
vs. Ariaen Gerretsen, Defendant

Plaintiff demands of defendant 44 gldrs. in sewan and
two sch. of wheat, for Antoni Coeck. Defendant admits the
debt. The hon. court orders defendant to satisfy plaintiff's demand.

Henderick Palingh, Plaintiff
vs. Tomas Teunissen, Defendant

Plaintiff demands of defendant 20 gldrs. 14 st. in sewan, light money. Defendant admits the debt, but excepts six gldrs. for delivered peas, having delivered to plaintiff six sch. of peas at five gldrs. which plaintiff is not willing to accept at more than four gldrs. The hon. court orders that defendant shall pay plaintiff 14 gldrs. 14 st., and plaintiff is refused the balance of six gldrs. because at the receipt of the six sch. of peas no mention was made of the price, whereas plaintiff has yet received said six sch. of peas at five gldrs. per sch.

Henderick Palingh, Plaintiff
vs. Antoni Delba, Defendant. Absent. Default.

Paulus Paulusen, Plaintiff
vs. Aert Martensen Doorn, Defendant

Plaintiff demands of defendant 10 sch. of wheat for wages, and a pistol which he bought of defendant, and paid for with work. Defendant answers that he engaged plaintiff till harvest time at eight sch. of wheat per month, and plaintiff in the mean time went away without reasons, and therefore asserts not to owe anything to plaintiff. Plaintiff answers saying, that they agreed that defendant should pay him every month, as long as there was grain to be threshed, and defendant refused him payment for the same, and requests payment as above. Defendant hereupon answers that he did not refuse payment to plaintiff, and asserts, as above, not to owe anything. The hon. court orders defendant to satisfy plaintiff's demand, considering that defendant did not pay plaintiff the monthly hire.

Evert Prys, Plaintiff
vs. Ariaen Gerretsen, Defendant

The account of plaintiff as well as defendant having been received by the hon. court, it is found from the bill of Evert Prys that there is coming to him: 29½ days wages having plowed and sowed for defendant at four gldrs. per day, 118 gldrs.; 17½ days wages during harvest, 105 gldrs.; contracted to cut the wheat with Palingh for 16 sch. of wheat, whereof, as per defendant's saying, six sch. were paid to Palingh, balance 10 sch., 60 gldrs.; for one sch. of buckwheat received by defendant, three gldrs.; for 9½ sch. of barley, loaned, 47 gldrs., 10 st.; for ½ sch. of gray peas, 2 gldrs., 10 st., to total: 336 gldrs. As to the further claim, viz., for ½ keg of beer to Mackum, and three pints of brandy paid to Joris Hal, plaintiff is required to prove that he paid the same at defendant's order, and the same having been proved, it is to be paid by defendant to plaintiff. And by defendant, Ariaen Gerretsen's, bill it is found that there is coming to him: For 20 sch. of buckwheat, 60 gldrs.; for 6 sch. of oats, 12 gldrs.; for the sowing and harrowing of two sch. of peas and two sch. of barley, 12 gldrs.; for three days board,

six gldrs., for a total of 90 gldrs. As to the further
claim for the use of his horses, and the boy to plow,
three days, defendant is ordered to prove that he contracted for wages, or else the claim will be refused him,
because he received ½ of the crop, and also because Henderick Palingh has declared that defendant offered the
use of his horses and his boy, provided he should receive
one half the crop of as much land, as plaintiff should be
able to sow.

Regarding the half acre of buckwheat which plaintiff
should have cut and harvested with his own buckwheat, defendant is ordered to prove that plaintiff did not plow
said half acre for himself, in which case plaintiff will
have to pay for said acre, according to valuation. In
regard to the declaration of Francois Le Cheer, it is decided that plaintiff as well as defendant will have to
bear one half the cost of mowing and carting, because
both of them received of the crop, or to the contrary, to
prove that the attestor, for Evert Prys specially, cut
the buckwheat and carted the peas, and in this case defendant is ordered to pay his share to plaintiff.

Jan Cornelissen Smits, Plaintiff
vs. Pieter Hillebrants, Defendant

Plaintiff demands of defendant 10 sch. of wheat for
wages. Defendant admits the debt and says that he cannot,
at present, pay the old debts, and requests that plaintiff
will wait till next harvest. Plaintiff replies saying
that he sympathizes with defendant, and requests now to
receive one-half of the debt, because he has to pay
others. For the other half he is willing to wait till
harvest time. The hon. court orders defendant to pay
plaintiff one-half, being five sch. of wheat, now, because plaintiff is willing to wait with the other half
till next harvest.

Henderick Albertsen, Plaintiff
vs. Pieter Hillebrants, Defendant

Plaintiff demands of defendant five sch. of wheat for
wages with the expenses. Defendant admits the debt, but
says it is a previous debt and says not being able to pay
till next harvest. Plaintiff replies saying not to be
able to allow him longer time, because he owes somebody
else. The hon. court orders defendant to satisfy plaintiff's demand with the costs.

Jan Hendericksen, Plaintiff
vs. Pieter Hillebrants, Defendant

Plaintiff demands of defendant 13 sch. of wheat, being five sch. of wheat and four gldrs., earned four years
ago, and 7½ sch. of wheat which his mother loaned him.
Defendant answers, and admits the five sch. of wheat and
the four gldrs., but says having a counterbill against
the 7½ sch. of wheat, and also says that it could be no
more than 6½ sch. of wheat. The hon. court orders de-

282

fendant to satisfy plaintiff for the five sch. of wheat
and the four gldrs., and concerning the further claim for
the 7½ sch. of wheat, plaintiff's mother shall settle with
defendant.

Pieter Hillebrants, Plaintiff
vs. Tjerck Claesen De Wit, Defendant

Roelof Swartwout in the place of Pieter Hillebrants,
as attorney for Aeltje Wygerts, last widow of Albert Gysbertsen, deceased, and at present wife of the aforesaid
Pieter Hillebrants, requests conveyance and transfer by
defendant of 20 morgens of arable land sold to the aforesaid widow's late husband Albert Gysbertsen, deceased, according to deed and obligation, on account of change of
government, either present or future. Defendant answers
to be willing to make out the deed as soon as nagivation
is again open, because he himself must yet receive a deed
of Jeronimus Ebbingh. And further requests the full payment of a sold horse, being a balance of 100 gldrs. in
grain, and further demands 14 sch. of wheat for damage sustained through the attachment of his horse, bought from the
estate of Aert Pietersen Tack at the Lord's execution, which
payment Albert Gysbertsen should have made for him, as is
shown by the contract. Plaintiff replies to defendant's
claim and shows a copy from the minutes dated Nov. 25, 1664,
where Tjerck Claesen as plaintiff requested execution in
regard to the above demand for payment for the horse, and
the same was delayed on account of nonconveyance of the
bought and paid for land, and further says notwithstanding
said claim for conveyance to be willing to pay, and has
shown a specification of the said /claim/ amounting to 205
gldrs. 5 st. Defendant answers and says to be satisfied
with what may be paid after sufficient proof and yet demands
the balance and 14 sch. of wheat for costs. The hon. court,
having heard parties, decides, and orders defendant to make
an effective conveyance and delivery of the land sold to
plaintiff, as soon as navigation is again open, or by default, to make good the damage and /loss of/ interest which
plaintiff might suffer on account of the same. And further in regard to plaintiff's presentation to pay for the
horse to defendant, parties are ordered to settle concerning
the difference. As to the costs, 14 sch. of wheat, demanded
by defendant, it is decided, whereas parties have been mutually negligent in living up to their contracts, therefore
said costs shall be mutually born one half by each.

Albert Jansen, Plaintiff
vs. Arent Jansen, Defendant. Absent. Default.
Thomas Harmensen, Plaintiff
vs. Aert Martensen Doorn, Defendant

Plaintiff demands of defendant 42 gldrs. 18 st. in
sewan for delivered goods. Defendant answers not to know
what he owes plaintiff. The hon. court orders parties to
settled with each other, and to pay the balance.

Thomas Harmensen, Plaintiff
vs. Warnaer Hoorenbeeck, Defendant
Plaintiff demands of defendant 13 gldrs. in sewan.
Defendant admits the debt. The hon. court orders defend-
and to satisfy plaintiff's demand.
Thomas Harmensen, Plaintiff
vs. Arent Jansen, Defendant. Absent. Default.
Paulus Cornelissen requests payment for freight on
materials for building the parsonage. As soon as the
treasury will allow, petitioner's request will be attended
to.
Henderick Jochemsen requests in a petition that he
may be permitted to surround with short palisades, for a
garden, the lot outside the Strand gate, deeded to him by
the former Dr. Genl. Petrus Stuyvesant, which request is
granted petitioner.

Ordinary Session, Tuesday, March 16, 1666.
Present: Willem Beeckman, Schout; Jan Willemsen
Hoochteylingh, Henderick Jochemsen, Evert Pels, Jan
Joosten, Commissaries.
Willem Beeckman, Schout, Plaintiff
vs. Jan Jansen Van Etten, Defendant
Plaintiff says that last year he rented the house of
Gerret Bancken, on account of back villages taxes, to defendant at one sch. of wheat per month. Already 13 months
have passed, and on this account demands 13 sch. of wheat.
Defendant answers and admits having taken the aforesaid
house but says that he is not able to pay. The hon.
court orders defendant to satisfy plaintiff's demand.
Roelof Swartwouth and Cornelis Barents Slecht,
guardians of the minor children of Mattys Jansen, deceased, Plaintiffs
vs. Thomas Chambers, Defendant
Plaintiffs demand, as at a previous session, of defendant a sum of 703 gldrs. 6 st. 14-- heavy money in
grain, the sch. of wheat at 50 st. for back rent of the
land of the children of Mattys Jansen, deceased, and interest as per account. Plaintiffs further demand of defendant the deed for the lands of the children of Mattys
Jansen, deceased, which deed plaintiffs, as guardians,
have put in his hands. Defendant answers, saying, that
in this country it has never been customary to pay interest for back rent, and therefore maintains that he does
not owe the same. Further asks whether it is law to pay
12 percent annually for interest? Defendant further says
whereas he has to keep two soldiers as for two farms, and
whereas he has leased the one farm of plaintiffs as guardians, therefore requests that the expenses for the one
soldier may fall on, and be born by, the plaintiffs, as
guardians. Defendant, also, further requests restitution
of the money paid for the redemption of the deeds; further

requests that plaintiffs may also share the expense for the
"doorsteeken" of a piece of land, this being also advanta-
geous to the lands of plaintiffs. And whereas at present
he is unable to pay, he requests time till October next.

Plaintiffs answer saying to be willing to deduct the
expenses incurred for the deed, and in regard to the further claims by defendant, request that said claims may be
refused defendant, and the rights of the orphans be vin-
dicated.

The hon. court, having heard parties, decides in regard to defendant's answers concerning the allowed interest of the back rent, to adhere to its previous decision,
on Feb. 17, 1665, for reasons adduced at said decision,
and orders defendant to pay proper interest on the same as
is customary in this country, being ten percent annually.
Further in regard to the expenses for keeping a soldier
for plaintiffs, it is decided whereas defendant, personally, is in possession of considerably more land than others
who are likewise burdened with two soldiers, therefore
defendant, on account hereof, cannot claim anything of
plaintiffs, unless he should be burdened with more soldiers.
Also in regard to the "doorsteeken" of a piece of land, it
is decided, if it can be proved that it tends to the im-
provement of the land of the orphans, defendant, after an
examination of the same, shall be entitled to a pro rata
compensation. And defendant is further ordered to satisfy
plaintiffs' demand for the above amount of gldrs. 703.6.14,
provided he may deduct of the interest charged in excess
by plaintiffs. And further orders defendant to return to
plaintiffs the deed of the land of the orphans they delivered to him, provided plaintiffs make restitution to
defendant of the money, advanced by him for said deed.

Albert Jansen, Plaintiff
vs. Arent Jansen, Defendant. Absent. 2nd Default.
Henderick Palingh, Plaintiff
vs. Antoni Delba, Defendant

Plaintiff demands of defendant six sch. of Indian
corn on account of Christoffel Davids. Defendant answers,
saying not to owe plaintiff, but Christoffel Davids 18
gldrs. in sewan, in place of Indian corn. The hon. court
orders plaintiff to show power of attorney of Christoffel
Davids, in regard to the above claim.

Aert Martensen Doorn, Plaintiff
vs. Paulus Paulusen, Defendant

Plaintiff requests revisal of a former judgment dated
Mar. 9, 1666, and says that he hired defendant since Dec.
1, 1665, up to harvest time, and that defendant, without
reasons, left before his bound time expired, and therefore
maintains that he /plaintiff/ is not obliged to pay him
/defendant/ the balance of his earned wages. Defendant
answers that plaintiff did not precisely pay him as per
contract, on account whereof he left his service. The

285

hon. court, revising the former judgment, orders plaintiff
to pay defendant the balance of the wages, being 10 sch.
of wheat and the pistol, because he did not pay defendant
monthly as per agreement, which defendant, on Mar. 9, did
not deny, and defendant is further ordered to remain with
plaintiff and serve his time, as per contract, till harvest, or in case he does not return to his service he shall
lose the 10 sch. of wheat because he left his service
without the knowledge of the hon. court. And plaintiff is
further obliged to satisfy defendant as per agreement.

Lysbeth Graffort, Plaintiff
vs. Severyn Tenhout, Defendant

Plaintiff demands of defendant seven sch. of wheat
for one year's wages for washing, and contracted with him
for nine sch. of wheat per year, and allowed him two sch.
Defendant answers saying that according to his agreement
with her husband he does not owe more than six sch. The
hon. court orders defendant to pay plaintiff the six sch.
of wheat.

Grietje Hendericks, Plaintiff
vs. Arent Jansen, Defendant

Plaintiff demands of defendant three sch. of wheat
on account of assigned money of the smith, and costs. Defendant admits the debt, and says not to be able to pay
just now. The hon. court orders defendant to satisfy
plaintiff's claim and costs.

Tjerck Claesen De Witt, appearing, requests revisal
of the former judgment on Mar. 9, in the case between him
and Pieter Hillebrants, and requests that Pieter Hillebrantsen may be made to bear the full amount of the damage for
the sold horse, for reasons that the payment for the horse
is in relation to the payment to Mr. Gysbert, deceased, but
has no connection with the delivery of the deed of the
land. The hon. court adheres to its former decision, and
once more orders parties to each bear one-half of the expense for the judicial sale of the horse, because parties
were both negligent in carrying out their contract.

Ordinary Seesion, Tuesday, March 23, 1666.
Present: Willem Beeckman, Schout; Jan Willemsen
Hoochteylingh, Henderick Jochemsen, Evert Pels, Jan
Joosten, Commissaries.

Willem Beeckman and Thomas Chambers, attorneys of the
Hon. Heer Petrus Stuyvesant, Plaintiffs
vs. Juriaen Westphael, Defendant

Plaintiffs, as attorneys of the hon. Heer Petrus
Stuyvesant, demand of defendant an amount of 1082 gldrs.
in beavers, being the balance of the back rent, and demand
the same as per agreement by "schepen knowledge," dated
Apr. 15, 1665. Defendant admits the debt and answers intending to deliver to plaintiffs this present week 100
sch. of wheat, and in case plaintiffs are not satisfied

with the same, they are at liberty to attach the farm with the crops of the same. Plaintiffs answer that defendant, in accordance with the "schout and schepen knowledge" must carry out his promise, and request, in accordance with the contents of said "schout and schepen knowledge," to be permitted to put threshers on defendant's floor, for the purpose of threshing as far as it is necessary, for the purpose of receiving the debt, and further request to permit the attachment, so that none of the harvested fruits of the land may be alienated. The hon. court, having heard the demand and answer of parties, orders defendant to satisfy plaintiffs' demand as per agreement by "schout and schepen knowledge" dated 18 Apr. 1665, and, by default, the plaintiffs by virtue of "schout and schepen knowledge" shall be permitted to put threshers on defendant's floor. And the attachment is permitted to plaintiffs, that they may receive payment.

Thomas Chambers, Plaintiff
vs. Roelof Swartwout and Cornelis Barentsen Slecht, guardians of the minor children of Mattys Jansen, deceased, Defendants

Plaintiff demands of defendants an accounting of their administration as guardians of the minor children of Mattys Jansen, deceased, the same to be rendered in presence of the hon. court, the plaintiff, and the minor children. Plaintiff further requests that defendants shall give security for what is already being administered by them, and for what may yet be administered. Defendants reply to the first demand, that they never refused to render an accounting of their administration, and are ready at any time so to do at the place to be designated in the presence of the hon. court, the plaintiff, and the minor children. To the second demand, defendants reply that they do not intend to furnish security for their administration, because, at the time, they were requested by the friends of the minor children to become guardians, and in case plaintiff does not like it to have said trust administered in this manner, he may hunt up and appoint other guardians who are willing to furnish security for said administration, provided, after they have rendered a proper accounting, they may be given receipt by the court, and further request that the expenses to be incurred on account of the accounting may not be charged to the minor children, but be born by plaintiff.

The hon. court orders defendants to render account and show the assets of their administration to plaintiff in the presence of the hon. court and the minor children inside of twice 24 hours, at the place they deem proper. The second point will be considered after the account shall have been rendered.

Willem Montagnie, Plaintiff
vs. Jan Jansen Van Amersfort, Defendant. Absent. Default.

Henderick Palingh, Plaintiff
vs. Aert Martensen Doorn, Defendant

Plaintiff demands of defendant 261 gldrs. in sewan light money for received merchandise. Defendant admits the debt, and answers having paid on the same 24½ sch. of wheat being 147 gldrs., therefore remaining 114 gldrs., being 19 sch. of wheat, and further excepts 21 gldrs. one half of the excise which has not yet fallen due. Plaintiff replies, saying that he is willing to wait for the 21 gldrs. till the expiration of his time as farmer, if he could only get the balance. The hon. court orders defendant to satisfy plaintiff for the balance of his claim.

Henderick Palingh, Plaintiff
vs. Jan Hendericksen, Defendant

Plaintiff demands of defendant 10 gldrs. for received merchandise. Defendant answers that he does not owe more than six gldrs. and if Ridsert Cage should say that he received 10 gldrs.' worth, he is willing to pay. The hon. court orders defendant to satisfy plaintiff's demand upon Ridsert Cage's word, because, during plaintiff's absence, he kept book of the received merchandise.

Evert Pels requests by petition, whereas he has taken some money at interest of the guardians of the minor children of Mattys Jansen, deceased, and he promised them to pay annual 12 percent interest, that the hon. court may be pleased to allow him to pay the proper interest as is customary in these countries. He further requests to be permitted to return said borrowed money to aforesaid guardians at the same price as he received the same, viz., the schepel of wheat at 50 st. in beavers.

The hon. court decides whereas the contract of "schepen knowledge" was at the time entered into with the consent of both parties, the aforesaid contract is to remain valid, as well in regard to the promised interest as to payment of the principal with the interest of the same, because it has no authority to change similar contracts.

Barent Holst requests by petition a piece of land about half a morgen in extent for a plantation, situated near Marten the mason's land. The hon. court decides, whereas it is not authorized to grant any land as property, therefore petitioner's request is refused until another time.

The guardians of the minor children of Mattys Jansen, deceased, request a proper salary for their administration as guardians of the minor children aforementioned, and that the domestic money cannot be valued at the same rate as the Holland money because it is permitted in Holland to draw the 40th and 60th penny. The hon. court decides, whereas in the fatherland at the sale of effects the 60th and for interest the 40th penny is allowed, therefore petitioners according to the custom in the fatherland, are permitted to draw double here.

To the judicial warning made to Aert Martensen Doorn
on account of Thomas Harmensen, plaintiff, on Mar. 9,
1666, he, Thomas Harmensen, in accordance with the given
answer of Aert Martensen Doorn, has judicially declared
that said Aert Martensen Doorn owes him the demanded
amount of 42 gldrs. 18 st. in sewan, and requests judicial
proceedings for the same. The hon. court orders the officer to proceed with the execution.

Ordinary Session, Tuesday, April 6, 1666.
    Present: Willem Beeckman, Schout; Jan Willemsen
Hoochteylingh, Henderick Jochemsen, Evert Pels, Jan
Joosten, Commissaries.
        Louwies DuBois and Antoni Crespel, Plaintiffs
            vs. Jan Willemsen Hoochteylingh, Defendant
    Plaintiffs demand of defendant payment for guarding
his cows of the amount of 20 sch. of wheat, or 120 gldrs.
in sewan as per contract made. Defendant answers that he
contracted with plaintiffs about his cows in such a manner, that they were to be guarded and pastured through the
whole of the forest just as was done by Willem Jansen Seba,
the former cowherder, which was neglected by plaintiffs,
and on this account he took the cows away from them.
    Plaintiffs reply, saying that they entered into no
agreement with defendant concerning the herding of the cows
other than the general conditions, and produce proof of all
the inhabitants that they have been satisfied with the manner in which their cattle were taken care of.
    Defendant replies to the same and says to adhere to
his former answer, and, if necessary, is ready to swear to
it.
    The hon. court decides whereas defendant has con-
sented, and has driven his cows once and yet a second time
to the herd of the other cattle, therefore he is obliged
to pay plaintiffs the full amount of the claim, also because, according to the testimony of the other inhabitants
who gave their cattle into plaintiffs' charge /said in-
habitants/ are well enough satisfied with the care taken
of their cattle, and therefore orders defendant to satisfy plaintiffs' demand.
        Cornelis Barentsen Slecht, Plaintiff
            vs. Tjerck Claesen De Wit, Defendant
    Plaintiff says that defendant was present at the mea-
suring of the land of the minor children of Mattys Jansen,
deceased, and of Thomas Chambers, and that he drew the
chain with the surveyor, that some part of said land remained unmeasured, and therefore requests that defendant
shall make a declaration concerning the same. Defendant
answers whereas he has been judicially requested /to do so/
he therefore declares that the extremity of the brandy
corner situated on the Kil has been left unmeasured, and,
further two small islands situated on Thomas Chambers'

land have also been left unmeasured and says that he was
present when the surveyor, about four years ago, measured
the land of Thomas Chambers and of the minor children of
Mattys Jansen, deceased, and is ready, if need be, to affirm the same under oath.

      Roelof Swartwout and Cornelis Barentsen Slecht,
    guardians of the minor children of Mattys Jansen,
               deceased, Plaintiffs
            vs. Thomas Chambers, Defendant

    Plaintiffs say whereas defendant, prior to this, has
requested of them an accounting of their administration of
the guardianship of the minor children of Mattys Jansen,
deceased, which they rendered in the presence of the hon.
court as chief guardians of the orphans, /they now/ judicially ask that defendant shall answer whether their administration has been done well or bad. Defendant answers
that the court messenger in his summons did not notify him
about what affair plaintiffs summoned him, therefore requests time to answer at the next session.

    Plaintiffs further say whereas after three warnings in
consequence of the judgment of Mar. 3, 1666, defendant has
refused payment of his rent and back interest, and also to
surrender the deed, they therefore request to be judicially sustained as guardians in the aforenamed rights of the
minor children, the more so because defendant himself on
Mar. 23, 1666, has requested the court to make them furnish
security for their administration, on account of which they
once more request to be upheld in their beforementioned
guardianship or to be released of the same. Defendant answers to refer to the relating of the court messenger, concerning plaintiffs' demand for the deed.

    The hon. court grants defendant time till the next
session, for the purpose of saying what he has to say
against plaintiffs concerning their account rendered about
administering /the estate/ of the minor children and orders
defendant, therefore, to answer at the next session.

    The guardians of the minor children of Mattys Jansen,
deceased, request, whereas Thomas Chambers is delaying his
business, and Evert Pels still has some money under him
with the interest thereon, and Jan Jansen Van Amersfoort
as guardian by right of blood has offered them his share,
being one-fourth part of the lands of the aforesaid minor
children; what they, petitioners, shall do in this regard,
the more so because said one-fourth of the lands can be
bought and paid for from the rent and back interest of
Evert Pels, and further that they, petitioners, may be not
made to suffer the damage in breaking new land.

    The hon. court decides that after Thomas Chambers
shall have filed his answer in regard to the demand concerning their administration of the estate, petitioner's
request shall be attended to.

Hendrick Palingh, Plaintiff
vs. Christoffel Davids, Defendant. Absent. Default.
Henderick Palingh, Plaintiff
vs. Jacob Barents Cool, Defendant. Absent. Default.
Joris Hael, Plaintiff
vs. Jacob Barents Cool, Defendant. Absent. Default.
Joris Hael, Plaintiff
vs. Pieter Pietersen, Defendant. Absent. Default.
Jacob Joosten, Plaintiff
vs. Cornelis Barentsen Slecht, Defendant. Absent. Default.
Jan Willemsen Hoochteylingh, Plaintiff
vs. Pieter Hillebrants, Defendant. Absent. Default.

Marten Hofman requests an attachment against the estate of Jan Albertsen Van Steenwyck, deceased, on account
of a claim he has on some money which the friends of the
deceased Jan Albertsen Van Steenwyck in the fatherland have
under them, and which belongs to his wife Amerens Claesen
De Wit, until the time that he shall have received further
information from his friends in Holland. The hon. court
grants petitioner's request, provided he shall, at the
first opportunity, present his claim.

The Rev. Hermanus Blom, preacher, requests, whereas
it is with difficulty that he receives his salary as
minister and preacher, each year, and he has not yet been
fully paid; to be either relieved of his charge, or that
the hon. court be pleased to see to it, that he shall receive his dues. And in case he cannot receive what is
owing him, enters a protest on account of the same before
God and the congregation, and /protests/ that the souls
which should perish in consequences of the discontinuance
of his ministry will have to be answered for, before God,
by the hon. court. The hon. court, at the request and
earnest solicitation of petitioner, will do its duty, as
it has been doing before, to collect as far as practicable
from the residents petitioner's back salary, and if not,
to judicially enforce the payment.

Jan Willemsen Hoochteylingh requests judicial proceedings against Aert Martensen Doorn, in consequence of
the judgment pronounced on Feb. 3, 1665, and costs of
same. The hon. court orders the officer to proceed with
the execution.

Thomas Chambers shows a petition of his stepsons Jan
Mattysen and Mattys Mattysen, signed by them, whereby the
hon. court is requested to allow them to themselves take
charge of their uncultivated land, notwithstanding they
are yet minors. The hon. court, having taken cognizance
of petitioners' request, deem it to be profitable for all
the minors that said uncultivated lands should be tilled,
the more so because some village taxes have to be paid for
the same, and in case petitioners know themselves efficient
and entirely able to direct their household and the farming
business, they will be permitted, with the knowledge of

and after consultation with their guardians, to take hold
of said affair, whether they can buy or lease from the
other partners their share, in such a manner as they shall
be able to agree about with the guardians.

Whereas in accordance with ancient usage, a change
will take place in the local magistrates through the re-
tirement of the two oldest magistrates about May, therefore
a double nomination has been made, for the purpose that
the Hon. Lord Govr. Genl. may elect two who are to serve
as youngest commissaries. And were nominated: Roelof
Swartwout, Cornelis Barents Slecht, Jacob Burhans, Henderick Aertsen.

Extraordinary Session at Wildwyck, Wednesday, April 28,
1666.
Present: Willem Beeckman, Schout; Evert Pels, Jan
Joosten, Commissaries.
Christoffel Davids, appearing before the hon. court,
shows an account he has kept in the transactions between
him and Andries Hop, deceased, in regard to the payment of
his half for the "Bronckenland" situated through the
Hellgate: "Account of what I, Christoffel Davids, have
paid on the one-half of 'Bronckenlant through the Hellgate,' amounting to one thousand gldrs. as per bill of
sale or deed. 1) Assigned Andries Hop, deceased, upon
Jacob Jansen Stol, and also received through him, 800
gldrs.; 2) Have once paid into the hands of Andries Hop,
at Fort Orange 5½ beavers, in the presence of Jacob Cop-
pen, 44 gldrs.; 3) Have further paid into Andries Hop's
own hands, 26 pieces of cloth at four for one beaver,
makes 6½ beavers, 52 gldrs.; 4) Have still paid to Andries
Hop two pairs of woollen stockings, at 1½ beavers, 12
gldrs.; 5) Further two roughly cured deer skins, into the
hands of the same, at ½ beaver, four gldrs.; 6) Further
a foxcoat of nine foxes into the hands of his wife, for
two beavers, 16 gldrs. Amounts to a total of 928 gldrs."
Which abovenamed amount of 928 gldrs. appearer declares to have thus paid on the aforesaid "Bronckenlant,"
and consequently has judicially affirmed the same under
oath.

Extraordinary Session, Tuesday, April 29/May 4, 1666.
Present: Willem Beeckman, Schout; Jan Willemsen
Hoochteylingh, Henderick Jochemsen, Evert Pels, Jan
Joosten, Commissaries; Daniel Broadhead, Captain of the
Militia.
Albert Heymans Roos, appearing before the hon. court,
complains of what has been done to him, yesterday, by five
soldiers, saying that he, plaintiff, returning from the
land, yesterday, for the purpose of taking the coulter
which was broken to the smith, for the purpose of having

292

the same fixed; and whereas the smith was not at home, he
was told by Jacob Joosten that the smith was at the house
of Louwies Dubois. Plaintiff going thither found the
smith there; and called him to the door, whereupon he /the
smith/ said that he would come right away. Plaintiff, in
the mean time, going away from the door, a soldier, named
Francois Vreeman, comes outside, walks up to where plaintiff stands, and immediately draws his sword without having word with or answer from plaintiff, and strikes twice
at plaintiff, whereupon plaintiff says to him, "You must
not do that anymore, or I shall go for you with the piece
of the coulter." He nevertheless lunged a third time at
plaintiff and hit him through his coat, whereupon he threw
the coulter at said François Vreeman, but did not hit him.
In the mean time Ridsert Hamer came out of the aforesaid
house, and hit plaintiff with his sword on the head.
Plaintiff, feeling this, takes hold of a stick or piece
of wood, which was laying handy, and therewith defended
his life, striking with it at Ridsert Hamer, aforenamed,
who, for the second time struck at him. Thereby still
came the third, Thomas Elger, who also struck at plaintiff,
and whom plaintiff, dealing him /Elger/ a blow with the
same stick, also turned off. Tomas Quinel, the fourth,
arriving, tried to pierce plaintiff from behind, whom
plaintiff, jumping about, hit with the same stick, so that
he tumbled to the ground. Francois Vreeman, now again at-
tacking plaintiff with the intention of sticking through
him, also received of plaintiff a thrust with the same
piece of wood, so that it dazed him, whereupon the fifth,
Robbert Pecock, appeared, and intended to pierce plaintiff.
Plaintiff, retreating, was followed by the aforesaid Pecock who tried to hit him, whereupon plaintiff ran under
his sword, and took hold of his body. In the mean time
the other four soldiers attacked plaintiff from behind and
wounded him five times, being three blows on the head and
two thrusts, one in his back, the other in the arm. Plaintiff, on account of this, requests justice, and that he, as
burgher, may not be molested by the soldiers and /be per-
mitted/ to follow his business without interruption.

Mattheu Blanchan, having been summoned as a witness
in the above case, declares that, yesterday, having taken
malt to the mill, he returned the wagon with the oxen to
Louwies Dubois, and says when arriving at the house of
said Dubois, he heard a noise in the house, on account of
which he did not want to enter, and that, in the mean time
Allert Heymans Roos arrived at the front of said house and
had the smith called outside for the purpose of fixing his
coulter. In the mean time Francois Vreeman came out of
the same house, and he saw that said Vreeman drew his
sword against Allert Heymans, and thrust at him, and that
thereupon, Allert Heymans threw the piece of the coulter
at him, but did not hit him. In the meanwhile Ridsert

Hamer attacked Allert Heymans, who was retreating to the
wagon, and struck at Allert Heymans, and has seen that
Ridsert Hamer's sword passed below Allert Heyman's left
arm, but does not know whether or not he wounded him.
Allert Heymans retreated from there to the house of
Louwies Dubois, and he saw that Allert Heymans took hold
of a stick there. While defending his life he /Heymans/
struck Ridsert Hamer (who intended to strike Allert Heymans) with the same stick on the arm, so that he dropped
the sword. And also saw that Thomas Elger appeared and
intended to hit Allert Heymans, whereupon Allert Heymans
hit the same with the stick so that he whirled around /or
grew giddy/. Francois Vreeman, appearing again, intended
to hit Allert Heymans, but Allert Heymans struck him down
with the same stick, and while Allert Heymans was pre-
paring to hit said Vreeman another blow, Tomas Quinel in
the mean time approached from behind with the sword a-
gainst Allert Heymans, but Allert Heymans with the same
stick, struck him down. Declares not having seen more,
and is prepared (if need be) to affirm the present under
oath.

Ridsert Hamer, appearing, declares having seen yesterday at the house of Lowys Dubois that Dirrick DeGoyer
drew his knife against Francois Vreeman. In the mean
while Francois Vreeman went outside, while Allert Heymans
was standing outside the door, he /Hamer/ has seen that
Allert Heymans struck said Francois Vreeman with the piece
of the coulter, so that he tumbled down, whereupon he, appearer, also went outside for the purpose of separating
them, and in the mean time Allert Heymans grasped a stick,
and beat appearer with the same. Meanwhile Ariaen Huyberts also came out of the said house with a bare knife,
hidden by his hand, and stuck him, appearer, with the same.
And says not to know more, and is ready (if necessary) to
affirm the present under oath.

Tomas Elger, appearing, declares having seen yesterday, at the house of Lowys Dubois that Dirrick DeGojer being outside the said house, had a bare knife in his hand.
Francois Vreeman, seeing this, drew his sword against Dirrick DeGojer. Allert Heymans, also standing in front of
the same door, threw the smallest piece of the broken coulter at aforesaid Vreeman, and taking the largest piece in
his hands, ran up to the aforesaid Vreeman for the purpose
of hitting him with the same, and does not know what cause
there was between Dirrick DeGojer and the aforesaid Vreeman. And says not to know any more, and is ready (if need
be) to affirm the present under oath.

Ariaen Huybertsen, appearing, he was notified that he
is accused by Ridsert Hamer of having, yesterday, stuck
said Ridsert Hamer with a knife, which Ariaen Huybertsen
denies, saying that, yesterday, he did not carry his
knife, but only the sheath of his knife, but says that he

has been at the house of Louwies Dubois, and has heard,
while still being in said house, that the soldiers were
fighting on the street with Allert Heymans, and upon coming outside, he saw that his uncle, Allert Heymans, was
bleeding, and intending to go to him, three soldiers with
drawn swords attacked him, without a word having been uttered on either side, with drawn swords, and cut through
his hat. In the mean time Captain Broadhead arrived and
pacified the soldiers and took him to the guardhouse under arrest. Arriving there, Corporal Ridsert Hamer, who
had arrested him, and taken to the guardhouse, immediately
hit him with his drawn sword in the head, and cut his
hand, and says that while under arrest he would have murdered him, if another soldier had not set him free. And
enters a complaint because he, a prisoner, was maltreated
and assaulted by Ridsert Hamer, and requests justice on
this account.

Louys Dubois declares that yesterday some residents
came to his house for a drink. In the meantime some soldiers also entered to have a drink. Coming from his inner
room he saw that Francois Vreeman being half mad had partially drawn his sword whom he requested to again sheath
his sword, which he did. Ridsert Hamer, in the meantime,
also being mad, said something which appearer did not understand, whom appearer requested not to make trouble in
his house, but to drink their wine in peace. Hereupon Ridsert Hamer, drawing his sword, appearer, with one hand,
took hold of the hilt and with the other hand held his
sleeve so that he could not entirely draw his sword, and
thus holding fast the sword; both of them got outside.
But Robbert Pekock, intervening, took hold of appearer,
and dragged him away from Ridsert Hamer, and being rid of
him, Ridsert Hamer struck appearer with the little stick
on the head. Thereupon Robbert Pecock again took appearer
in the house, and was followed by Ridsert Hamer, who, still
standing before the door, struck at appearer with the same
little stick, whereupon appearer's wife asked Ridsert Hamer
why he beat her husband? Thereupon he twice beat his wife
with the same little stick. Ridsert Hamer at the same time
exclaimed, "I want my gloves, or I shall kill your husband,"
whereupon appearer answered, "Come inside and look for your
gloves." Francois Vreeman, then, being in the house, again
entirely unsheathed his sword, not knowing with whom he had
a quarrel. Appearer, seeing this, took hold of aforesaid
Vreeman's arm, and threw him outdoors. Thereupon he was
followed by the greatest part, English as well as Dutch,
and appearer then closed his door. And as to the drawing
of any knife, he appearer, has not seen that the same was
done in his house. And says not to know any more, and (if
required) is ready to affirm the present under oath.

Frederick Pietersen, appearing, declares, whereas yesterday he has been present at the house of Louwies Dubois,

he has not seen that a knife was drawn by Dirk DeGojer,
and neither knows that there were any differences in the
aforesaid house between soldiers and inhabitants. And
further says that he was outside the door of the aforesaid
house when Allert Heymans arrived with the broken coulter
and called the smith outside the said house, and has seen
that Francois Vreeman came out of the aforesaid house, and
further that said Vreeman drew his sword against Allert
Heymans, whereupon Allert Heymans said, "Look out what you
do," and at the same time Vreeman struck twice at Allert
Heymans, and while he was striking at him a third time,
Allert Heymans threw a piece of the coulter at aforenamed
Vreeman, but did not hit him with the same. In the meanwhile the corporal Ridsert Hamer came out of the aforesaid
house, drew his sword and struck at Allert Heymans who defended himself with a stick he had there found and parried
as much as he could for the purpose of defending his life.
And then there arrived one Thomas Elger with his sword
drawn, and also struck at Allert Heymans who also parried
him with said stick. Thereupon came Thomas Quinel, also
with his drawn sword against Allert Heymans, and struck at
him who was also parried with the same stick. At last Robbert Pecock also appeared against Allert Heymans, with his
sword drawn, and struck at him, under whose sword Allert
Heymans ran and took hold of his body. In the meanwhile
Allert Heymans was wounded by the four other soldiers. Then
Captain Broodhead came and ordered the soldiers to desist.
And says not to know any more and (if need be) is prepared
to affirm the present under oath.

Decree prohibiting trafficking on Sundays with the
savages:

Whereas, prior to this, the irregularity has been
noticed among the residents here, of trafficking and dealing with the savages on Sundays and days of prayer, on
account of which actions the savages might find opportunity
on said Sundays and days of prayer to surprise the village,
because the larger portion of the people is unarmed at
church, therefore, for the purpose of preventing this, the
hon. court, here resolves and decides, and orders in the
name and by the authority of his Royal Majesty of Great
Britain, etc., that nobody, whatever business he may conduct, shall venture on Sundays and days of prayer to, in
any manner, traffic or deal with any male or female savage
under penalty, on violation, of 100 gldrs. fine for every
time. Let everybody look out for himself. Thus enacted
at the session of the hon. court at Wildwyck, May 4, 1666.

And further, also, all residents here are warned to
pay heed to the discharge of a cannon which shall be a
sign or signal of alarm, and then as quickly as possible
to arrive at the village. Enacted as above.

The captain of the burgher guard, Thomas Chambers, is ordered to command the guard, keeping watch on Saturday night, to make the rounds on Sundays during religious services, fully armed.

Extraordinary Session, Wednesday, May 12, *1666.
Present: Willem Beeckman, Schout; Jan Willemsen Hoochteylingh, Henderick Jochemsen, Evert Pels, Jan Joosten, Commissaries.
The hon. schout proposes, whereas great multitudes of savages are again appearing in our village, not only of Esopus but also of other nations of savages, that also during the daytime a burgher guard may be kept in the village. The hon. court orders the captain of the burgher guard, Thomas Chambers, to have two men keep a daily watch, which /two men/ shall continually make the rounds of the village during the daytime. Also that, through the corporal, he shall warn every resident, when going to the field to work, to every one carry his gun, for the purpose of being better guarded against the savages.

Ordinary Session, Tuesday, May 18, 1666
Present: Willem Beeckman, Schout; Jan Willemsen Hoochteylingh, Henderick Jochemsen, Evert Pels, Jan Joosten, Commissaries.
  Eduard Wittiger and Joris Porter, Plaintiffs
          vs. Mattheu Blanchan, Defendant
Plaintiffs demand of defendant compensation for the damage suffered on account of defendant's cattle, last year, to their Indian corn, and say, if defendant is inclined to amicably settle about the same that they will be very reasonable; if not, they demand compensation for the entire damage. Defendant answers that he drove his cattle into the wood, and could not watch it in the wood, and further says that, as per the regulations here, everybody is obliged to have proper fences around his land and plantation, and therefore maintains not to be obliged to repair the damage, the more so because Thomas Chambers' gate was open on his land, and consequently defendant's cattle followed the cattle of aforementioned Chambers. Plaintiffs answer saying that they warned defendant three or four times to watch his cattle and to keep it back, because their fences are /not/ in a good condition, so that it should not cause them any more damage, which defendant did not do, and on account hereof plaintiffs claim compensation for the suffered damage. Defendant answers hereupon that plaintiffs ought to have obeyed the orders which have been issued in this regard, to have the fence lawfully examined. Plaintiffs say they did not know of any order · in this regard, because they are strangers, and assert that it was sufficient having warned defendant three or four times.

The hon. court refers parties to two good men, viz.,
to Tjerck Claesen De Wit and Aert Martensen Doorn, for the
purpose of settling (if possible) the differences between
parties, and, if not, that parties shall again, at the
next session, address themselves to the hon. court, with
the report of the aforementioned good men.

Eduard Wittiger and Joris Porter, Plaintiffs
vs. Jan Jansen Van Amersfort, Defendant. Absent. Default.

Eduard Wittiger and Joris Porter, Plaintiffs
vs. Lambert Huybertsen, Defendant. Absent. Default.

Ridsert Cage, Plaintiff
vs. Gerret Fooken, Defendant

Plaintiff, holding a procuration of Michiel Sea, late
servant of defendant, demands of defendant 30 gldrs. in
beavers, or 90 gldrs. in sewan for wages at harvest time
in the year 1663. Defendant answers that he and his deceased partner, Jan Gerretsen, have hired said Michiel Sea
for one month, in the month of May of the year 1663 for 28
gldrs. in sewan for the purpose of plowing which is known
to several people here, and thereupon paid to Harmen Hendericks for said Michiel Sea six gldrs. in sewan for the
trouble of getting him out of the woods, when he had lost
his way. And whereas his partner, Jan Gerretsen, deceased,
was killed in the same year during the troubles with the
savages and they were absolutely ruined, therefore defend-
and maintains that he does not owe more to aforesaid
Michiel Sea than one-half, after deduction of the six
gldrs. paid to Harmen Hendericks. The hon. court decides
whereas defendant, during the troubles with the savages in
the year 1663 lost all his effects, and, besides, his partner, Jan Gerretsen, was killed during the same troubles,
and Michiel Sea was hired by both of them for 28 gldrs. in
sewan which can be proved, and, also, said Michiel Sea has
not been able to serve his full month, the hon. court having
considered all this, therefore orders defendant to pay
plaintiff one-half of the monthly wage, provided he may
deduct the six gldrs. in sewan, paid to Harmen Hendericks.

Antoni Crespel, Plaintiff
vs. Paulus Paulusen, Defendant. Absent. Default.

Roelof Swartwout and Cornelis Barentsen Slecht,
guardians of the minor children of Mattys Jansen, deceased, Plaintiffs
vs. Thomas Chambers, Defendant. Absent. Default.

Whereas necessity requires it to examine the fences
around the lands about Wildwyck, so that no damage may be
caused to the crops by pigs or cattle, therefore schout and
commissaries at Wildwyck elect and appoint for this purpose
in the place of Aert Jacobsen, deceased, besides the formerly appointed Tjerck Claesen De Witt and Juriaen Westphael, Henderick Aertsen to examine said fences every 14
days or three weeks and to fine the negligent after one
warning, as they shall find things.

Extraordinary Session, Monday, June 7, 1666.
Present: Willem Beeckman, Schout; Jan Willemsen
Hoochteylingh, Henderick Jochemsen, Evert Pels, Jan
Joosten, Commissaries

Willem La Montagnie requests by a petition that, at
the request of many residents here, he may be permitted to
keep a day and evening school here, and besides, that no
other schools may be permitted but his, and also that he
may be exempt from lodging soldiers. The hon. court
grants petitioner's request under condition that he shall
be reasonable in his charges of school money and be obliged
to keep up the school for one year.

Extraordinary Session, Monday, June 21, 1666.
Present: Willem Beeckman, Schout; Jan Willemsen
Hoochteylingh, Henderick Jochemsen, Evert Pels, Jan
Joosten, Commissaries.

On this date the appointed two new commissaries,
viz., Thomas Chambers and Roelof Swartwout, took their
proper oath, the two oldest commissaries Jan Willemsen
Hoochteylingh and Henderick Jochemsen retiring.

Ordinary Session, Tuesday, June 22, 1666.
Present: Willem Beeckman, Schout; Evert Pels, Jan
Joosten, Thomas Chambers, Roelof Swartwout, Commissaries;
and Capt. Daniel Broodhead.
Eduard Wittiger and Joris Porter, Plaintiffs
vs. Jan Jansen Van Amersfoort, Defendant. Absent. Default.
Eduard Wittiger and Joris Porter, Plaintiffs
vs. Lambert Huybertsen, Defendant. _Absent. 2nd Default.
Was received /the report about/ the case between
Eduard Wittiger and Joris Porter, plaintiffs, vs. Mattheu
Blanchan, defendant, presented to the court on May 18
last, which case had been referred to the decision of two
good men, viz., Tjerck Claesen DeWit and Aert Martensen
Doorn. Said good men /say in/ their written report that
they could not make parties settle /the case/, because
plaintiffs demand 150 gldrs. for the damage suffered to
their corn of last year, and defendant sticks to the answer given by him. On account hereof the hon. court, besides Capt. Broodhead, once more refer parties to two
impartial men, and the parties themselves shall be allowed to each choose one man for the purpose of finally
settling their differences. And in case the two good men
elected by the parties themselves cannot succeed in agreeing, they shall choose a third to finally settle the differences. And parties shall submit themselves to and be
satisfied with such impartial decision.
Tjerck Claesen De Wit, Plaintiff
vs. Andries Pietersen Van Leeuven, Defendant
Plaintiff says that defendant refuses to fence in
his portion of the common fence running from Aert Marten-

sen Doorn's land till the fence of Wassemaker's land, and
requests that defendant may be made to fence in his portion,
beside himself. Defendant answers that he does not refuse
to make the common fence mentioned by plaintiff, and says
that plaintiff besides others bordering on the common fence
also ought to assist in fencing in the back portion of his
land, where also damage is to be expected. The hon. court
decides and orders that defendant besides others bordering
with their land on the common fence, shall together erect
/said fence/ from the land of Aert Martensen Doorn till
Wassemaker's land, and continue to keep the same in repairs. And further /orders/ plaintiff besides the others
whose land borders on his fences, to assist in erecting defendant's fence of the back part of his land, until the
new village shall be again inhabited.

   Andries Pietersen Van Leeuven, Plaintiff
    vs. Allert Heymans Roos, Defendant

  Plaintiff says that defendant uses a wagon road through
his /plaintiff's/ hired land, and therefore requests that
defendant may be prohibited from using said wagon road,
because defendant's lands are situated under the new village, and /plaintiff/ on this account suffers damage. Defendant answers that heretofore he was permitted by plaintiff to use a wagon road to his lands, and that, when requested to do so, he assisted in the work on the bridge.
The hon. court decides that plaintiff, for the present and
as long as necessary shall allow defendant a wagon road to
his lands, provided defendant shall return to plaintiff a
dry sheaf for a green sheaf in case the latter should sustain any damage. Nor is defendant permitted to allow any
loose horses or colts to pass along said road, for fear
that they may cause damage.

  In consequence of the request and proposition of Capt.
Broodhead that the fences commencing from Wassemaker's
land through the Kil and further across the Kil till Allert Heymans's fences, ought to be repaired, so as to prevent any damage, the hon. court orders the following persons, viz., De Heer Beeckman, Jan Joosten, Tjerck Claesen,
Allert Heymans, Aert Martensen, Henderick Aertsen, Pieter
Hillebrants, Andries Pietersen, Jan Jansen Van Oosterhout,
Lambert Huybertsen, Jan Willemsen Hoochteylingh, the widow
of Aert Jacobsen and Ariaen Gerretsen Van Vliet, to assist
in making the aforementioned fence on Saturday next, being
June 26, under penalty, for those being absent, of a fine
of one Flemish pound for the benefit of those who shall
have done the work. And said Capt. Broodhead promised and
accepted to keep in proper repairs the further fence of
Wassemaker's land. And, for the above purpose the abovenamed are ordered to call on Saturday morning at the house
of Allert Heymans which Allert Heymans is authorized to
see to it that the aforesaid fence be properly made /or
repaired/.

Louwies Du Bois requests that the judgment pronounced on Apr. 6, 1666, against Jan Willemsen Hoochteylingh, may be judicially enforced. The hon. court orders the officer to proceed with the execution.

Extraordinary Session, Wednesday, August 4, 1666.
Present: Willem Beeckman, Schout; Evert Pels, Thomas Chambers, Roelof Swartwout, Commissaries.
The hon. schout proposes to reduce the burgher guard, and thus to relieve them, because the residents, here, have complained several times, and have requested the above on account of the present harvest.
In regard to the above proposal the hon. court, the captain and the lieutenant of the burghers decide that the watch by the residents shall be lightened and decreased to one-half of each half corporal's guard, because many of the strange savages have each departed for their own land. And in case we should be informed of any gathering of savages again taking place about this neighborhood, the watch shall again be reinforced as the circumstances may require.

Extraordinary Session, Saturday, August 14, 1666.
Present: Willem Beeckman, Schout; Evert Pels, Jan Joosten, Thomas Chambers, Roelof Swartwout, Commissaries; Daniel Broodhead, captain of the militia.
In regard to the order given by the hon. court on June 22, last, that in the case between Eduard Wittiger and Joris Porter vs. Mattheu Blanchan the decision was to be made by good men selected by themselves, Eduard French and Eduard Wittiger request that the third /person necessary/ for the final decision or judgment be chosen from the court. And for this purpose is selected by the court the commissary Roelof Swartwout.
Was farmed out the tapster and burgher excise of the wines and beers to be consumed during the next current year, at public auction.
Bidders for the tapster excise: Henderick Palingh, 400 gldrs.; Henderick Palingh, increases the same to 450 gldrs.; Daniel Broodhead, increases the same to 500 gldrs.; Henderick Palingh, increases the same to 550 gldrs.; Daniel Broodhead, increases the same to 575 gldrs.
Was increased /by the auctioneer/ with 200 gldrs., the increased 575 remaining fixed, and runs down to 0 gldrs., and remains farmer Daniel Broodhead, for the amount of 575 gldrs.
Bidders for the burgher excise: Laurens Jansen, 200 gldrs.; Henderick Palingh increases the same to 250 gldrs.; Henderick Cornelissen increases the same to 300 gldrs.; Capt. Broodhead increases the same to 350 gldrs.; Henderick Palingh increases the same to 375 gldrs.; Henderick Cornelissen increases the same to 400 gldrs.

    Was increased /by the auctioneer/ with 100 gldrs.,
the increased 400 gldrs. remaining fixed, and runs down
to six gldrs., and remains farmer Henderick Cornelissen,
Lyndraejer, for the sum of 406 gldrs.

Extraordinary Session, Saturday, September 4, 1666.
    Present: Willem Beeckman, Schout; Evert Pels, Jan
Joosten, Thomas Chambers, Roelof Swartwout, Commissaries.
    The hon. court resolved to post decrees /containing/
that nobody shall be permitted to pick or gather the
hop growing wild in the woods before September 10/20, and
so continually every year, under penalty for those picking
the hop before this designated period, of a fine of 100
Rixdollars for every violation. Further to forbid, by the
said decree, anybody from venturing to pick the hop standing or growing on the farming lands without the owner's
consent, upon penalty as the case may require, and further
that nobody shall undertake to steal from the gardens
within or without the village, or from the outside plantations, under penalty of bodily punishment as the case may
require, and reads as follows:

    Whereas some residents of the village of Wildwyck, as
well as others not being residents, annually go out for
the purpose of picking and gathering hop, growing wild, in
which picking and gathering of the hop many, being possessed by avidity pick and gather said hop before the time,
before it is and can be ripe, and has been found and is
being complained about, because said hop is not fit for
proper merchandise, wherewith the buyer is defrauded, and
on which account the other good and valuable hop gathered
by others in this place is also under-rated, the hon.
court of this village of Wildwyck desirous of preventing
in the name and by the authority of the Royal Majesty of
Great Britain, any future fraud or deception in the hop,
therefore the said hon. court by the authority of the Royal
Majesty of Great Britain above named, orders and commands
that from now on and subsequently every year nobody,
whether residents or non-residents of this village, shall
undertake to pick and gather the hop, growing wild in the
wood, before September 10/20, and the same, as mentioned
before, year after year, under penalty for those, who shall
be found to have picked or gathered the hop before the
stipulated time, of 100 rix dollars for every time.
    Also, in regard to the complaint of those having hop
on their own land, that many, before this have ventured
without the consent of the owner, to pick said hop on his
land like the hop growing wild in the woods, the said hon.
court in the name of the above mentioned royal majesty
orders and prohibits anybody from venturing to pick the hop
standing or growing on the lands of the residents here,
without the consent of the owner of the said land, under

302

penalty of being punished for the same as thieves, as the
case may require.
   And in regard to the complaint, that prior to this,
some have dared, and still dare, to invade the gardens in
as well as outside the village, and also the plantations
and to plunder and rob them, opening /the gates/ or breaking the fences of the gardens and plantations /so that/
pigs and other animals invade /the same/, trampling down
and crushing through this thieving and robbing the other
fruits in the gardens and plantations, therefore the hon.
court, wishing to put a stop to this abuse (being theft),
orders and prohibits, in the name of the above Royal
Majesty, anybody from daring to plunder and rob aforenamed
plantations and gardens without or within this village, of
whatever fruits they may contain, under penalty to the
person found to have committed such robbery, of corporal
punishment, as an example for others. Thus enacted at the
session of the hon. Heeren judges at Wildwyck, this
August 25/September 4, 1666.

Ordinary Session, Wednesday, October 6, 1666.
      Present: Willem Beeckman, Schout; Jan Joosten,
Thomas Chambers, Commissaries.
            Henderick Palingh, Plaintiff
vs. Tjerck Claesen De Wit, Defendant. Absent. Default.
            Henderick Palingh, Plaintiff
            vs. Ariaen Gerretsen, Defendant
   Plaintiff demands of defendant a sum of 86 gldrs. 16
st. in light money, as also a sum of 107 gldrs. as per
note, and whereas defendant has neglected /to obey/ the
judgment of the hon. court and also to pay a note issued
/by him/, /plaintiff/ demands the entire amount of 193
gldrs. 16 st. Defendant being absent, he is represented
by his wife who admits the debt. The hon. court orders
defendant to pay plaintiff his claim of 86 gldrs. 16 st.
besides the 107 gldrs. which, according to the note, should
have fallen due on the month of December, because defendant has neglected to pay a portion of the note, notwithstanding plaintiff has allowed defendant a considerable
reduction.
         Henderick Cornelissen, Lyndraejer, Plaintiff
            vs. Arent Teunissen, Defendant
   Plaintiff demands of defendant 16 sch. of white peas
and 10 sch. of oats which have been destroyed by the pigs
upon the land, said damage having been caused on account
of defendant's fence as is shown by the appraisal of the
examiners of the fences, as also by the declaration of
Albert Goverts. Whereas the bench is not quite complete,
therefore this case is adjourned till the next session.
            Willemtje Jacobs, Plaintiff
vs. Pieter Hillebrants, Defendant. Absent. Default.
   Aert Otterspoor requests that he may be allowed a

fixed amount of money for the trouble of catching wolves.
The hon. court, in regard to the abovenamed request, allows petitioner for every wolf caught by him, whether male
or female, ten guilders. Petitioner further requests to
be shown where, on the cultivated land outside the curtain,
he may build a small house for his convenience. The hon.
court first wants to find out who has been granted the
preference for the little corner of land.

Ordinary Session, Tuesday, October 19, 1666.
Present: Willem Beeckman, Schout; Evert Pels, Roelof
Swartwout, Commissaries.

Willem Beeckman, Plaintiff
vs. Pieter Hillebrants, Defendant. Absent. Default.

Roelof Swartwout, Plaintiff
vs. Aert Martensen Doorn, Defendant. Absent. Default.

Roelof Swartwout, Plaintiff
vs. Pieter Hillebrants, Defendant. Absent. Default.

Tjerck Claesen, Plaintiff
vs. Claes Claesen, Defendant
Plaintiff demands that defendant shall carry out his
agreement concerning grain sold, and demands security or
payment, and by default of security he has attached the
grain and the earned wages at Annetje Gerrets's, and requests that the arrest may be declared valid. Defendant
answers that he cannot find sureties. The hon. court orders defendant to give security for the grain sold /to
him/ of else the attachment shall remain valid.

Henderick Palingh, Plaintiff
vs. Pieter Hillebrants, Defendant. Absent. Default.

Willemtje Jacobs, Plaintiff
vs. Pieter Hillebrants, Defendant. Absent. 2nd Default.
Plaintiff says that defendant had his sister board
with her /plaintiff/ before the last war with the savages,
when he was living on the Great Piece, and demands 7½ sch.
of wheat for five weeks' board.

Magdalena Dirricks, Plaintiff
vs. Ridsert Cage, Defendant. Absent. Default.
Henderick Palingh requests that the judgment pronounced on Oct. 6, 1666, against Ariaen Gerretsen may be
judicially enforced. The hon. court orders the officer,
in compliance with the above request, to proceed with the
execution.

Cornelis Barents Slecht requests by a petition to be
relieved of boarding a soldier on account of his poverty
and heavy debts, because it is impossible for him to further board a soldier, and also because he is a single inhabitant, and requests that he may be burdened the same as
every other single resident. At petitioner's request the
hon. court decides that petitioner, as a matter of relief
in boarding a soldier, shall board the same every third
month, and are joined with him in boarding a soldier:

Pieter Cornelissen and Jan Jansen Van Oosterhout.

Ordinary Session, Tuesday, October 16, 1666.
    Present: Willem Beeckman, Schout; Evert Pels, Jan
Joosten, Roelof Swartwout, Commissaries.
                 Willem Beeckman, Plaintiff
              vs. Pieter Hillebrants, Defendant
    Plaintiff demands of defendant 30 sch. of wheat for
grain furnished him, and the taking over of debts, and
still 11 sch. of wheat for summonses and "eygen pandem" of
decrees of execution. Defendant admits the above debts
and says that he has a claim against the hon. court of
eight sch. of wheat on account of the journey made last
winter to Fort Orange, and requests that the same may be
deducted from the amount claimed in the above demand.
Plaintiff replies that he, personally, is not obliged to
pay the above eight sch. of wheat, and therefore claims
the full amount. The hon. court decides that plaintiff, in
accordance with defendant's own admission, must be satisfied for the full claim. In regard to the eight sch. of
wheat which defendant says the court owes him, the hon.
court orders defendant, at the next session, to produce
proof of the same, and he shall be paid in accordance with
the finding in the case.
                 Willem Beeckman, Plaintiff
              vs. Pieter Hillebrants, Defendant
    Plaintiff demands of defendant an amount of 25 gldrs.
fine on account of a dead dog which defendant dragged outside the gate. Defendant answers that plaintiff has relieved him of said fine, and further says that plaintiff
has cheated him in the purchase of a horse. Plaintiff
says that defendant shall prove that he cheated him in said
transaction. The hon. court orders defendant to prove at
the next session of the court that plaintiff made him a
present of the 25 gldrs. fine, and also to prove in which
plaintiff has cheated him.
                 Willem Beeckman, Plaintiff
    vs. Albert Govertsen, Defendant. Absent. Default.
                 Gerret Fooken, Plaintiff
    vs. Pieter Hillebrants, Warnaer Hoorenbeeck, and
                 Jan Hendericks, Defendants
    Plaintiff demands of defendants an amount of 26 sch.
of wheat, on account of the sale of the crops in the new
village in the year 1664, according to a signed contract.
Defendants answer that plaintiff sold them grain, and
coming on the great piece on the field, defendants did not
find grain worth the cutting, and further say that defendants can be free with the "wyncoop" which they offer to
prove. The hon. court orders defendants at the next session of the court to produce their proof.
                 Gerret Fooken, Plaintiff
              vs. Pieter Hillebrants, Defendant

Plaintiff demands of defendant 15 gldrs., owing to
advanced grain. Defendant admits the debt. The hon.
court orders defendant to satisfy plaintiff's demand.

Cornelis Barents Slecht, Plaintiff
vs. Annetie Gerrets, Defendant

Plaintiff demands of defendant nine sch. of wheat,
wages for brewing a half-barrel of good beer. Defendant
says that one-half of the wages for brewing belongs to her,
the other half to Andries Pietersen. She consents to paying for the half-barrel of good beer. Plaintiff answers
that he was asked by her to brew. The hon. court orders
defendant to satisfy plaintiff for his full claim. In regard to the other half of the /wages/ for brewing, defendant will have to get the same of Andries Pietersen.

Cornelis Barents Slecht, Plaintiff
vs. Pieter Hillebrants, Defendant

Plaintiff demands of defendant 8½ sch. of wheat,
balance of an account coming to him. Defendant admits the
debt. The hon. court orders defendant to satisfy plaintiff's claim.

Willemtje Jacobs, Plaintiff
vs. Pieter Hillebrants, Defendant

Plaintiff demands, as per a previous demand on Oct.
19, 1666, 7½ sch. of wheat, board for his sister. Defendant answers that it is true that he had his sister
lodge at the house of her husband, for which her husband
demanded of him, defendant, in payment 1½ days' driving,
which he has not yet been able, up to now, to conveniently
do, and offers to do it yet. Plaintiff answers that she
is not satisfied with driving, but demands payment in grain.
The hon. court decides, whereas defendant agreed with her
husband concerning the board of his sister, to drive for
the same, and consequently refers to him, therefore plaintiff's husband, at the next session of the court, shall
appear in regard hereof before the hon. court, for the
purpose of giving information.

Magdalena Dirricks, Plaintiff
vs. Ridgert Cage, Defendant. Absent. 2nd Default.

Plaintiff demands of defendant wages of ½ year's
washing, being five sch. of wheat.

Warnaer Hoorenbeeck, Plaintiff
vs. Aert Martensen Doorn, Defendant

Plaintiff demands of defendant a sum of 108 sch. of
wheat, being a portion for earned wages, and a portion for
advanced money. Further demands a suit of clothes for
which he paid more than three years ago. Defendant answers that he claims against the above demand one year's
board, being 1½ sch. of wheat weekly. The hon. court orders parties to themselves select two good men for the
purpose of settling their various accounts.

Aert Otterspoor requests the court to show him a
spot where he may erect a small house for his convenient

use, because age and ill health are rendering him weak.
The hon. court allows petitioner to possess and use during
his life time the point near the little water gate at
Wildwyck, and to cover the same with a beard roof, provided petitioner shall keep said point properly closed
with curtain-palisades, and further that the structure,
after his departure or his death, shall remain village
property.

Walran DuMont requests that the chosen guardians of
the minor child of Jan Arents, deceased, viz., Jan
Joosten and Louwies Dubois, may be confirmed by the hon.
court. The hon. court, being aware of the suitableness of
the guardians selected by Walran DuMont for the minor
child of Jan Arents, deceased, viz., Jan Joosten and Louwies DuBois, confirms the same by the present, and advises
said guardians to deport themselves in this their administration with all uprightness and reasonableness.

Jan Joosten requests the hon. court to deed to him
certain woodland, covered with shrubs, extending from the
extremity of the lands of Evert Pels and along the lands
of Aert Martensen Doorn, to the land of Tjerck Claesen,
containing about 10 or 12 morgens, for a plantation, because he is a resident of this place, and up to the present
does not yet possess any land. Whereas the hon. court
does not deem itself qualified to deed away any land,
therefore petitioner is referred to the Hon. Lord governor
general at New York.

Extraordinary Session, Friday, October 29, 1666.
        Present: Willem Beeckman, Schout; Evert Pels, Jan
Joosten, Thomas Chambers, Roelof Swartwout, Commissaries.
        On this day the meeting resolved about the measures
to be taken for finding the preacher's salary for the year
1666 among the congregation, amounting, as per the orders
of the hon. Ld. Govr. Genl. to 1,000 gldrs., whereof are
to be deducted 200 gldrs. which had been paid in excess of
the salary for 1665. And it was resolved to appraise the
mudde of wheat at one beaver, and other grains in proportion, in paying the preacher's salary. In order to find
said salary the morgen of arable land is taxed one gldr.,
draft horses and draft oxen and milch-cows /shall be taxed/
30 stivers a piece, and the house lots the same as in the
previous year 1665.

Ordinary Session, Tuesday, November 2, 1666.
        Present: Willem Beeckman, Schout; Evert Pels, Jan
Joosten, Thomas Chambers, Roelof Swartwout, Commissaries.
                Gerret Fooken, Plaintiff
        vs. Jan Hendericksen, Defendant. Absent.
        Plaintiff demands of defendant one-third of the 26
sch. of wheat, and the costs of same. Defendant is absent. Whereas defendant, at the last session, engaged to

have proof against plaintiff, and consequently defendant
was also ordered by the hon. court to produce proof in his
case, and whereas defendant has remained absent, and did
not appear before the hon. court, therefore defendant is
ordered by the hon. court to satisfy plaintiff's full demand, with the costs of the same.

Magdalena Dirricks, Plaintiff
vs. Ridsert Cage, Defendant. Absent. 3rd Default.

Plaintiff demands of the defendant five sch. of
wheat for a half year's wages for washing with the costs
of the same. Defendant is absent. The hon. court orders
defendant, because he contemptuously defaulted three times,
to satisfy plaintiff's full demand, with the costs for
same.

Henderick Cornelissen, Plaintiff
vs. Arent Teunissen, Defendant

Plaintiff demands of defendant 16 sch. of white
peas, and 10 sch. of oats which have been destroyed by the
pigs on the field, said damage having been caused on account of defendant's fence, as is shown by the appraisal
of the examiners of the fences, and by the declaration of
Albert Govertsen. Defendant answers that he is not obliged
to repair plaintiff's fences around the latter's land, and
that he can leave his own land unfenced, in case he does
not want to sow in it or to cultivate it. The hon. court
decides that defendant is obliged to properly keep in repair his fences, in accordance with the decree of Nov. 18,
1661, and /sentences him/ to pay plaintiff for the damage
as per the valuation by the examiners of the fences.

Joris Hael, Plaintiff
vs. Aert Martensen Doorn, Defendant. Absent. Default.
Joris Hael, Plaintiff
vs. Frederick Pietersen, Defendant. Absent. Default.
Joris Hael, Plaintiff
vs. Jan Hendericks, Defendant. Absent. Default.
Joris Hael, Plaintiff
vs. Paul Paulusen, Defendant. Absent. Default.
Joris Hael, Plaintiff
vs. Harmen Hey, Defendant. Absent. Default.
Joris Hael, Plaintiff
vs. Evert Pels, Defendant

Plaintiff demands of defendant 61 gldrs. for received
merchandise. Defendant admits the debt, and agrees to
satisfy plaintiff next week. The hon. court orders defendant to satisfy plaintiff's demand.

Joris Hael, Plaintiff
vs. Jacob Barents Cool, Defendant

Plaintiff demands of defendant 58 gldrs. for received merchandise. Defendant answers that he owes plaintiff 20 gldrs., and his brother owes him 38 gldrs. And he
has agreed to pay for his brother, when he can receive it
for him. The hon. court orders defendant to satisfy

plaintiff's demand.

Joris Hael, Plaintiff

vs. Severyn Tenhout, Defendant. Absent. Default.

Eechie Ariaens, Plaintiff

vs. Jacomyna Cornelis, Defendant

Plaintiff says that she hired out her daughter to defendant for one summer, being from May till All Saint's Day, and in the meantime she /who?/ becoming sick, plaintiff had her daughter return home and demands the hire of two shirts, two aprons and a pair of shoes. Defendant answers that plaintiff's daughter left her in the latter part of August, it being the busiest period of harvesting, and therefore maintains not to owe anything. The hon. court orders defendant to satisfy plaintiff for as much as her daughter earned of her during her service.

Roelof Swartwout requests by a petition that the hon. court may grant him possession of the little corner of land about three morgens in extent situated between the lands sold by Juffr. Ebbings of the 160 morgens, and those she still possesses, being a small island, for the purpose of supporting out of the proceeds of the same his large family, which little island, up to the present, is empty and sterile for lack of cultivation. Whereas the hon. court is not qualified to deed away any lands, petitioner is therefore referred to the Govr. Genl. at New York; said little island or corner of land having been claimed by Johanna De Laet, wife of Jeronimus Ebbingh who, on Nov. 18, 1664, has shown to the hon. court a bill of sale for the said little island. Roelof Swartwout further requests that he may be given a copy of the minutes, dated Nov. 18, 1664, in the case of Johanna De Laet and Evert Pels, which is allowed him.

Ordinary Session, Tuesday, November 16, 1666.

Present: Willem Beeckman, Schout; Evert Pels, Roelof Swartwout, Commissaries.

Whereas the bench is incomplete, Jan Joosten, Commissary, being out of town with knowledge /of the court/, and the Commissary Thomas Chambers is absenting himself, though having been cited by the court messenger, therefore this ordinary session was adjourned till tomorrow, and the parties, 16 in number, notified by the court messenger to return tomorrow. /And it was decided/ to again cite the commissary Thomas Chambers through the court messenger, by form of protest, to occupy his seat on the bench. Which protest reads as follows:

The hon. Schout and the Commissaries now present, having met on this day for the purpose of hearing parties according to oath and duty, and whereas you have now and several times before been negligent in attending the sesseions, and on account hereof we have again been obliged

to dismiss the parties without having been able to trans-
act any business, therefore this present session has been
adjourned till tomorrow, on which account you are ordered
to be present tomorrow for the purpose of filling the
bench, and if not, we shall be compelled to complain about
your absence.

Ordinary Session, Wednesday, November 17, 1666.
    Present: Willem Beeckman, Schout; Evert Pels, Thomas
Chambers, Roelof Swartwout, Commissaries.
              Nicolaes De Meyer, Plaintiff
           vs. Roelof Swartwout, Defendant
    Plaintiff demands of defendant an amount of 45½ sch.
of wheat, as per "schepen knowledge" wherein interest for
three years besides expenses incurred for an extraordinary
session of the court, amounting to 32 gldrs. 4 st. in sewan
with the costs of the same. Defendant admits the debt, but
excepts the expenses made on account of the extraordinary
session of the court on Nov. 25, 1665. The hon. court orders defendant conform to his admission, to pay plaintiff
the aforesaid claim of 45½ sch. of wheat. And in regard to
defendant's exception concerning the costs incurred by
plaintiff for an extraordinary session of the court, the
hon. court is of the opinion that defendant shall pay said
expenses to plaintiff because said expenses are in regard
to the demand for mortgage to the amount of 423 gldrs. in
beavers and 18 sch. of wheat, passed on Nov. 28, 1665, and
therefore orders defendant to satisfy plaintiff in regard
to the costs claimed, with costs.
              Nicolaes De Meyer, Plaintiff
       vs. Jan Jansen Van Amersfoort, Defendant. Absent.
    Plaintiff requests, because defendant is absent, that
he may be permitted to convoke an extraordinary session
against defendant because he is a stranger. The hon. court
grants plaintiff at his request an extraordinary session
against defendant, because defendant, at plaintiff's request, has been summoned a second time by the court messenger, and has been unwilling to appear.
              Daniel Broodhead, Plaintiff
     vs. Henderick Dirricksen, Defendant. Absent. Default.
              Jacobus Visch, Plaintiff
           vs. Thomas Chambers, Defendant
    Plaintiff says that, during the late troubles with
the savages, he left a looking glass at defendant's house,
for defendant to take care of, and because he /plaintiff/
left for Fort Orange has not been able to return to get it
again, and requests defendant to return the same to him,
because plaintiff received said looking glass as security
of one Arent Isaacsen. Defendant answers that plaintiff,
at his departure, left said looking glass with him, and
promised him to indemnify him for board and lodging, received of him, and either to send said payment down from

Fort Orange or to bring it himself, and whereas plaintiff
did not do so defendant demands three beavers for lodging
and board. Plaintiff answers, saying that he arrived here
with officers of the Company, for pleasure, for the purpose of taking a trip with them, and therefore denies
owing anything for board, and in consequence demands of
defendant a bill for the time he was with him. The hon.
court decides that defendant shall return to plaintiff the
looking glass he left with him for safe keeping, and that
plaintiff shall agree with defendant about the lodging and
board.

Jacobus Visch, Plaintiff
vs. Jan Jansen Van Amersfoort, Defendant. Absent. Default.
 Plaintiff demands of defendant 15 gldrs. in beavers,
originating from sheets sold him, and requests payment,
and expenses.

Roelof Swartwout, Plaintiff
vs. Pieter Hillebrants, Defendant. Absent. Default.

Joris Hael, Plaintiff
vs. Warnaer Hoorenbeeck, Defendant. Absent. 2nd Default.
 Plaintiff demands of defendant 63 gldrs. in sewan.

Joris Hael, Plaintiff
vs. Severyn Tenhout, Def⋯nt
 Plaintiff demands of defendant ⋯ gldrs., with the
costs. Defendant answers that, yesterday, he offered barley to plaintiff, but he was unwilling to accept the same,
and offers to pay plaintiff in other grains, as soon as he
shall have threshed. The hon. court orders defendant to
satisfy plaintiff's demand with costs.
 Samuel Olivier, Plaintiff, vs. Jan Jansen Van Amersfoort, Defendant; have settled.

Jannetie Fransen, Plaintiff
vs. Cornelis Vernoy, Defendant
 Plaintiff says that she sold defendant a cow for 140
gldrs. in sewan and a sch. of peas which her husband has
received, and further says that defendant delivered her a
silver belt for the 140 gldrs., which having been appraised
by the silversmith Henderick Ahasuerus, was by him valued
at 80 gldrs. in sewan, and therefore demands payment of
140 gldrs. sewan, because the silver belt is not worth as
much. Defendant answers that he did not furnish said silver belt to plaintiff by weight, but upon a voluntary
agreement, and says that plaintiff's husband was satisfied
with the silver belt and the sch. of peas, in payment of
the cow, and having further been asked whether, first of
all, he did not buy the cow for 140 gldrs. in sewan, and
a sch. of peas, answers, "Yes," and that afterward they
agreed upon the belt. The hon. court orders defendant to
pay plaintiff the 140 gldrs. in sewan, or else to prove
that plaintiff's husband accepted the silver belt as full
payment for the cow in place of the 140 gldrs.

Jan Cornelissen, Plaintiff
vs. Lambert Huybertsen, Defendant
Plaintiff demands of defendant five sch. of wheat,
wages for putting on share and coulter. Defendant answers
that Ariaen Gerretsen detached said share and coulter, and
that aforesaid Ariaen Gerretsen took it upon himself to pay
for the same. The hon. court orders defendant to satisfy
plaintiff's demand, because he agreed to pay for the repaired plow and coulter in case Ariaen Gerretsen should
fail to pay plaintiff.

Lambert Huyberts, Plaintiff
vs. Ariaen Gerretsen, Defendant. Absent. Default.

Arent Teunissen, Plaintiff
vs. Gommert Paulusen, Defendant
Plaintiff demands of defendant a sch. of wheat for
taking care of his cow. Defendant answers that he did not
contract with the cowherder for his animal. The hon.
court refuses plaintiff's demand.

Gommert Paulusen, Plaintiff
vs. Sara Gillissen, Defendant
Cornelis Hoogeboom requests that the attachment levied by
Reyndert Pietersen, at Thomas Chambers', on his money may
be repealed, because he does not know about having any difference with Reyndert Pietersen and he is very much inconvenienced by the same. Whereas the attachment has not been
properly sued for at the right time and place by Reyndert
Pietersen, and he has not given reasons for the same,
therefore the (arrest) attachment, at Thomas Chambers',
against Cornelis Hoogeboom is repealed.

Extraordinary Session, Friday, November 19, 1666.
Present: Willem Beeckman, Schout; Evert Pels, Jan
Joosten, Roelof Swartwout, Commissaries.
Nicolaes De Meyer, Plaintiff
vs. Jan Jansen Van Amersfoort, Defendant. Absent.
Plaintiff demands of defendant, as per an assignment
issued to Thomas Chambers which has not been accepted, an
amount of 130 gldrs. four st. in beavers, and also an
amount of 74 gldrs. 14 st. in sewan, originating from
"schepen knowledge" dated Apr. 3, 1664, and whereas defendant has now as well as formerly remained absent and did not
appear, therefore plaintiff further demands an amount of
50 gldrs. besides the expenses for the extraordinary and
previous ordinary /sessions/ by virtue of a promise by defendant, as is shown by "schepen knowledge" dated Nov. 18,
1664, and requests speedy justice, for the purpose of being
enabled to receive his money. Defendant is absent. The
hon. court decides whereas defendant shows contempt by not
appearing, therefore he shall satisfy plaintiff's full demand with the costs for the same inside of three times 24
hours, which he is also warned by the hon. court to do, or
by default of payment the officer is ordered to proceed
with the execution.

Jacobus Visch, Plaintiff
vs. Jan Jansen Van Amersfoort, Defendant. Absent.
Plaintiff demands of defendant 15 gldrs. in beavers,
originating from cloth sold him in the year 1657, with
the expenses for the same. Defendant is absent. Whereas
defendant has suffered the second default to take place
and has shown contempt by not appearing, and plaintiff is
a stranger and is about to depart, therefore defendant is
condemned by the hon. court to satisfy plaintiff's demand
with expenses.

Ordinary Session, Tuesday, November 23, 1666.
Present: Willem Beeckman, Schout; Evert Pels, Jan
Joosten, Thomas Chambers, Roelof Swartwout, Commissaries.
Frederick Philipsen, Plaintiff
vs. Aert Martensen Doorn, Defendant
Plaintiff demands the balance on a note, dated Apr.
3, 1665, 33½ sch. of wheat. Defendant admits the debt,
and says having delivered five sch. of peas more than he
has been credited with. Plaintiff replies that defendant
last year delivered the five sch. of peas at the house of
Jan Jansen Van Amersfoort and agreed to replace the same
in the fall, because they were no good. The hon. court
orders defendant to satisfy plaintiff for his full demand.
Frederick Philipsen, Plaintiff
vs. Cornelis Barents Slecht, Defendant
Plaintiff demands of defendant an amount of 675 gldrs.*
11 st. in beavers, originating from a "schepen knowledge"
to the amount of 563 gldrs. in grain, beavers value, a
barrel of mackerel and a keg of butter worth 24 sch. of
wheat, a deed worth eight gldrs. in beavers and three
years' interest, amounting to 132 gldrs. in beavers. Defendant admits the debt of 563 gldrs. in beavers value,
and makes exceptions to the interest of the aforesaid
amount, because he did not promise interest, and also to
the eight gldrs. for the deed. The hon. court refuses
plaintiff's demand for interest up to date, as also the
payment for the deed, unless plaintiff can prove that defendant, when he conveyed the lots, promised to deliver
him a deed, and orders defendant to satisfy plaintiff's
demand in regard to the note provided he may deduct the
draft on the hon. company amounting to 125 gldrs. 9 st.
in beavers.
Cornelis Barents Slecht, Plaintiff
vs. Allert Heymans Roos, Defendant
Plaintiff demands of defendant nine sch. of wheat,
wages for brewing. Defendant admits the debt, and says to
intend to pay him in two or three days. And /also/ says
having a counter claim for a boy who is at Fort Orange for
whom he is attorney. The hon. court orders defendant to
satisfy plaintiff's demand.

Cornelis Barents Slecht, Plaintiff
vs. Juriaen Westphael, Defendant

Plaintiff demands of defendant 23 sch. of wheat, as
per balance. Defendant admits the debt, and says not being able to pay at present, because he has no opportunity
therefor. The hon. court orders defendant to satisfy
plaintiff's demand.

Roelof Swartwout, Plaintiff
vs. Juriaen Westphael, Defendant

Plaintiff demands of defendant an amount of 250 gldrs.
for fines /he had been/ condemned to pay in the year 1663,
owing to a decree issued on Aug. 4 of said year, and
whereas defendant asked leave to appeal, and did not avail
himself of it, therefore demands execution of the sentence
dated Oct. 9, 1663. Defendant answers not being obliged
to satisfy the above demand, because the promises given
him were not kept while mowing in the year 1663. Whereas
plaintiff was dilatory in his office, neglecting to
speedily execute the sentence of Oct. 9, 1663, at the
time, therefore parties are referred to two impartial good
men whom they may themselves choose, for the purpose (if
possible) of settling their differences, or else to again
address the court.

Roelof Swartwout, Plaintiff
vs. Aert Martensen Doorn, Defendant. Absent. Default.

Roelof Swartwout, Plaintiff
vs. Annetie Gerrets, Defendant. Absent. Default.

Roelof Swartwout, Plaintiff
vs. Pieter Hillebrants, Defendant

Plaintiff demands of defendant 18 sch. of wheat for
wages and delivered butter. Defendant answers that plaintiff assigned said claim to Nicolaes De Meyer. And
Nicolaes De Meyer, having been called on account of the
same, says he accepted it. Plaintiff further demands of
defendant security for the carting of four loads of wood,
for breaking four morgens of new land, and still five or
six prepared beams he has loaned defendant as per obligation on Nov. 5 last, and to satisfy the aforementioned demand in the middle of the month of May 1667, because defendant has disposed of his horses. Defendant admits the
above obligation. The hon. court refuses plaintiff the
above demand for security of defendant, because defendant's
time, as per the obligation, has not yet expired and no
security was stipulated in the same.

Lambert Huyberts, Plaintiff
vs. Ariaen Gerrets, Defendant

Plaintiff demands of defendant reparation of coulter
and share, amounting to five sch. of wheat, which share
and coulter he loaned defendant last year. Defendant answers that he, also, loaned other things to plaintiff, and
if plaintiff wants to be indemnified for share and coulter, he /defendant/ also wants to be indemnified by

plaintiff for objects loaned him. The hon. court decides
whereas parties mutually have loaned each other things,
therefore plaintiff must prove that defendant agreed to
have said share and coulter repaired, and that defendant
shall produce a bill against plaintiff for the things he
has loaned him /plaintiff/.

Nicolaes De Meyer, Plaintiff
vs. Cornelis Barents, Defendant

Plaintiff demands of defendant as per a letter of attorney by Cornelis Van Dyck, five beavers for physician's
fee and shaving, besides a sch. of wheat with the costs of
the same. Defendant admits the annual money for two
years, being two beavers and a sch. of wheat for tobacco,
but denies owing three beavers doctor's fee. The hon.
court decides that Cornelis Van Dyck shall prove that defendant promised him to pay the physician's fee, and orders defendant, as per his admission, to pay plaintiff two
beavers and a sch. of wheat.

Henderick Palingh, Plaintiff
vs. Tjerck Claesen De Wit, Defendant. Absent. Default.

Magdalena Dirricks, Plaintiff
vs. Pieter Hillebrants, Defendant

Plaintiff demands of defendant seven sch. of wheat
for two pairs of shoes and other /merchandise/. Defendant
admits the debt, and says not to be able to pay right away
and offers to pay as soon as possible. The hon. court
orders defendant to satisfy plaintiff's demand.

Magdalena Dirricks, Plaintiff
vs. Harmen Hey, Defendant. Absent. Default.

Warnaer Hoorenbeeck, Plaintiff
vs. Jan Jansen Van Oosterhout, Defendant

Plaintiff demands of defendant 13 sch. of wheat,
balance for a wagon. Defendant admits the debt, and
agrees to pay the 13 sch. of wheat in eight or ten days.
The hon. court orders defendant to satisfy plaintiff's
demand.

Joris Hael, Plaintiff
vs. Harmen Hey, Defendant. Absent. 3rd Default.

Plaintiff demands of defendant 23 gldrs. with costs.
Defendant is absent. The hon. court orders defendant to
satisfy plaintiff's demand with costs, because he shows
contempt by not appearing and has committed the third default.

Jacob Barents Cool, Plaintiff
vs. Evert Pels, Defendant

Plaintiff demands of defendant on account of his
brother 24 sch. of oats and 17 gldrs. in sewan, in payment
of wages earned by his brother. Defendant admits the
debt. The hon. court orders defendant to satisfy plaintiff's demand.

Nicolaes De Meyer requests judicial enforcement of
the sentence dated Nov. 17, 1666, against Roelof Swartwout,

and further requests that the effects mentioned in the
"schepen knowledge" of Nov. 25, 1665, may not be permitted
to be disposed of or alienated by Roelof Swartwout, because Roelof Swartwout threatened to be obliged to sell
some cows for victuals, and that the same was to be made
known by bills. Roelof Swartwout answers that he did not
threaten Nicolaes De Meyer to sell some of the mortgaged
cows, and does not permit said Meyer to affix bills
against him, and requests, because he has lost his effects in the troubles with the savages, and therefore is
powerless, that he may simply pay the interest according
to the aforesaid sentence, which plaintiff has requested
to have judicially enforced. The officer, by virtue of
Nicolaes De Meyer's request, is ordered to proceed with
the execution, and is further ordered to take care of the
mortgaged effects of Roelof Swartwout as per the past
"schepen knowledge."

Jannetie Francen requests judicial enforcement of the
sentence dated Nov. 17, 1666, against Cornelis Vernoy.
The officer is ordered to proceed with the execution.

Decree for the purpose of having confirmed the deeds
issued on the aforementioned date. (A Copy)

At the general court of Assizes held at New York on
Oct. 1 by authority of his Majesty, in the 18th year of
the reign of our Souvereign Lord Charles II by the Grace
of God King of England, Scotland, France and Ireland,
Protector of the Faith, etc., and in the year of our Lord
1666. This assembly, having taken cognizance of the fact
that both villages and private individuals are negligent
in turning in their charters and deeds for the purpose of
having the same confirmed, nor even come to fetch or request new ones, because the same are defective and void
in consequence of the order issued previously, and besides having taken into serious consideration that several
villages and persons in this government, English as well
as Dutch, have possession of their land and houses upon
condition that they are subjects of the States General of
the United Provinces, which is contrary to the oath and
duty to his majesty, Orders that all charters and deeds
issued prior to this shall be delivered up for the purpose
of being confirmed or renewed by authority of his royal
highness the duke of York, and those having, up to now, no
deed shall be furnished one about the first day of April
next, after which time neither village nor private individual whether English or Dutch shall be anymore permitted
to submit in court similar old charters, deeds or letters
of sale, but shall be considered and deemed as of no value.

Below was written, Thus enacted by the order of the
governor and court of Assizes.

Ordinary Session, Tuesday, December 14, 1666.

Present: Willem Beeckman, Schout; Evert Pels, Jan
Joosten, Thomas Chambers, Roelof Swartwout, Commissaries.
Willem Beeckman, Schout, Plaintiff
vs. Pieter Gillissen, Defendant
Plaintiff says that defendant about two years ago
misbehaved by wounding a savage and consequently demands
of defendant an amount of 63 gldrs. 10 st., being 28 gldrs.
as per sentence pronounced on Feb. 17, 1665, 18 gldrs. for
"eygenpandinge" in the case with Thomas Harmensen, 10
gldrs. for costs incurred in arresting defendant, six
gldrs. for breaking a lock, one gldr. 10 st. for a knife
and costs. Defendant answers that he assigned plaintiff
to Juriaen Westphael for the payment of 28 gldrs. as per
demand on Feb. 17, 1665, and denies plaintiff's further
demand. Plaintiff answers that he was not paid by Juriaen
Westphael, because he did not actually take it upon himself to pay, and whereas the payment was not made, therefore he, defendant, ought to pay. The hon. court decides
that defendant shall satisfy plaintiff in accordance with
the sentence dated Feb. 17, 1665, amounting to 28 gldrs.
as also the 18 gldrs. which plaintiff advanced as officer
in the case of Thomas Harmensen, and the one gldr. 10 st.
for the knife, and costs. The further demand for the 10
and six gldrs. is refused plaintiff.
Henderick Cornelissen, Farmer, Plaintiff
vs. Joris Hael and Henderick Palingh, Defendants
Plaintiff demands of defendants, on account of refusal to pay him what is due him for the small excise:
confiscation of the wines and fivefold fine for the same,
being for Joris Hael 2½ ankers of brandy, and for Henderick
Palingh seven ankers of brandy, and requests to be upheld.
Defendants answer having declared their wines to the tapsters excise, and maintain that they are not obliged to
pay to the burgher excise, because neither one of them is
citizen of this place. The hon. court decides, whereas
defendants have declared their wines to the tapster excise
and have neglected to also pay the burgher excise, therefore defendants are ordered to satisfy plaintiff for his
just claim for the burgher excise, according to the conditions of the farm, made with approbation of the hon.
Lord Gov. Genl. His further claim is refused to plaintiff.
Henderick Palingh, Plaintiff
vs. Evert Pels, Defendant
Plaintiff demands of defendant 100 gldrs. in sewan.
Defendant denies the debt, but says owing 72 gldrs. from
which are to be deducted six gldrs. for carting a load,
and requests bill of defendant for received wines. The
hon. court orders plaintiff to send in an account to defendant, and orders defendant to satisfy plaintiff for
the amount of the bill.

Henderick Palingh, Plaintiff
vs. Aert Martensen Doorn, Defendant. Absent. Default.
Lambert Huybertsen, Plaintiff
vs. Ariaen Gerretsen, Defendant

Plaintiff demands of defendant the amount of 86 gldrs., being 30 gldrs. for a share and coulter loaned him, and which he, defendant, was to have repaired, eight gldrs. for a hatchet bought of and paid for to defendant, but which /plaintiff/ did not receive, and 48 gldrs. for rent of two horses for eight days. Defendant answers that he is not obliged to have the coulter and share repaired for plaintiff on account of using them; in regard to the hatchet says, "there is the hatchet"; the 48 gldrs. rent for the horses defendant admits. The hon. court orders defendant, in consequence of his admission, to pay plaintiff the 48 gldrs. for rent of the horses; in regard to the coulter and share, plaintiff is ordered to prove that defendant agreed to pay the smith for the same, and in regard to the hatchet plaintiff shall prove that defendant has again sold the same to the wheelwright.

Harmen Hendericks, Plaintiff
vs. Joris Hael, Defendant. Absent. Default.
Mattheu Blanchan, Plaintiff
vs. Reyndert Pietersen, Defendant

Plaintiff says there is a dispute between him and defendant concerning 50 boards which plaintiff says had been settled for at a previous balancing of accounts, and whereas defendant denies said settlement, plaintiff requests that defendant shall swear to it, in accordance with the liquidation and settlement which took place on May 28, 1666. Defendant agrees to affirm under oath that plaintiff is indebted to him for the 50 boards, besides what plaintiff owes him as per the aforesaid settlement. In regard to the aforenamed affair, defendant took the proper oath.

Tomas Harmensen, Plaintiff
vs. Ariaen Gerretsen, Defendant

Plaintiff demands of defendant ten sch. of wheat as per assignment by Aeltje Sybrants, by virtue of a previous suit on Nov. 18, 1664. Defendant answers having received of Aeltje Sybrants value amounting to seven sch. of wheat and has a claim against her for 30 sch. of wheat, wages for carting stone and wood. The hon. court refuses plaintiff's demand and refers him to Aeltje Sybrants, for the purpose of enforcing his claim against her.

Arent Cornelissen Vogel, Plaintiff
vs. Ariaen Gerretsen, Defendant

Plaintiff demands of defendant a cow which defendant is keeping for him. Defendant answers that he bartered with plaintiff a heifer and a bull for the aforenamed cow upon condition that plaintiff shall give him 15 sch. of wheat besides, and that defendant shall keep exchanged

heifer four years more, for one half of the natural increase. Plaintiff replies, and denies absolutely that he
swapped, because defendant did not want to promise him
butter, and further says that defendant told him to deliver a holland breed of cattle, and that the heirer should
be three years old next May. The hon. court orders defendant to prove at the next session of the court that he
bartered the cow to plaintiff upon said conditions.

Jan Willemsen Hoochteylingh requests that nine gldrs.
in grain may be ordered to be deducted from his village
taxes, for wages at the parsonage. This request is granted
petitioner. He also requests by petition that those
living near his lands may be ordered to each assist him
in proportion in erecting his fences, and that he, petitioner, may be exempt from /assisting at/ the common
fence. The hon. court decides, if petitioner is successful in having his neighbors erect fences at each individual's land, he is permitted to have done the same.
As to being released from /assisting at/ the common fence,
the hon. court judges it necessary to yet keep the same in
repairs until the time that the land shall be differently
protected.

Ordinary Session, Tuesday, January 8/18, 1667.
    Present: Willem Beeckman, Schout; Evert Pels, Jan
Joosten, Thomas Chambers, Roelof Swartwout, Commissaries.
            Aert Otterspoor, Plaintiff, Absent
        vs. Henderick Albertsen, Defendant. Absent.
            Harmen Hendericks, Plaintiff
        vs. Joris Hael, Defendant. Absent. 2nd Default.
    Plaintiff demands of defendant eight sch. of wheat
for earned wages for chopping wood, with costs.
            Harmen Hendericks, Plaintiff
     vs. Pieter Hillebrants, Defendant. Absent. Default.
            Warnaer Hoorenbeeck, Plaintiff
     vs. Pieter Hillebrants, Defendant. Absent. Default.
            Joris Hael, Plaintiff
  vs. Aert Martensen Doorn, Defendant. Absent. Default.
            Joris Hael, Plaintiff
        vs. Leendert Barents, Defendant
    Plaintiff demands of defendant 17 gldrs. and costs.
Defendant admits the debt and says being unable to pay until he shall /himself/ have received payment. The hon.
court orders defendant to satisfy plaintiff's demand, with
costs.
            Joris Hael, Plaintiff
        vs. Ariaen Gerretsen, Defendant
    Plaintiff demands of defendant 23 gldrs. Defendant
answers that plaintiff has in his possession a pewter can
and a fayence can and a candle-stick and requests restitution of the same. Plaintiff replies, saying that about two
years ago he took said goods as security for an amount of

21 gldrs. and that the demand for 23 gldrs. is the balance
of last summer. The hon. court orders defendant to produce at the next session of the court an exact bill for
the foregoing.

                Arent Cornelissen Vogel, Plaintiff
vs. Pieter Hillebrants, Defendant. Absent. Default.
                Eechie Ariaens, Plaintiff
                vs. Barbara Jansen, Defendant
     Plaintiff demands of defendant the hire of her daugh-
ter, being a balance of 15 sch. of wheat, because defendant discharged her daughter before the time was up. Defendant denies having discharged her /plaintiff's/ daughter, and further says that her daughter remained away from
her house and service without reason or cause, and further
requests that her daughter shall serve the full time. The
hon. court orders plaintiff to produce witnesses in her
suit.

                Henderick Palingh, Plaintiff
vs. Aert Martensen Doorn, Defendant. Absent. 2nd Default.
     Plaintiff demands of defendant 15 gldrs.
                Pieter Gillissen, Plaintiff
                vs. Tjerck Claesen, Defendant. Absent. Default.
                Leendert Barents, Plaintiff
                vs. Evert Pels, Defendant
     Plaintiff demands of defendant 33 sch. of wheat, less
one gldr. Defendant denies this claim, and is willing to
compare accounts with plaintiff and to pay him this week.
The hon. court orders parties to mutually liquidate their
accounts and orders defendant to satisfy plaintiff for
what defendant may be found to owe plaintiff.

                Evert Prys, Plaintiff
                vs. Evert Pels, Defendant
     Plaintiff demands of defendant an amount of 115 gldrs.
blance as shown by account handed in. Defendant refers to
the account delivered by him to plaintiff, and on account
whereof plaintiff claims a balance of defendant of two
gldrs. 12½ st. which is shown by the account which was
produced by defendant, and defendant agrees to prove that
plaintiff, at harvest time, did not work more than 10½ days
and in the barn not more than 4½ days. Defendant also demands a copy of plaintiff's bill. Defendant is permitted
a copy of plaintiff's bill for the purpose of proving, as
he has agreed to do, the mistakes in plaintiff's account.

     Cornelis Barentsen Slecht requests judicial enforce-
ment against Juriaen Westphael for the amount of 23 sch.
of wheat, as per the minutes of Nov. 23, 1666. The officer is ordered to proceed with the execution.

     Albert Gerretsen requests payment from the bankrupt
estate of Aert Pietersen Tack, which has been sold by
judicial process.

     Henderick Cornelissen, Lyndraejer, requests a deed
of the barn of Aert Pietersen Tack, bought at the judicial

sale. For the purpose of liquidating said estate next Friday is designated in the presence of the commissaries Jan Joosten and Roelof Swartwout.

At the request of Albert Jansen, court messenger, he is permitted to charge for burying, announcing the death of, and officiating; for an adult four sch. of wheat when the great bier is used, and for the little bier three sch. of wheat, and for a child which is carried under the arm two sch. of wheat, or the value of the same. In regard to the second request of Albert Jansen, court messenger, he is allowed ¼ of the "stiver money" at all public sales, provided he assist the vendue-master in collecting the money, and in properly regulating the same /vendue/ at the place where it is held.

The letter of Domine Hermanus Blom having been read by the hon. court, the court is sorry to see that very little has been collected toward the salary of the writer, Domine Blom. On account of which the Heer Officer with some of the commissaries shall do their duty, visit the residents and sharply admonish them to pay in their share.

Ordinary Session, Tuesday, January 15/25, 1667.
Present: Willem Beeckman, Schout; Evert Pels, Jan Joosten, Thomas Chambers, Roelof Swartwout, Commissaries.
Thomas Chambers, Plaintiff
vs. Tjerck Claesen De Wit, Defendant
Plaintiff demands of defendant 16 sch. of wheat, originating from a balancing of accounts in the year 1664. Defendant says having a counter-claim, and requests time till the next session of the court. The hon. court grants defendant time for the purpose of producing his arguments against plaintiff at the next session.
Thomas Chambers, Plaintiff
vs. Aert Martensen Doorn, Defendant. Absent. Default.
Pieter Gillissen, Plaintiff
vs. Tjerck Claesen De Wit, Defendant
Plaintiff demands of defendant five sch. of wheat, balance of wages during the last harvest. Defendant answers that he paid plaintiff for his labor and also says that plaintiff earned half wages during harvest time, and that on account hereof he paid him four gldrs. a day, and maintains not to owe plaintiff any more, because plaintiff is not able to fully perform his work, or at least has not done so. And both parties admit that they did not make a contract in regard to the wages to be paid during harvest time. The hon. court orders plaintiff to prove at the next session that he was fully competent at harvest time to perform his work as well as others, and this having been proved, he shall be paid the same wages, earned by any other man or hand who satisfactorily serves at harvest.
Henderick Palingh, Plaintiff
vs. Christoffel Davids, Defendant. Absent. Default.

Henderick Palingh, Plaintiff
vs. Louwies Dubois, Defendant
Plaintiff demands of defendant the money for burgher
excise of 24 ankers which defendant retailed during plaintiff's tenure of the farm, being two gldrs. eight st. for
each anker. Defendant answers that he does not owe the
same because, when declaring the first anker declared by
him, plaintiff did not claim more than 14 gldrs. per
anker, and plaintiff having been questioned by defendant,
the former said that he did not need to pay him any more.
The hon. court decides, whereas in accordance with the
conditions of the farming, plaintiff is entitled to the
burgher as well as the tapster excise, therefore defendant
is ordered to satisfy plaintiff for his full claim of the
burgher excise, being 45 st. light money per anker.
Henderick Palingh, Plaintiff
vs. Aert Martensen Doorn, Defendant. Absent. 3rd Default.
Plaintiff demands of defendant 15 gldrs. light money
and costs. Defendant is absent. The hon. court, on account of defendant's contemptuous conduct in not appearing, sentences defendant to satisfy plaintiff's demand
with costs.
Henderick Palingh, Plaintiff
vs. Frederick Pietersen, Defendant. Absent. 3rd Default.
Eduard Wittiger and Evert Prys, Plaintiffs
vs. Jan Broersen, Defendant. Absent. Default.
Eechie Gerrets, Plaintiff
vs. Jan Willemsen Hoochteylingh, Defendant
Plaintiff produces the witnesses in the case between
her and defendant, being Jacob Van Elmendorp, young man,
and Magdalena Blanchan, young woman, who declare that they
were both present when plaintiff's daughter appeared before defendant's door, saying that her daughter first
knocked at the door for the purpose of being admitted in
the house, and that her mistress did not want to let
plaintiff's daughter enter the house, whereupon the girl
said, "Mistress, then I am going to my mother to sleep,"
and defendant's wife answered, "Go away, you must never
more return," and declare further that this took place in
the evening, after the beating of the drum. Cornelis
Hoogeboom, as witness, declares that plaintiff on the day
following, entered defendant's house, and heard that defendant's wife did no longer want plaintiff's daughter to
serve her, though plaintiff was willing to permit her
daughter to stay in her service. Plaintiff, having been
asked who hired her daughter, answers that defendant's
wife hired her daughter, but not defendant, which defendant does not deny, but says it was done with his knowledge.
Defendant further answers that plaintiff's daughter shall
serve out her time with him, and is then willing to pay
her wages. The hon. court decides whereas defendant's
wife was unwilling to admit plaintiff's daughter to the

house, but said that she should go to her mother and never
more return, as per declaration and testimony of Jacob
Elmendorp and Magdalena Blanchan and also through the
testimony of Cornelis Hoogeboom which testimony confirms
the declaration of the first witnesses that defendant's
wife said the following day when plaintiff had called at
defendant's house, that she would no longer have her
daughter in her service, therefore defendant is sentenced
to satisfy plaintiff's demand of January 8/18 last, being
15 sch. of wheat, because, according to defendant's admission, defendant's wife has hired plaintiff's daughter.

Warnaer Hoorenbeeck, Plaintiff
vs. Pieter Hillebrants, Defendant

Plaintiff demands of defendant 7½ sch. of wheat for
advance grain, and one sch. of wheat for wages, both owing
since the year 1663, and requests payment. Defendant answers there was only 6½ sch. of grain loaned to him, with
one sch. for wages, together 7½ sch. Plaintiff is satisfied with defendant's answer. The hon. court orders defendant to pay plaintiff 7½ sch. of wheat.

Arent Cornelissen Vogel, Plaintiff
vs. Pieter Hillebrants, Defendant

Arent Cornelissen, absent, his son, Cornelis Arents,
appears in his place, who demands of defendant 7 sch. of
wheat as per balance. Defendant admits the debt. The hon.
court orders defendant to satisfy plaintiff's claim.

Tomas Harmensen, Plaintiff
vs. Warnaer Hoorenbeeck, Defendant

Plaintiff demands of defendant 31 gldrs. light money
with costs. Defendant answers not to owe any more than 13
gldrs. Plaintiff answers that he attached on Arent Jansen,
Wheelwright, his claim of three sch. of wheat, for which
attachment defendant has become surety. Defendant answers
that he became security for as far as he should have received the three sch. of wheat of Aert Martensen Doorn on
account of Arent Jansen. The hon. court orders defendant,
as per admission, to satisfy plaintiff for the 13 gldrs.
with costs, and that defendant, as per his own confession,
shall be obliged to receive the three sch. of wheat of
Aert Martensen Doorn, and after having received them to
pay the same to plaintiff.

Andries Pietersen Van Leeuve, Plaintiff
vs. Annetje Gerrets, Defendant

Plaintiff demands of defendant the amount of 332
gldrs. in wheat for earned wages as per obligation. Defendant admits the debt, and says that, on account of a
bad harvest, it is impossible for him to pay. The hon.
court orders defendant to satisfy plaintiff's demand.

Femmetje Alberts, Plaintiff
vs. Juriaen Westphael, Defendant

Plaintiff demands of defendant per balance of account the amount of 294 gldrs. light money for earned

wages of her son, Jan Hendericks Westercamp. Defendant
answers having a counter claim, viz., that 12 sch. of
wheat are to be deducted from said account, which 12 sch.
he took it upon himself to pay to Niclaes De Meyer, as
also one month's hire of nine months' hire. The hon.
court sentences defendant to satisfy plaintiff's demand,
provided he may keep the 12 sch. of wheat till the arrival
of Nicolaes De Meyer, and that plaintiff shall prove that
her son has paid the one month's hire to defendant, which
defendant wants to deduct.

Evert Prys, Plaintiff
vs. Evert Pels, Defendant

Plaintiff demands of defendant satisfaction of the
judgment of January 8/18 when defendant obliged himself
to show the mistakes in plaintiff's days of labor. Also
demands costs. Defendant produces a specified account of
plaintiff's days of labor. Plaintiff, replying, is not
satisfied with defendant's special account, but demands
proof as per previous judgment. The hon. court orders defendant to adduce proof as per previous judgment at the
next session of the court, under penalty of sentence.

Harmen Hendericks, Plaintiff
vs. Joris Hael, Defendant

Plaintiff demands of defendant seven sch. of wheat for
seven months' wood chopping. Defendant answers not to owe
the debt, because with plaintiff he contracted for two
sch. of wheat, with Capt. Boodhead's knowledge, which he
has paid plaintiff. The hon. court decides whereas plaintiff contracted with defendant for two sch. of wheat,
therefore plaintiff is refused his demand, but out of sym-
pathy with plaintiff the hon. court will pay him 2½ sch.
of wheat out of its treasury.

Joris Hael, Plaintiff
vs. Aert Martensen Doorn, Defendant. Absent. 2nd Default.

Plaintiff demands of defendant 42 gldrs.

Joris Hael, Plaintiff
vs. Ariaen Gerretsen, Defendant. Absent.

Plaintiff shows as per previous judgment dated Jan.
8/18 last the account between him and defendant, and it
was found that per balance of account defendant owed him
in the year 1664 21 gldrs. which he has allowed to stand
against the claim for the cans, and further shows by a
specified account that for delivered merchandise since May
last defendant owes him 23 gldrs. which he demands by the
present of defendant with costs. Defendant is absent.
The hon. court orders defendant to satisfy plaintiff's demand for 23 gldrs. with costs.

Henderick Palingh requests by a petition that the
hon. court will allow and grant him in ownership the
sloping soil (afhangende grond) outside the palisades for
his share of repairing the curtains in this village of
Wildwyck, situated opposite his lot. This "afhangende

324

grond" perhaps means: "soil bordering upon."_7_
     Whereas Thomas Chambers, some years ago, has already
taken possession of a portion of the soil belonging to the
curtains, by erecting a brewhouse, opposite petitioner's
house, and the hon. court is neither authorised to grant
in ownership the further soil outside the curtains which
has not yet become private property, and therefore petitioner is referred to the Lord Dir. Genl. Ridsert Nicolls
at New York.
     Mattheus Capito, Secretary, requests by petition,
whereas the hon. court on Jan. 8/18 last has allowed the
court messenger one-quarter of the "stivers money" of all
vendues, which greatly diminishes petitioner's income, and
whereas petitioner's salary is small, and other sources of
income are also very scarce and few, therefore, he requests that from now on he may be permitted to demand and
receive for every written page three to one in sewan, viz.,
for the necessary copies from the minutes, and also for
copies from other writings, whereas before this he did not
receive more than 12 st. sewan for every copy from the
minutes. Petitioner is permitted from now on to charge
and receive 24 st. light money in place of 12 st. light
money for every page of writing.

Decree against desecrating the Sabbath.
     Whereas desecrating the Sabbath is greatly on the in-
crease among many, and mostly in this village notwithstanding the several stringent decrees issued by the Magistrates and the previous heavy punishments of wars, bad
harvests and other misfortunes to the inhabitants here
which the great God has sent us, and again threatens and
has threatened to visit us with, on account of the disobedience against His will and command not to desecrate the
Sabbath or Sunday, but ardently to observe the same, therefore Schout and schepenen of this village of Wildwyck,
hoping to be freed from, and to escape, the great coming
punishments of the great God, on account of the desecra-
tions of the Sabbath heretofore committed and yet to be
committed, order and command in the same of the Royal
Majesty of Great Britain, etc., most urgently everyone and
particularly the inhabitants of this village, that nobody
from the present shall be permitted on Sundays, great holy
days, and days of prayer, to drink to excess, to go out for
pleasure drives with wagons, sleighs or horses, nor to commit any other improprieties, on which account, also, the
public innkeepers are forbidden, on Sundays, high feast
days and days of prayer to serve drinks until sunsent, under penalty to those who shall be found drunk on Sundays,
high feast days and days of prayer, of 50 gldrs. fine. And
those driving for pleasure on said days, whether with
wagons, sleighs or horses, six gldrs. for every person;
and for the public innkeeper serving drinks on said days

25 gldrs., and for every customer six gldrs. And whereas
daily experience has also shown that many residents here
are sometimes not satisfied with remaining whole days in
the public inns, but even spend entire nights there, and
then upon leaving the public inns, behave most noisily and
boisterously in the streets, like mad people, for the purpose of preventing and removing said improprieties, the
aforesaid Schout and schepenen, in the aforenamed Majesty's
name order and command that no public innkeeper shall serve
drinks after 4:00 o'clock in the evening or after the beating of the drum, under penalty for the public innkeeper of
a fine of 12 gldrs. for every violation, and of six gldrs.
for every customer, and for those found behaving noisily
and boisterously on the streets at night, for every time
also six gldrs. Let every one look out for himself.
　　Thus enacted at the session of schout and schepenen
of the village of Wildwyck, this January 15/25, 1667.

Ordinary Session, Tuesday, January 29/February 8, 1667.
　　Present: Willem Beeckman, Schout; Evert Pels, Jan
Joosten, Thomas Chambers, Roelof Swartwout, Commissaries.
　　　　　　Thomas Chambers, Plaintiff
　　　　vs. Tjerck Claesen De Wit, Defendant
　　Plaintiff demands of defendant 16 sch. of wheat, as
per previous demand on January 15/25 last. Defendant produces a written answer and claims of plaintiff an amount
of 291 sch. of wheat, originating from four days' carting
/of grain or hay/ in the year 1663, being 16 sch. of wheat;
and for three mowers for four days which defendant supplied to plaintiff, besides his implements, in the aforesaid year, and therefore demands, the expenses being deducted, 275 sch. of wheat on account of loss of time of
said mowers, and says that he did not offer said claim at
the past settlement. Plaintiff, replying, denies the
counter claim of defendant, and further demands, as per
settlement made on Mar. 21, 1664, of defendant an amount
of 25 sch. of wheat, 4½ gldrs. in sewan, besides two sch.
of peas whereof defendant has paid four sch. of wheat and
eight sch. of barley, so that there is yet a balance of 16
sch. of wheat. Defendant answers, and requests that plaintiff shall affirm under oath that he did not hold back the
aforesaid claim for four days' carting and of three mowers
for the four days, when liquidating accounts. The hon.
court decides whereas it is plain from plaintiff's book
that on Mar. 21, 1664, he clearly settled accounts with defendant, in the presence of a witness, to the amount of 25
sch. of wheat and 4½ gldrs. in sewan, and thereupon yet
delivered to defendant two sch. of peas and defendant paid
therefore to plaintiff eight sch. of barley and four sch.
of wheat, therefore defendant is sentenced to satisfy
plaintiff for the balance, being 10 sch. of wheat. And in
regard to the claim against plaintiff which defendant kept

back, as he pretends, defendant is ordered to affirm the
same under oath, and then give further information concerning said affair.

Thomas Chambers, Plaintiff
vs. Aert Martensen Doorn, Defendant

Plaintiff demands of defendant the amount of 181 gldrs.
16 st. in beavers or in grain beavers' value, as per note
on Mar. 19, 1664. Defendant admits the debt, and on the
other hand demands of plaintiff in reduction of the aforenamed amount, for the use of his brewkettle and brewing
tubs for the time of two years, as per contract with every
brewer, as when plaintiff paid the brewer five gldrs. and
when another person brewed himself, the rent for the kettle
and brewing tubs half and half. Plaintiff answers against
defendant's counter claim that when putting up the brewkettle the wages for brewing were included in the contract,
viz., to be received half and half from outsiders, and that
defendant, besides plaintiff, shall also try to collect
the wages for brewing. And requests that defendant shall
pay him interest for the above amount since Mar. 19, 1664,
because the note has remained unpaid by defendant. Defendant does not admit the interest, because in the note
no interest was mentioned. The hon. court orders defendant
as per admission to satisfy plaintiff's demand for the note
and plaintiff's demand for interest is refused because no
interest was mentioned in the note. In regard to defendant's counter claim for the use of the brewkettle and brewing tubs, parties are ordered to each examine the same, and
to liquidate, and as far as is known to plaintiff to impart information in regard to the brewing done.

Evert Pels, Plaintiff
vs. Jacob Barents Cool, Defendant

Plaintiff demands of defendant 15 sch. of wheat for
Jan Verbeeck, by virtue of a power of attorney, and requests that the attachment levied at Albany by the court
messenger there on Jan Cornelissen Smith for the amount of
10 sch. of wheat, may be declared valid. Defendant admits
the debt, and says that about four years ago he paid on it
to Jacob Joosten four sch. of wheat as attorney for Jan
Verbeeck, to be paid to Jan Verbeeck, and further says that
he told Jan Cornelissen, before he went to Albany this
winter, that he would pay 10 sch. of wheat on his account
to Reyndert Pietersen, and promises to pay the balance as
soon as possible to Jan Verbeeck. Jan Cornelissen, having
been cited on this account, and having been asked whether
he agreed to pay 10 sch. of wheat to Reyndert Pietersen on
the account of Jacob Barents Cool, before he went to Albany, answers that he was not specially charged to pay
Reyndert Pietersen these 10 sch., but only that in a dis-
course he was told by Jacob Barents that he, Jacob Barents,
owed Reyndert Pietersen. The hon. court decides, whereas
at Jan Cornelissen's at Albany, 10 sch. of wheat have been

attached by Jan Verbeeck, and defendant admits the debt,
therefore said attachment is declared valid.

Mattheus Capito, Plaintiff
vs. Jan Jansen Van Amersfoort, Defendant. Absent. Default.

Thomas Harmensen, Plaintiff
vs. Jan Jansen Van Amersfoort, Defendant. Absent. Default.

Henderick Cornelissen, Plaintiff
vs. Ariaen Gerretsen, Defendant. Absent.

Plaintiff requests that the attachment at Matheus
Capito's for the amount of six sch. of wheat against defendant may be declared valid. The hon. court decides
that the attachment of the six sch. of wheat at Mattheus
Capito's is valid, because plaintiff has obtained a judgment against defendant.

Reyndert Pietersen, Plaintiff
vs. Jacob Barents Cool, Defendant

Plaintiff demands of defendant 25 sch. of wheat for
sold and delivered merchandise, and further says that Jan
Cornelissen was to deliver to him 10 sch. of wheat for
defendant. Defendant admits the debt. The hon. court orders defendant to satisfy plaintiff's demand, and whereas
plaintiff has been negligent in accepting the 10 sch. of
wheat of Jan Cornelissen, even before the attachment executed by Jan Verbeeck on the 10 sch. of wheat, therefore
plaintiff is refused his claim of assignment by Jan Cornelissen for the 10 sch. of wheat.

Jan Willemsen Hoochteylingh, Plaintiff
vs. Eechie Gerrets, Defendant

Plaintiff requests revisal of the previous sentence
of Jan. 15/25 last, and produces in writing the following
reasons: that plaintiff's daughter had received permission
of her mistress to go out with the young folks, but that
her daughter stayed out longer than the time allowed by
her mistress, and therefore maintains not to be liable for
defendant's previous claim. Defendant refers to the previous sentence, and further demands the costs for the same.
The hon. court, having examined plaintiff's writing, and
also the previous judgment on Jan. 15/25 last, judges in
accordance with the declarations that defendant's demand
is just, and the hon. court therefore adheres to this
judgment, and condemns plaintiff to satisfy defendant for
the previous demand and costs.

Warnaer Hoorenbeeck, Plaintiff
vs. Ariaen Gerretsen, Defendant. Absent.

Warnaer Hoorenbeeck demands payment by defendant of
the amount of 116 gldrs. on account of an assignment of
Aert Martensen Doorn, from the grain bought at the vendue
of Aert Martensen Doorn. The vendue master is instructed
to assist plaintiff in judicially enforcing the payment
thereof by defendant.

Joris Hael, Plaintiff
vs. Aert Martensen Doorn, Defendant. Absent. 3rd Default.

Plaintiff demands of defendant 42 gldrs. and costs.
Defendant is absent. The_hon. court sentences defendant,
owing to contempt by /not/ appearing to satisfy plaintiff's
demands, with costs.

Joris Hael, Plaintiff
vs. Antoni Crespel, Defendant

Plaintiff demands of defendant four gldrs. Defendant admits the debt. The hon. court orders defendant to
satisfy plaintiff's demand.

Femmetie Alberts, Plaintiff
vs. Juriaen Westphael, Defendant

Plaintiff produces, as per a previous sentence, a
declaration signed by Jacob Jansen Van Etten and Teunis
Jacobsen who declare having heard of Jan Hendericks, deceased, that he served with defendant nine or 10 days less
than his legal time. Defendant answers that declarers
could not very well take their oath in regard to the above
named declaration, and further says that nine or 10 days'
serving would matter very little, and complains of his
indigence, so that he cannot well satisfy plaintiff's previous demand. The hon. court refers to its previous sentence, provided plaintiff shall permit defendant to deduct
10 days' wages from the nine months' hire.

Henderick Jochemsen, Plaintiff
vs. Teunis Jacobs, Defendant

Plaintiff demands of defendant 120 gldrs. balance of
account originating from the lease of a horse for 10 days
each day six gldrs. and for five days' ploughing. Defendant answers that he used plaintiff's horse only three
days and agrees to prove the same, the other days were un-
fit for carting, on account of the rain. Concerning the
ploughing, he says not having ploughed as many days, and
neither having contracted for as much money. Plaintiff
answers that defendant by verbal contract was obliged to
plough as many days for him, as he has ploughed for defendant which defendant did not do, and therefore he demands payment for five days' ploughing, three sch. of wheat
for each day. The hon. court refers parties to two good
men, one of which each of the parties is permitted to
choose himself, for the purpose, if possible, to settle
their difference; if not, parties shall again have to address the court, with the report of the good men, chosen
by themselves, and clearer proof of accounts.

Marietje Simons, Plaintiff
vs. Jannetie Pels, Defendant

Plaintiff demands of defendant 17 gldrs. for wages.
Defendant answers and asks plaintiff how many days she
worked for her. Plaintiff answers that she does not actually remember the days, and has off and on worked for
her, and still demands the aforenamed amount of 17 gldrs.
Defendant thereupon says, if plaintiff can prove the days
of her labor, she is willing to satisfy her. The hon.

court orders plaintiff to show at the next session how
many days she worked for defendant, or else to affirm her
demand under oath.

Evert Prys, Plaintiff
vs. Evert Pels, Defendant

The accounts and documents of both parties having been
received, the hon. court has found that plaintiff has a
claim against defendant for work on the barn, six days,
36 gldrs.; for five days' threshing while he was in de
Koningh's employ, 18 gldrs. 15 st.; for five days' chopping wood, 15 gldrs.; for 11 days' threshing, 33 gldrs.;
for 11 days' harvesting, 66 gldrs., amounting to a total
of 168 gldrs. 15 st. Plaintiff is ordered to prove the
further claim for 1½ days' harvesting. Defendant's counter claim is as follows: for seven weeks' board at 10
gldrs. per week, 70 gldrs.; for two days' threshing, six
gldrs.; and still one week's board when plaintiff had hurt
his leg, 10 gldrs., amounting to a total of 86 gldrs. He,
defendant, having been asked whether he was ready to affirm his difference with plaintiff's account under oath,
answered, "No." Therefore, plaintiff has a balance in his
favor of 82 gldrs. 15 st., after having deducted from
plaintiff's amount of 168 gldrs. 15 st. defendant's claim
of 86 gldrs. And therefore defendant is ordered to pay
plaintiff the balance, being 82 gldrs. 15 st. and the costs.

Antoni Crespel requests that the judgment, dated
Dec. 16, 1664, against Jan Jansen Van Amersfoort, may be
judicially enforced. The hon. court orders the officer at
petitioner's request to proceed with the execution.

Albert Jansen Van Steenwyck and Harmen Hendericks request that they may be granted a written statement by the
hon. court of the little island situated on the farm of
the hon. Heer Petrus Stuyvesant, for the purpose of getting, in the spring, a deed for the same of the hon. Heer
Gov. Genl. Petitioners are ordered to prove that said parcel of land has been given and granted them as property by
the hon. Heer Petrus Stuyvesant.

Louwies Dubois complains in a petition to the hon.
court of the sentence in favor of Henderick Palingh, farmer, saying that according to the farmer's claim during his
period of farming he fully satisfied him, and he did not
then demand of him the burgher exicse. On account hereof
petitioner (because Farmer Palingh neglected to collect of
him the burgher excise during the period in which he had
the farm) maintains that he is not obliged to pay the
burgher excise. Petitioner is ordered to prove that the
farmer, Henderick Palingh, acquited him of the burgher excise or that he /petitioner/ has paid the same. And without that, the hon. court refers to its pronounced judgment.

The hon. Heer Willem Beeckman, Elder, and Jan Joosten,
deacon, both as members of the Consistory, notify the hon.
court that on Jan. 18/28, at the meeting of the Consistory,

Domine Hermanus Blom requested to be relieved on Mar. 5
next of his office as preacher, on which date one-half
year of this current year would have expired. The further
time during his stay here before his departure he was
willing to officiate as preacher out of charity, to which
it was answered that the same would be made known at the
next session /of the court?/. The hon. court refers Domine
Hermanus Blom, concerning this affair, to the hon. Heer
Gov. Genl. Ridsert Nicolls.

Decree against running at the ring, and the pulling of
roosters and geese:
    Whereas the rod of the great God is suspended over
our head, and is threatening us with further disasters of
war and other punishments on account of our misdeeds and
disobedience, and for the purpose of escaping the same we
are obliged to meet the great and good God with a contrite
heart, and to pray Him to avert the threatened heavy
punishments which are to follow, Schout and schepenen of
this village of Wildwyck for the purpose of observing the
same therefore earnestly prohibit, in the name of the Royal
Majesty of Great Britain, etc., each and everyone of the
residents of this village of Wildwyck, that from now on
nobody shall undertake (for the purpose of preventing
drunkeness and all other misdeeds originating from in-
toxication) to engage in running at the ring, drawing or
clubbing goose or rooster, or to do anything similar, under
penalty to those having been found to have acted contrary
to this, of a fine of 25 gldrs., but that everybody in
place of thus uselessly spending his time, had better
exercise his Christian religion with holy prayers and
decent conduct. Let everybody look out for himself. Thus
enacted at the session of the hon. Schout and Schepenen of
the village of Wildwyck, this Jan. 29/Feb. 8, Anno 1667.

Extraordinary Session, Monday, February 4/14, 1667.
    Present: Willem Beeckman, Schout; Evert Pels, Jan
Joosten, Thomas Chambers, Roelof Swartwout, Commissaries.
    The wife of Cornelis Barents Slecht and her daughter
express their grief and complain that their husband and
father has been assaulted and wounded in his house by
Capt. Broodhead, and also that said captain has arrested
him and taken him to the guard house. On account hereof
dissatisfaction has arisen among the burghers, and they
have armed themselves, and in regard to this the burghers
request the hon. court that Cornelis Barents Slecht shall
be liberated from his arrest. To this it is answered that
the hon. court is not authorized to proceed with violence
against the militia, and in the meantime Capt. Broodhead,
having been requested through the court messenger to appear at this meeting, the court messenger returned with
the message, If the commissaries wanted to speak to him,

they should come to him. And for the purpose of preventing more difficulties, because the militia as well as the
burghers are in arms, the hon. court resolved that two
commissaries should visit said captain, and for this purpose are chosen the commissary and captain of the burghers
Thomas Chambers and the commissary Evert Pels, in order to
acquaint the aforenamed captain with the request of the
burghers, that Cornelis Slecht, their sergeant, arrested
by him, may be again liberated from his arrest, for the
purpose of preventing further difficulties and disasters.
And in the case the aforenamed Cornelis Slecht, burgher
sergeant, has in any manner offended the said captain,
that he shall summon him as per the order of the hon. Lord
Gov. Genl. to appear on this account before the local
magistrate, for the purpose of then examining and correcting the differences. These aforementioned deputed commissaries repaired to the central guard house and having,
at the house of Joris Hael, acquainted capt. Broodhead with
the aforenamed request, /he/ answered that he would keep
said Cornelis Slecht as long as he liked, and in case the
burghers wanted to liberate the arrested man by force that
he would expect them. In regard to the above, it was resolved to pacify the burghers be force of reasoning, because the hon. court does not find itself authorized to
proceed with violence against the militia, and to command
everyone of them to go where his business obliges him to
go, for the purpose of preventing disasters and difficulties. The hon. court, having, in a body, met the burghers
where they were assembled under arms, acquainted them with
the above, and ordered them to keep quiet and not to undertake anything against the militia, and told them that
the hon. court, concerning the case of Cornelis Slecht,
would address the hon. Ld. Gov. Genl. /The burghers/ replied that capt. Broodhead and several other soldiers have
threatened today and more times to set fire to the village
which induces them to act on the defensive against the
militia, and requested authority for this of the hon.
court, which was absolutely refused and forbidden them by
the hon. court, for reasons as stated above.

Ordinary Session, Tuesday, February 12/22, 1667.
        Present: Willem Beeckman, Schout; Jan Joosten, Thomas
Chambers, Roelof Swartwout, Commissaries.
                Willem Beeckman, Plaintiff
vs. Henderick Jochemsen, Juriaen Westphael, Claes Claesen,
        Defendants. Absent. Default.
    Cornelis Slecht and Aert Martensen Doorn, Plaintiffs
        vs. Evert Pels, Defendant. Absent. Default.
    Plaintiffs request to be relieved from the security
for defendant, for the principal and interest of the children of Mattys Jansen, deceased.
        Roelof Swartwout and Cornelis Barentsen Slecht,

332

guardians of the minor children of Mattys Jansen,
deceased, Plaintiffs,
vs. Evert Pels, Defendant. Absent. Default.
Plaintiffs demand of defendant, though absent, payment as per "schepen knowledge" of the amount of 1,537
gldrs. 12 st. in beavers, or in case of default, immediate
judicial enforcement with costs.

Jan Tyssen, son of Mattys Jansen, deceased, also requests that Evert Pels' debt may be paid, in the same manner as the aforenamed guardians have demanded the same.
For reasons, defendant has been cited by the court messenger to appear, and to defend his cause. He answers that
he knows the affair very well, as well in regard to the
sureties, as to the guardians, and that, on this account,
he is awaiting the judgment of the hon. court, and will
submit to the same. The hon. court orders defendant to
satisfy plaintiffs' demand with costs, because as per the
court messenger's report, defendant has admitted to have
nothing to say against it in defense, and plaintiffs are
permitted, in case of nonimmediate payment, to judicially
proceed against defendant.

Henderick Cornelissen, Farmer, Plaintiff
vs. Ridsert Cage, Defendant. Absent. Default.
Plaintiff requests to be upheld in his farm, because
defendant Ridsert Cage has refused to declare his beers for
the burgher excise, and on this account plaintiff has even
requested the officer, in the presence of Jan Joosten,
commissary, to confiscate said Cage's beers, and maintains
that said beers have been smuggled.

Grietje Hendericks, Plaintiff
vs. Eldert Gerbertsen, Defendant
Plaintiff demands of defendant 97 gldrs. heavy money
in grain, the sch. of wheat at three gldrs., for earned
wages by her former husband Jan Arents, deceased, on which
have been paid, as per account sent in, four sch. of maize.
Defendant answers not to have anything against the account
but says that upon his order by his farmhand who was at the
time living at Catskil, some ironwork was /caused to be/
made, and therefore does not know how much by said farm-
hard was paid on this bill, and he will, in regard to this,
make inquiries of his late hand, and is willing to pay
what, upon inquiry, he shall find has not been paid. Plaintiff answers that she has given defendant time till May
next for the purpose of enquiring concerning the same of
his late*farmhand, provided defendant shall give her security for what is coming to her. Defendant answers being
willing to give plaintiff security for what is coming to
her. The hon. court orders defendant, as per agreement,
to give security to plaintiff for what is coming to her.

Thomas Harmensen, Plaintiff
vs. Jan Jansen Van Amersfoort, Defendant. Absent. 2nd
Default.

Plaintiff demands of defendant 1) 3 sch. of wheat, and
further for an obligation for laying a ceiling with the
materials, 59 gldrs. in sewan.

Joris Hael, Plaintiff
vs. Jan Jansen Van Amersfoort, Defendant. Absent. Default.

Joris Hael, Plaintiff
vs. Jacob Jansen Van Etten, Defendant

Plaintiff demands of defendant three sch. of wheat
for received goods. Defendant admits the debt. The hon.
court orders defendant to satisfy plaintiff's demand.

Joris Hael, Plaintiff
vs. Pieter Hillebrants, Defendant. Absent. Default.

Joris Hael, Plaintiff
vs. Pieter Gillissen, Defendant

Plaintiff demands of defendant 50 gldrs. for received
goods. Defendant admits the debt. The hon. court orders
defendant to satisfy plaintiff's demand.

Jacob Jansen Van Etten, Plaintiff
vs. Juriaen Westphael, Defendant. Absent. Default.

Henderick Palingh, Plaintiff
vs. Jan Jansen Van Amersfoort, Defendant. Absent. Default.

Henderick Palingh, Plaintiff
vs. Christoffel Davids, Defendant. Absent. Default.

Evert Prys produces two declarations against Evert
Pels by virtue of the order of the hon. court on Jan. 29/
Feb. 8 last, whereby he proves having cut oats for Evert
Pels in the year 1666 during 1½ day, and Evert Pels is
consequently ordered to pay plaintiff for 1½ day harvest-
ing, being nine gldrs.

Evert Prys requests that the judgment dated Jan. 29/
Feb. 8 last as also his foregoing proof of the 1½ day's
wages during harvest time against Evert Pels shall be judicially enforced. The officer is ordered to proceed with
the execution.

Paul Paulusen, Plaintiff
vs. Evert Prys, Defendant

Plaintiff demands of defendant two sch. of wheat,
which he has advanced for defendant. Defendant denies the
debt. Plaintiff answers that he is ready to prove the
same. The hon. court orders plaintiff at the next session of the court to produce proof in his case.

Joris Hael requests that the judgment of Jan. 15/25
last, against Ariaen Gerretsen, may be judicially enforced.
The officer is ordered to proceed with the execution.

Femmetie Alberts requests that the judgment, dated
Jan. 15/25 last, against Juriaen Westphael may be judicially enforced. The officer is ordered to proceed with the
execution.

Lambert Huybertsen requests that the judgment dated
Dec. 14, 1666, against Ariaen Gerretsen may be judicially
enforced. The officer is ordered to proceed with the
execution.

Eechie Gerrets requests that the judgment dated Jan.
29/Feb. 8 last, against Jan Willemsen Hoochteylingh, may
be judicially enforced. The officer is ordered to proceed
with the execution.

Paulus Cornelissen requests payment for carting materials for the parsonage. The hon. court will find out
who still owes anything for building the parsonage and
will then assign petitioner so that he may receive his
money.

Harmen Hendericks requests that the attachments levied
against Ridgert Cage for the amount of eight gldrs. with
Roelof Swartwout and for the amount of 12 gldrs. with Jan
Cornelissen may be declared valid. The hon. court consents
to bring the business concerning these attachments before
capt. Broodhead.

Harmen Hendericks produces, in regard to his request
to take possession of, and to obtain a deed for, the little
island situated on the farm of the hon. Heer Petrus Stuyvesant under the fort from the hon. Heer Gov. Genl. two
witnesses, viz., Juriaen Westphael and Henderick Cornelissen, who declare that the hon. Heer Petrus Stuyvesant has
granted said little island to Harmen Hendericksen. Petitioner is ordered to prove that the hon. Heer Petrus
Stuyvesant granted him the exclusive right of possession
to said little island.

Ordinary Session, Tuesday, Feb. 19/Mar. 1, 1667.
Present: Willem Beeckman, Schout; Evert Pels, Jan
Joosten, Thomas Chambers, Roelof Swartwout, Commissaries.
Willem Beeckman, Plaintiff
vs. Henderick Jochemsen, Defendant
Plaintiff demands of defendant 87 gldrs. eight st.
balance of account sent to him, as well for the purchase
of a mare from the vendue at Aert Tack's as for other items
with costs. Defendant answers not to have anything against
the sale of the horse and further says that he kept back
a mudde of wheat for the rent of the barn of Aert Martensen Doorn, against the other account. Plaintiff replies
that he does not owe any rent for the barn, because he was
permitted by Aert Doorn to stable his cattle in a part of
the barn, and even used said part of the barn before Aert
Doorn leased the barn to defendant. The hon. court, having
heard parties, decides that defendant shall satisfy plaintiff's above demand with costs, on account of which he is
thus ordered. And in case Aert Doorn leased defendant the
barn under condition that he might demand rent of plaintiff for stabling his cattle, the hon. court then decides
that defendant will have to claim the same from Aert Martensen Doorn, but not from plaintiff.
Willem Beeckman, Plaintiff
vs. Frederick Pietersen, Defendant. Absent. Default.
Willem Beeckman, Plaintiff
vs. Claes Claesen, Defendant. Absent. 2nd Default.

Jan Willemsen Hoochteylingh, Plaintiff
vs. Eechie Gerrets, Defendant

Plaintiff demands from defendant two sch. of wheat
for which about three years ago she received goods, further
two sch. of wheat which defendant demands as hire for her
daughter in excess of what she contracted for. Defendant,
speaking improperly in the presence of the court, will not
be heard, until she shall have paid to the hon. court the
fine of one pound Flemish.

Jan Willemsen Hoochteylingh, Plaintiff
vs. Evert Prys, Defendant

Plaintiff demands of defendant three sch. of wheat
for delivered goods, and two sch. of buckwheat he loaned
him for sowing, with costs. Defendant admits the debt.
The hon. court orders defendant to satisfy plaintiff's demand with costs.

Evert Prys, Plaintiff
vs. Jan Willemsen Hoochteylingh, Defendant

Plaintiff demands of defendant 20 sch. of buckwheat
on account of damage sustained in his buckwheat in the
year 1665 which has been thus appraised by two impartial
men. The defendant refers to the judgment pronounced on
Nov. 3, 1665, in regard to the same case against Ariaen
Gerretsen, he having the buckwheat in partnership with
plaintiff and said Ariaen Gerretsen. Plaintiff answers
that defendant shall prove that more other horses than defendant's have been in said buckwheat. Defendant answers
that his partner at the time of the aforesaid sentence
ought to have been sued, would then also have provided
proof. The hon. court refers to the judgment pronounced
on Nov. 3, 1665.

Tjerck Claesen, Plaintiff
vs. Thomas Chambers, Defendant

Plaintiff produces a declaration signed by Pieter
Hillebrants that he besides two other mowers, besides yet
a binder, in regard to his kept open action in the year
1663 by defendant, with plaintiff's implements have mowed
four days. Defendant adheres to his denial at the previous
suit on Jan. 29/Feb. 8, 1667, that he admitted to plaintiff
the claim for plaintiff's right which he did not submit,
and in regard to the same demands that plaintiff shall affirm the same under oath, and then he will reply to the former demand. The hon. court persists in its previous judgment on Jan. 29/Feb. 8, 1667. And in regard to his declaration by plaintiff, Tjerck Claesen, that at the settlement
between him and defendant he did not submit a certain claim
or pretence, plaintiff has made his proper oath. Plaintiff
having made the proper oath, further demands of defendant,
as per a written claim, the amount of 291 sch. of wheat,
being 16 sch. of wheat for driving four days in the year
1663, and 275 sch. of wheat for the loss of the services
of three mowers during four days in the same year. Defendant denies the entire above claim, saying not to owe

the same, saying further that plaintiff did not loan him
mowers. Parties arguing concerning this case make known
that it had been agreed that each one should have his turn
in proportion of the land, in having and using the mowers,
binders and "hockers," during said harvest time, the one
after the other. The hon. court orders plaintiff to adduce
clearer and more evidence in writing concerning this affair against defendant and (the same having been shown to
and seen by the hon. court) they shall in writing communicate with each other and sue in legal form.

Joris Hael, Plaintiff
vs. Jan Jansen Van Amersfoort, Defendant. Absent. Second
Default

Joris Hael, Plaintiff
vs. Pieter Hillebrant, Defendant

Plaintiff demands of defendant 31 gldrs. and costs.
Defendant admits the debt. The hon. court orders defendant to satisfy plaintiff's demand with costs.

Henderick Jochemsen, Plaintiff
vs. Evert Prys, Defendant

Plaintiff demands of defendant 16 gldrs. 10 st.
balance of account in the year 1663, Feb. 12, in the presence of good men. Defendant denies the debt. The hon.
court orders plaintiff to show evidence of the verdict of
the good men.

Thomas Harmensen, Plaintiff
vs. Jan Jansen Van Amersfoort, Defendant. Absent. 3rd
Default

Plaintiff demands of defendant 1) three sch. of
wheat, 2) for being obliged to make the ceiling, with the
materials 59 gldrs. in sewan, and for two years' damage
sustained by plaintiff on account of negligence in making
the ceiling at the lease and which were deducted from his
rent, every year four sch. of wheat, with costs. Defendant is absent. The hon. court orders defendant, owing to
his contempt by not appearing, to satisfy plaintiff's a-
forenamed demand, with costs.

Thomas Harmensen, Plaintiff
vs. Jan Cornelissen, Defendant. Absent. Default.

Thomas Harmensen, Plaintiff
vs. Claes Claesen, Defendant. Absent. Default.

Thomas Harmensen, Plaintiff
vs. Severyn Tenhout, Defendant. Absent. Default.

Henderick Palingh, Plaintiff
vs. Christoffel Davids, Defendant

Plaintiff demands of defendant the amount of 330
gldrs. for received goods. Defendant demands an account
of plaintiff, debit as well as credit, and is willing to
pay what he owes by a proper account. The hon. court orders plaintiff to render a proper account to defendant at
the next session of the court.

Roelof Swartwout and Cornelis Barents Slecht, guardians of the minor children of Mattys Jansen, deceased, re-

337

quest approval by the hon. court in regard to the purchase
of Evert Pels' farm on Feb. 15/25, 1667, bought by them in
the presence of Thomas Chambers, stepfather, and Margarita
Hendericks, mother of said minor children. The hon. schout
Willem Beeckman advises that said guardians shall show that
said purchase is to the advantage of the minors, because
the children last year and also at the last session petitioned to collect the money of Evert Pels for the purpose of exploiting and tilling of the uncultivated lands.
Jan Joosten, commissary, also advises the preceding.
Evert Pels, commissary, as seller of the farm, cannot give
advice concerning the same. Thomas Chambers, commissary,
as stepfather of the minors, cannot give advice in the
case.
      Cornelis Barents Slecht complains that Daniel Brood-
head on Feb. 4/14 last has maltreated, beaten and hacked
him in his house and without cause arrested him, and also
took his sword away from his house, requests to be sustained in his burgher rights and restitution of his sword.
The hon. court in regard to this will request capt. Broodhead to return the sword and further, at the earliest opportunity, communicate the whole affair to the hon. Lord
Gov. Genl. Ridsert Nicolls, and make him acquainted with
the same.

Ordinary Session, Tuesday, February 26/March 8, 1667.
      Present: Willem Beeckman, Schout; Evert Pels, Jan
Joosten, Thomas Chambers, Roelof Swartwout, Commissaries.
                  Willem Beeckman, Plaintiff
vs. Frederick Pietersen, Defendant. Absent. 2nd Default.
                  Willem Beeckman, Plaintiff
  vs. Claes Claesen, Defendant. Absent. 3rd Default.
      Plaintiff demands of defendant 21 gldrs. 16 st.
balance of account, with costs. Defendant is absent.
The hon. court orders defendant, owing to his contempt in
not appearing, to satisfy plaintiff's demand with costs.
                  Henderick Palingh, Plaintiff
  vs. Cornelis Hoogeboom, Defendant. Absent. Default.
                  Joris Hael, Plaintiff
      vs. Jan Jansen Van Amersfoort, Defendant
Plaintiff demands of defendant 15 gldrs. with costs.
Defendant admits the debt. The hon. court orders defendant to satisfy plaintiff's demand with costs.
                  Reyndert Pietersen, Plaintiff
            vs. Jan Gerretsen, Defendant
Plaintiff demands of defendant 101 gldrs. for received
goods, as per obligation. Defendant admits the debt. The
hon. court orders defendant to satisfy plaintiff's demand.
                  Reyndert Pietersen, Plaintiff
            vs. Evert Pels, Defendant
Plaintiff demands of defendant the amount of 145 gldrs.
in beavers, as per balance. Defendant answers having a
bill against this, and says the above settlement can be

paid in sewan, and further that he paid five beavers and
30 planks on said bill. The hon. court refers parties to
two good men and impartial, viz., to Henderick Jochemsen
and Willem Montagnie, for the purpose, if possible, to
settle the differences between parties, and, if not, parties shall again address the court at the next session
with the report of the good men.

Reyndert Pietersen, Plaintiff
vs. Jan Jansen Van Amersfoort, Defendant

Plaintiff demands of defendant 25 sch. of wheat for
delivered goods, as per obligation, with the interest of
the same being 10 percent annually. Defendant admits the
debt. The hon. court orders defendant to satisfy plaintiff's demand with the interest as per obligation.

Henderick Jochemsen, Plaintiff
vs. Juriaen Westphael, Defendant

Plaintiff, attorney for Geertruyd Pietersen Vossenborch, demands of defendant 16 sch. of wheat, balance as
surety for Jan Van Bremen. Defendant admits the debt and
says that he took it upon himself to pay Geertruyd Vossenborch for Jan Dirrickson Van Bremen 29 sch. of wheat whereof he paid 13 sch. of wheat, and that Jan Dirricksen Van
Bremen left with him as security for the same an old mare
for the purpose of using the same till Geertruyd Vossenborch shall have been fully paid, and shows, besides, Jan
Van Bremen's note. The hon. court orders defendant, as
per admission, to satisfy plaintiff's demand, provided
defendant is permitted to hold on to the old mare, or to
sue Jan Dirricksen Van Bremen himself.

Evert Pels, Plaintiff
vs. Juriaen Westphael, Defendant

Plaintiff as attorney for Jan Dirricksen Van Bremen,
demands of defendant the amount of 150 gldrs., as per obligation, for one-half share of a young mare. Defendant
produces in regard to this Jan Dirricksen Van Bremen's obligation to Geertruyd Pietersen Vossenborch amounting to
29 sch. of winter wheat shown in the signed security of
the old mare of Jan Dirricksen Van Bremen which paper he
says has been mislaid at the time of the sharing of the
young mare. Defendant further shows a bill against Jan
Dirricksen for food and drink for himself and daughter for
an entire winter, a balance of four sch. of wheat, and for
stabling during the winter of a colt 10 sch. of wheat, on
which he has received three casks of tar, and in consequence
demands the balance of plaintiff. The hon. court orders
plaintiff to communicate defendant's answer and counter-
claim as soon as possible to his employer /or client/ and
is permitted to take copy of defendant's written answer,
and thereupon further action will be taken in regard to the
case of parties.

Evert Pels, Plaintiff
vs. Aert Martensen Doorn, Defendant. Absent. Default.

Tomas Harmensen, Plaintiff
vs. Claes Claesen, Defendant. Absent. 2nd Default.
Tomas Harmensen, Plaintiff
vs. Severyn Tenhout, Defendant
Plaintiff demands of defendant three sch. of wheat.
Defendant admits the debt. The hon. court orders defendant to satisfy plaintiff's demand.
Tomas Harmensen, Plaintiff
vs. Henderick Albertsen, Defendant
Plaintiff demands of defendant 27 gldrs. 12 st. Defendant admits the debt, and says that he told plaintiff
to come and receive his payment. The hon. court orders
defendant to satisfy plaintiff's demand.
Evert Pels and Henderick Jochemsen, Plaintiffs
vs. Tjerck Claesen, Defendant
Plaintiffs demand of defendant 50 sch. of oats as per
a note by Swerus Teunissen, on account of the estate of
Jan Albertsen Van Steenwyck, with the costs. Defendant
admits the debt and says that in the spring he will pay to
Henderick DeBacker upon his arrival. Plaintiffs further
demand that defendant shall make out to them a note for
the money with him, in regard to the separation and division of /the estate/ of Jan Albertsen, deceased. The
defendant consents to passing an obligation, provided the
same shall be deposited with the hon. court. The hon.
court orders defendant to satisfy plaintiffs' demand with
costs.
Evert Pels and Henderick Jochemsen, Plaintiffs
vs. Roelof Swartwout, Defendant
Plaintiffs demand of defendant the amount of 107 gldrs.
4 st. in sewan, and the interest, as per obligation, in regard to the estate of Jan Albertsen Van Steenwyck, deceased, and costs. Defendant admits the debt. The hon.
court orders defendant to satisfy plaintiffs' demand with
costs.
Tjerck Claesen requests, because the hon. court, last
session, ordered him to produce more proof in the case between him and Thomas Chambers, that he may be granted time
until navigation is open for the purpose of then procuring
proof from the persons at present living at the Manhatans.
Petitioner is granted his request by the hon. court.
Tjerck Claesen requests whereas he is suffereing
great damage to his own land on account of the fenceless
condition of Marten the mason's land, that said land of
Marten the mason may be appropriated for the purpose of
fencing the same, and also to receive his money. The hon.
court will first examine how _____/a break/____.
Thomas Chambers requests that the 16 sch. of wheat for
pronounced sentence dated Jan. 29/Feb. 8, 1667, in his
favor against Tjerck Claesen may be delivered. Petitioner's
request is granted.

Jan Gerretsen, Plaintiff
vs. Juriaen Westphael, Defendant

Plaintiff demands of defendant 25 sch. of wheat and
one sch. of oats for wages, with costs. Defendant admits
the debt. The hon. court orders defendant to satisfy plaintiff's demand with costs.

Cornelis Hoogeboom, Plaintiff
vs. Juriaen Westphael, Defendant

Plaintiff demands of defendant 17 sch. of wheat,
whereof he paid four sch. of oats. Defendant admits the
debt. The hon. court orders defendant to satisfy plaintiff's demand.

Willem Montagnie, Plaintiff
vs. Aert Martensen Doorn, Defendant. Absent. Default.

Willem Montagnie, Plaintiff
vs. Harmen Hey, Defendant. Absent. Default.

Jan Willemsen Hoochteylingh produces a declaration
signed by Cornelis Slecht and Juriaen Westphael containing
that Ariaen Gerretsen, in the year 1665, plowed too much
of his hired land, which the court, on Nov. 3, 1665, had
ordered him to prove. Whereas the aforenamed attestors,
in their deposition, declare to know the boundary line between the land of Jeronimus Ebbingh and of the hon. Heer
Stuyvesant, therefore said attestors are ordered by the
hon. court to show the boundaries of said lands, and also
to make an estimate of Jeronimus Ebbingh's land plowed up
by Ariaen Gerretsen.

Thomas Harmensen requests that the judgment pronounced
on Feb. 24/Mar. 1, 1663, against Jan Jansen Van Amersfoort
shall be judicially enforced. The hon. court orders the
officer to proceed with the execution.

Henderick Palingh, Plaintiff
vs. Christoffel Davids, Defendant

The accounts between Henderick Palingh, plaintiff,
and Christoffel Davids, defendant, having been received by
the hon. court, it was found, after both had been examined,
that Christoffel Davids still owes Henderick Palingh an
amount of 109 gldrs. six st. in sewan (the difference of
60 gldrs. which Christoffel Davids mentioned in regard to
Evert Prys, was declared by Henderick Palingh with a formal oath, to have been before settled and paid) and therefore defendant Christoffel Davids is ordered to pay plaintiff Henderick Palingh the above amount of 109 gldrs. six
st. in sewan.

Thomas Chambers requests that the judgment dated
Jan. 29/Feb. 8, 1667, against Aert Martensen Doorn shall be
judicially enforced. The hon. court orders the officer to
proceed with the execution.

Whereas on Feb. 16/26 ult. Henderick Cornelissen,
Lyndraejer, has been wounded in the abdomen by Willem
Visscher, soldier, and on Feb. 21/Mar. 3 next died of this
wound, and deceased, leaving neither friends nor last will,

therefore Mattheus Capito, having been in copartnership
with deceased, requests the hon. court to appoint curators
for the estate left by the deceased. In compliance with
the above request Roelof Swartwout and Willem La Montagnie
are requested by the hon. court, and authorized /to act
as/ curators of the estate left by the deceased Henderick
Cornelissen, Lyndraejer

Ordinary Session, Tuesday, March 12/22, 1667.
    Present: Willem Beeckman, Schout; Evert Pels, Jan
Joosten, Thomas Chambers, Roelof Swartwout, Commissaries.
            Willem Beeckman, Plaintiff
        vs. Frederick Pietersen, Defendant
    Plaintiff demands of defendant a sum of 145 sch. of
oats for the sale of a suit of clothes and an uppershirt.
Defendant admits the debt, and requests time until the return of Rynier Vander Coche from the Manhattans who will
satisfy plaintiff for the amount claimed. The hon. court
orders defendant to satisfy plaintiff's demand, as per
his admission, unless plaintiff be willing to grant defendant the time requested.
            Willem Beeckman, Schout, Plaintiff
        vs. Henderick Palingh, Defendant
    Plaintiff demands of defendant, as per balance, 330
gldrs. 14 st. light money for farm by order of the hon.
Heer Gov. Genl. and further for excise on 7 ankers of rum,
98 gldrs. light money. Defendant objects to the demand
for 330 gldrs. 14 st. and requests to be upheld in his
rights as farmer, saying that captain Broodhead has received 12 half barrels of good beer, on which said Broodhead has been unwilling to pay the excise, and therefore
demands said excise plus the fine for the same, in accordance with the excise law. And in regard to the demand
for 98 gldrs., he says that he is not obliged to pay
plaintiff, as collector of the excise, the 98 gldrs., and
if anybody, in his quality of farmer, comes to him and
demands said amount of him, he will pay it, unless the
hon. Heer Gov. Genl. should order him to pay the same to
plaintiff.
            Reynier Pietersen, Plaintiff
        vs. Evert Pels, Defendant
    Plaintiff demands of defendant the same as by a previ-
ous demand, the amount of 145 gldrs. in beavers, as per
settlement and note on July 18, 1659. Defendant gives in
a counter-claim, amounting to 95 gldrs. in beavers and 55
gldrs. 16 st. in sewan. Plaintiff replies and denies the
entire counter-claim, except seven English shillings for
14 gldrs. in sewan, and the 18 lbs. of pork at nine gldrs.
16 st. in sewan, and requests that defendant shall prove
the rest of his counter-claim, or affirm the same under
oath. Defendant, having been asked whether after the
balancing of accounts, he has delivered such goods to

plaintiff and for the amounts as drawn out in the counter
bill, and whether he is willing to enforce said counter
claim under oath, says, "Yes," and consequently took the
required oath. The hon. court orders defendant to pay
plaintiff the balance of his counter claim, being 31 gldrs.
8 st., with costs.

Jan Willemsen Hoochteylingh, Plaintiff
vs. Claes Claesen, Defendant

Plaintiff demands of defendant two sch. of wheat and
two sch. of oats. Defendant admits the debt. The hon.
court orders defendant to satisfy plaintiff's demand.

Henderick Jochemsen, Plaintiff
vs. Aert Martensen Doorn, Defendant

Plaintiff demands of defendant four sch. of wheat on
account of inconvenience in the rented barn by Mr. Willem
Beeckman for stabling his cattle. Defendant denies the
debt. The hon. court orders plaintiff to prove his claim
at the next session.

Evert Pels, attorney for Jan Dirricksen Van Bremen,
Plaintiff
vs. Aert Martensen Doorn, Defendant

Plaintiff demands of defendant a sum of 100 gldrs. in
sewan, as per note, and costs. Defendant admits the debt.
The hon. court orders defendant to satisfy plaintiff's demand, with costs.

Dirrick Jansen Schepmoes, Plaintiff
vs. Jan Joosten, Defendant

Plaintiff says that about 2½ years ago, while
wrestling, defendant's son broke plaintiff's leg, and requests that defendant shall pay the doctor's bill for the
same, being according to the claim of Willem Montagnie,
guardian for the minor children of Gysbert Van Imbrock,
deceased, six sch. of wheat. Defendant answers if plaintiff had right away acquainted him with the same, he might
then have given him into the doctor's care on as advan-
tageous terms as possible. The hon. court decides, whereas plaintiff broke his leg by wrestling, therefore he is
denied his demand.

Jan Lootman, Plaintiff
vs. Pieter Hillebrants, Defendant

Defendant demands of plaintiff 25 sch. of wheat and
one sch. of white peas, for wages, and costs. Plaintiff
admits the debt. The hon. court orders defendant to satisfy plaintiff's demand, with costs.

Roelof Swartwout and Cornelis Slecht, guardians of
the minor children of Mattys Jansen, deceased, Plaintiffs
vs. Thomas Chambers, Defendant

Plaintiffs demand of defendant first an amount of
1,093 gldrs. 3 st. in wheat, the schepel at 50 st., as per
bill sent to his house, originating from back rent and
borrowed money, and interest of the same, because, before
this, they made out some assignments on defendant, and de-

fendant returned the same. Defendant denies, and says not
to owe anything except 50 gldrs., which he borrowed for
received goods, because he has paid out to the children
their paternal inheritance, and he, as father, is entitled
to receive the interests of the principal, until the time
of their majority, for the education of the children.
Plaintiffs deny defendant's answer, and first of all re-
peat their previous claim, amounting to 1,091 gldrs., 3
st. in wheat, the sch. at 50 st. The hon. court orders
plaintiffs to adduce clearer proof at the next session,
because defendant denies the entire claim except for 50
gldrs. which he has borrowed.

Joris Hael requests that the judgment pronounced on
Feb. 26/Mar. 8, 1667, against Jan Jansen Van Amersfoort
shall be judicially enforced. The officer is ordered to
proceed with the execution.

Thomas Harmensen requests that the sentence, dated
Mar. 8, against Henderick Albertsen, shall be judicially
enforced. The officer is ordered to proceed with the
execution.

The curators of the estate of Henderick Cornelissen,
deceased, request that the money of Christoffel Davids in
the custody of Evert Pels, from the suit of H. Cornelissen
and Christoffel Davids, amounting to 100 gldrs., shall be
attached by the officer, and said attachment having taken
place, that the attachment shall be declared valid.
Whereas Christoffel Davids has been beaten*by the plaintiff,
Henderick Cornelissen, as per judgment, therefore said attachment, after having been executed by the officer, is
declared valid by the hon. court.

Juriaen Westphael requests that the attachment executed at the hon. Heer Willem Beeckman's against Jan Dirricksen Van Bremen for the amount of 20 sch. of wheat shall be
declared valid till the arrival of Jan Dirricksen Van
Bremen, on account of a claim for security for 29 sch. of
wheat. At petitioner's request, the executed attachment
is declared valid by the hon. court.

Henderick Palingh requests that the judgment against
Christoffel Davids, dated Feb. 26/Mar. 8, 1667, shall be
judicially enforced. The officer is ordered to proceed with
the execution.

Henderick Palingh requests that the judgement dated
Jan. 15/25, 1667, against Louwies DuBois, shall be judicially enforced. The officer is ordered to proceed with the
execution.

Aert Martensen Doorn requests by a petition that he
may be given time in the case between him and Thomas Chambers, for the purpose of learning from one Jacobus, now
brewer for Jeremias Van Rentselaer for whom and how many
times he brewed in the year 1663. Petitioner, at his request, is granted and permitted three weeks' time, for the
purpose of enquiring of Jacobus the brewer, and to bring

an answer concerning the same, and by default or expiration
of the period mentioned, the officer shall proceed with the
execution.

Ariaen Gerretsen Van Vliet requests the corner opposite the house of Tjerck Claesen for the purpose of building a cottage there. The hon. court judges that the curtains shall not be built on and petitioner in consequence
is referred to the hon. Lord Gov. Genl. for the purpose of
requesting a site for a house outside the curtains of the
village.

Thomas Chambers requests that the hon. court be
pleased to examine a projecting corner of woodland and
valley which he intends to request the hon. Lord Gov. Genl.
to grant him in ownership. The hon. court, at petitioner's
request, will enquire into the foregoing.

Roelof Swartwout requests the hon. court to have measured his lot bought at Wildwyck, and the lot granted him
by the late Hon. Lord Dr. Genl. Petrus Stuyvesant, for the
purpose of obtaining from the hon. Ld. Gov. Genl. Ridsert
Nicolls the confirmation for the same. The hon. court
grants petitioner's request, provided he shall have said
lots surveyed in the presence of two commissaries.

Arent Teunissen requests the court to allow him a site
for making rope /ropery/. The hon. court provisionally allows petitioner to make the ropery in the cross street
near the house of Gerret Bancker.

Pieter Hillebrants requests the hon. court to permit
him to build on his own lot outside the western point of
the curtains. The hon. court refers petitioner's request
to the hon. Lord Gov. Genl.

Evert Pels requests whereas he has bought Christoffel
Davids's house and land on the strand, that he may be permitted to live there with his family. Petitioner is granted his request, after approbation of the hon. Lord Dir.
Genl., the more so because the hon. court is aware that it
does not concern the village of Wildwyck.

The hon. court resolves, whereas the soldiers again
mount guard at the redoubt, and the savages are again expected to arrive, therefore a half corporal's guard of the
burghers shall from now on mount burgher guard during the
night, and one-half of said half corporal's guard shall
also watch during the day, and the meeting point shall be
at every guard corporal's or "Landpassaet" in order to then
go to their watches in a body.

Ordinary Session, Tuesday, March 19/29, 1666/7.

Present: Willem Beeckman, Schout; Evert Pels, Jan
Joosten, Roelof Swartwout, Commissaries.

Louwies Dubois shows a declaration against Henderick
Palingh, farmer, signed by Arent Teunissen, who declares
having heard last year at the house of Jan Joosten, that
Henderick Palingh did not ask more of petitioner's wife

than 14 gldrs. To which is given the following answer:
Received by the hon. court the abovementioned declaration
which is not fully accepted by the same, because there is
only one attestor, and said declaration has also been shown
too late, because previous to the same Palingh, farmer, has
been granted execution. And the hon. court is unable to
see that the aforementioned declaration favors the petitioner, because miscalculation of the farmer is not payment.

Evert Pels, attorney for Jan Dirricksen Van Bremen,
requests that the judgment dated Mar. 22, 1667, against
Aert Martensen Doorn shall be judicially enforced. The
officer is ordered to proceed with the execution.

Extraordinary Session, Thursday, March 21/31, 1667.
Present: Willem Beeckman, Schout; Jan Joosten, Thomas
Chambers, Roelof Swartwout, Commissaries.
The letter of the hon. Lord Gov. Genl. dated Mar. 9
having been read and received on Mar. 19/29 through a
savage, this belowmentioned decree was affixed at the
gates of this village, of the following contents:
Pursuant to an order and letter of the hon. Lord
Gov. Genl. Ridsert Nicolls to the hon. local court, all
residents of this village are ordered by the present in
the name of his Royal Majesty of Great Britain that not a
single one among them shall undertake to proceed, assist
or appear in any act of hostility, whether with or without
their arms, to the molestation or annoyance of his Majesty's garrison, stationed here, under penalty of death.
Thus given in the village of Wildwyck, this March 21/31,
1667.

Ordinary Session, Tuesday, March 26/April 5, 1667.
Present: Willem Beeckman, Schout; Jan Joosten, Thomas
Chambers, Roelof Swartwout, Commissaries.
Willem Beeckman, Plaintiff
vs. Tjerck Claesen DeWit, Defendant. Absent. Default.
Willem Beeckman, Plaintiff
vs. Tomas Teunissen Quick, Defendant
Plaintiff demands of defendant 43 gldrs. 16 st. in
sewan, for delivered goods. Defendant admits the debt.
The hon. court orders defendant to satisfy plaintiff's demand.
Willem Beeckman, Plaintiff
vs. Evert Pels, Defendant. Absent. Default.
Willem Beeckman, Plaintiff
vs. Ridgert Cage, Defendant
Plaintiff, as collector, demands of defendant 62
gldrs. for excise, and for himself personally 14 gldrs.
which defendant agreed to pay for Tomas Quinel. Defendant
admits the excise debt. In regard to the 14 gldrs., personal, says that he never heard of it, except now. The

hon. court orders defendant, as per his admission, to pay
the excise amounting to 62 gldrs., and in regard to the 14
gldrs., personal claim, plaintiff is ordered to prove his
personal claim at the next session.

Allert Heymans Roos, Plaintiff
vs. Thomas Chambers, Defendant

Plaintiff demands of defendant 60 sch. of wheat, as
per assignment by Cornelis Hoogeboom. Defendant admits the
debt. The hon. court orders defendant to satisfy plaintiff's demand, as per his acknowledgement.

Jan Jansen Van Oosterhout, Plaintiff
vs. Claes Claesen, Defendant

Plaintiff demands of defendant 20 gldrs. Defendant
admits the debt. The hon. court orders defendant to satis-
by plaintiff's demand.

Jan Willemsen Hoochteylingh, Plaintiff
vs. Pieter Gillissen, Defendant

Plaintiff says that he hired defendant for the time
of one year, and whereas defendant left his service inside
said time, he requests that defendant shall serve out his
time, because he principally hired him to watch his cows
during the summer. Defendant admits having hired himself
out to plaintiff for a year. The hon. court orders defendant to serve out his contracted time with plaintiff, and
in case of default, the officer, Heer Beeckman, in compliance with plaintiff's request, is ordered to do his duty
concerning the same.

Ridsert Cage, Plaintiff
vs. Evert Prys, Defendant

Plaintiff demands of defendant 28 gldrs. Defendant
answers having assigned 16 gldrs. to Thomas Mattheu, and
for the 12 gldrs. worked 1½ day in the maize, boarding himself, and he also loaned plaintiff a razor, and he agrees
to pay the balance when the razor and 1½ day wages shall
have been paid him. Plaintiff replies that he did not accept the assignment to Thom Mattheu, nor did he set him to
work. The hon. court orders plaintiff to prove his claim
at the next session of the court.

Ridsert Cage, Plaintiff
vs. Jan Cornelissen Smith, Defendant

Plaintiff demands of defendant 18 gldrs. Defendant
answers having paid six gldrs. to Walran DuMont, and says
in regard to the 12 gldrs. that Magdalena Dirricks executed
an attachment against plaintiff by virtue of a "scheepen
judgment" and when the attachment has been released, defendant is ready to satisfy plaintiff. The hon. court orders plaintiff to summon Magdalena Dirricks, for the purpose of giving reasons for the attachment levied.

Ridsert Cage, Plaintiff
vs. Roelof Swartwout, Defendant

Plaintiff demands of defendant eight gldrs. Defendant
answers that an attachment was levied against said eight

gldrs. by Magdalena Dirricks, by virtue of a "scheepen
judgment" against plaintiff, and is ready to satisfy plaintiff as soon as the attachment shall have been removed.
The hon. court orders plaintiff to summon Magdalena Dirricks, for the purpose of giving reasons for the attachment
levied.

Claes Claesen, Plaintiff
vs. Annetie Gerrets, Defendant

Plaintiff demands of defendant two sch. of wheat and
two sch. of oats. Defendant admits the above debt. The
hon. court orders defendant, as per admission, to satisfy
plaintiff's demand.

Jan Lootman requests that the judgment dated Mar. 22,
1667, against Pieter Hillebrants shall be judicially enforced. The hon. court orders the officer to proceed with
the execution.

Jan Dirricksen Van Bremen has levied an attachment
under the hands of Henderick Jochemsen against such moneys
as said Henderick Jochemsen shall have received or shall
yet receive for Geertruyd Pietersen Vossenburch, and requests that said attachment may be declared valid. The
hon. court declares the levied attachment valid, provided
petitioner shall proceed with his case against Geertruyd
Vossenborch inside of two months.

Willem Beeckman requests whereas Evert Pels did not
appear after the summons of demand of debt and is indebted
to the amount of 70 gldrs. which he accepted /to pay/ of
the back farm money for the farmer Palingh, and whereas he
is now about to leave and has sold most of his real and
personal estate, that /petitioner/ may therefore be permitted, for the purpose of securing his claim, to arrest
his person. Whereas Evert Pels is still possessed of sufficient property which has remained unsold and does not remove with his entire family outside the limits of this
village, therefore the arrest of the person of Evert Pels
is not permitted by the hon. court.

These four below-named persons are nominated by the
commissaries from among the community, that the hon. Lord
Gov. Genl. may appoint two from among them as incoming com-
missaries /in place of/ retiring present commissaries Evert
Pels and Jan Joosten, viz., Cornelis Barents Slecht, Allert
Heymans Roos, Jan Willemsen Hoochteylingh, Henderick
Jochemsen.

Extraordinary Session, Saturday, April 6/16, 1667.
Present: Willem Beeckman, Schout; Evert Pels, Jan
Joosten, Thomas Chambers, Roelof Swartwout, Commissaries.
Received by the hon. court a letter from the hon.
Lord Gov. Genl., dated Apr. 2/12, 1667, and in accordance
with its contents were summoned Allert Heymans Roos, Hen-
derick Jochemsen and Antoni D'Elba, and after having been

acquainted with the order of the hon. Lord Gov. Genl., the
aforesaid persons were, by the officer Willem Beeckman,
arrested and taken to the watch in the guardhouse. Arriving
there, Antoni D'Elba said to the officer Beeckman, according
to his report, "If you don't want to go on my bail, then I
shall not remain here in the guardhouse." On account of
which Antoni D'Elba being a single man, the officer Beeckman is ordered to shackle the person of Antoni D'Elba until
he shall have procured bail. And shortly afterward became
surety: Jan Willemsen Hoochteylingh for Allert Heymans
Roos, Tjerck Claesen DeWit for Henderick Jochemsen, Francois Lecheer for Antoni D'Elba, that the aforenamed persons
shall appear before his honor, or before such /other or
others/ as his honor shall be pleased to appoint, after
having been admonished at their houses six hours previously
/to answer for/ such crimes as they shall be charged with.

Extraordinary Session, Monday, April 29/May 9, 1667.
    Present: Willem Beeckman, Schout; Evert Pels, Jan
Joosten, Thomas Chambers, Roelof Swartwout, Commissaries.
    Cornelis Barentsen Slecht, in obedience to a verbal
order of the hon. Lord Gov. Genl., shows to the hon. court
against Thomas Chambers, divers documents as well of purchase of, and conveyance by, the aborigines of a parcel of
land situated under the village of Wildwyck, besides a
declaration signed by Juriaen Westphael, Geertruyd Andriesen and Jacob Jansen Stoutenborch who declare that it
is known to them that the aforesaid Cornelis Barents
Slecht has bought the abovenamed parcel of land from the
natives, and further a certified village tax bill by which
said Cornelis Slecht is required to contribute towards the
building of the parsonage here in the ratio of 25 morgens
of his own claimed land as morgen money; and further a certified bill of the aforesaid tax of one rixdollar per morgen, issued by the late hon. Lord Dr. Genl. Petrus Stuy -
vesant on Nov. 12, 1661. The measuring of the aforesaid
land is also certified to by the sworn surveyor Jaques
Corteliou. And whereas Thomas Chambers on May 12, 1664,
obtained a deed of said land from the late hon. Lord Dr.
Genl. Petrus Stuyvesant, for his step children, therefore
requests that the land bought by him from the savages here
as shown by the aforenamed documents may be restored to
him and deeded to him.
    Thomas Chambers replies that the abovenamed declara-
tions have not been confirmed under oath, and further says
that Cornelis Barentsen Slecht has no proof of approbation
for the purpose of the land by the late hon. Lord Dr. Genl.
Petrus Stuyvesant, and that he refers to the deed, by the
beforenamed Hon. Lord Petrus Stuyvesant, to his stepchildren on May 12, 1664, and says that the late Hon. Ld. Dir.
Genl. in place of the said claimed land has offered to
Cornelis Slecht, a parcel of land beyond the new village.

Cornelis Slecht replies that such a parcel of land was
offered him by the late Hon. Ld. Dr. Genl. in writing, for
14 morgens of land which Thomas Chambers claimed his stepchildren were short, and therefore claims the remaining
eight morgens of the aforesaid claimed lands.

Whereas the hon. court was not shown the approbation
of the late Hon. Ld. Dr. Genl. Petrus Stuyvesant for the
purchase of said claimed land by Cornelis Barentsen Slecht
and it is neither known that he took possession of said
land, but on the contrary it appears that the stepchildren
of Thomas Chambers were granted a deed on May 12, 1664, for
the abovementioned land, notwithstanding the aforesaid Cornelis Barents Slecht in the year 1661 was taxed for building the parsonage, for the aforesaid claimed land at two
gldrs. 10 st. per morgen, and not further for the preacher's
salary, but that the aforenamed children were taxed for
contributing to the salary of the preacher here for the
above land from Sept. 5, 1664, till Mar. 5, 1667, when the
preacher severed his connection, and whereas the hon. court
is not qualified to pronounce judgment in this case,
therefore parties are referred for a decision in the above
to the hon. Ld. Gov. Genl. Ridsert Nicolls.

Aert Martensen Doorn and his wife Geertruyd Andriesen
request that for the child from another marriage of Geertruyd Andriesen, viz., Jan Jacobs Slyckkoten, the hon. Heer
Willem Beeckman, Schout, and Roelof Swartwout, commissary,
shall be appointed guardians. The hon. court approves of
the aforenamed persons as guardians of the aforenamed minor
child, Jan Jacobs Slyckkoten, and commend them to acquit
themselves of their trust with all uprightness and reasonableness.

Evert Pels requests whereas he is about to remove from
here, that another shall be appointed in his place as
guardian and curator of the estate of Jan Albertsen Van
Steenwyck, deceased, besides Henderick Jochemsen. The hon.
court in regard to this requests and appoints Jan Willemsen Hoochteylingh as curator of said estate.

Evert Pels requests whereas on his bill he is taxed
for 25 morgens, and he has not possessed more than 20 morgens, to have the overcharge deducted which is allowed him
by the hon. court.

He also requests for the use of his barn for the ministry some compensation, and consequently the hon. court allows him 125 gldrs. in sewan, in reduction of his village
taxes.

Ordinary Session, Tuesday, May 14/24, 1667.
Present: Willem Beeckman, Schout; Jan Joosten, Thomas
Chambers, Roelof Swartwout, Commissaries.

At the written petition by Geurt Hendericksen, uncle
and blood guardian of the minor children of Jan Hendericksen, his deceased brother, living at Albany, that guardians

shall be appointed for the aforesaid children, for the purpose of taking them under their supervision, /therefore/ in obedience to the abovementioned request are appointed and invited as guardians by the hon. court Jan Willemsen Hoochteylingh, elder, and Henderick Aertsen, deacon.

The hon. scout Willem Beeckman complains about Harmen Hendericks, saying that about five weeks ago said Harmen Hendericks appeared at his house with his watch, for the purpose of demanding a fine, and taking the same from his son Hendericus, for neglecting the watch, as Harmen Hendericks said. And whereas his son had not been ordered by the superior officers to take the watch, and Harmen Hendericks has done the same upon his own authority, and has even further insulted and threatened plaintiff, therefore he requests that said Harmen Hendericks shall be disciplined for said insults and threats.

On this date, in place of the retiring commissaries Evert Pels, Jan Joosten, and Roelof Swartwout, have taken their proper oath as incoming commissaries: Jacob Burhans and Henderick Aertsen (Henderick Jochemsen, the third, being absent), in accordance with the appointment of the Hon. Ld. Governor Genl., from a previous nomination.

Grietje Hendericks, wife of Walran DuMont, requests that the attachment levied on 16 sch. of buckwheat, in the possession of Tjerck Claesen, shall be declared valid, and that she may be permitted to dispose of said 16 sch. of buckwheat, because Elbert Gerbertsen, as per his own acknowledgment on Feb. 4/14 last, admitted to owe her as much, and was consequently ordered by the hon. court, on the same date, to give security for said amount, and also says that said Elbert Gerbertsen has neglected his right in the allowed time. The hon. court grants petitioner's above request, provided she shall wait, if, by the first yacht, payment should arrive from Elbert Gerbertsen for what is coming to her.

Roelof Swartwout, attorney for Dom. Hermanus Blom, requests, whereas he has levied an attachment on 10 sch. of wheat, in the hands of Frederick Pietersen, on account of Pieter Hillebrants' indebtedness, that said attachment shall be declared valid. The hon. court declares the aforenamed attachment valid.

On May 27/June 6 of the year 1667 were legally married by schout and commissaries at Wildwyck Cornelis Aertsen Fynhout, young man, and Neeltje Aertsen, young daughter of Aert Jacobs, deceased.

Extraordinary Session, Tuesday, May 28/June 7, 1667.
Present: Willem Beeckman, Schout; Thomas Chambers, Henderick Jochemsen, Jacob Burhans, Henderick Aertsen, Commissaries.

On this date Henderick Jochemsen (being absent at the last session) took the proper oath as incoming commissary.

Wyntie, the wife of Allert Heymans Roos, requests a
certificate of the hon. court concerning the conduct of
her husband here at Wildwyck, and she was given the following certificate:

"In compliance with the request made to us Schout and
Commissaries at Wildwyck, by Wyntie the wife of Allert Heymans Roos, the following certificate is granted by us, in
regard to the life and conduct of her husband Allert Heymans Roos, aforenamed, at Wildwyck: 1) Said Allert Heymans Roos, in the year 1662, he being at the time commissary of the hon. court, had arrested by the schout one
Pieter Van Hael, a poor resident of this place, and did not
permit him to leave his arrest on bail, but was afterwards
permitted to leave the schout's house and serve out his arrest in his own house, where he was obliged to board at his
own expense a soldier for the purpose of guarding him, because the aforesaid Pieter Van Haal had said that he did
not get full weight of some butter received from said Allert
Heymans Roose, said /proceedings/ being illegal; further,
also, said Allert Heymans Roos, in the year 1663, opposed
the order of the hon. Ld. Dr. Genl. in regard to the taking
care of the cattle, he being at the time burgher-sergeant
in the troubles and war with the savages here, on which account an uprising among the burghers could easily have
originated; furthermore, said Allert Heymans Roos has opposed the decree of the council of war and the burgher
court here, during the same year who gave a safe conduct,
the council of war as well as the burgher court, to two
highland savages which two savages he intended to intercept
outside the gate with a loaded gun for the purpose of
shooting them dead, contrary to the said resolution. Also
at the time when the burghers here were tumultuous, on
Feb. 4/14, 1667, and we went among them for the purpose of
pacifying and calming them, the aforesaid Allert Heymans
Roos treated us very contemptibly by despising our authority as laid down in our instruction, and furthermore has
often behaved disrespectfully in opposing decrees issued
here. Which certificate, above named, concerning the aforesaid Allert Heymans Roos, having been legally asked for by
Wyntie, wife of said Allert Heymans Roos, we, according to
honor, duty and oath, have not been able to give to her and
her husband any other than the one written above.

"On which account we have subscribed to the present
with our own hand, at our session on the day and in the
year as mentioned before.

"Was signed by the aforesaid Scout and Commissaries."

Extraordinary Session, Friday, June 21/July 1, 1667.
    Present: Thomas Chambers, Henderick Jochems, Jacob
Burhans, Henderick Aertsen, Commissaries.
    Captain Daniel Broodhead and some other soldiers who
are tilling Wassemaker's land, complain that a portion of

the fence of said land is insufficient, on account of which a large number of horses entered, and caused some damage to the maize and other summer crops, and request that said fence shall be repaired by the residents here, that they may not be caused any further damage through cattle or horses, and also request compensation for the sustained damage.

Tjerck Claesen DeWit and Juriaen Westphael, the appointed examiners of the fences, having examined the said portion of the aforesaid land, declare having found that the fence of the aforenamed end is insufficient. Therefore, the hon. court orders that, tomorrow, each one of the farmers, for the purpose of putting said end of the aforementioned fence in good shape, shall send one man thither with tools, and shall put the same in such shape that no complaints shall be made concerning the same, under penalty to those remaining absent, and on which account the work should have been left undone, of making good the damages, which should afterward be caused. In regard to making good the damage suffered by plaintiffs, /this/ is suspended till next session.

Ordinary Session, Tuesday, June 26/July 5, 1667.
Present: Willem Beeckman, Schout; Thomas Chambers, Henderick Jochems, Jacob Burhans, Henderick Aertsen, Commissaries.

Thomas Chambers, Plaintiff
vs. Henderick Palingh, Defendant

Plaintiff accuses defendant of calling him a knave or boef, and asks him for reasons for saying so. Defendant admits and says that plaintiff is a knave because he has caused trouble in his house, and that he called his fellow-soldiers "rogues." Plaintiff takes it upon himself to prove at the next session that he did not molest defendant in his house. Defendant requests that Henderick Jochemsen shall be made to declare under oath whether he did not hear Thomas Chambers say at the house of Harmen Hendericks that the English who are at present here were banished from England and sent to an island, and that the English took their course to the Manhatans without authority of the King of England, and that Stuyvesant has surrendered the country to them.

Henderick Jochemsen, having been judicially questioned about the above under oath, says that he did not hear this out of Thomas Chambers' mouth, but only /says/ that a year ago last Shrove-tide he heard from the mouth of Thomas Chambers at the aforesaid house that some English behave in such a manner, cursing, swearing and blustering, as if they were bandits, which he has also confirmed under oath.

Harmen Hendericks, having been interrogated under oath at the request of Henderick Palingh, declares under oath having heard at his house (he having forgotten the time) out of the mouth of Thomas Chambers, that these

Englishmen who are now here, are a party of bandits, and
had been sent to some island, and that they thus came
here, and that Stuyvesant has given the land to them.

Henderick Palingh further says that he heard from
Eduart Wittiger that Thomas Chambers said, "I do not esteem
my commission, because I did not take the oath of office,
and therefore I may say what I please." Thomas Chambers
denies all of the above declarations saying that Harmen
Hendericks cannot be a witness in this case because Henderick Palingh heard out of the mouth of Harmen Hendericks
that which Harmen Hendericks has declared above, and that
Harmen Hendericks has declared his own case. Henderick
Palingh further requests that Harmen Hendericks' wife shall
also be heard as witness in the aforenamed case, and whereas she cannot now be present on account of being confined
in child bed, that she shall be examined concerning this
affair in her own house.

The hon. court besides the commander of the militia
here, Christoffel Berrisfort, having heard Henderick
Palingh's complaint, and Harmen Hendericks's declaration,
find that Harmen Hendericks is passionately prejudiced
against Thomas Chambers, which he showed before the court
here. On this account Henderick Palingh is ordered to
produce better proof in this, his case, against Thomas
Chambers for the purpose of then the better presenting it
to the hon. Ld. Gov. Genl.

Thomas Chambers, Plaintiff
vs. Michiel Mot, Defendant

Plaintiff demands of defendant his reasons for pur-
suing him last Thursday, being June 20/30, on the road
while he was going home in company with Robbert Pekock, and
brings as witness the wife of Joris Hal who saw defendant
go outside the gate. She makes the following declaration:
Defendant asked her where she was going. She answered that
she went after her husband for the purpose of taking him
home, so that he should not get in trouble. Hereupon defendant answered, "You need not go after your husband, Mr.
Palingh is as good a man as your husband, and better when
he has a sword." Defendant went before her, until she
found Thomas Chambers prostrated on the ground in the road;
he then left her for the woods in the direction of Mr.
Palingh, who stood on the knoll of the underwood and she
saw both defendant and Mr. Palingh return home. Defendant
answers having gone outside the gate for the purpose of seeing how the trouble would end.

Frederick Hossy, David Grafford, Antoni Coeck, Willem
Houghton and Onfre Fargeson request to be compensated for
the damage caused to their crops on Wassemaker's land which
has been occasioned by the horses entering upon their sowed
and tilled land, and thereby request that said land shall
be better protected, because they, in running after the
horses, have neglected much in their plantation, and it is

now high time to clean the maize. In regard to the above
request, the examiners of the fences are recommended and
requested to view today or tomorrow the damage done to the
crop, and to appraise said damage. And it is further ordered that each one of the householders early tomorrow at
6:00 o'clock shall send a man with tools for the purpose
of erecting a garden fence on the aforenamed land, under
penalty for those who neglect /their duty/ of 10 gldrs.
fine.

Mattheus Capito requests, whereas he has attached 49
gldrs. under the hands of Annetje Gerrets, of Cornelis
Barents, that said attachment may be declared valid. The
hon. court grants petitioner's request, and declares the
levied attachment valid.

Willem Beeckman, Schout, Plaintiff
vs. Harmen Hendericks, Defendant

Plaintiff, having on May 14/24 ult. made complaint
before the court against defendant Harmen Hendericks, how,
about five weeks ago, defendant came to his house with his
watch for the purpose of demanding and receiving a fine of
his son Henricus on account of neglecting his watch, and
whereas plaintiff's son had not been ordered by the higher
officers to mount guard, and defendant did the same by his
own authority, and even further insulted and threatened
plaintiff, and when plaintiff, later on, on the same day
acquainted Capt. Thomas Chambers with this occurrence, defendant in the meanwhile arrived and said, in case plaintiff had come before the door he would have saluted him
with the hammer, therefore requests that defendant on account of said insults and threats shall be punished.

Defendant answers that he came to plaintiff's house
for the purpose of getting the fine from his son, for
neglecting his watch, he having orders from the superior
officers to make plaintiff's son mount guard and that
plaintiff said to him and his watch, "You buffalo's, get
out of my house," and thereupon he departed with his
watch.

Capt. Thomas Chambers, having been called and questioned whether he had given orders to Harmen Hendericks to
have plaintiff's son mount guard, answers, "No," and in
regard to the above molestation by defendant to plaintiff,
defendant asked him, if he would be permitted to keep
plaintiff's son in his watch, and /Chambers/ answered not
until he should have given orders to defendant.

The hon. court, having heard plaintiff's accusation
and defendant's answer, and also the captain's answer to
the same, decides that defendant, on account of speaking
evil to plaintiff and of treating him badly, and further
because he had no order from the superior burgher officers
to press plaintiff's son for the watch, but has done the
same by his own authority, shall first appear at the next
session and in the presence of the court beg plaintiff's

pardon, and, besides, pay a fine of 50 gldrs. for the poor
to which he is sentenced, and defendant is also further ordered not to commit any such further act under penalty of
a higher fine.

    Roelof Swartwout and Cornelis Barentsen Slecht,
    guardians of the minor children of Mattys Jansen,
                 deceased, Plaintiffs
            vs. Thomas Chambers, Defendant

    Whereas on Mar. 12/22 ult. the hon. court has ordered
plaintiffs to produce better proof in regard to the demand
of 1,091 gldrs. 3 st. in wheat, the sch. at 50 st., and defendant denied the whole claim except 50 gldrs. which he
borrowed, therefore plaintiffs produce as proof, for the
purpose of sustaining their above demand, the contract of
"uytcoop" of the paternal estate, and that defendant relieved himself from the aforesaid children, and gave them
in their care, and further that about five or six months
after the "uytcoop" defendant hired said children from
them, and therefore demand the aforesaid amount, with costs.
Defendant still persists in his former answer, saying that
he is entitled to the proceeds from the capital until the
children shall have attained to their majority. The hon.
court finds and judges that defendant, Thomas Chambers, was
entitled to the enjoyment of the returns from the capital
up to the time that he relieved himself and surrendered
the children to the care of plaintiffs, and further that
defendant contracted with plaintiffs to hire said children
from them for his service, and also to hire the designated
land from plaintiffs, and even paid them something without
raising any issue about claiming the proceeds, wherefore
the hon. court judges that defendant cannot claim any more
of the proceeds than before stated, on which account defendant is ordered to satisfy plaintiffs for the balance
of the rent and the borrowed money with the interest of the
same.

    Jan Tyssen requests whereas he is betrothed to a young
daughter that he may be permitted to demand of his guardians his share, and to enjoy the same. Petitioner is permitted by the hon. court to draw his share from his guardians, as soon as it shall be shown that his banns have been
registered.

    The commissary Henderick Jochemsen reports that about
eight days ago Jan Jansen Van Oosterhout complained to him
that Joris Porter, his soldier, coming home drunk, made
trouble with him, and went for him with drawn sword without
having any cause against him.

    Decree against those catching other people's horses
without their permission, use and ride on them.

    "Whereas schout and commissaries here have been ac-
quainted with and complained to about that some residents
here when going in search of their horses, take and use

356

another man's horses until they have found their own with
the same, and then they sometimes do not take back the
horse they have thus used to its former pasture, but allow
it to run in unknown places to the inconvenience of the
owner who, when wanting to use his own horses, is obliged
to go in search for them at distant and strange places.
And further that some have dared to use the horses of other
people, without the permission of the owners, in their work,
this being a species of theft. For the purpose of preventing this, schout and commissaries of this village of Wildwyck in the name and by the authority of the Royal Majesty
of Great Britain stringently order and command all and every
body that from now on none of the residents here shall
undertake to catch other people's horses without the permission of the owners, for the purpose either of searching
for their horses with the same or to use them in their own
work, under penalty of 50 gldrs. for every time this shall
be found to have been done. Let every body look out for
damage. Thus enacted at the session of schout and commissaries of this village of Wildwyck this June 25/July 5,
1667.

Extraordinary Session, Friday, June 28/July 8, 1667.
        Present: Willem Beeckman, Schout; Henderick Jochem-
sen, Jacob Burhans, Henderick Aertsen, Commissaries.
        Harmen Hendericksen, having been summoned to appear at
the session, and having been made acquainted with the
previous sentence dated June 25/July 5 ult., answers not to
intend to submit to said sentence, with which answer the
hon. schout Willem Beeckman is not satisfied, and for the
purpose of upholding the authority of hon. local court here
intends to himself go before the hon. Heer Gov. Genl. and
to inform him of the obstinacy of the aforesaid Harmen Hendericks. On account of said obstinacy of Harmen Hendericks
the hon. court resolves to send said Harmen Hendericks to
N. York to the hon. Lord Gov. Genl. Ridsert Nicolls, with
the yacht of Reyndert Pietersen, at present laying here,
for the purpose of there answering the demand which the
hon. schout shall there make against him.
        The commissary Henderick Jochemsen complains that
Harmen Hendericksen has called him and Capt. Thomas Chambers rascals and liars, and in regard to the same shows a
declaration signed on June 27/July 7, 1667, by Jacob Burhans and Reynier Van der Coele. Said declaration having
been read to Harmen Hendericksen, he answers that plaintiff
has also called him names. The hon. schout Willem Beeckman is advised and requested by the hon. court to show
plaintiff's complaint, with the declaration, to the hon.
Ld. Gov. Genl., and to request him to vindicate /plaintiff/.

Extraordinary Session, Saturday, June 29/July 9, 1667.
        Present: Willem Beeckman, Schout; Henderick Jochem-

sen, Jacob Burhans, Henderick Aertsen, Commissaries.

Harmen Hendericks produces a declaration signed by
Tjerck Claesen De Wit, dated June 27/July 7 inst. /contain-
ing/ that about three months ago (he having forgotten the
exact time) he, attestor, being at the house of Mattheus
Capito with Capt. Thomas Chambers, he, petitioner, complained to him and Thomas Chambers, that the schout Willem
Beeckman had called him, petitioner, "a buffalo," because
he came to collect from his son the fine for the watch,
whereupon Thomas Chambers answered petitioner, "Just remember, for he is no better than any other farmer's son."
Capt. Chambers, having been called in on this account, and
been acquainted with the foregoing, admits having said the
above. The aforenamed Harmen Hendericks produces another
declaration signed by Joost Ariaens, dated June 27/July 7,
who declares that in the month of April last, he not having
remembered the exact date, being at the house of Henderick
Martensen, at his departure, petitioner spoke to Capt.
Thomas Chambers about drawing the son of the schout Willem
Beeckman in the watch, and heard the aforesaid Capt. order
petitioner to draw the said son of Schout Willem Beeckman
in the watch, saying besides, "If Willem Beeckman is Schout,
his son shall not be any more exempt than had been his,
the captain's, son." The aforenamed captain answers to
this that he had ordered the lieutenant to draw all the
young men, being 16 years of age, in the watch.

Jan Hendericks is also presented by Harmen Hendericks.
The declarer, having heard in front of Harmen Hendericks's
house, while Capt. Thomas Chambers was passing said house,
that Harmen Hendericks spoke to said captain /and told him/
that he had warned the son of schout Willem Beeckman twice
to mount guard, to which said captain answered him: "Just
remember," and then the captain went on. Captain Thomas
Chambers admits the above. Henderick Palingh, as witness
for Harmen Hendericks, declares having heard, at the house
of Henderick Jochemsen, that Capt. Thomas Chambers ordered
his lieutenant Henderick Jochemsen to draw the son of the
schout Willem Beeckman in the watch. Capt. Thomas Chambers
answers that he ordered his lieutenant to draw all the
young men, 16 years of age, in the watch. Henderick
Palingh further declares having heard at the house of Harmen Hendericks that Capt. Thomas Chambers ordered his officers to draw the son of schout Willem Beeckman in the
watch, and that he the captain was fully responsible for
the fine, if he took security therefor from the house.
Capt. Thomas Chambers denies the above.

Jannetje Hillebrants, wife of Francois LeCheer, declares having heard at the house of Henderick Martensen, he
being about to depart, that Henderick Jochemsen should
have said, "Wny should not Beeckman's son watch as well as
my son?" not knowing to whom Henderick Jochemsen should have
said the same. Henderick Jochemsen answers, that it is

quite well possible that he should have said the same, but
cannot tell to whom. These aforenamed declarations thus
having been heard by the hon. court, Harmen Hendericks requests copy of what has been written above. The hon. court,
at his request, allows Harmen Hendericks a copy, and the
hon. court further refers to the previous judgment dated
June 28/July 8, 1667. This pronounced judgment having now
been communicated to Harmen Hendericks, Harmen Hendericks
requests that Capt. Thomas Chambers and Lieutenant Henderick Jochemsen shall go down with him. This further request of Harmen Hendericks is not granted him by the hon.
court, but it adheres to its former decision. The hon.
court, having informed Harmen Hendericks about the difficulties which might result from the aforementioned question, the aforenamed Harmen Hendericks admits before it
that he was wrong, requesting the schout that the question
shall be mutually forgotten, and thus they both, after
shaking hands, buried their differences. And in regard
to the 50 gldrs. fine for the poor, the hon. court, out of
consideration, because Harmen Hendericks himself needs
them, for this time remits the same and absolves him /from
paying the same7.

Extraordinary Session, Thursday, July 25/August 4, 1667.
     Present: Willem Beeckman, Schout; Thomas Chambers,
Henderick Jochems, Jacob Burhans, Henderick Aertsen, Commissaries; Christoffel Berisfort, Commander of the Militia.
     The commander of the militia here, Christoffel Berris-
fort, has shown to the court a letter from the hon. Lord
Gov. Genl. Ridsert Nicolls, dated July 5/15 last, wherein
his hon., in regard to the difference between Capt. Thomas
Chambers and Henderick Palingh, passed upon by the hon.
court on June 25/July 5, recommends that the same be erased
from the minutes, because he has found out that the declaration of Harmen Hendericks, in favor of Henderick Palingh,
is nul and of no value, and that the aforenamed commander
shall punish Henderick Palingh, so that he shall never more
commit such and similar offences against the bench.
     /With this entry ends the handwriting of Secretary
Capito.
     The following entries are more difficult to read than
his. Made by Schout Beeckman.7

     August 6/16, took place the farming out of the tapster
and burgher excise, according to the conditions read before,
at public auction for 12 months.
     Offers made for the tapster excise: Reyner Van
Coelen, 200 gldrs.; is increased by Swartwout to 300 gldrs.;
still by the same to 350 gldrs.; Reyner Van Coelen increases
the same to 400 gldrs., draws two sch. of wheat; Aert Otterspoor increases it to 450 gldrs., draws two sch. of
wheat; Reynier Van Coelen increases it to 500 gldrs., and

again draws two sch. of wheat. The 500 gldrs. remain fixed;
this is increased by the auctionner with 300 gldrs., and
runs to nothing, so that Reynier Van Coelen becomes farmer
for the amount of 500 gldrs.

After the condition of the burgher excise had been
read, offers were made by: Claes Claes, 200 gldrs.; Reynier Van Coelen, 225 gldrs.; Claes Claes increased it to
250 gldrs.; Reyner Van Coelen again to 275 gldrs., draws
one sch. of wheat; Claes Claesz increases it to 300 gldrs.,
draws one sch. of wheat; Reyner Van Coelen increases it to
325 gldrs., draws one sch. of wheat; Claes Claesz increases
it to 350 gldrs., draws one sch. of wheat; Tomas Hermens
increases it to 375 gldrs. These 375 gldrs. remain fixed,
and this is increased by the auctioneer with 200 gldrs.,
but runs down to nothing, so that Tomas Hermens becomes
farmer at the above amount of 375 gldrs., but in his place
it is taken by Reyner Van Coelen at the above amount of 375
gldrs.

Ordinary Session, August 27/Sept. 6, 1667.

Present: the entire bench except Henryck Aertsen.

Resolved to reissue the decree dated Sept. 4, 1666,
in regard to picking hop.

Willem Beeckman, vs. Reyn. Van Coelen, defendant,
default.

Willem Beeckman, vs. Roelof Swartwout. Plaintiff
complains that defendant does not keep his fence in proper
repairs, and further says that last Wednesday he missed a
pig there, he and his people having heard a shot on defendant's land, on account of which he maintains that the
missing pig must have been shot there, and requests that
defendant shall keep his fence in proper condition, the
same having been found, yesterday, to be not sufficient to
keep out pigs and cattle. Defendant answers and denies
having caused damage to him, but says that plaintiff's
horses caused damage to his land. The hon. court orders
defendant to properly repair his fence, so that other
people's pigs and cattle shall not be damaged, defendant's
fence having been found, by the examiners, to be inefficient
for excluding pigs and cattle.

Thomas Chambers vs. Tomas Hermens, Defendant. Absent.
Default. Arien Gerrits Van Vliet, having been summoned as
witness by Tomas Chambers in the suit of Tomas Chambers
vs. Tomas Hermens, declares having heard about three weeks
ago .... Case is adjourned till next session.

Willem LaMontagne vs. ....

Evert Prys vs. Reyner Van Coelen, Defendant. Plaintiff as attorney for Geleyn Verplancken demands of defendant a sum of 315 gldrs. in sewan or beavers at 25 gldrs. a
piece, as per obligation. Defendant admits the debt, and
requests time till his grain shall have been threshed.
The hon. court orders defendant, as per his note and obligation, to satisfy plaintiff's demand.

Roelof Swartwout requests by petition to be appointed grain measurer. The hon. court answers petitioner that his request will be considered at the proper time or occasion.

Willem La Montagnie asks by petition for salary because in the absence of a preacher he is filling both places that of fore-reader and fore-singer in the church here. Petitioner is granted by the hon. court for his office of fore-reader, in the absence of a preacher, an annual salary of 500 gldrs. light money, over and above his salary as fore-singer, besides free rent; petitioner is permitted to occupy the front part of the village-house and one-half of the upper floor, the hon. court reserving the back portion of the house besides the other half of the upper floor and the cellar to its own use, petitioner's salary to commence from the time that Dom. Blom severed his connection with the congregation here and departed.

Fredryck Hussy and David Crafford send in a bill for damage caused by village cattle at Wassemaker's land to soldiers having planted there, amounting to 1,040 gldrs. The hon. magistrates having seen the unreasonable demand, and their own appraisal, to the amount of 1,040 gldrs., by soldiers and David Crafford who have planted on Wassemaker's land, judge that not as much damage has been caused. On account hereof the aforesaid soldiers and David Crafford are ordered to specially point out in which they have been caused so much damage, and the aforesaid soldiers and Crafford shall set a time, and give notice the evening before, to Mr. Berisford, the commissary Hendrick Jochems, besides Tierk Claessen de Wit and Jan Joosten, that they may specially value the caused damage and acquaint the local magistrates with the same.

On Sept. 1/11 were lawfully married before the hon. court Jan Matthysen, young man, and Magdalena Blangon, young daughter.

On Sept. 3/13 were lawfully married before the Magistrates Antene Kouk, young man, being a soldier in the service of the King of England, and Jannetie Crafford, young daughter.

Ordinary Session, Tuesday, Sept. 24/Oct. 4, 1667.
Present: Schout Beeckman, Thomas Chambers, Hend. Jochems, Jacop Burhans, Commissaries.
Reynier Van Coelen, Plaintiff
vs. Hend. Palingh, Defendant
Plaintiff demands of defendant 729 gldrs. as per obligation. Defendant answers that he will pay plaintiff the amount of the obligation when it becomes due in December next. Plaintiff further says that defendant accosted him on the street, and said that he had a claim against him for 1,400 gldrs., whereof he requests account and proof. Defendant demands, per account, 415 gldrs. and im-

mediate payment. Reynier Van Coelen answers having received the 415 gldrs. in reduction of the bill. Defendant
Hendrick Palingh denies having sold and delivered anything
in reduction of the bill. The hon. court orders Reynier
Van Coelen to prove that he received the 415 gldrs. of
Palingh for the debt of the obligation, or if not is ordered
to pay the 415 gldrs.

Willem Beeckman, Plaintiff
vs. Reyner Van Coelen, Defendant

Plaintiff demands of defendant 21 whole beavers,
balance of a note for the sale of negroes, with costs. Defendant admits owing only 20 to plaintiff. The hon. court
orders defendant to pay plaintiff 20 good beavers, with
costs.

Reynier Van Coelen, Plaintiff
vs. Tomas Hermens, Defendant

Plaintiff demands of defendant satisfaction of conditions in regard to the sale of oats on Wassemaker's land.
Defendant answers having stipulated at the sale of the oats
that plaintiff should have it cut at the proper time which
he has not done, but on the contrary has allowed the same
to get overripe. Plaintiff replies, saying that when they
were cutting the oats, he offered Tomas to pay him two sch.
of wheat above the three sch. he had promised him at the
sale, which thus relieves him. Agrees to prove the same.
Parties are ordered to prove their assertions at the next
session, and to each produce his witnesses and proofs before the court.

Tomes Hermens, Plaintiff
vs. Reyner Van Coelen, Defendant

Plaintiff demands two barrels of cider which defendant
ought to have delivered to him in the month of July and 200
gldrs. damage for the nondelivery. Defendant answers that
he did not absolutely sell him more than he delivered to
him, but promised him to deliver two more barrels to him
upon his return from Manhatans. Again coming at Manhatans,
he discovered that the cider leaked out of the barrels in
his cellar, and therefore did not bring any with him.
Plaintiff is ordered to prove that defendant absolutely
sold him the demanded wine or two barrels of cider or by
default his further claim will be refused him. Tomas Hermens, Reyner Van Coelen for several times' calling the
bench names, were told by the officer that he would have
them fined on that account. Are therefore sentenced to pay
six gldrs. fine each.

Willem Beeckman, Plaintiff
vs. Matth. Coenraets, Defendant. Default.

Willem Beeckman, Plaintiff
vs. Jacob Elders, Defendant

Plaintiff requests that defendant shall be ordered
to serve out his legal two months, or by default will be
obliged to sue him for damages for neglect in threshing his

seed corn. Defendant answers that he can never do enough
work, and therefore refuses to stay with plaintiff. The
hon. court orders defendant to serve out his two months
with plaintiff, and to do his work as it ought to be done.

Harent Cornelisse Vogel, Plaintiff
vs. Arien Gerrits, Defendant

Plaintiff demands of defendant restitution of a cow
he had delivered to defendant to take care of during the
winter, and which cow he chased in the wood before there
was grass. Defendant says that he asked plaintiff how to
act with the cow, whether or not he should give her in the
care of the cowherder, and he answered, "Just drive her
outside Tomesen's gate and let her go, she will certainly
find her food," and when he let her go, most of the village
cattle were being sent into the woods to pasture. Plaintiff replies that early in April he went to Fort Orange,
and that he did not say so, because at the time there was
no grass yet. The hon. court decides whereas defendant
sent the cow in question into the wood at the time when
most of the village cattle were being driven thither,
therefore he is not responsible for the animal's loss.

Thomas Chambers, Plaintiff
vs. Jacob Janssen Van Etten and Jan Broersen, Defendants.

Plaintiff says that four pigs of his escaped from his
own land through the Great Kill, and that last Friday in
or near defendants' plantation two pigs were pierced and
wounded, one of which remained behind. Therefore, he maintains that defendants must have wounded the same. Defendants answer not having hurt pigs with either knife or gun
because they did not have either. Defendants, having been
questioned under oath whether they had not seen that some
body wounded the pigs, answer, "No, only the dogs."

Jacob Janssen and Jan Broerssen, Plaintiffs
vs. Wessel Wessels, Defendant

Plaintiffs produce defendant as a witness to declare
that they did not do anything to Capt. Chambers' pigs as
is being said. Defendant says when he heard the pigs
squealing he went with plaintiffs to deliver them, but he
did not see that plaintiffs hurt them. Wessel Wessels,
having been questioned under oath, whether he did not see
anybody in their company hurt the pigs, answers, "No,
only the dogs."

Jacob Jansen and Jan Broerssen, Plaintiffs
vs. Paul Paules, Defendant

Plaintiffs demand payment of five sch. of peas for
damage to peas which defendant burnt by accident, because
his fellow originators of the fire have agreed to pay five
sch. of peas for their share. Defendant answers that the
fire was caused by accident in the straw, and thus spread
to the peas, therefore judges not being obliged to pay, but
will submit to the judgment of the court. Defendant is ordered to pay plaintiffs as much as his partners have paid

or promised to pay.

Ordinary Session, Tuesday, October 15/25, 1667.
    Present: Schout Beeckman, Mr. Berisfoord, and Commissaries.

    At this session, a chief of the Esopus savages, Tamirewackingh, appears, who complains that for the last two years his maize on his plantation has been eaten and destroyed by the pigs from this village, and therefore requests that some of the Magistrates shall be sent to examine the damage, before they set out on their hunting expeditions. /This undoubtedly means the Indians./ It is resolved that Mr. Beresford, besides the commissaries Hend. Jochems and Hend. Aertsen, shall go with petitioner for the purpose of inspection.

The Schout Willem Beeckman, Plaintiff
vs. Roelof Swartwout, Defendant

    Plaintiff accuses defendant that he sold some strong drink to savages, in accordance with a declaration of the savages in the presence of Mr. Berisford and commissaries, Hend. Jochems, Jacob Burhans and Hend. Aertsen, and consequently demands the fine conform to the decree. Defendant answers that he knows nothing about it. Plaintiff replies and says that the farmer Van Coelen was present when defendant's wine was examined in his cellar, and /the gauger/ only found seven cans, about, in the anker, which anker of wine he had received only seven or eight days ago. The hon. court, having proposed to defendant to purge himself with an oath, defendant answers that this is against the law. The hon. court adjourns the case until it shall have enquired of the hon. Heer Gov. Genl. whether the declaration of a savage or savages is deserving of belief in deciding the case, because the decree of the hon. Lord Gov. Genl. does not contain mention of the same.

Mrs. Brodhad, Plaintiff
vs. Reyner Van Coelen, Defendant

    Plaintiff requests payment of a certain quantity of oats which defendant, without plaintiff's permission, had harvested and threshed on the field at Wassemaker's. Defendant answers that he contracted for the same with Mr. LaVall, in the presence of Capt. Chambers and Lieut. Hend. Jochems. Capt. Chambers and Lieut. Jochems deny that a final contract was made, but say that they were only having a talk about it on board the yacht in the presence of Mr. LaVall. Parties request that the case shall be submitted to two members of the court for the purpose of settling it, if possible, for which purpose commissaries Thomas Chambers and Jacob Burhans are selected, who report that Van Coelen shall pay to Widow Brodhads eight sch. of oats for her claim, to be paid when the other oats shall have been sold.

The Widow Brodhads, Plaintiff
vs. Matth. Coenraets, Defendant

Plaintiff demands 30 gldrs. for delivered stockings and shoes. Defendant says that he promised to pay her when the last yacht shall sail. The hon. court orders defendant to pay the claimed 30 gldrs.

The Schout Beeckman, Plaintiff
vs. Reyner Van Coelen and Evert Prys, Defendants
Evert Prys Default

Reynier Van Coelen, Plaintiff
vs. Thomas Hermens, Defendant

Plaintiff still demands payment for oats sold on Wassemaker's land. Defendant yet answers that he bought the oats under condition that it should be harvested at the proper time, and produces a declaration signed by Freryck Peters that he warned plaintiff to harvest the oats, and defendant further produces a declaration of Matth. Coenraets who says having heard Van Coelen say that he had sold one-half of the oats at Wassemaker's land to Thomas Hermens under condition that the same should be cut at the proper time. Hend. Palingh declares having heard at the same day of the sale that Van Coelen said, "I have sold one-half of the oats to Thomas Hermens, and will have to cut the same at the proper time, and cart home with my horses." Says that such is true, and defendant holds being sufficiently discharged from the purchase, because he had the oats cut when they were overripe and mostly spoiled. Plaintiff Van Coelen brings before the court Albert /Sabaers? Rosky?/ who declares having heard when busy cutting the oats that Van Coelen offered to Thomas Hermens to discharge him from the purchase of the oats in case he was willing to pay him 10 sch. of wheat (?) and that he could earn the same harvesting or threshing. The court, having considered the case, judges, according to defendant's declarations, that defendant is discharged from the purchase of one-half of the oats, unless plaintiff be able to legally refute the witnesses.

Hend. Jochems, Plaintiff
vs. Jannetie Pels, Defendant

Plaintiff says having levied an attachment, for Philip Schyler under Reynier Van Coelen, for a claim for 20 beavers which plaintiff says Evert Pels owes him /Philip Schyler/. Defendant demands proof of debt, and says that she now came from Albany and that Philip Schuyler did not speak to her about it. The hon. court refuses the attachment because plaintiff has no power of attorney and neither can he show the origin of the debt.

Arien Gerrits, Plaintiff
vs. Harent Cornelis, Defendant

Plaintiff demands 10 sch. of wheat for taking care of a cow during the winter and for washing. Defendant admits owing for washing, being two sch. of wheat, and further says that he shall first return him his cow, and that then he is willing to pay for taking care of her during the winter.

The hon. court decides whereas the question concerning
the restitution of the cow had been settled at the last
session, therefore defendant is ordered to pay plaintiff
the above claim.

Tierck Claessen De Wit, Plaintiff
vs. Poul Polsen, Defendant

Plaintiff demands of defendant 5½ days' labor for
which he paid him last fall. Also demands a sch. of wheat
for linseed. Defendant says that last spring he presented
himself two or three times to go to work, because plaintiff had him called, and that, then, it did not again suit
plaintiff. Agrees to prove the same, and also agrees to
pay plaintiff the sch. of wheat for the linseed. Defendant
is ordered to prove his assertion at the next session of
the court.

Freryck Peters, Plaintiff
vs. Warner Horenbeeck, Defendant. Default.

Hend. Palingh, Plaintiff
vs. Tierck Claesen, Defendant

Plaintiff demands of defendant 43 sch. of wheat for
/goods/ delivered to him for Michiel Mot. Defendant says
owing 27 sch. for earned wages during harvest. Further
says that he did not fulfill his contract for the balance
by chopping trees around his land. If he had done so, he
would, as per settlement, only owe him 41 sch. Plaintiff
answering says that he wants immediate payment of the acknowledged 27 sch. of wheat. The hon. court orders defendant to pay plaintiff the acknolwedged 27 sch. of wheat.

Hend. Palingh, Plaintiff
vs. Cornelis Fynhout, Defendant. Default.

Henry Palingh, Plaintiff
vs. Marietie Hans, widow of Jurn. Westphael, Defendant.
Default.

Hend. Palingh, Plaintiff
vs. Hend. Jochems, Defendant

Plaintiff demands of defendant nine sch. of wheat.
Defendant admits the debt and agrees to pay as soon as possible. The hon. court orders defendant to pay the demanded nine sch. of wheat.

George Hall, Plaintiff
vs. Reyner Van Coelen, Defendant. Default.

George Hall, Plaintiff
vs. Marretie Hans, Defendant. Default.

George Hall, Plaintiff
vs. Hendryck Van Wye, Defendant. Default.
and Hermen Hey, Defendant. Absent.

Madaleen Dircx, Plaintiff
vs. Annetie Adriaens, Defendant

Plaintiff complains that defendant yesterday came to
her house with the intention of making trouble, whereupon
she was told to leave the house. She not being willing to
do so, plaintiff took hold of her sleeve, and said to her

that she should go outside, whereupon defendant attacked
her, and beat her so that her flesh became discolored in
her house. Defendant says that she came to her house for
the purpose of paying Jannetie Pels for a sch. of apples,
and that then a few words were said which caused the trouble.
Jannetie Pels and Henry Palingh declare, at the request of
plaintiff, that they were at the house and that they saw and
heard that plaintiff did not treat defendant badly, or give
her cause for the assault. The hon. court recommends parties to keep the peace, or else it will be obliged to punish
according to law.

Willem Beeckman, Schout, requests that the judgment
pronounced against Freryck Peters shall be judicially enforced. The officer is ordered to proceed with the execution.

Said Beeckman requests that the judgment pronounced in
his favor against Van Coelen shall be judicially enforced.
The officer is ordered to proceed with the execution.

The hon. court orders that the schepels which are in
the village shall, tomorrow, be examined and gauged. The
messenger is ordered to notify the people of said /decision/.

It was resolved and ordered to look more closely after
the improving and keeping in repair of the village palisades, and that the schout shall pay close attention to this
matter, and to fine those who are negligent, to the amount
of 25 gldrs.

Ordinary Session, Tuesday, November 1, 1667.
Present: Willem Beeckman, Schout; Thomas Chambers,
Hend. Jochems., Jacob Burhans., Hend. Aertsen, Commissaries.
Schout Beeckman, Plaintiff
vs. Rynier Van Coelen and Evert Prys, Defendants.
Both defendants default.
Schout Beeckman, Plaintiff
vs. Francoys Le Schier, Defendant
Plaintiff says that defendant has behaved very badly
against Michiel Verbruggen, and has badly pushed and beaten
him, and has hurt his ribs, on which account he lodged a
complaint, and demands a fine, in consequence of 100 gldrs.
Defendant admits having beaten Michiel Verbrugge with a
stick so that he fell to the ground. The hon. court orders
defendant, for his insolence committeed against Michiel
Verbrugge, to pay a fine of 50 gldrs.
Eva Ringhouts, Plaintiff
vs. Geertruyt Andries, Defendant
Plaintiff demands of defendant 86 gldrs. sewan and 12
sch. of wheat which she has borrowed, besides the expenses
for two trips hither amounting to 56 gldrs. sewan. Defendant admits the debt. The hon. court orders defendant to
pay plaintiff the above claim for advanced moneys and 40
gldrs. for expenses made.

George Hall, Plaintiff
vs. Cornelis Fynhout, Defendant.   Default.
George Hall, Plaintiff
vs. Jacob Stoutenborch, Defendant.   Absent.
George Hall, Plaintiff
vs. Jan Tyssen, Defendant

Plaintiff demands of defendant 111 gldrs. 10 st. Defendant admits the debt with the exception of /a claim for/
three days' threshing which he deducts. The hon. court
orders defendant to pay the balance.

George Hall, Plaintiff
vs. Cornelis Hogeboom, Defendant

Plaintiff demands of defendant 24 gldrs. for himself
and 30 gldrs. for Dr. Tideman. Defendant admits the debt.
The hon. court orders defendant to pay plaintiff the above
claims.

George Hall, Plaintiff
vs. Peter Jellissen, Defendant

Plaintiff demands of defendant 25 gldrs. for delivered
goods. Defendant admits the debt and is therefore ordered
to satisfy the demand.

George Hall, Plaintiff
vs. Dirck Hindericx, Defendant.   Absent.
George Hall, Plaintiff
vs. Matth. Coenraets?, Defendant

Plaintiff demands of defendant 20 gldrs., which defendant admits owing, and is therefore ordered to pay to
plaintiff.

George Hall, Plaintiff
vs. Albert Gerrits, Defendant

Plaintiff demands of defendant 43 gldrs., personally,
and for Dr. Tideman 12 gldrs. Defendant admits the debt,
but requests time. The hon. court orders defendant to pay
the above claim.

George Hall, Plaintiff
vs. Warner Horenbeeck, Defendant

Plaintiff demands of defendant 13 gldrs. 4 st. Defendant admits the debt, says he will pay next week. Defendant is ordered to satisfy plaintiff's demand.

Henry Palingh, Plaintiff
vs. Tierck Claesen, Defendant

Plaintiff demands of defendant 114 gldrs. Defendant
admits the debt. The hon. court orders defendant to satisfy plaintiff.

Henry Palingh, Plaintiff
vs. Marretie Hansen, Defendant

Plaintiff demands of defendant 130 gldrs. 6 st. Defendant admits the debt and is in consequence ordered to
pay plaintiff the demanded 130 gldrs. 6 st.

Hend. Palingh, Plaintiff
vs. Jan Hend., Defendant.   Default.

Mrs. Brodhad, Plaintiff
vs. Cornelis Fynhout, Defendant. Default.
Mrs. Brodhad, Plaintiff
vs. Severyn Ten Hout, Defendant

Plaintiff demands of defendant 46 gldrs., 10 st. Defendant admits the debt. The hon. court orders defendant to satisfy plaintiff's demand.

Mrs. Brodhad, Plaintiff
vs. Hermen Hey, Defendant. Default.
Mrs. Brodhad, Plaintiff
vs. Jacomine Slecht, Defendant

Plaintiff demands of defendant 11 gldrs. Defendant admits the debt, but says that her deceased husband plowed one day for Capt. Brodhad, and demands six sch. of wheat for the same. Plaintiff says that he did the plowing for friendship's sake besides others, and that defendant should have made the claim during her husband's life and that she has owed her more and prior to this, but never spoke about it. The hon. court decides whereas defendant did not claim the wages for plowing before Capt. Broadhad and family departed from here, and they have also had previous accounts, therefore defendant is ordered to pay plaintiff the above claim.

The Widow of Capt. Brodhad, Plaintiff
vs. David Crafford, Defendant

Plaintiff demands of defendant 223 gldrs. Defendant admits owing only 192 gldrs. The hon. court orders defendant to pay plaintiff the admitted 192 gldrs., and Mrs. Brodhad is ordered to prove that defendant or his wife bought the stuff for aprons in question and, if so, defendant is also ordered to pay for the same.

Mrs. Brodhad, Plaintiff
vs. Aert Peters, Defendant. Default.
Willem Haton, Plaintiff
vs. Reyner Van Coelen, Defendant

Plaintiff demands of defendant 72 gldrs. 10 st. for wages. Defendant says that not so much is coming to defendant. It is ordered that defendant shall pay plaintiff as much as by settlement he shall be found to owe.

Freryck Peters, Plaintiff
vs. Warner Horenbeeck, Defendant

Plaintiff demands of defendant a balance of 104 sch. of oats and costs. Defendant admits the debt, and in consequence is ordered to satisfy the demand.

Jan Tyssen, Plaintiff
vs. Marretie Hansen, Defendant

Plaintiff demands of defendant 20 sch. of wheat for wages. Defendant admits the debt. The hon. court orders defendant to satisfy plaintiff.

Albert Gerrits, Plaintiff
vs. Marretie Haften, Defendant

Plaintiff demands of defendant nine sch. of wheat which

defendant admits owing. The hon. court orders defendant
to satisfy plaintiff's demand.

Hermen Hend., Plaintiff
vs. Gerrit Aertsen, Defendant. Default.

Hermen Hendricx, Plaintiff
vs. Hermen Hey, Defendant. Absent.

Tierck Claessen De Wit, Plaintiff
vs. Poul Poulsen, Defendant

Plaintiff still demands 5½ days' labor, according to
an agreement for the purchase of an ax. Defendant brings
Severyn Ten Hout who says that he was sent last winter by
Tierck to tell Poul to come and chop wood, and when he came
in the morning, had to go home again. Plaintiff answers
that the ax, then had not yet been sold, and that the same
was for chopping palisades. The hon. court orders plaintiff to prove that when he called upon him to work, the
ax had not yet been sold, because defendant says the
contrary.

Reyner Van Coelen, Plaintiff
vs. Hend. Palingh, Defendant

Plaintiff requests that defendant shall affirm under
oath that which on last session of the court he declared
at the request of Thomas Hermens. Defendant, being present,
took the same in regard to said case, as also Matth. Coenraets in regard to the same case.

Cornelis Slecht, Plaintiff
vs. Mrs. Brodhad, Defendant

Plaintiff demands payment for two half barrels of good
beer and one-half barrel small beer, and besides one beaver for services rendered. Defendant says that she paid in
sugar for the services, and that he should have demanded
her husband's debt during his life. Plaintiff says that he
asked Capt. Brodhad several times for it, but could not get
it. Parties are ordered to settle their accounts, and what
shall be shown the one to owe the other, he is ordered to pay.

Cornelis Hogeboom, Plaintiff
vs. Reyner Van Coelen, Defendant

Plaintiff demands of defendant 11½ sch. of wheat for
delivered stone and for wages. Defendant says that he has
a counter bill. Parties are ordered to liquidate. What
shall be found to be owing, defendant shall be obliged to
pay plaintiff, with costs.

Aert Martens, Plaintiff
vs. Thomas Hermens, Defendant

Plaintiff demands of defendant 51 sch. of wheat for
delivered cider, to be paid when the winter wheat was in
the ground. Defendant admits the debt, but says having a-
greed to pay next January. Plaintiff is ordered to prove
that the time for payment has appeared.

Thomas Hermens, Plaintiff
vs. Aert Martens, Defendant

Plaintiff demands of defendant payment of 62 gldrs.

five st. for a debt he took it upon himself to pay. Defendant denies having taken such an obligation. The hon. court orders plaintiff to prove that defendant agreed to pay the debt, and that the time as expired.

Henry Palingh requests that his previous judgment against Tierck Claessen shall be judicially enforced. The officer is ordered to proceed with the business and the execution.

Ordinary Session, Tuesday, November 8, 1667, New Style.
Present: the Schout Willem Beeckman; Thomas Chambers, Hend. Jochems., Jacob Burhans, Hend. Aertsen, Commissaries.

The Schout Beeckman, Plaintiff
vs. Reyner Van Coelen and Evert Prys, Defendants.

Plaintiff says that defendants on August 7 engaged in a fight, and that Evert Prys in the schout's presence wounded Reyner Van Coelen in the shoulder, and therefore demands the fine, set upon wounding anybody, amounting to 300 gldrs. Defendant Van Coelen says that he took orders to the schout. In the meantime, his servant, Evert Prys, also arrived, drunk and having much talk, and calling names, whereupon he ordered him to go home and sleep. He called more names, whereupon /Van Coelen/ hit him with the halbert and then called in the guard to take charge of him. They, however, did not do so, and said Evert Prys, in the mean time, went for a sword, again met him in front of the schout's door, and hit /Van Coelen/ in the shoulder. Evert Prys is absent, third default.

Thomas Chambers, Plaintiff
vs. Henry Palingh, Defendant

Plaintiff demands of defendant 1,388 gldrs. sewan or grain sewan's price, originating from the purchase of house and brewery. Defendant demands first 77 gldrs. for repairs made to the malt floor at the time he was renting said brewery. Plaintiff replies: "In case it is shown by the contract of the lease that any repairs made by the lessee on the brewery must be repaid, I shall submit to the same," and further says that the dwelling as well as the brewery are mortgaged for the purchase money. Defendant answers that he paid for the dwelling but has not been deeded to him as per contract, and therefore he has no right, yet, to mortgage the same. Plaintiff replying says that he still adheres to said conditions as well in regard to the sale as to the lease. The hon. court, having read the lease of the brewery, finds that it was not stipulated that the lessor should have to pay for what the lessee should want to make for his own convenience; therefore, defendant Henry Palingh is refused his claim for 77 gldrs. Further, having examined the conditions of sale and having read them to parties, the conveyance of the house and lot took place on Dec. 21, 1665, and was accepted by Hendk. Palingh, as shown by his signature, so that the hon. court is of the opinion that

plaintiff Thomas Chambers was not negligent in performing
the contract, on which account defendant is sentenced to
pay plaintiff the demanded 1,388 gldrs.

Francoys Le Schier, Plaintiff
vs. Michiel Verbrugge, Defendant

Plaintiff says that defendant should have said to Albert Gerrits that he had broken a horn of his cow and
beaten his calf, on which account it remained behind and
got lost. Defendant answers having said that he treated
him tyrannically and beat him; he may have done the same
to cattle. Plaintiff agrees to prove his assertion.

Michiel Verbrugh, Plaintiff
vs. Francoys Le Schier, Defendant

Plaintiff demands payment for doctor's fee, pain, and
lost time for seven days, on account of the maltreatment
committed against him without reasons. Also demands wages
for having taken care of the cows, alone, for seven days at
six gldrs. per day. Defendant also demands proof of his
having killed Hend. Aertsen's calf, of which plaintiff accuses him. Plaintiff says he did not say that he killed
said calf, but that he hung up the pieces of a skin. Defendant agrees to prove his assertion. Plaintiff is ordered to bring in a specified account of the doctor's bill
at the next session.

Matthys Coenraets, Plaintiff
vs. Reyn. Van Coelen, Defendant

Plaintiff demands of defendant ¼ year's hire, amounting to 20 sch. of wheat. Defendant shows per account that
plaintiff received of him 98 gldrs. 10 st., and further
says that plaintiff did not serve with him during ¼ of a
year, and agrees to prove the same. Plaintiff admits having received 98 gldrs. 10 st. in wheat, and demands the
balance. Defendant Van Coelen is ordered to prove his assertion at the next session or by default to pay the balance to plaintiff.

Severyn Ten Hout, Plaintiff
vs. Tierck Claessen, Defendant. Default.

Cornelis Slecht, Plaintiff
vs. Tierck Claesen, Defendant. Default.

Mrs. Brodhad, Plaintiff
vs. Hermen Hey, Defendant

Plaintiff demands of defendant 21 gldrs. 4 st. for delivered merchandise and requests quick justice, because she
is about to depart, and defendant is a single man. Defendant's second default. Whereas defendant Hermen Hey does
not appear for the purpose of answering, it is ordered that
he shall give security for the demanded amount to plaintiff
under penalty of arrest.

Mattheu Blanchan appeared at this session, notified
the court that a certain amount of money was owing to him
by Hend. Cornelis Lynd., deceased, and that Roelof Swartwout, having been appointed curator of the deceased's es-

tate, is a man without means, and all his property having
been mortgaged he is, on that account, poor, wherefore he
is not fit to administer other people's estates, and for
the sake of securing himself and other creditors, requests
to have him discharged or dismissed. Mattheu Blanchan will
have to address the appointed curators Swartwout and Montagnie in regard to his claim, and in case of refusal of
payment can address the court for the purpose of forcing
them.

Jan Tysen requests that the judgment pronounced in his
favor against Marretie shall be judicially enforced. The
officer is ordered to proceed with the execution.

George Hall requests that the judgment pronounced in
his favor on Nov. 1 against Warener Horenbeeck, Albert Gerrits, Mattys Coenraets and Cornelis Hogeboom shall be judicially enforced. The officer is ordered to attend to the
same and to proceed with the execution.

The schout Willem Beeckman shows to the hon. court the
answer received from the Ld. Gov. Nicolls to the decision
of the hon. court, and the accusation of Swartwout in regard to the sale of strong drink to savages, to find out in
how far the declaration of savages has to be accepted, and
is answered that it has been declared and decided by the
general court or diet held on Sept. 27, 1666, at New York
that the testimony of savages shall be accepted, when the
case is fortified by other circumstances, and whereas in
the presence of the commander of the militia and of three
commissaries at the house of Swartwout those savages and
the wine were introduced or shown, and it is also known
that he, Swartwout, eight days before he was proceeded a-
gainst for this affair, had received an anker of wine on
burgher-excise and that on the same anker no more than seven
or eight cans were found, and it was so nearly consumed,
and further the circumstance that the hon. court proposed
to him on Oct. 15/25 to clear himself under oath which he
did not accept, on this account he still demands, conform
to the decree, the fine of five pounds sterling. Defendant, having been summoned to appear at the session, having
been acquainted with the answer and the schout's conclusion,
defendant Roelof Swartwout requests time till next session
for the purpose of filing his answer. Defendant is granted
this request till next session, for reason that he makes
the excuse of not having had a copy, and not knowing anything about the case.

Ordinary Session, Tuesday, November 5/15, 1667.
      Present: the Schout Beeckman and all the Commissaries.
            Willem Beeckman, Plaintiff
        vs. Thomas Quick, Defendant. Absent.
            Willem Beeckman, Plaintiff
        vs. Jan Willems, Defendant. Default.

Nicolaes De Mayer, Plaintiff
vs. Aert Martens, Defendant
Plaintiff demands of defendant 285 gldrs. 12 st. sewan or wheat as per "schepen knowledge" and account, with
costs, and further 125 gldrs. in sewan per account of Frans
Barents Pastoren, as per obligation, with costs. Plaintiff further says that he has seized 22½ sch. of wheat belonging to Aert Martens, under Marretie Hans, and requests
that the same shall be declared valid. Defendant admits
the debt, agrees to pay as soon as possible. The hon.
court orders defendant to satisfy plaintiff's above demand
with costs. The levied attachment is declared valid.
Nicolas Majer, Plaintiff
vs. Reyner Van Coelen, Defendant
Plaintiff demands of defendant a sum of 1,466 gldrs.
one st. and 1½ year interest, amounting to 229 gldrs. 16
st., amounting together to 1,695 gldrs. 17 st., as per obligation in braided sewan. Further still as per balance
of account 243 gldrs. sewan or wheat, with costs. Defendant admits the debt, but says that he will not allow him
the interest. The hon. court orders defendant to satisfy
plaintiff, as per obligation shown, besides the 243 gldrs.,
with costs.
Anna Hardenbroeck, Plaintiff
vs. Reynr. Van Coelen, Defendant
Plaintiff shows an obligation against defendant amounting to 747 gldrs., and says that her husband has more than
once settled here at Esopus with defendant, so that he still
owes honestly 641 gldrs., which plaintiff at present demands.
Defendant admits having passed the obligation, and says
having paid 250 gldrs. on the same, and demands account and
satisfaction for 358 lbs. of sole leather and upper leather
delivered to her husband, still 30 pairs of men's shoes,
further still delivered 358 of upper leather, further some
calf skins, also a mirror with four silver plates. Plaintiff replies and still demands the balance of 641 gldrs.
with costs, and says that defendant shall go to Manhatans
and that her husband, in the presence of impartial shoe-
makers, shall give him the remaining shoes and satisfaction
for the delivered leather. Regarding the mirror, says that
defendant's wife gave the same to her to take care of, is
ready to return the same. The hon. court orders defendant
to pay plaintiff the demanded 641 gldrs. with costs, because Willem Montagne declares that when he wrote the obligation at the request of Abel Hardenbroeck in the presence
of Reyner Van Coelen for the remaining debt of 641 gldrs.,
said Van Coelen was satisfied with the same. But what defendant is able to prove having paid after said date, he
is permitted to deduct. In regard to his pretence about
the delivered leather, defendant is referred to Abel Hardenbroeck to whom he delivered the same, for the purpose
of settling with him, because /the court/ only sees a bill

of defendant but no contract of what defendant says Abel
Hardenbroeck has agreed about with him.

Matth. Capito, vendue-master, ex-officio, Plaintiff
vs. Roelof Swartwout, Defendant

Willem Montagnie appeared because Matt. Capito is absent. Demands of defendant for the sale of a horse, bought
at vendue, the amount of 60 sch. of wheat; which horse had
been mortgaged by Pieter Hillebrants to N. De Mayer for 44
sch. of wheat. Defendant says having bought the horse direct of Pieter Hillebrants, but not at vendue or as highest
bidder, and says in regard to this matter not to have anything to do with Matt. Capito, unless he has a power of attorney of Pieter Hillebrants, but admits having bought the
same for 60 sch. of wheat, and still to owe 34 sch. of
wheat for the same, because Pieter Hillebrants owed him 26
sch. of wheat. Plaintiff requests in case it shall be proved
that the horse was bought at vendue, defendant shall be ordered to pay. Defendant Swartwout is ordered to pay the
admitted 34 sch. of wheat to Mr. Nicolas De Meyer, or by
default, Mr. De Meyer is authorized to have the horse again
publicly sold by virtue of his mortgage.

Roelof Swartwout, Plaintiff
vs. Reyner Van Coelen, Defendant

Plaintiff demands of defendant 204 gldrs. for delivered
garden produce and wages. Defendant admits the debt, but
says that plaintiff is in partnership with him as farmer
/excise/, and finding that they shall lose on the same, he,
on that account, wanted to keep back the demanded amount
from plaintiff. The hon. court orders defendant to satisfy
plaintiff for the demanded amount, and in case any shortage
should exist in the matter of the partnership for the farming, he may demand what shall be found to be short.

Reyner Van Coelen, Plaintiff
vs. Roelof Swartwout, Defendant

Plaintiff demands of defendant his dues in regard to
the complaint made by the schout against defendant that,
according to the admission of the savages, he sold wine to
them. Defendant says that he knows nothing about it, and
that /plaintiff/ shall prove the same. In regard to said
misdeed, that Roelof Swartwout sold strong drink, contrary
to the decree of the hon. Lord Gov. Genl. Nicolls, he has
on this account been ex-officio examined by the schout,
here, so that it /the court/ does not consider the plaintiff
qualified.

Cornelis Slecht, Plaintiff
vs. Tierck Claessen, Defendant

Plaintiff demands payment of 25 gldrs. for the use of
the bridge across the Kil, during the war. Defendant says
that he, besides all the neighbors here in the village, used
the road or bridge during the war. Parties are ordered to
select two good men, for the purpose of settling their difference, if possible, or else to report to the court.

Matths. Blanchan, Plaintiff
vs. Mrs. Brodhad, Defendant. Absent.
Michiel Mot, Plaintiff
vs. Marretie Hanse, Defendant
Plaintiff demands of defendant 43 gldrs. for wages.
Defendant admits a debt of 42 gldrs., will show having paid
him one gldr. The hon. court orders plaintiff to accept
of defendant 42 gldrs.
Willem Beeckman, Plaintiff
vs. Evert Prys, Defendant
Plaintiff demands of defendant 51 gldrs. 12 st. for
delivered merchandise. Defendant admits owing no more than
37 gldrs. 4 st. Says not to know of any more. Plaintiff
replying says that he sent others for some wine, according
to his wife's statement; she forgot by whom, because it is
already long ago. The hon. court orders defendant to pay
plaintiff the acknowledged 37 gldrs. 4 st., with costs, and
plaintiff is to furnish proof of the rest.
Schout Beeckman, Plaintiff
vs. Rejner Van Coelen and Evert Prys, Defendants
Plaintiff says that defendants on Oct. 7 engaged in a
fight, and that Evert Prys, with a sword, cut his fellow-
defendant, Van Coelen, in the shoulder, in the presence of
the schout, for which plaintiff asks the fine of 300 gldrs.,
as per law. Vander Coelen says that he intended to take
the order to the officer, and that Evert Prys then came,
and called him names, whereupon he struck him with the pike
on the arm. Thereupon Evert Prys went away and fetched a
sword, "he then again met me and struck me in the shoulder."
Defendant Evert Prys answers that his master Reynr. Van
Coelen ordered him to go home, whereupon, "I said there was
neither beer nor water to drink, whereupon my master Van
Coelen answered, 'You lie like a rascal,' whereupon I again
said: that he lied like a rascal, whereupon he immediately
took hold of the half pike and beat me with the same on the
arms, so that the pike broke in three pieces, then he drew
his sword, and I took flight." The hon. court, having considered the case, sentences Evert Prys to pay a fine of 50
gldrs., and Reyner Van Coelen a fine of 30 gldrs., to be
paid to plaintiff.
Reynier Van Coelen presents a petition in which he
requests to be permitted to open a village inn, with the
privilege of alone keeping a public house. The hon. court
allows petitioner Reynier Van Coelen to open an inn besides
others.

Ordinary Session, Tuesday, Nov. 12, 1667.
Present: the hon. Schout Willem Beeckman; Thomas
Chambers, Hendrick Jochems, Jacob Burhans, Commissaries.
Schout Beeckman, Plaintiff
vs. Reynier Van Coelen, Defendant
Plaintiff demands of defendant for the magistracy half

a year's back farm money of burgher and tapster excise as per conditions with the costs. Defendant admits owing ¼ year's farm money, and promises to take measures for paying. Defendant is ordered to fulfill the conditions of the farm, and to pay what is owing.

Henry Palingh, Plaintiff
vs. Thomas Chambers, Defendant

Plaintiff demands of defendant 2,400 gldrs. for delivered goods during the years 1665, 1666, and 1667. Defendant says that he does not owe plaintiff, but on the contrary that plaintiff Hend. Palingh owes him for a house he bought of him, and for rent of a brewery, and for the purchase of a brewery, as is shown by a contract dated Nov. 8, N. S. Plaintiff Henry Palingh says that the conditions regarding the sale of the house are void; the conditions have not been fulfilled, because the condition says that it was to be delivered on Christmas 1665, free and unencumbered, which grantor did not do, and that there can be no delivery without a deed, therefore he contends not to owe for the house. Defendant Thomas Chambers further says that he conveyed to plaintiff Henry Palingh as per condition the house and lot, as is further shown by Palingh's signature, though at the time of the sale he had no deed of the lot, but has now received one of the hon. Lord Gen. Nicolls, and is ready when the house shall have been fully paid for to make a further conveyance, by virtue of the deed. The hon. court, having considered the dispute and case in question between parties concerning the condition of the purchase of the house and lot on Nov. 8, N. S., has found that Thomas Chambers's demand was right, and parties are referred by the magistrates to the judgment pronouned on Oct. 28/Nov. 8.

Henry Palingh, Plaintiff
vs. Peter Peters, Defendant

Plaintiff demands of defendant 77 gldrs. for delivered goods. Defendant admits owing 74 gldrs. The hon. court orders defendant to pay plaintiff the admitted 74 gldrs.

Anna Hardenbroeck, Plaintiff
vs. Rynier Van Coelen, Defendant

Plaintiff requests judicial enforcement of the judgment, obtained Nov. 5/15 last. Defendant Van Coelen requests that the money for which he was sentenced in behalf of the plaintiff shall remain in consignment here till he has settled with her husband for his claim for the delivered leather. The hon. court consents to the execution under condition that the money shall be put in the custody of the officer here, and Van Coelen is specially ordered, as soon as the river is navigable to go and settle with Abel Hardenbroeck, concerning his claim for the delivered leather, and in case of neglect plaintiff is permitted to draw and receive the money from the officer.

Jan Tyssen, Plaintiff
vs. Roelof Swartwout, Defendant

Plaintiff demands an accounting of defendant's guardianship. Defendant answers being busy making up the account, and receiving the money, and guardian Swartwout
further requests that after the accounting he shall also be
relieved of the daughter Annete, she having attained her
majority. Defendant is ordered to render an accounting of
his guardianship. His request is granted, if the daughter
has attained her majority.

Jan Hendricks, Plaintiff
vs. Reynier Van Coelen, Defendant

Plaintiff demands payment of 230 sch. of wheat or its
value, owing to the sale of the crop on the field, in accordance with conditions or contract. Defendant admits the
debt, but says whereas he has been notified by the schout,
in the name of the court, that he should take care /to pay/
the arrears of the village taxes for his purchased land
that therefore he shall pay the same from the demanded a-
mount, because the demanded 230 sch. of wheat have been
transferred to Aert Martens, the seller of the farm. Plaintiff replies and says that defendant has no authority to
administer his money without his consent. Parties are ordered to state their case more explicitly at the next session, and then the same shall be disposed of upon the evidence.

The schout Beeckman notifies having attached under
the hands of Rynier Van Coelen, what Evert Prys may have
to claim of him, and specially eight sch. of wheat for delivered maize, and further wages, by virtue of a "schepen
knowledge" dated Nov. 8, amounting to 87 gldrs. The hon.
court declares the attachment valid.

Rynier Van Coelen, Plaintiff
vs. Jan Hendricks, Defendant

Plaintiff demands of defendant 94 gldrs. 14 st. for
delivered goods. Defendant admits the debt. The hon.
court orders defendant to satisfy plaintiff's demand.

Reynier Van Coelen, Plaintiff
vs. Aert Martens, Defendant

Plaintiff demands of defendant 766 gldrs. 10 st., and
still seven gldrs. advanced money. Defendant says not yet
to know whether he or plaintiff is in debt. The hon. court
orders parties to settle with each other and to show each
other their claims.

Reynier Van Coelen, Plaintiff
vs. Roelof Swartwout, Defendant

Plaintiff demands of defendant his share of the excise, because he is his partner in the farm, and plaintiff
has been notified by Schout Beeckman to pay the due three-
monthly amount. Defendant answers not to be in partnership, but that he contracted concerning the profit or loss
of the farm, and in case of a loss is ready to pay his share
at the end of the year. Defendant is ordered to pay his
share of the loss, as it shall be found to exist.

Roelof Swartwout, Plaintiff
vs. Rynier Van Coelen, Defendant
Plaintiff makes known that on Nov. 5/15 last he obtained judgment against defendant amounting to 203 gldrs.
in regard to which defendant up to now has been negligent--
on which account he has caused plaintiff great damage and
plaintiff therefore is obliged to proceed against defendant
for damage caused. Defendant says having replied at the
serving of the summons that he should go with him and make
out the excise account, and pay besides him, what should
be short. The hon. court consents to the execution on the
obtained judgment against Van Coelen, amounting to 203
gldrs. and costs.
Jan Martens, Plaintiff
vs. Jan Jansen Amersfort, Defendant
Plaintiff demands of defendant 18 gldrs. Defendant
admits the debt. The hon. court orders defendant to satisfy plaintiff's demand for 18 gldrs.
Jan Martens, Plaintiff
vs. Christoffer Davids, Defendant. Absent. Default.
Roelof Swartwout requests whereas the horse bought by
him of Peter Hillebrants has, by virtue of a mortgage, now
again been sold by N. Meyer, by Lord's execution, on account whereof he suffered great loss, for which horse I
had promised /to pay/ 60 sch. of wheat, and I had a claim
against Peter Hillebrants of 26 sch. of wheat, therefore
requests the hon. court to be permitted to retain the 26
sch. of wheat. The hon. court, having considered the case,
permits petitioner to retain the 26 sch. of wheat.
Nicolas Meyer requests that the judgment obtained on
Nov. 5/15 against Van Coelen and Aert Martens shall be ju-
dially enforced. The officer is ordered to proceed with
the execution.

Ordinary Session, Tuesday, December 3/13, 1667.
Present: Willem Beeckman, Schout; Thomas Chambers,
Hend. Jochemsen, Jacob Burhans, Hend. Aertsen, Commissaries.
Schout Beeckman, Plaintiff
vs. Jan Joosten, Hermen Hendrics, Jan Cornelis, Roelof
Swartwout, Meyndert Jansen, Van Coelen, Lammert Hyberts,
Frerick Peters, Jacomine Slecht, and Anders Pers
The Schout complains that defendants, in obedience to
the order of the hon. court, do not attend to their duty
in closing their palisades around the village, and on account thereof demands the fine. The hon. court resolves,
after adjournment of the session, to go in a body on a tour
of inspection, and those being negligent shall be fined.
Willem Beeckman, Plaintiff
vs. Jan Jansen Amersfort, Defendant
Plaintiff demands of defendant an amount of 80 gldrs.
10 st. as per account, with costs. Defendant admits the
debt, except 30 gldrs. salary for services rendered as

officer in judicial actions. The hon. court orders defendant to pay the full claim as per bill produced, with costs.
　　　　Schout Willem Beeckman, Plaintiff
　　vs. Thomas Hermens and Michiel Verbrugh, Defendants.
　　Plaintiff says having been informed that last Saturday
evening a door of his house was broken open by Michiel Verbruggen and that two hams and an anker of wine were carried
away. Defendant says not to know who broke his door open
and carried away his goods, but that Michiel Verbruggen excused himself with having been drunk. Michiel Berbruggen
is absent, and not to be found in the village.
Thomas Chambers, as attorney for his stepchildren, Plaintiff
　　vs. Roelof Swartwout and Cornelis Slecht, their
　　　　　　guardians, Defendants
　　Plaintiff produces a written complaint in regard to
the 780 gldrs. in wheat at 2 gldrs. 10 st. per sch. charged
by defendants to the children as claimed salary, which
shows a bad administration. Defendants answer that they
cannot verbally answer the produced complaint, and therefore request copies of the same, but the summoned guardian
Swartwout further says, in case the hon. court wants to reduce the charged salary, he will not object, because he does
not intend to plead any further. The hon. court, having
considered the case, orders plaintiff to furnish defendants
with a copy of his opposition against their administration,
and defendants to furnish copy of their bill for 780 gldrs.
for salary, and further that defendants shall reply at the
next session.
　　　　Christopher Berrisford, as attorney for
　　　　　　Mrs. Brodhad, Plaintiff
　　　　vs. Reyner Van Coelen, Defendant
　　Plaintiff demands of defendant the hired horses of
Capt. Brodhad, and leased by defendant to Freryck Peters,
contrary to contract. Defendant says because he was o-
bliged to remove the hired horses from his stable, and he
takes their risks upon himself, and that he will return
them in better condition than he received them. Plaintiff
Mr. Berrisford is satisfied with defendant's promise.
　　　　Mr. Christoffer Berisfoord, Plaintiff
　　　　vs. Hermen Hey, Defendant
　　Plaintiff in his quality as above demands of defendant
28 (or 216) gldrs. Defendant admits the debt and says
that he had agreed with Mr. Brodhad to pay during the winter before navigation sets in, and that Tierck Claesen became surity for the same. The hon. court orders defendant
to satisfy the debt to plaintiff according to his admission.
　　　　Peter Jillesen, Plaintiff
　　　　vs. Reyner Van Coelen, Defendant
　　Plaintiff demands first, six sch. of wheat loaned to
defendant and further 34 sch. of wheat for his full hire
because he sent him away without reasons. Defendant answers, and on the contrary demands 62 gldrs. 10 st. Fur-

ther says that he hired plaintiff and that he was one
month in his service, and in the meanwhile misbehaved by
calling his wife a whore, etc., and on this account he discharged him. Plaintiff replies and says that the woman
first called him names. Defendant brings Richard Cage and
Thomas Quinal, who declare having heard that Peter Jelli-
sen called Reyner Van Coelen's wife a whore. The hon.
court, having heard the case from both sides, orders defendant Van Coelen to return to plaintiff the loaned six
sch. of wheat, and to pay him his hire in proportion to
the services rendered by him.

Thomas Quick, Plaintiff
vs. Reyner Van Coelen, Defendant

Plaintiff says that defendant hired him till May for
40 sch. of wheat and that defendant has now discharged him
without reasons. Therefore, he demands his full hire. Defendant says that he hired his man Thomas Quick till May
and that he ordered him to cart wood which he refused, and
that he several times fed clean wheat to the horses, which
he did to cause trouble. Plaintiff denies having fed the
horses clean wheat. Defendant agrees to prove the same and
produces his threshers Jacob Van Etten and Jan Broerssen,
who declare having seen several times wheat in the horses'
manger. Leendert Barents also a thresher declares having
taken a quantity of wheat out of the horses' manger and all
the threshers together say that said Thomas Quick has
several times fed the threshed wheat against their will to
the horses. The hon. court, having considered the case,
orders defendant to pay plaintiff in proportion of his
rendered services and time.

Tierck Claessen, Plaintiff
vs. Annetie Gerrits, Defendant

Plaintiff says that he was security for 27 gldrs. 6
st. at an auction for one Cornelis Barents, and that he
still has a claim against said Cornelis Barents, and whereas he has at this place yet a blanket in the custody of defendant, he requests to seize said blanket for the purpose
of recoverying his claim. Defendant shows a bill wherefrom
it appears that said Cornelis Barents still owes her 16
sch. of wheat for advanced money. The hon. court orders
that the blanket shall be appraised by impartial men, and
what it shall be found to be worth more than the 27 gldrs.
6 st. in payment of the auction shall be divided among them
in proportion to their claim.

George Hall and Matth. Blanchan send in a petition in
which they say that Reynier Van Coelen is a retailer of
liquor, contrary to the law, because he, Van Coelen, is a
farmer of his Majesty's excise and that the same on this
account is defrauded. The hon. court has permitted Reynier
Van Coelen, besides others, to retail strong drink, because
he complained that after the first quarter he was much out
with the farm. Further no farmer yet, either in this

country or anywhere else, has ever been prohibited to retail strong drink, and cannot see wherein his Majesty's excise is being defrauded, for the farmers have to pay the
promised and contracted for amount, whether there are few
or many retailers. The court judges this answer to be
sufficient.

Roelof Swartwout produces before the session certain
bill for costs, on account of suit for debt against Reyner
Van Coelen, owing to nonpayment. He claims that he has to
pay certain expenses owing to the sale of a horse "by
Lord's execution" which /horse/ because Swartwout could not
pay was again sold by the auctioneer, and requests approval
of the same. The hon. court allows him the costs incurred
over and above his further claim against Reyner Van Coelen,
amounting to 5 gldrs.

Ordinary Session, Tuesday, December 10/20, 1667.
Present: Willem Beeckman, Schout; Thomas Chambers,
Hend. Jochems, Jacob Burhans, Hend. Aertsen, Commissaries.
Roelof Swartwout, Plaintiff
vs. Reyner Van Coelen, Defendant
Plaintiff still demands of defendant for damage caused
him by nonpayment on account of the judicial sale of the
horse, and others as per bill, besides some running interests to Nicolas De Mayer, amounting as per account to 75
gldrs. 4 st. Defendant says that he did not give cause for
the judicial sale of the horse, but only delayed on account of the excise farm money, because he is his partner,
and he has accepted to pay plaintiff's claim of 204 gldrs.,
as per his assignation to Nicolas De Mayer. The hon. court
decides that Van Coelen shall yet pay the demanded amount
of 204 gldrs. to Mr. Mayer with the interest from the judgment till the day of payment if Mayer demands the same,
besides the five gldrs. costs, and the expenses for the
present.
Severyn Ten Hout, Plaintiff
vs. Tierck Claessen, Defendant. 2nd Default.
Roelof Swartwout and Cornelis Slecht as guardians of
the children of Matth. Jansen, deceased, submit in accordance with the order of the hon. court their answer to the
last complaint of Mr. Thomas Chambers, as attorney for his
stepchildren, now having reached their majority. The submitted answer having been read to the attorney, Mr. Chambers, he rejects and opposes the same, and says that it
does not touch upon the points of the complaint, and therefore requests that the guardians shall give security for
the judgment by the court, before he will proceed further.
The hon. court decides that parties, in its presence, shall
try to agree; if not, shall both furnish security before
proceeding further.
Roelof Swartwout, Plaintiff
vs. Cornelis Slecht, Defendant

382

Plaintiff shows a protest against defendant, who
stored some grain in Evert Pels' barn, on account of which
repairs could not be made, which caused the roof to fall
in, and he therefore protests, owing to the costs and
damage. Defendant Cornelis Slecht answers that Thomas
Chambers told him in his house that the barn was propped
and that therefore it did not matter whether the grain
should lay there a little longer. The damage has been
examined and valued at 100 gldrs. sewan, which is to be
paid by the guardians.

After the demise of Secretary Matth. Capito, schout
and commissaries have inventoried all the writing books,
and papers (as well those belonging to the village as to
himself), found, and delivered them to the Schout Beeckman with the request to administer the village affairs,
the vendues and the private property of Matth. Capito,
provided he shall draw a proper salary as well for the
outstanding vendue-debts as for the estate.

(End of Volume I)

www.ingramcontent.com/pod-product-compliance
Lightning Source LLC
Chambersburg PA
CBHW060133280326
41932CB00012B/1501